Understand the Bible for yourself

Understand the Bible
for yourself

Tecwyn Morgan

**Christadelphian Bible Mission,
404 Shaftmoor Lane,
Birmingham, B28 8SZ
UK**

"Understand the Bible for Yourself" – 2006 – © **CBM**

First Printing – 2006

ISBN 085189 170 5

ACKNOWLEDGEMENTS

Cover
Photos.com
Bible Quotations
Scripture quotations are from the *The Holy Bible, English Standard Version,* published by Harper Collins Publishers © 2001 by Crossway Bibles, a division of Good News Publishers. Used by permission. All rights reserved.
Illustrations
Clipart.com; Christian Clipart; Paul Wasson; Darren Storey; Dynamic Graphics; Doug Hardy; John Norcross. All rights reserved.
Preparation
Thanks to Sue Mathias, John S Roberts, Andrew E Walker and John Morris, for their assistance and advice.

Further copies are available from the Publishers:

Christadelphian Bible Mission,
404 Shaftmoor Lane,
Birmingham, B28 8SZ
UK

Printed by:
Printland Publishers,
GPO Box 159,
Hyderabad, 500001,
India

Printland Publishers is the Printing and Paper Division of Culcreuch Exports Pvt Ltd, India

Contents

Preface

If the front door of a building swung shut leaving you locked outside, you would soon know how important a key really is. With it you could gain easy access again. Without it you would be unhappy, for it could take you quite a while to get back in.

But what if someone then arrived with the key? How welcome that would be! As it turned in the lock, you would probably be resolving never to be without your own key again. And all that just about gaining access to a building! How would you feel if someone arrived with the key to eternal life? If you were told you could get into God's House – somewhere you could live forever – wouldn't that mean much?

That key exists and you may well have it already. The Bible is the key that God has given to show us how to live for ever. Understand for yourself what it really teaches and, with God's help, you can live for ever in a perfect world. Without the key, however, you will be shut out of all that is due to happen when God puts the final phase of His rescue plan into effect.

Several times in the past, God has intervened in human affairs and the outcome has always been dramatic and hugely important. He is about to do the same again; this time on a bigger scale than ever before. The whole world is going to be changed and a new society will be formed out of the wreckage of the old one. All the indications are that this change is about to begin. We need to think about it, and what it means for us and our families.

This book will explain what is about to happen and why. But, even more importantly, it will show you how to find the key that will let you into God's new world. This book is not the key. The Bible is the key and this is a book about the Bible. It can help you understand what the Bible teaches and help you read the Bible for yourself. It will tell you what the author thinks is true Bible teaching, and what the church he belongs to teaches. But this book is not about him or about his church. It is about you – to help you read and understand the Bible – a book that many people find confusing and difficult.

It will give you things to think about; suggest some answers and show you how to work things out for yourself. It invites you to check your own understanding against the conclusions presented here.

It does not start at the beginning of the Bible and work its way through. There are other books that do that. This one looks at one New Testament letter, which happens to contain a summary of the gospel of God. Then it looks elsewhere in the Bible to see where those ideas came from and to find out more about what they really mean. We hope you will find this a challenging and informative read.

1

The Gospel of God

When the second part of the Bible was being written – what is now called the "New Testament" – the Romans ruled the earth. They had established a powerful empire which had an iron grip on the developed world, in and around the Mediterranean Sea. Within that empire was the tiny but troublesome country known as "Israel", which occupied the eastern coastline of the Mediterranean.

The nation of Israel has had a really up-and-down history. The Jewish people were descendants of Abraham. They had gone to live in Egypt where, after many years, they had been made slaves. From there God rescued them to become His people,[1] a nation that would be especially privileged. There were about 600,000 adult Jewish men in Egypt at that time, about 3500 years ago, and God asked them and their families to undertake a huge challenge.

He said that He would be their God if they would be His people, and they readily agreed. They made a formal agreement together – called a "covenant" or "testament" – which is what the first part of the Bible is all about. That's why it's called the "Old Testament". It is mainly about God's dealings with the nation of Israel, while the second part, the "New Testament", is about God's great offer of salvation to all nations. It's really one Bible, in two parts, not two Bibles. And we need both parts to understand God's message to us. That message came first through the people of Israel and then through the work of Jesus and his followers.

It is the coming of the Lord Jesus Christ that makes the difference and separates the two parts of the Bible. That difference was becoming clear when the apostle Paul picked up his pen to write a letter to believers who lived in Rome – the capital city of the Roman empire. He wrote that he

---

[1] *You can read all about this in the Book of Exodus, second book in the Old Testament part of the Bible (the first part).*

1

hoped to visit them but, before he did this, he wanted to explain his understanding of the purpose of God. Paul was a very colourful character and had become a believer in very dramatic circumstances.[2] The letter had a particular purpose when it was written and contains details about certain things that were happening at that time.[3] But because it contains Paul's detailed explanation of what he believed, the Letter to the Romans is a wonderful help to us today. It gives us a summary of the gospel as it was believed and taught by the apostles, so we can work out for ourselves just what true Christianity is all about.

Before we look at that summary, remember that this is about First Century Christianity. This is when Jesus was born and when he taught his followers, and the whole of the New Testament was written within sixty or so years of his death. That was a long time ago, but if you want to understand what Jesus and his immediate followers taught, you have to go back to their original words and not rely on what other people might tell you. If it turns out that Paul's teaching does not fully match up with what you believe, you will need to think that through. If you have no personal views or beliefs about Christianity at this stage, then everything will be new to you.

Here's a useful tip at the very start. Try to approach the Bible as though it was the first time you had ever read it. Be ready to learn what it teaches – not what you think it teaches – and there is every likelihood that you will understand it better than if you have already made up your mind about what it says. That's not always easy to do, especially if you already have strong views, but it will undoubtedly prove helpful if you can manage to do that.

Letter to the Romans

You might want to take some time now to read the letter for yourself, before or after this summary. Notice how the letter begins and what the apostle is setting out to achieve. Here

---

[2] *The record of Paul's conversion is contained in the Acts of the Apostles, chapter 9.*

[3] *See, in particular, Romans 15:14-16:23 where Paul writes about his own work, including a big fund-raising collection that was then being taken for the believers in Jerusalem, and all the personal greetings he sent to people he knew in Rome. In this part he encourages Jews and Gentiles to live peacefully together, which might suggest that they had been falling out.*

2

are the opening verses:

> *"[1] Paul, a servant of Christ Jesus, called to be an apostle, set apart for the gospel of God, [2] which he promised beforehand through his prophets in the holy Scriptures, [3] concerning his Son, who was descended from David according to the flesh [4] and was declared to be the Son of God in power according to the Spirit of holiness by his resurrection from the dead, Jesus Christ our Lord, [5] through whom we have received grace and apostleship to bring about the obedience of faith for the sake of his name among all the nations, [6] including you who are called to belong to Jesus Christ. [7] To all those in Rome who are loved by God and called to be saints: Grace to you and peace from God our Father and the Lord Jesus Christ" (Romans 1:1-7 ESV).*[4]

If you are not familiar with the Bible you may be pleasantly surprised how easy it is to read and how readily it can be understood. Notice also how much information it contains in just a few verses.[5] Here is a short summary of what we learn from these introductory verses. It illustrates how you can gain information, almost without realising what is happening.

❖ Paul introduces himself as someone who serves Jesus Christ and who has been called to be his spokesperson, or *"apostle"* (verse 1).

❖ He says that his function, as an apostle, is to explain the *"gospel of God"*, which 'good news' was set out first in the Old Testament – the Jewish Holy Scriptures (verse 1 again).

❖ Central to this good news is what happened to the *"Son of God"* – the Lord Jesus Christ – who has a twofold ancestry. He was connected to the Jewish race because

---

[4] *This book uses the **English Standard Version** of the Bible in most places because it is a recent English translation which combines accuracy of translation – from the original Hebrew and Greek in which the Scriptures were written – with ease of understanding. The choice of translation is something that will be discussed later, in Chapter 3, when considering how best to read the Bible.*

[5] *The whole of the Bible has been divided by translators into chapters and verses fo easy reference: there were no such divisions when the original manuscripts were written.*

he was King David's descendant – through his mother Mary. And he was connected to God both because God was his Father and because God raised him from the dead (verses 3 and 4).

❖ Jesus shows *favour* to all of us – the meaning of the word *"grace"* – provided we believe the gospel and obey his commandments. Through the gospel, or good news, we are all called to belong to Jesus and to separate ourselves to God. This invitation comes because God loves us, and because He wants to show us favour, however undeserving we might be. He is offering us peace, just as it was first offered to the believers in Rome (verse 7).

Notice how straightforward it is to understand what at first seems to be a difficult passage of New Testament teaching. This little example is typical of how to obtain information, either from:

✓ letters like the one Paul wrote to Rome,
✓ narratives – like the Gospels or Acts,
✓ poetry – like the Psalms in the Old Testament,
✓ historical records – like the book of Kings
✓ ancient prophecies – like the book of Isaiah.

The approach is always the same: to read carefully and to take note of what you are being told. A notebook can be helpful, especially if you are looking for teaching about a certain topic. For example, if you want to find out what the Bible says about any hope of life after death, a page of Bible references that you have written down for yourself as you have been reading will be of more direct help than a lot of comments made by someone else. This is because you will have been looking at the original material, uncluttered by what other people, with their own ideas, might want you to think.

Notice that writing out what a verse is saying is different from just writing out the verse itself, useful though that can be at times. Here we are trying to note down the teaching of a particular verse and this book contains several worked examples of how that might be done.

Regular Bible reading is by far the best way to understand Bible teaching and it is exactly the way God means us to come to understand His Word. A daily Bible reading planner is the best way to make sure that you work your way systematically through the entire library of books

4

which make up the Bible. There are 66 books altogether in the two Testaments. Two different planners are included later which you may like to try.[6] But before you begin a systematic study it is important to think about the best way to approach it, so that you understand what you are reading.

Here is one approach to try. If you sit down and read right through the letter the apostle Paul wrote to the believers at Rome and then write down the key points he makes, you might come up with something like this.[7]

---

[6] *The first is in Chapter 3, on pages 34 & 35; the other is a more comprehensive daily reading table and that can be found in Chapter 28, on pages 436 & 437.*

[7] *If you want to stop and read the Letter and then summarise its teaching for yourself, you can then compare your findings with those listed below. But you may not be quite ready for that yet. Do what seems comfortable for you.*

Romans – Chapter and Verse	Summary of Contents
1:1-7	Introduction – Paul is writing about the gospel of God to all in Rome who have been called by God to receive His grace through Jesus Christ.
1:8-17	He explains that he was hoping to visit them sometime and that he is preaching the good news about Jesus, because it can give salvation to everyone who believes it.
1:18-32	Now he says why that salvation is needed. God is angry with mankind because it ignores the evidence of His existence and is behaving in a godless and shameful way. Mankind is depraved: people not only do wrong but they rejoice in doing those things.
2:1-16	God is going to judge the world for its godless behaviour and that means individuals will be held responsible for their actions, unless they do something about it.
2:17-29	This coming judgement will affect Jews and non-Jews alike.[8] Having been born as a Jew, and having lived as a Jew, will be no protection. Something more than that is needed. What matters is what a person is like inside.
3:1-20	Jews were given a head start over the rest of mankind because they got to know God during Old Testament times. But their Scriptures explain that all mankind has disobeyed God (disobeying God is what the Bible calls "sin"). Everybody has broken God's law; everybody is guilty before God.

[8] *Non-Jews are called "Gentiles" in the Bible.*

3:21-31	God has an escape plan. Belief in Jesus Christ can enable a person to be saved from eternal death, but without this belief it is inescapable. Jesus died to set people free from sin and make them right with God. Jesus is at the centre of God's plan.
4:1-25	Belief in God has been shown in the past to be what God wants. [9] It was the secret of Abraham's success, when all else seemed hopeless, and it was the only thing that King David had left when his life went badly wrong. We should follow the example of these faithful men and learn from them.
5:1-11	If we believe in God we can live at peace with Him, because of what Jesus has done for us. Belief will give us hope and make life bearable, whatever happens. For we will come to realise that Christ died for us and that we can be saved through him.
5:12-21	Where the first man Adam failed, the Lord Jesus has now succeeded. Adam's actions brought disaster upon the human race, but Jesus has made recovery possible. Through Jesus it is possible to obtain forgiveness so that we can be counted right with God which, in turn, can make eternal life available to us. [10]
6:1-23	Forgiveness comes by baptism, an act which identifies us with the work of Jesus. As he was killed, buried and then rose again, so in baptism we re-enact these actions. We are buried in water and raised to a new life, having resolved to put our past life to death. The outcome is that we promise to live for Jesus, not for ourselves, and to live holy or separate lives, seeking always to please God and the Lord Jesus Christ. Baptism is part of the way in which we escape from sin and death and find eternal life.

[9] *The Bible term for belief in God is "faith" and Paul uses that word a lot in his writings.*

[10] *The technical term for being 'right with God' is that we can be made "righteous". There are more than 40 occurrences of that phrase in this letter.*

7:1-25	Things don't change overnight! We can expect there to be a lot of inward turmoil and tension. It's as though we lost one partner and found another, with all the upheaval that can bring. There is likely to be a struggle inside us, between our old and new natures. The old one tries to get us to carry on living as before and the new nature that is developing within us tries to get us to do right things. We will know what we ought to do, and sometimes will want to do that, but often we will do things that belong to our life before baptism. It can be a real struggle at times!
8:1-17	As our spiritual life develops and we get to understand more and more what God has done for us, through Jesus Christ, we will begin to develop a way of thinking and living which is increasingly pleasing to God. We will come to realise more and more what a privilege it is to be members of God's family – brothers and sisters in Christ.
8:18-39	All this will give us a better view of life, with all its present unfairness and hardship. We will understand that God doesn't want it to be like this: He wants everything set free from sin, suffering and death. God is at work to achieve things that are good and which will change the world for the better. He means to fill it with people who are like His Son, the Lord Jesus, and He can help us overcome all our difficulties. When the time is right God will destroy all that opposes Him and establish a free and perfect society.
9-11	Although God called Israel to be a special nation and gave it great privileges, the Jews rejected His offer of salvation. God has the right to choose whoever He wants and to reject whoever He chooses to; after all, God made everybody and He is in charge of everything! But the Jews' failure was due to their conviction that they could earn a place in God's favour simply by being descendants of Abraham. They did not understand that belief in God and His promises was the key factor.

	For the moment, they have stumbled and lost their way; but it is part of God's purpose that the nation should be reinstated to favour. Jerusalem and the Jewish people still have an important part to play in the purpose of God.
12-15:13	God's gracious purpose has become known to us and we should live in a way which shows true appreciation for all He has done. We should live in a way that properly honours and worships God. Every day we should try to purify our minds and find out what God wants of us. We should use our God-given abilities to His glory, learning to love one another and becoming submissive and obedient. We should live as good citizens, accepting the rule of law and complying with what the state requests (provided it accords with God's law, which is our first priority). We should help one another, be understanding and tolerant of one another's weaknesses and failings, live at peace, and seek to live a Christ-centred and Christ-like life. Our lives should seek to glorify God in all things.
15:14-16:27	*Conclusion:* Paul explains his own position as someone who has been commanded to preach, especially to Gentiles. He tells the congregation at Rome that he hopes to come to see them soon, asks for their prayers and sends lots of personal greetings to believers whom he has met elsewhere on his travels. Thus the letter ends by giving us an insight into the Christian family of believers and the warmth and affection they felt towards one another.

"For I am not ashamed of the gospel, for it is the power of God for salvation to everyone who believes, to the Jew first and also to the Greek" (Romans 1:16)

Checklist

This brief summary of the Letter to the Romans serves at least three purposes.

1 It demonstrates how you can work your way through the Bible and broadly summarise the main teachings it contains. There is, of course, a lot more contained in the Letter to the Romans than is summarised here – as our earlier more in-depth look at the Introduction (Romans 1:1-7) showed. But it gives an overall view of the apostle's preaching – what he calls the "gospel of salvation".

2 It enables you to look for yourself at the various parts of the letter to see if the summary is fair and accurate. Remember the aim of this book is to help you understand the Bible for yourself. Your own Bible reading is a vital part of that process. You are only going to be convinced about Bible truth when you have seen it for yourself in the pages of the Bible. This book can help, but it is not a substitute for your own reading and thinking.

3 It provides a checklist of teachings against which you can compare your own beliefs. For example, ask yourself these questions:

   a Do you know why belief (or "faith") is so important to God, and what it is that we must believe, if we want to please Him?

   b Do you know who is to blame for the depraved state of mankind, and whether or not God will count us responsible for that?

   c Do you know what Abraham and David believed, which made them right with God? Do you believe those things, whatever they are?

   d What exactly was the result of Adam's failure and how did the death of Jesus put things right?

   e Is baptism essential for salvation and, if it is, what must you believe before being baptised? [11]

---

[11] *Notice that in Romans chapter 6, Christian Baptism is defined as a burial in water, not an act of sprinkling or pouring.*

f   Does the nation of Israel, or the city Jerusalem, feature in your present understanding of God's purpose in its final phase? If not, why not?

You may find some of those questions a bit baffling at this stage, but don't worry. This book is going to look in some detail at those issues. Because the Letter to the Romans sets out what Paul understands the gospel to be all about, we will use that letter as the framework for our thinking.[12]

We will work step-by-step through the apostle's explanations and follow his argument. The journey to explore what First Century Christianity is about will take us to many other parts of the Bible, as all 66 books of the Bible are part of God's message to mankind. In that way we shall find the key to eternal life.

Things to Read

📖   Why not read right through the Letter to the Romans, all 16 chapters?

📖   If that's a bit much at this stage, pick one section of the Letter that looks interesting – using the Summary of Contents above – and read through that. See if you agree with the suggested summary for that part. If not, write your own.

Questions to Consider [13]

1.1   What did Paul say to the Roman believers (Christians) about where the good news from God (the gospel) had first been promised? (Romans 1:2)

1.2   What did he say about the origin and nature of the Lord Jesus Christ? (Romans 1:3-4)

1.3   How did he describe the gospel, and what effect did he say it could have in our lives? (Romans 1:16)

---

12 *Paul calls the gospel: "the power of God for salvation to everyone who believes" (Romans 1:16).*

13 *The questions at the end of each chapter are to help you think things through for yourself. There are answers, in Chapter 30, should you want to check your findings, or you can correspond with someone if you want to discuss things or get further help. More details can be found on page 451.*

2

The Holy Scriptures

Before we spend a lot of time learning to understand the Bible, we need to be sure about one thing – that the Bible is really God's Word. If it is full of myths and fables, as some people suggest, we could be wasting our time. But if it is a message from God, we would be foolish to ignore it. Many religions have their sacred Scriptures, or holy writings. How can we be sure about what is written in the Bible? This chapter looks at something the apostle Paul says right at the start and from there examines the authority and accuracy of the Bible.

❖ Word of Prophecy

Right at the start of Paul's Letter to the Romans[1] he refers to his calling as an apostle of Jesus Christ,[2] and then he says something about the gospel which might surprise some readers. He says this:

> *"Paul, a servant of Christ Jesus, called to be an apostle, set apart for the gospel of God,* **which he promised beforehand through his prophets in the holy Scriptures***" (1:1,2).*

Paul is saying that the gospel is not just a New Testament message; it is contained in both the Old and New Testaments. You can find the gospel throughout the Bible. That's another of the challenges the Bible presents to its readers. Ask yourself if your understanding of the purpose of God is just about the life and work of Jesus. Does it include things that are taught in the 39 books of the Jewish part of the Bible – the Old Testament? As a simple check:

---

[1] *From now on we are going to refer to the Letter to the Romans as just "Romans".*

[2] *Paul says that an apostle is someone "set apart for the gospel of God".*

1   What do you understand by the phrase Jesus used lots of times when he taught about *"the kingdom of God"?* [3] Do you realise that this kingdom once existed in Old Testament times?

2   What do you make of these verses?

> *"And the Scripture, foreseeing that God would justify the Gentiles by faith,* **preached the gospel beforehand to Abraham***, saying, 'In you shall all the nations be blessed' " (Galatians 3:8);*

> *"Therefore, while the promise of entering his rest still stands, let us fear lest any of you should seem to have failed to reach it.* **For good news came to us just as to them***, but the message they heard did not benefit them, because they were not united by faith with those who listened" (Hebrews 4:1,2).*

First we are told that Abraham had the gospel preached to him. A specific passage is referred to (Genesis 12:3) which is said to be a part of the gospel.[4] Then the writer of another New Testament letter says that the Jewish nation had the gospel preached to them. However they were unable to receive what God had promised because they did not believe His promises. Then he warns us about the same danger. So you will see that both Testaments claim to have the same message from God. It follows that we must read and understand both parts of the Bible. The whole Bible is necessary for our salvation.

❖ What Paul told Timothy

One of the early companions of the apostle Paul was a young man named Timothy who had been brought up in a mixed home. He had a Gentile father but a Jewish mother – and he became a devoted follower of the Lord Jesus. Writing to him on one occasion, Paul said this about his upbringing:

> *"But as for you, continue in what you have learned and have firmly believed, knowing from whom you learned it*

---

[3] *See, for example, Matthew 6:33; 19:24; 21:31,43; Mark 1:15; 4:26, 30 and Luke 4:43; 7:28.*

[4] *Genesis 12:3 says "...in you all the families of the earth shall be blessed".*

and how from childhood you have been acquainted with
the sacred writings, which are able to make you
wise for salvation through faith in Christ Jesus. *All*
Scripture is breathed out by God *and (is) profitable for*
teaching, for reproof, for correction, and for training in
righteousness, that the man of God may be competent,
equipped for every good work" (2 Timothy 3:14-17).

This shows us how important the Old Testament is.
Timothy lived at a time when the New Testament had not
yet been written, or when only parts of it were in circula-
tion. His Scriptures, which he had been brought up to read
and respect, were the Old Testament. They are what the
apostle calls *"the sacred writings"* – and they held the key
to his spiritual education. They had a lot to teach him; they
could reprove and correct him; they could train him in
righteousness – in right living before God. These Scriptures
could make him acceptable to God by bringing him to *"faith*
in Christ Jesus".

The reason given for this remarkable power of the
Scriptures is that *"**All Scripture is breathed out by God**"*.
In some versions of the Bible the translation reads that the
Scriptures are *"inspired"* by God, or given by *"inspiration"*,
but the ESV uses a more literal rendering.[5] Scripture
claims to have come out of the mouth of God, just as our
words come from our mouths.

❖ Jesus' Use of Scripture

This was something that Jesus also taught. Once he was
tempted to turn stones into bread and whilst resisting the
temptation he said this about the Word of God:

*"It is written, 'Man shall not live by bread alone, but **by***
every word that comes from the mouth of God'"
(Matthew 4:4).

In his reply Jesus quoted from the Old Testament
Scriptures, thus endorsing their claims and showing that
he accepted them fully. The verse he used is from the Book
of Deuteronomy. It was written of the occasion when the
nation of Israel was wandering in a wilderness. It was a
time when the people were fed miraculously by food that

---

[5] *For example, the King James Version says: "All scripture is given by inspi-*
ration of God, and is profitable for doctrine, for reproof, for correction, for
instruction in righteousness" (2 Timothy 3:16).

God supplied daily for them.

> *"He (God) humbled you and let you hunger and fed you with manna, which you did not know, nor did your fathers know, that he might make you know that man does not live by bread alone, but man lives by every word that comes from the mouth of the LORD"* (Deuteronomy 8:3).

If we think for a moment about what we have learned from these words of the Lord Jesus, we can see that:

✓ Jesus believed the Old Testament absolutely, as something that had come *"from the mouth of the LORD"*; [6]

✓ He used it in the way God had intended, to 'equip him for every good work' and to help him resist temptation;

✓ He believed in the wilderness experience of Israel after its miraculous Exodus experience – when the infant nation escaped from slavery in Egypt;

✓ He believed in the miraculous provision of Manna – something that happened daily for forty years, to keep the wanderers alive.

At this point it is worth asking whether your approach to the Scriptures is the same as that of the Lord Jesus Christ – the founder of Christianity. Do you believe in the history of the Bible, in the possibility of miraculous events occurring as part of God's programme of events, and are you willing to accept that Scripture is God-given or God-breathed? These straightforward questions would catch out a lot of people. Many people reckon that the Bible is mainly myth and legend, handed down over centuries and thus substantially distorted before the various books were written down. Would you rather follow them or believe what the Lord Jesus believed? There really is no choice!

---

6 *When the Bible uses all capital letters to describe "the LORD" it does so to show that the original Hebrew language uses the special name of God, which is translated "Yahweh" and sometimes "Jehovah" in different Bible versions. This is God's covenant name, a name which explains that He is a Redeemer and Deliverer of His people.*

❖ Jesus Believed the Scriptures

If we collect together a few of the sayings of Jesus about the Scriptures, it will soon show us exactly what he believed. Evidently he was schooled in the Old Testament, as many Jewish boys would have been in his days. He had a wonderful understanding of the people who featured there, the things they said and, even more importantly, what they meant by what they said. His grasp of Bible teaching was so extensive that he could easily out-think his accusers and leave them totally confused.

Some people said of Jesus that: *"No one ever spoke like this man!" (John 7:46).* Jesus had an outstanding grasp of Old Testament truth because he was God's Son and had come with God's message. He was the God-given Saviour of the world, so we need to pay the most careful attention to what he said and believed.

Here are some of the things Jesus said about the Old Testament Scriptures:

"(Jesus) rolled up the scroll and gave it back to the attendant and sat down. And the eyes of all in the synagogue were fixed on him. And he began to say to them, **"Today this Scripture has been fulfilled in your hearing"** *(Luke 4:20,21)*

"And taking the twelve, he said to them, 'See, we are going up to Jerusalem, and **everything that is written about the Son of Man by the prophets will be accomplished.** *For he will be delivered over to the Gentiles and will be mocked and shamefully treated and spat upon. And after flogging him, they will kill him, and on the third day he will rise.' But they understood none of these things. This saying was hidden from them, and they did not grasp what was said" (Luke 18:31-34).*

"The Son of Man goes as it is written of him, *but woe to that man by whom the Son of Man is betrayed! It would have been better for that man if he had not been born" (Matthew 26:24).*

"For I tell you that **this Scripture must be fulfilled in me:** *'And he was numbered with the transgressors.' For what is written about me has its fulfilment" (Luke 22:37).*

"And he said to them, 'O foolish ones, and slow of heart to believe all that the prophets have spoken! Was it not necessary that the Christ should suffer these things and enter into his glory?' **And beginning with Moses and all the Prophets, he interpreted to them in all the Scriptures the things concerning himself"** *(Luke 24:25-27).*

"You search the Scriptures because you think that in them you have eternal life; and it is they that bear witness about me, yet you refuse to come to me that you may have life ... Do not think that I will accuse you to the Father. There is one who accuses you: Moses, on whom you have set your hope. If you believed Moses, you would believe me; **for he wrote of me.** *But if you do not believe his writings, how will you believe my words?" (John 5:39-47).*

❖ Life History in Advance

There are many more examples of similar statements made by Jesus. These few provide a flavour of the Lord's absolute conviction that the Old Testament Scriptures were inspired and prophetic accounts. As Jesus understood matters, they spoke of him because they predicted his coming and his life history. A very considerable list of such prophecies can be compiled, which show beyond doubt that the Bible can predict the future. On the next page are listed just a few, all about the life of Jesus.

Then Jesus said to them, "These are my words that I spoke to you while I was still with you, that everything written about me in the Law of Moses and the Prophets and the Psalms must be fulfilled" (Luke 24:44)

Old Testament	Prophecy	Fulfilment
Micah 5:2	Jesus to be born in Bethlehem	Matthew 2:6
Isaiah 60:3,6	To be visited by Wise Men	Matthew 2:11
Hosea 11:1	To go into Egypt	Matthew 2:15
Jeremiah 31:15	To have his life threatened (by Herod)	Matthew 2:18
Isaiah 9:1,2	To base his work in Galilee	Matthew 4:15,16
Isaiah 35:5; 42:7	To perform miracles	Matthew 12:18-20
Psalm 69:9	To cleanse the Temple at Jerusalem	John 2:17
Psalm 22:6	To be persecuted	Mark 15:29-32
Zechariah 9:9	To enter triumphantly into Jerusalem	Matthew 21:5
Psalm 41:9	To be betrayed by his friend	John 13:18
Zechariah 11:12	For thirty pieces of silver	Matthew 26:15
Zechariah 13:7	To be deserted by his disciples	Matthew 26:31
Isaiah 53:7	To be silent under accusation	John 19:9

Old Testament	Prophecy	Fulfilment
Psalm 35:15,21; Isaiah 50:6	To be insulted, hit, spat upon and scourged	**Mark 15:19**
Psalm 22:14,17	To be crucified	**Matthew 27:35**
Isaiah 53:9,12	To be crucified with wrongdoers	**Luke 23:33**
Psalm 34:20	Not a bone of his body to be broken	**John 19:36**
Zechariah 12;10; 13:6	To have his hands and feet pierced	**Matthew 27:35**
Isaiah 53:9	To be buried with the rich	**John 19:38-42**
Psalm 16:8-10; 110:1-3	To be raised from the dead and be exalted to God's right hand in heaven	**Acts 2:22-28**

That table gives some idea of the range of Old Testament prophecy about just one subject – the life history of the Lord Jesus. These prophecies were written hundreds of years before his birth and come from many different time periods and many different writers. But they speak with one voice because the message is God's, not man's. The prophets were impelled to speak and write as God's messengers: *"No prophecy of Scripture comes from someone's own interpretation. For no prophecy was ever produced by the will of man, but men spoke from God as they were carried along by the Holy Spirit"* (2 Peter 1:20).

❖ Detailed Predictions

We will get an even better idea of the Bible's remarkable accuracy by looking at just one prophetic passage. Psalm 22 was written by King David, who lived about 1000 years before Jesus was born. In it he predicts what was to happen to the promised descendant who would, one day, occupy David's throne in Jerusalem.

David wasn't just a poet; he was a prophet. In his own words, just before he died he said how grateful he was that: *"The Spirit of the LORD speaks by me; his word is on my tongue. The God of Israel has spoken, the Rock of Israel has said to me ..." (2 Samuel 23:2,3).* The results of that process of inspiration are breathtaking. They achieve a remarkable blend of God's message with some personal characteristics of the prophet. Look at the scenario described in Psalm 22 as it depicted what would happen in the life of David's successor. Bear in mind that at the time of writing crucifixion was unknown – it was a form of public execution introduced much later, one which was perfected by the Romans. Yet King David, inspired by God, could write about this. His successor would:

↘ Feel forsaken by God at a crucial time in his life when he was in dire trouble (Psalm 22:1) – these are the very words spoken by Jesus on the cross (Matthew 27:46).

↘ He would be despised and rejected by his fellows, who would openly mock him and challenge him to save himself, if he could (verses 6-8) – these were precisely the taunts that were hurled at Jesus.

↘ He would suffer the agony of feeling that his entire body was being pulled apart (verses 14-17), would have an intense thirst, and would be a public spectacle. This is a quite remarkable depiction of crucifixion well ahead of its time, including the piercing of hands and feet.

↘ His clothing would be divided between others who would cast lots for his garments – exactly as the soldiers did (verse 18 and John 19:24).

↘ The suffering one would not lose hope. He would continue to put his faith in God, in the firm belief that he would be able to bear witness to a lot of people that God is a Saviour and Redeemer (verses 21-31). This was something that Jesus began to do after his resurrection, when he was seen by more than 500 people (1 Corinthians 15:6), but the complete fulfilment of those words is still to come (see Zechariah 12:10).

❖ **Remarkable Book**

So far we have taken just one topic – the way that writers of the Bible could foretell the future, because they were inspired by God. And we have looked at just one subject – the life history of the Lord Jesus Christ, which was written in advance. We have seen that:

✓ the Bible was able to predict exactly what would happen in precise detail;

✓ the Lord Jesus valued the Old Testament Scriptures and used them in his own life to obtain guidance and help; and

✓ he clearly believed what he read in those Scriptures.

We saw some of the things that the Bible foretold about how Jesus would live and die (there are many more of those prophecies we did not consider). We looked at just one prophetic passage (Psalm 22) to see a remarkable prophetic picture of the crucifixion that Jesus would suffer, and the way he would overcome it with God's help.

❖ More from Jesus

But we have still only scratched the surface. If we were just to consider more fully the testimony of Jesus, we would discover that he relied upon the authority and accuracy of God's Word to such an extent that he:

↻ Could base his argument on just a word (John 10:35);

↻ Rely on just the tense of the original Hebrew (Mark 12:26,27); [7]

↻ Accepted as absolutely historical fact:

   ↻ the creation of *Adam and Eve* (Matthew 19:4-6),

   ↻ the death of *Abel* (Matthew 23:35),

   ↻ the flood at the time of *Noah* (Luke 17:26,27),

   ↻ the destruction of Sodom and Gomorrah (17:28-32), and so on.

---

[7] *In Mark 12:26,27 Jesus proved the resurrection by explaining that God used the present, not the past, tense when describing himself as the God of Abraham. He explained that God said "I **am** the God of Abraham", and not "I **was** the God of Abraham". That shows the remarkable confidence Jesus had in the authority of God's Word given to Moses.*

And there are still lots of things the Lord said about the Scriptures that we haven't considered, such as:

> *"Do not think that I have come to abolish the Law or the Prophets;* **I have not come to abolish them but to fulfil them. For truly, I say to you, until heaven and earth pass away, not an iota, not a dot, will pass from the Law until all is accomplished"** *(Matthew 5:17,18), or*

> *"If he called them gods to whom the word of God came – and* **Scripture cannot be broken** *– do you say of him whom the Father consecrated and sent into the world, 'You are blaspheming,' because I said, 'I am the Son of God'?" (John 10:35,36).*

The example of Jesus is very important in working out our approach to the authority of Holy Scripture. If we want to know what the Bible *really* teaches, the lead that Jesus gives is one of the very best ways of finding a correct understanding. Jesus accepted the Bible as the inspired and wholly accurate Word of God.

❖ God has Spoken

When Jesus came he was a further link in the chain of Divine revelation. From the very beginning of His dealings with mankind, God communicated with His creation. He gave Adam and Eve instructions about how to live; told Noah when to build an ark; made great promises to Abraham and his family; gave Israel a code of laws through Moses, as well as many prophecies about their future. This was part of an almost continuous process of communication in which God made known His will to mankind.[8] A New Testament writer says this:

> *"Long ago, at many times and in many ways,* **God spoke to our fathers** *by the prophets, but in these last days* **he has spoken to us by his Son"** *(Hebrews 1:1).*

The Old and New Testaments are that record of God communicating with mankind and they leave us in no

---

[8] *There is a gap of some 400 years between the Old and New Testaments during which there was no communication from God. That gap was broken when John the Baptist appeared to herald the coming of Jesus, the Messiah.*

doubt about that. Over and over again the prophets declared that they were speaking on God's behalf. Here's just one sample in which the prophet Haggai makes that point repeatedly:

> *"Yet now be strong, O Zerubbabel, **declares the Lord**. Be strong, O Joshua, son of Jehozadak, the high priest. Be strong, all you people of the land, **declares the Lord**. Work, for I am with you, **declares the Lord of hosts**, according to the covenant that I made with you when you came out of Egypt. My Spirit remains in your midst. Fear not. For **thus says the Lord of hosts**: Yet once more, in a little while, I will shake the heavens and the earth and the sea and the dry land. And I will shake all nations, so that the treasures of all nations shall come in, and I will fill this house with glory, **says the Lord of hosts**. The silver is mine, and the gold is mine, **declares the Lord of hosts**. The latter glory of this house shall be greater than the former, **says the Lord of hosts**. And in this place I will give peace, **declares the Lord of hosts**"* (Haggai 2:4-9).

The prophets were God's spokesmen. The expression *"says the Lord"* occurs over 500 times in the Bible because, time and again, the various writers of the Bible want us to know that their message was not theirs, but God's. Even Jesus repeatedly made that same claim:

> *Jesus answered them, "My **teaching is not mine, but his who sent me**. If anyone's will is to do God's will, he will know whether the teaching is from God or whether I am speaking on my own authority"* (John 7:16,17);

> *Jesus said to them, "When you have lifted up the Son of Man, then you will know that I am he, and that **I do nothing on my own authority, but speak just as the Father taught me**"* (John 8:28).

❖ Internal Harmony

Notice that wherever you look in the Bible – whether it's the prophet Haggai, or the words of the Lord Jesus – there is an unmistakable consistency so far as the message is concerned. The 66 books that make up the Bible were written over a time span of more than 1500 years, and by more than 40 different writers. They came from quite different backgrounds and lived in quite different times, yet the message has a remarkable harmony and unity. For there is only one author – Almighty God.

People have written entire books about the unity of the Bible, or the way in which incidental details tie in wonderfully with one another. Here is just one snippet from a book about the Bible, which will give you a flavour of the way in which these arguments could be extended:

> *"The Bible, at first sight, appears to be a collection of literature – mainly Jewish. If we enquire into the circumstances under which the various Biblical documents were written, we find that they were written at intervals over a space of nearly 1400 years. The writers wrote in various lands, from Italy in the west to Mesopotamia and possibly Persia in the east. The writers themselves were a heterogeneous number of people, not only separated from each other by hundreds of years and hundreds of miles, but belonging to the most diverse walks of life. In their ranks we have kings, herdsmen, soldiers, legislators, fishermen, statesmen, courtiers, priests and prophets, a tent making Rabbi and a Gentile physician, not to speak of others of whom we know nothing apart from the writings they have left us. The writings themselves belong to a great variety of literary types. They include history, law (civil, criminal, ethical, ritual, sanitary), religious poetry, didactic treatises, lyric poetry, parable and allegory, biography, personal correspondence, personal memoirs and diaries, in addition to the distinctively Biblical types of prophecy and apocalyptic."* [9]

❖ A Book from God

This book is not written to show you *why* the Bible is the Word of God. We have not considered the way in which the Bible:

✓ predicted the future of various nations;

✓ was in advance of its time;

✓ contains accurate historical data which has been shown to be true when historians and archaeologists have made further discoveries; or

---

[9] *This extract is from "The Book and the Parchments" by F.F.Bruce.*

✓ has a message which has been remarkably preserved, so that we can be sure about its accurate transmission.

Enough has been written in this chapter, however, to show that it is very worthwhile to seek to understand the Bible for yourself. It is a quite remarkable book – a book from God – and it has a message which is unlike anything else that has ever been written. It was written by eyewitnesses of the events that are recorded. It is utterly frank about the weaknesses and failures of the people it describes, for the Bible was not written to glorify man, or to magnify the nation of Israel, from which most of the writers came. It was written to glorify God and to explain His gracious purpose.

The Bible is a Holy Book, because it has come from God. For that reason it is set apart from all other books. And it has been written to help to make us holy. Remember that it is *"able to make you wise for salvation through faith in Christ Jesus. All Scripture is breathed out by God and profitable for teaching, for reproof, for correction, and for training in righteousness, that the man of God may be competent, equipped for every good work"* (2 Timothy 3:15-17).

Guidebook for Life

The Bible is a deeply moral book. It shows us the difference between right and wrong in every aspect of life: it defines what God considers right and describes both what He says is wrong and what will happen to us if we do wrong things. That is why there is so much history in the Bible. It is the record of God inviting men and women to walk in His way and then observing them doing the very opposite and getting into trouble – sometimes into big trouble. But if it was no more than that, the Bible would make very depressing reading. It would be a catalogue of disasters, and it is certainly not that.

The Bible is our Guidebook for Life. It shows us what God is like, what He wants to do with us and with our world. It shows what we must do if we want to be part of that gracious purpose, and how we can achieve a Christlike life. Most people think of improving themselves in terms of getting things and getting on. God wants us to learn to live differently; to accept His standards as those by which we will live, and to model ourselves on the way the Lord Jesus lived.

This remarkable book from God can help us achieve

25

those God-given objectives. It is a word of life which has the power to transform the way we think and then the way we behave. As we get to understand for ourselves what the Bible says about our situation and what God really offers – as opposed to what many people think God offers – we will come to realise how the Bible can change our lives. For the moment here is the testimony of one of its inspired writers, a fisherman whose life was entirely transformed by his encounter with the Lord Jesus Christ. This is what the apostle Peter wrote:

> *"Having purified your souls by your obedience to the truth for a sincere brotherly love, love one another earnestly from a pure heart, since **you have been born again, not of perishable seed but of imperishable, through the living and abiding word of God**; for 'All flesh is like grass and all its glory like the flower of grass. The grass withers, and the flower falls, but the word of the Lord remains forever' And **this word is the good news that was preached to you**"* (1 Peter 1:22-25).

Peter wrote to people whose previously impure lives had been made pure by their obedience to the things they now understood and believed. They were people who had found a new life in Christ. The way in which this had come about was that they had been reborn through the effect of the *"living and abiding word of God"* in their lives. That same transformation awaits us as we continue our journey of understanding.

Things to Read

📖 This chapter is full of Bible references and you might look some of them up, both to become familiar with the layout of the Bible – where the different books are located – and to check out the setting or context of the passages referred to. It is always a good thing to check up Bible references, rather than just taking them for granted.

📖 To see how the Bible exposes the weaknesses of its writers, so that we can learn from their mistakes, read 2 Samuel chapter 11 – about King David's big mistakes – and then Psalm 51, in which he fully repents of what he had done.

Questions to Think About

2.1 How do you know that the apostle Paul still believed the Old Testament prophecies after he had become a follower of the Lord Jesus? (Acts 17:2; 24:14 and 28:23)

2.2 Nowadays some people say that much of the Old Testament is myth and legend and that parts of it, like the Book of Genesis, were written very many years after the events there described. What help do we get from the way the Lord Jesus Christ viewed the Scriptures? (Mark 1:44; Matthew 15:4 and Mark 7:10; Matthew 19:3-9 and Luke 20:37)

2.3 Did the New Testament writers claim to write inspired Scripture? (John 14:26; 1 Thessalonians 2:13; 2 Peter 3:15-16; 1 Corinthians 14:37)

3

On Reading the Bible

God has communicated with mankind in a quite remarkable way. His Book is a unique revelation – unlike anything else that has ever been written. It lays bare the lives of many of its writers, showing us just what they were like, including their faults. It presents a portrait of the greatest man who ever lived – the Lord Jesus Christ – and it thus portrays life at its very best. Yet, in describing what happened to him, it also shows us human nature at its very worst.

❖ A Book to Read

Such a book has to be read. It cannot be neglected or overlooked yet, more often than not, that is what happens. Many people have Bibles; only a few read any of it and very few people read the entire Bible on a regular basis. Some people may have favourite parts of the Bible that they read quite often, but if we want to know God's message for mankind, the entire Bible must be read. And, because it is a long and sometimes complicated book, we need to read it and keep on reading it. This is a book that can give us a new life, but it is going to take a while to understand it entirely.

Everybody wants to know about the mysteries of life, which is why, in some countries, there is such interest in fortune telling or witchcraft. Is there any life after death? Is the world going to end sometime? Why do people suffer? Questions like that are not easily answered, but the Bible has the answers – because it contains God's message and God's answers. So how do we get to know what those answers are?

This book will work through those questions and seek the answers to them as we follow the apostle Paul's Letter to the Romans. But it has already become clear that, to understand the Bible for ourselves, we need to do some more Bible reading of our own. At the end of each chapter in this book you will find some suggestions about further

Bible reading. If you follow these they will help to increase your understanding of Bible teaching and will help you check up on what we will look at in Romans.

It is a good Bible-based practice to check things out, not just to take them for granted. When the apostle Paul made his first visit to Europe, he met some fierce opposition in different places. He came across a group of people in a place called Berea, of whom it was said:

> *"These Jews were more noble than those in Thessalonica; they received the word with all eagerness, **examining the Scriptures daily to see if these things were so**. Many of them therefore believed, with not a few Greek women of high standing as well as men" (Acts 17:11,12).*

You might want to work out a pattern of daily Bible reading that suits your own needs. Different readers of this book will be at quite different stages of understanding. Some will be quite familiar with the Bible already; others might never have looked seriously at it. So a variety of ideas are suggested here and you can pick something that seems appropriate. But first, here are some general observations.

❖ Bible Versions

This book uses the English Standard Version of the Bible, which is a quite recent translation into English.[1] The ESV updates the Revised Standard Version of the Bible, which itself was a revision of earlier versions going back to the 1611 King James Version. The reason for using it is that the ESV combines a fairly literal approach to Bible translation with a pleasant and readable style. Other versions will be referred to from time to time, where that translation is a little clearer, and it does not matter too much which version you have available or choose to use.

The Old Testament of the Bible was mainly written in Hebrew (with just a small part in Aramaic) and the New Testament was written in Greek. All translations do the best they can to render the original languages into English,

---

[1] *It is customary for Bible Versions to be abbreviated to just their initials, so the English Standard Version is known as the ESV, the King James Version as the KJV (or sometimes as the AV, as it is also known as the 'Authorised Version'), the New International Version as the NIV and the Good News Bible as the GNB.*

and some are bound to do it better than others. Be sure you are using a translation and not a paraphrase, as some versions – like *"The Living Bible"* or *"The Message"* – set out to be a very free rendering, more chatty and conversational than accurate.

A Bible with Cross References can be a great help. These are references that appear in the margin, or at the bottom of the page. They point you to other passages of Scripture which are similar, or which deal with similar subject-matter. As you become more familiar with the message of the Bible you will want to make use of those extra helps. But, for the moment, what matters is how to start.

Read through the Gospel of Mark if you want a gentle introduction to the Life of Jesus. You will quickly realise how different things were two thousand years ago. The events that are described in the Bible happened in the Middle East, in an agricultural society where Roman law controlled the life of the citizens and Jewish law regulated the way people worshipped. The more you read the easier it becomes, but it is always worth remembering that life was somewhat different in Bible times. These are writings that belong to ancient history. The marvellous thing is that they are still relevant and meaningful today. The Bible is an old book with a really up-to-date message.

❖ Two Different Parts

The structure of the **New Testament** is quite easy to follow. The life of Jesus is told four times, in the gospel accounts by Matthew, Mark, Luke and John. Then comes the story of the early church – mainly centred on the preaching of the apostles Peter and Paul. That is contained in the Acts of the Apostles, which was written by the gospel writer Luke. The Acts account refers to many places that the apostles visited and the various letters, which make up the rest of the New Testament, were written during or after their journeys.

The letters were the way the various apostles kept in touch with new congregations that had been established. Sometimes they were letters of general encouragement; sometimes they dealt with specific problems or issues that had arisen. As we have already seen, Romans was written to set out Paul's understanding of the gospel of salvation prior to his intended visit, as well as dealing with some local problems the church in Rome had.

The **Old Testament** Scriptures are longer. They make up about two thirds of the Bible and include history, poetry and prophecy. The historical or narrative accounts start in the first Book – Genesis – and go right up to the Book of Esther – 17 books in all, out of 39. The first 11 chapters of Genesis describes the creation of the world, then tells how things went wrong, the coming of a worldwide flood and the building of the Tower of Babel. After that the record follows the story of one family – that of Abraham, and his descendants.

Those descendants eventually became a nation (Israel), and were rescued from slavery in Egypt, led by Moses. After a period of wandering in the desert they entered the Promised Land and began to live as God's chosen nation, learning to obey and follow His Law. First they had a God-given leader Joshua, after that they were given judges to save them from particular situations, and then they were given kings, somewhat like the other nations.

The Kingdom established in Israel did not, however, run very smoothly. After initial success, under King David and his son Solomon, the kingdom split into two – North and South. The Northern kings abandoned the true worship of God and devised a completely man-made system of calf-worship. They had false priests and made up their own rules and regulations. That arrangement lasted for about 200 years before the Northern Kingdom was taken captive to Assyria and all the people were deported. The Southern Kingdom of Judah fared a little better. Altogether it lasted for about 350 years before it too abandoned the worship of God and paid the price. By then, about 600 B.C., Babylon was the ruling power in the Middle East, having conquered the Assyrians, and the people of the Southern Kingdom were deported there, to the country we now know as Iraq.

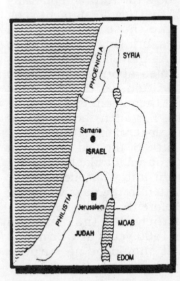

Map of Israel and Judah in the time of the Kings

Seventy years later a group of Jewish[2] exiles returned from Babylon – which had, in the meantime, been conquered by the Persians. They started to rebuild their nation and the city Jerusalem. This part of their history is covered in the books of Ezra and Nehemiah. Four hundred years after that – by which time the Romans were the ruling power – the New Testament begins, with the birth of Jesus.

❖ Wonderful Variety

Now you have some idea of the variety and fascination of the library of books which make up the Bible. There are books full of **poetry** and proverbial **wisdom**. The Book of Psalms is the hymn book that was used in temple worship. There are the wise sayings of King Solomon and of others; love poetry; and a reasoned treatise about the best way to live before God. There is also the Book of Job which explains how someone can become right in the sight of God, an insight that came about when Job was severely tested.

Then there is **prophecy**, which makes up a large proportion of the Bible. Someone has worked out that over one quarter of the Old Testament predicts the future in one way or another (and over one fifth of the New Testament too). There are large prophecies – like those of Isaiah and Jeremiah – and twelve shorter ones, bringing us right up to the times of Ezra and Nehemiah. As the Book of Acts gives us a guide in New Testament times about when and to whom the various letters were written, so the historical parts of the Bible help us work out the meaning of the message that God's prophets brought. For often their message had an immediate as well as a longer-term significance.

If you would like to sample a little of the Old Testament after reading the Gospel of Mark, you might like to read the Book of Ruth to give you an insight into what life was like in those times. That book was written in the days when the Judges ruled (about 1250 years before the birth of Jesus).

It's a marvellous feature of the Bible that such an ancient book – written down over 1900 years ago – can still be so interesting and relevant. It should be no surprise

[2] *Because the people who returned were mainly from the tribe of Judah – the small tribe that had been living in and around Jerusalem – from now on the people in the land are known as Jews (a word which originally referred to members of the tribe of Judah).*

since, as we have seen, this is a book from God. Its various writers wrote as they were inspired by God. They did not make things up. They could never have achieved such a superb result without the help of God. As the apostle Peter once said:

*"We have something more sure, the prophetic word, to which you will do well to pay attention as to a lamp shining in a dark place, until the day dawns and the morning star rises in your hearts, knowing this first of all, that **no prophecy of Scripture comes from someone's own interpretation. For no prophecy was ever produced by the will of man, but men spoke from God as they were carried along by the Holy Spirit**"* (2 Peter 1:19-21).

Daily Bible Reading

If you decide you would like to read a part of the Bible every day, to work your way through everything that God has included in His message, you will find a daily Bible Reading planner helpful. It is designed to give you an introduction to different parts of the Bible and it will take you a year to work through, reading one chapter each day.

If you think that is a bit too much for you at this early stage of your understanding, you can think about starting it later on, as your knowledge grows about the Bible's overall message. If you want something more detailed, which will take you through the whole Bible in the course of a year, there is another Bible Reading plan towards the end of this book. But you need to pace yourself so that you can read more as your level of understanding increases.

*"These Jews were more noble than those in Thessalonica; they received the word with all eagerness, **examining the Scriptures daily to see if these things were so**"* (Acts 17:11)

Bible Reading Planner
Read a chapter a day for 12 Months

Step	Week	Sunday	Monday	Tuesday	Wednesday	Thursday	Friday	Saturday
1	1	Psalm 18	Genesis 1	Luke 2	1 Cor 13	Mark 4	Ecclesiastes 3	2 Tim 3
2	2	Genesis 2	Genesis 3	Genesis 4	Genesis 5	Genesis 6	Genesis 7	Genesis 8
	3	Matthew 1	Matthew 2	Matthew 3	Matthew 4	Matthew 5	Matthew 6	Matthew 7
3	4	Genesis 11	Genesis 12	Genesis 13	Genesis 14	Genesis 15	Genesis 17	Genesis 19
	5	Matthew 8	Matthew 9	Matthew 10	Matthew 11	Matthew 12	Matthew 13	Matthew 14
	6	Genesis 22	Genesis 26	Genesis 27	Genesis 28	Genesis 29	Genesis 30	Genesis 31
4	7	Matthew 15	Matthew 16	Matthew 17	Matthew 18	Matthew 19	Matthew 20	Matthew 21
	8	Genesis 32	Genesis 33	Genesis 37	Genesis 39	Genesis 40	Genesis 41	Genesis 42
	9	Matthew 22	Matthew 23	Matthew 24	Matthew 25	Matthew 26	Matthew 27	Matthew 28
	10	Genesis 43	Genesis 44	Genesis 45	Genesis 46	Genesis 47	Genesis 49	Genesis 50
5	11	Mark 1	Mark 2	Mark 3	Mark 6	Mark 7	Mark 8	Mark 9
	12	Exodus 1	Exodus 2	Exodus 3	Exodus 4	Exodus 5	Exodus 6	Exodus 7
	13	Mark 10	Mark 11	Mark 12	Mark 13	Mark 14	Mark 15	Mark 16
	14	Exodus 8	Exodus 9	Exodus 10	Exodus 11	Exodus 12	Exodus 13	Exodus 14
	15	Luke 1	Luke 2	Luke 4	Luke 5	Luke 7	Luke 9	Luke 10
	16	Exodus 16	Exodus 17	Exodus 19	Exodus 20	Exodus 24	Exodus 25	Exodus 32
	17	Luke 11	Luke 12	Luke 13	Luke 14	Luke 15	Luke 16	Luke 17
	18	Leviticus 8	Leviticus 10	Leviticus 16	Leviticus 17	Leviticus 23	Leviticus 25	Leviticus 27
	19	Luke 18	Luke 19	Luke 20	Luke 21	Luke 22	Luke 23	Luke 24
	20	Numbers 14	Numbers 17	Numbers 20	Numbers 21	Numbers 22	Numbers 23	Numbers 24
	21	John 1	John 3	John 4	John 10	John 11	John 15	John 17
	22	Deut 1	Deut 2	Deut 3	Deut 6	Deut 8	Deut 18	Deut 28
	23	Acts 1	Acts 2	Acts 3	Acts 4	Acts 5	Acts 6	Acts 7
	24	Joshua 1	Joshua 2	Joshua 3	Joshua 4	Joshua 6	Joshua 20	Joshua 24
	25	Acts 8	Acts 9	Acts 10	Acts 11	Acts 12	Acts 13	Acts 14
	26	Judges 4	Judges 7	Judges 14	Ruth 1	Ruth 2	Ruth 3	Ruth 4

Bible Reading Planner
Read a chapter a day for 12 Months

Step	Week	Sunday	Monday	Tuesday	Wednesday	Thursday	Friday	Saturday
7	27	Acts 15	Acts 16	Acts 17	Acts 18	Acts 19	Acts 20	Acts 21
	28	1 Samuel 1	1 Samuel 2	1 Samuel 3	1 Samuel 8	1 Samuel 9	1 Samuel 10	1 Samuel 15
	29	Acts 22	Acts 23	Acts 24	Acts 25	Acts 26	Acts 27	Acts 28
	30	1 Samuel 16	1 Samuel 17	2 Samuel 1	2 Samuel 2	2 Samuel 5	2 Samuel 7	2 Samuel 24
	31	Romans 5	Romans 6	Romans 8	Romans 9	Romans 10	Romans 12	Romans 13
	32	1 Kings 3	1 Kings 5	1 Kings 12	1 Kings 17	1 Kings 18	2 Kings 5	2 Chron 36
	33	1 Corinth 1	1 Corinth 2	1 Corinth 3	1 Corinth 10	1 Corinth 11	1 Corinth 13	1 Corinth 15
	34	Psalm 1	Psalm 2	Psalm 6	Psalm 16	Psalm 19	Psalm 22	Psalm 23
	35	2 Corith 11	Galatians 1	Galatians 2	Galatians 3	Galatians 4	Galatians 5	Galatians 6
	36	Psalm 32	Psalm 37	Psalm 45	Psalm 46	Psalm 48	Psalm 49	Psalm 51
	37	Ephesians 4	Ephesians 5	Ephesians 6	Philippians 1	Philippians 2	Philippians 3	Philippians 4
	38	Psalm 67	Psalm 72	Psalm 88	Psalm 90	Psalm 91	Psalm 95	Psalm 96
	39	1 Thess 1	1 Thess 2	1 Thess 3	1 Thess 4	1 Thess 5	2 Thess 1	2 Thess 2
	40	Psalm 103	Psalm 104	Psalm 110	Psalm 122	Psalm 146	Psalm 149	Psalm 150
	41	1 Timothy 1	1 Timothy 2	1 Timothy 6	2 Timothy 1	2 Timothy 2	2 Timothy 3	2 Timothy 4
	42	Isaiah 1	Isaiah 2	Isaiah 9	Isaiah 11	Isaiah 25	Isaiah 26	Isaiah 32
	43	Hebrews 1	Hebrews 2	Hebrews 3	Hebrews 4	Hebrews 5	Hebrews 10	Hebrews 11
	44	Isaiah 40	Isaiah 42	Isaiah 52	Isaiah 53	Isaiah 55	Isaiah 60	Isaiah 61
	45	Hebrews 12	Hebrews 13	James 1	James 2	James 3	James 4	James 5
	46	Jeremiah 1	Jeremiah 17	Jeremiah 30	Jeremiah 31	Jeremiah 33	Jeremiah 36	Jeremiah 38
	47	1 Peter 1	1 Peter 2	1 Peter 3	1 Peter 5	2 Peter 1	2 Peter 2	2 Peter 3
	48	Ezekiel 2	Ezekiel 3	Ezekiel 18	Ezekiel 36	Ezekiel 37	Ezekiel 38	Ezekiel 39
	49	1 John 1	1 John 2	1 John 3	1 John 4	2 John	3 John	Jude
	50	Daniel 2	Daniel 3	Daniel 5	Daniel 6	Daniel 7	Daniel 9	Daniel 12
	51	Hosea 13	Joel 3	Micah 5	Zechariah 8	Zechariah 12	Malachi 3	Malachi 4
	52	Revelation 1	Revelation 2	Revelation 3	Revelation 5	Revelation 19	Revelation 21	Revelation 22

Things to Read

📖 This chapter has suggested that you sample the New Testament by reading the whole of the Gospel of Mark (all 16 chapters) and the Old Testament by reading the Book of Ruth (just 4 chapters). Don't rush them; take your time and work carefully through the passages.

📖 You may, however, prefer to start with the Bible Reading Planner which includes both Mark and Ruth within its suggested readings, as part of Step 5.

📖 There are also suggested readings with each chapter of this book, so you can decide what is best for you. Perhaps you will prefer to start regular Bible reading after you have finished this book, for there are suggestions about helpful passages at the end of each chapter.

📖 If you note anything especially interesting or difficult, make a note of it, or scribble down a question or two, and that will help you develop a logical and thoughtful approach to the Scriptures.

Questions to Think About

3.1 Even the Kings of Israel were commanded to read the Bible and to make their own copy of part of it, so that it was available for their ready reference. Every family in Israel was to talk about and teach the Scriptures in their homes, so that these things would be their daily delight. What does that indicate to us about daily Bible reading? (Deuteronomy 17:18-20; 6:6-12)

3.2 How did the Scriptures help Jesus to learn about the will of God and what does his experience teach us about the progress we are likely to make? (Luke 2:40-47,51-52; 4:3-12; 16-21)

4

Why God is Angry with His World

We have been thinking about the wonder of God's revealed Word and the need for us to read it for ourselves. This has prepared us for the apostle Paul's Letter to the Romans, in which he set out his understanding of the gospel of God. We needed to understand at the outset how special and how different these writings are. Paul was not writing to explain his own understanding of the gospel. Far from it! His clear emphasis was upon the fact that this:

✓ was the gospel promised by the prophets in God's Holy Scripture (Romans 1:1,2);

✓ concerned the Lord Jesus Christ who is the centre of God's plan and purpose (1:3,4); and that

✓ it was Jesus who had called him to be an apostle (1:5).

The Good News, he explained, was God's, not his; and it puts Jesus at the centre of everything.

❖ God is Angry

No sooner has the apostle made those introductory remarks than he launches into an explanation that must have startled and troubled his first century readers. It should trouble us as well. The gospel can save you, he says, if you believe it (Romans 1:16,17), but without it you and all the inhabitants of the world are in deep trouble. Here are his actual words:

"For the wrath of God is revealed from heaven against all ungodliness and unrighteousness of men, who by their unrighteousness suppress the truth" (Romans 1:18).

Paul says either, we are considered right with God, because of the things we believe, or we are very definitely in the wrong. None of us likes being in the wrong – with our parents, or relatives or our employer – but it's a much more

37

serious and dangerous thing to get on the wrong side of God. None of us wants to be the subject of God's righteous anger. So why is God so angry with the world He has made, and what can we do about it for ourselves? A careful look at Romans chapters 1 and 2 will explain all we need to know and will show us what avoiding action we should take. But take a moment to stop to think about something.

At the very start of his letter Paul tells his readers that there is a real problem facing mankind. Why does he do that, instead of spelling out the gracious plan of salvation that God has been carefully working out from the very beginning?

Do you go to the doctor or the clinic when you are feeling all right? Of course not! You only go when you think there is something wrong with you that needs to be put right. And that's exactly how the apostle is approaching the question of our spiritual health. If we think that everything is all right, it is unlikely that we will pay God's Word the attention it deserves. It is only when we know that the situation is serious that we will recognise that we need God's help.

❖ Wake-Up Call

The news that God is angry with mankind is designed to alert all mankind. It should tell us that things are seriously wrong in our lives so far as God is concerned and that we need to give this our most urgent attention. If your employer was angry with you, you would want to know straight away what had upset him or her. As it turns out, it is quite easy to work out from Paul's letter what is upsetting God. He is angry about people who:

⊻ **Are ungodly and unrighteous** – people who suppress that truth that God has revealed (Romans 1:18);

⊻ **Ignore the evident truth all around them** – they do not acknowledge that the world has been created by God. If they opened their eyes they would be bound to see the evidence that God made everything, because the design apparent in creation points to the great Designer, just as it was intended to (1:19-21);

⊻ **Know of God's existence but choose to worship other things.** Many cultures and civilisations have a sense of the existence of God, but many people deliberately suppress those senses. Instead of worshipping

God they choose to please themselves, or worship possessions or things that they have made (1:22-23).

❖ Divine Designer

This penetrating analysis goes right to the heart of the matter. One of the earliest arguments given in support of God as Creator was that of design. As long ago as 1800 a writer[1] argued that if he happened to be walking along and found a watch on the ground he would immediately wonder whose it was. It would never occur to him that it might just have happened into existence: that would have been absurd! A stone perhaps: a watch never! In the same way, he said, finding the world to be so wonderfully constructed and so carefully made, we should be asking ourselves – *"Whose world is this?"* and *"Who made it?"*

❖ Bible Prophecy

Of course, there are a lot more arguments that can be advanced to demonstrate that God exists apart from that of God the designer of the Universe. We have been thinking about one of them already when looking at the wonderful revelation contained in the Bible. Who but a divine and all-seeing God could have given such marvellous advance notice about the coming of His Son, the Lord Jesus. Hundreds of years before his birth, a detailed picture of his

---

1 *"In crossing a heath, suppose I pitched my foot against a stone and were asked how the stone came to be there, I might possibly answer that for anything I knew to the contrary it had lain there forever; nor would it, perhaps, be very easy to show the absurdity of this answer. But suppose I had found a watch upon the ground, and it should be inquired how the watch happened to be in that place, I should hardly think of the answer which I had before given, that for anything I knew the watch might have always been there. Yet why should not this answer serve for the watch as well as for the stone? Why is it not as admissible in the second case as in the first? For this reason, and for no other, namely, that when we come to inspect the watch, we perceive – what we could not discover in the stone – that its several parts are framed and put together for a purpose ... This mechanism being observed – it requires indeed an examination of the instrument, and perhaps some previous knowledge of the subject, to perceive and understand it; but being once, as we have said, observed and understood – the inference we think is inevitable, that the watch must have had a maker – that there must have existed, at some time and at some place or other, an artificer or artificers who formed it for the purpose which we find it actually to answer, who comprehended its construction and designed its use"* (William Paley, *"Natural Theology"*).

life was given so that when he came people would know this was the Coming One. It says a lot about the perversity and blindness of mankind that the Lord was despised and rejected when he came, instead of being readily accepted and followed.

Bible prophecy is a marvellous testimony to the existence of God, as it is intended to be. Who but a divine creator could have predicted the future of a mighty city in the ancient world that was, in its day, the equivalent of Washington or New York in today's world. Yet the prophet Isaiah said:

> *"Babylon, the glory of kingdoms, the splendour and pomp of the Chaldeans, will be like Sodom and Gomorrah when God overthrew them. It will never be inhabited or lived in for all generations; no Arab will pitch his tent there; no shepherds will make their flocks lie down there. But wild animals will lie down there, and their houses will be full of howling creatures; there ostriches will dwell, and there wild goats will dance" (Isaiah 13:19-21).*

That was precisely what happened to this mighty city of the ancient world – the one with the hanging gardens that was one of the wonders of the world. It fell into absolute decay and ceased to be inhabited. In time it was lost under the sand dunes of Iraq and was only rediscovered after careful search was made for it. Exactly as predicted, the Bedouin came to regard the site with superstitious dread and would not even pitch their tents there.

If you think that remarkable, as indeed it is, consider what God said about the Jewish nation when he described their history and that of the city of Jerusalem. Through many different prophets, and at many different times, the Jews were told that if they disobeyed God they would suffer the consequences. Moses, for example, said that this would happen:

> *"The Lord will scatter you among all peoples, from one end of the earth to the other, and there you shall serve other gods of wood and stone, which neither you nor your fathers have known. And among these nations you shall find no respite, and there shall be no resting place for the sole of your foot, but the Lord will give you there a trembling heart and failing eyes and a languish-*

ing soul. Your life shall hang in doubt before you. Night and day you shall be in dread and have no assurance of your life. In the morning you shall say, 'If only it were evening!' and at evening you shall say, 'If only it were morning!' because of the dread that your heart shall feel, and the sights that your eyes shall see" (Deuteronomy 28:64-67).

Moses spoke those words nearly 3500 years ago and they have become remarkably and horribly true over the last 2000 years. When the Romans brought the troublesome Jewish state to an end and dispersed all its inhabitants, they left the land and the city of Jerusalem desolate.[2] By doing this they started the process that Moses had warned about. The Jews became a homeless people, scattered throughout the entire world. To this day there are Jews in most places of the world, and now there are Jews back in the land their forefathers once inhabited. The nation that was dispersed is now being regathered, again just as the prophets of God predicted would eventually happen. Here's just one of those prophecies:

*"For thus says the Lord GOD: Behold, I, I myself will search for my sheep and will seek them out. As a shepherd seeks out his flock when he is among his sheep that have been scattered, **so will I seek out my sheep, and I will rescue them from all places where they have been scattered on a day of clouds and thick darkness. And I will bring them out from the peoples and gather them from the countries, and will bring them into their own land**" (Ezekiel 34:11-14).*

Who would have been able to predict this remarkable happening, except Almighty God, who both knows the future and controls world events? The Jews had been away from their former land for more than 1800 years, and had suffered generations of abuse and ill-treatment during that exile. The climax of their suffering was the horror of the Nazi concentration camps, where some six million Jews perished. But now the nation is back in its ancient land –

---

2 *The Romans applied the principles of "sword and fire" to subdue the rebellious Jews and the result was devastation and death everywhere throughout the land.*

just as God promised – and exists as a political state which is now recognised among the nations. And their ancient capital city Jerusalem is back under Jewish control.

❖ Mankind Astray

We have looked at just two pointers to the existence of God – the evident design that exists all around us, that points to a Designer; and the remarkable way in which God's Word foretells the future, across hundreds and then thousands of years. Again, it would be possible to spend a lot of time thinking about that subject, but we need to get back to the apostle's prime concern.

Having made the point that God's existence is clearly demonstrated by the world that He has made, Paul now charges mankind with the crime of wilful ignorance. What should have been obvious to everyone has been deliberately ignored. They are *"ungodly"*, *"unrighteous"* and take no notice of these great truths, and deliberately suppress their God-given sense of someone or something which is above and beyond them.[3] But we need to look a little more closely at the apostle's description of mankind in its present godless state. Using just the first two chapters of Romans, this is how the apostle summarises the unhappy state of people:

> *"They **became futile in their thinking**, and their **foolish hearts** were darkened" (Romans 1:21);*

> *"God gave them up to a **debased mind** to do what ought not to be done. They were **filled with all manner of unrighteousness, evil, covetousness, malice. They are full of envy, murder, strife, deceit, maliciousness. They are gossips, slanderers, haters of God, insolent, haughty, boastful, inventors of evil, disobedient to parents, foolish, faithless, heartless, ruthless"** (1:28-31);*

> *"Because of your **hard and impenitent heart** you are storing up wrath for yourself on the day of wrath when God's righteous judgement will be revealed" (2:5);*

> *"For those who are **self-seeking and do not obey the**

---

[3] One writer has called this inbuilt instinct *"the religious instinct in man, which makes him desire to worship something or someone"*.

truth, but obey unrighteousness, *there will be wrath and fury"* (2:8).

This is only one section of Scripture, and we need to base our understanding on all that God has revealed. But even this brief summary contains a clear picture of what has gone wrong with mankind. Notice first that the problem is one of a futile or debased *"mind"* and a foolish, hard or impenitent *"heart"*. Something has happened to human nature that has made it both insensitive to and estranged from the will of God. Instead of being inclined towards the obvious conclusion – that since God exists He should be worshipped – mankind now takes the contrary position. Men and women live to serve themselves; their natural inclination is to glorify mankind. They prefer to worship things – the created rather than the Creator. Or, in Paul's inspired words:

"Although they knew God, they did not honour him as God or give thanks to him, but they became futile in their thinking, and their foolish hearts were darkened. **Claiming to be wise, they became fools, and exchanged the glory of the immortal God for images resembling mortal man and birds and animals and reptiles"** *(1:21,22).*

This is why God is angry with His world and its people. He gives them everything and they give Him nothing back, not even the recognition of His existence. Most people make no attempt to seek God and find Him, despite having every opportunity to do so. The apostle Paul once addressed some thoughtful and influential people in Athens and summed up the situation like this:

"The God who made the world and everything in it, being Lord of heaven and earth, does not live in temples made by man, nor is he served by human hands, as though he needed anything, since **he himself gives to all mankind life and breath and everything ... that they should seek God, in the hope that they might feel their way toward him and find him"** *(Acts 17:24-27).*

❖ What Went Wrong?

It was never meant to be like this, so far as God was concerned, and His righteous anger is directed at mankind because man has gone so far astray from what God wants to happen. God did not make men and women with characteristics like those Paul has described – hard and impenitent hearts, futile minds, self-seeking and self-serving, and suchlike. Quite the contrary: the Scripture says that God made the first man and woman:

> *"In his own image, in the image of God he created him; male and female he created them" (Genesis 1:27).*

The reference to *"male and female"* shows us that we are not being told that this was a physical image, for there are physical differences between the sexes. Instead it was a spiritual likeness, something to do with the mental and emotional condition of the created pair. They were made to worship God and to be His companions; so they had all the attributes needed to make that relationship possible. But they were also given an opportunity to make their own choices and develop their own preferences. God made them free agents. He did not create robots or automatons. He put them in a situation where they could develop characters and learn to overcome challenges. The garden eastward in Eden was a place of learning and growing where mankind could learn and develop spiritually. But wrong choices were made and the result has been disastrous.

Later in the Letter to the Romans, Paul will carefully analyse what Adam did in Eden which brought sorrow and sadness, death and disaster into the world. As he later explains, this was the dreadful mistake that Jesus came to put right. For the moment we need to notice that two things occurred in Eden which changed human nature. God had given a Law – the first one ever given, and one which gave Adam and Eve the opportunity to show their willingness to obey God. It was such a simple thing that nowadays people joke about it, but it was a very important issue. They could eat of any tree of the garden except for one. That forbidden fruit – on the one tree that showed the difference between "right" and "wrong" – was therefore called *"the tree of the knowledge of good and evil"* (Genesis 2:17). Eat it and suffer the consequences; or resist the temptation and continue to live in harmony with God – that was the challenge!

❖ Return to Dust

Adam's failure was an act of wilful disobedience – the New

Testament makes that clear, as we shall see in due course. There were two consequences of that act of rebellion. First, it resulted in the sentence of death being passed upon Adam as God had indicated: *"Of the tree of the knowledge of good and evil you shall not eat, for in the day that you eat of it you shall surely die" (Genesis 2:17).* This sentence was not just restricted to Adam however, it passed to all mankind for all are descended from Adam and have inherited his mortality:

> *"To Adam he said, 'Because you have listened to the voice of your wife and have eaten of the tree of which I commanded you, "You shall not eat of it," cursed is the ground because of you; in pain you shall eat of it all the days of your life; thorns and thistles it shall bring forth for you; and you shall eat the plants of the field. By the sweat of your face you shall eat bread,* **till you return to the ground, for out of it you were taken; for you are dust, and to dust you shall return'"** *(Genesis 3:17-19).*

The whole of Adam's life was changed as a result of this action and so is ours. Whereas he might have continued to live with no fear of death, now Adam would die, and so would his descendants. God delayed the punishment, but it came in due course. His death is listed in the same chapter which contains a long list of his successors (Genesis chapter 5), all of whose life-histories end with the words *"and he died"*. They died and we still do: death is a universal experience and God's words clearly mean what they say.

Death is the end of life – it is a process of turning to dust and that is how it is understood all through the Bible. The lie that was first put to Eve suggested that she would not die (Genesis 3:4), but that breaking God's law would be advantageous. It was said that would do them both some good. Curiously, that is what a lot of people have come to believe about death – that it is a gateway to another and better life; that it commences another existence in heaven, or suchlike.

In Chapter 5 – *The Problem of Sin and Death* – we will look at these questions in more detail and will see that some popular ideas about the afterlife have no support in the Bible. For the moment, note that when God said death would result if His law was broken, He meant that Adam and Eve would cease to exist if they broke His commandments. Their lives would end; and so they did.

❖ Change of Nature

There was something else too that happened at that time –
a second consequence of Adam's disobedience. Again it is
something which affects us also. Just as we inherit a mortal nature[4] because of what Adam did, we also inherit
Adam's tendency to please himself, rather than God. He
was not created with that tendency, for God made both
Adam and Eve, and all creation, in a condition which is
described as *"very good"* (Genesis 1:31). But once he had
disobeyed God[5] it seems that this became a principle by
which he chose to live. Adam had the capacity to become
like God in some respects,[6] but he chose a different path.
From then on all his descendants developed the tendency
to move away from God, rather than towards Him. By
nature, they preferred to disobey rather than to obey Him.

We can see this moral change very early in the Bible
account. The third son born to Adam and Eve was called
Seth. The inspired record records that he was born in
Adam's *"own likeness, after his image"* (Genesis 5:3). Adam
had been made in God's likeness, with the possibility of
becoming godlike in his actions and attitudes. But all
Adam's children were born with a tendency in a different
direction – they were self-centred. Cain, Adam and Eve's
first child, demonstrated what that meant in practice in a
most tragic way. He and his brother Abel were encouraged
to worship God: Abel did this in the way that God had indicated, by bringing an animal offering. Cain brought vegeta-
bles instead, disregarding what God required. God accepted
Abel but rejected Cain, and Cain promptly killed his brother and then lied to God about what he had done. You can
read about it in Genesis chapter 4.

Two chapters further on, and 1600 year later, the world

---

[4] *The word "mortal" just means that we die; it is the opposite of "immortal",
which means never dying. The Bible says that God alone is immortal by
nature (1 Timothy 6:16).*

[5] *The idea that he should disobey God would never have occurred to Adam
or to Eve naturally, for they were made "very good", but the thought was
put to them by an outsider – a serpent (Genesis 3:1). Notice that the serpent
is held responsible for what he had done and was cursed by God as a consequence (3:14).*

[6] *God wanted mankind to become godly or Godlike: to reflect his image
(Genesis 1:26).*

was already totally godless. Everybody was following Adam's lawless example: they were all choosing to please themselves rather than obeying God. As it turns out, there were only eight people left in the entire society at that time who were willing to listen to God's commandments and to obey Him. All the rest are described in this way:

> *"The LORD saw that the wickedness of man was great in the earth, and that every intention of the thoughts of his heart was only evil continually. And the LORD was sorry that he had made man on the earth, and it grieved him to his heart. So the LORD said, 'I will blot out man whom I have created from the face of the land, man and animals and creeping things and birds of the heavens, for I am sorry that I have made them.' But Noah found favour in the eyes of the LORD"* (Genesis 6:5-8).

The Bible never wastes words, so when it uses all those words to describe the human condition – *"the wickedness of man was **great** in the earth, and that **every intention of the thoughts of his heart was only evil continually**"* – you can see how serious the situation had become. God decided to destroy the entire society and to start again with Noah and his small family, and that is why the flood came. God was angry with the people in the world that existed before the flood. He was sorry that He had put man on the earth and it grieved Him to His heart – and He is equally angry with our world.

❖ 21st Century World

Remember that the words used to describe our modern society are much the same as those that occur in early Genesis, before the flood. People today are *"futile in their thinking"*, their hearts are *"foolish"* and *"darkened"*; their minds are *"debased"*; they are filled with *"all manner of unrighteousness, evil, covetousness, malice. They are full of envy, murder, strife, deceit, maliciousness. They are gossips, slanderers, haters of God, insolent, haughty, boastful, inventors of evil, disobedient to parents, foolish, faithless, heartless, ruthless"*. They are *"self-seeking and do not obey the truth, but obey unrighteousness"*. All these are expressions we found in Romans chapters 1 and 2, and there is something else too.

Three times the apostle says what God is doing about all

this. Nothing! Paul tells us that God has determined to let the world alone for the time being so that the full effects of sinful and disobedient behaviour will become apparent. Our immoral world has long-since left behind the laws of God. It has made its own rules for living and set its own standards. God's values and laws are now challenged by many people who wish to determine for themselves what they accept as "right" and "wrong". Here is the divine assessment of today's society:

> *"**God gave them up** in the lusts of their hearts to impurity, to the dishonouring of their bodies among themselves, because they exchanged the truth about God for a lie and worshipped and served the creature rather than the Creator, who is blessed forever! Amen. For this reason **God gave them up** to dishonourable passions. For their women exchanged natural relations for those that are contrary to nature; and the men likewise gave up natural relations with women and were consumed with passion for one another, men committing shameless acts with men and receiving in themselves the due penalty for their error. And since they did not see fit to acknowledge God, **God gave them up** to a debased mind to do what ought not to be done" (Romans 1:24-28).*

God by no means approves of many of the things that are happening today, which are contrary to His revealed Law. In this passage express mention is made of homosexual and lesbian practices which are declared impure, dishonouring and contrary to nature. The fact that these things are now being tolerated in society does not mean that they are right. It merely shows that God is biding His time, and is still giving some people the opportunity to choose a different way of life. His *"kindness"*, *"forbearance"* and *"patience"* are being shown to us to give us a chance to come to repentance (Romans 2:4).

❖ Two Classes of People

God has allowed men and women to behave as they wish for a period, but the Scripture says that God will not tolerate this for ever, and all the indications are that He will intervene very soon. So there is no time to lose if you want to take advantage of God's gracious invitation to change direction and choose the things that please Him. We all have to decide where we stand. Either we go the way of the world by accepting its values and adopting its attitudes, or we find a way that is right with God. Paul says this about that class of people:

> "*He (God) will render to each one according to his works:* **to those who by patience in well-doing seek for glory and honour and immortality,**[7] **he will give eternal life**; *but for those who are self-seeking and do not obey the truth, but obey unrighteousness, there will be wrath and fury. There will be tribulation and distress for every human being who does evil, the Jew first and also the Greek, but* **glory and honour and peace for everyone who does good,** *the Jew first and also the Greek. For God shows no partiality" (Romans 2:6-11).*

So there is a different way: one that will bring us back into God's favour. It is the way that will result in life and not death; the one in which we can be reckoned to be right in God's sight, not wrong. As we progress in our reading of Romans we shall see what this involves and what we can do to be found on God's side, when He brings this present evil age to an end and starts again with something which is so much better.

Things to Read

📖 If you haven't already read the Letter to the Romans then read chapters 1 and 2. This will help you to see the way in which Paul presents his logical and well-reasoned arguments.

📖 As everything starts in Genesis, and as Paul will later have such a lot to say about Adam's failure, reading Genesis chapters 2-4 will give you a lot of helpful background.

Questions to Think About

4.1 The events at the time of the Flood in Noah's day are very similar to what is about to happen. What can we learn from the Flood which will help us? (Matthew 24:34-42; Hebrews 11:6-7; 2 Peter 3:3-15)

---

[7] *Notice how the Scripture gently points out that we are mortal creatures by advising us to "seek for immortality"; we do not yet possess it.*

4.2   The Bible says that right at the end of human govern-
      ment, before God takes direct control, things will be
      very bad on earth. Why do you think that we may
      have reached that time now? (1 Timothy 4:1-5; 2
      Timothy 3:1-7)

*"From childhood
you have been
acquainted with the
sacred writings,
which are able to
make you wise for
salvation through
faith in Christ Jesus"
(2 Timothy 3:15)*

5
The Problem of Sin and Death

The apostle now emphasises the points he has been making for his readers. He has already said that mankind is going its own godless way and has warned that the result will be destruction unless people choose to follow God's way. He has spelled out why God is angry about the godless and sinful way that people are now living. He has warned both Jews and Gentiles that they must change their ways if they want to escape God's judgements. Now he takes his readers through the Old Testament Scriptures to show that everybody, without exception, has lived in a way which is wrong in the sight of God.[1] This includes every one of us as well.

The apostle strings together a lot of verses to prove very important point:

> *"None is righteous, no, not one; no one understands; no one seeks for God. All have turned aside; together they have become worthless; no one does good, not even one ... Now we know that whatever the law says it speaks to those who are under the law, so that every mouth may be stopped, and the whole world may be held accountable to God. For by works of the law no human being will be justified in his sight, since through the law comes knowledge of sin"* (Romans 3:10-20).

In this passage (of which only the beginning and the end are shown above) there are many quotations from the Old Testament, mainly from the Psalms, which demonstrate Paul's key teaching.[2] All through Bible history the inspired writers have declared men and women to be wrong in the

---

[1] *Notice how important the Old Testament is for the apostle as a source of information about the will and purpose of God. It needs to be read and understood just as much as the New Testament.*

[2] *This is, in fact, the longest single string of quotations in the whole of the New Testament, which again demonstrates Paul's appreciation of the value of the Old Testament.*

51

sight of God. Everyone has turned aside to do evil. No one does what is good. People speak and say wrong things, so their lives are ruined and miserable because they have disobeyed God's commandments. In the law court of God, if God was to sit as Judge, every one of us would be found *"Guilty!"*

Don't be too depressed about this. The apostle needs to show that we have a huge problem to face up to before he can be sure that we will take our condition seriously. Remember, it's a bit like going to the doctor – you only go when you know you've got problems. The key problem Paul has identified is not a popular one today. It is the problem of *"sin"* which will lead inevitably to *"death"*, unless we take immediate avoiding action, with God's help. To demonstrate further Paul's concern about these two problems, look how often he talks about sin and death in this letter:

❖ Sin and Death

*"Therefore, just as **sin** came into the world through one man, and **death** through sin, and so death spread to all men because all **sinned**" (5:12);*

*"Now the law came in to increase the trespass, but where **sin** increased, grace abounded all the more, so that, as sin reigned in death, grace also might reign through righteousness leading to eternal life through Jesus Christ our Lord" (5:21);*

*"Do you not know that if you present yourselves to anyone as obedient slaves, you are slaves of the one whom you obey, either of **sin, which leads to death,** or of obedience, which leads to righteousness?" (6:16);*

*"For **the wages of sin is death**, but the free gift of God is eternal life in Christ Jesus our Lord" (6:23);*

*"Did that which is good, then, bring death to me? By no means! It was **sin, producing death in me** through what is good, in order that **sin** might be shown to be **sin**, and through the commandment might become **sinful** beyond measure" (7:13);*

*"For the law of the Spirit of life has set you free in Christ Jesus from **the law of sin and death**" (8:2).*

For the moment, don't worry about what all of these verses mean, we shall come to them in due course. But just notice how important the connection is between *"sin"* and its partner *"death"*. We *sin* and therefore we *die* – they are *cause* and *effect*. Sin is like an employer who pays us the wages we deserve – death; like a slave master who does with us whatever he chooses; or like a king who reigns over us and then gives us death as an inheritance. It's a pretty grim picture, and that is exactly what the inspired apostle wants us to understand. [3]

❖ Sin

> *"**Sin** came into the world through one man, and **death** through sin" (Romans 5:12).*

That's the way Paul describes what we have already been considering. The first act of wilful disobedience was committed by Adam when Eve suggested to him that he should eat the fruit she had already eaten. We are told that Eve was deceived by the serpent – that she did not know what she was doing when she agreed with his suggestion (see 1 Timothy 2:14). This is why Adam is held responsible for the first act of deliberate disobedience. He was not deceived – he knew what he was doing: breaking God's law and accepting the consequences, whatever they were. God had said that in the day he ate of that fruit he would die, so it was his sin that brought death to the human race.

Sin is an act of rebellion against God: a deliberate refusal to do what God says. This is how the Bible defines it:

> *"Whoever knows the right thing to do and fails to do it, for him it is sin" (James 4:17).*

> *"Everyone who makes a practice of sinning also practises lawlessness; sin is lawlessness" (1 John 3:4).*

> *"All wrongdoing is sin" (1 John 5:17).*

So acts of deliberate disobedience, or the failure to do what God wants, are equally wrong and the Bible uses sev-

---

[3] *Notice that this is picture language to help us visualise both Sin and Death, which otherwise are quite difficult things to think about. See Romans 5:14-17 (where death is pictured as a king) and 6:16-17 (where sin is pictured as a slave-master).*

eral different words to spell this out. The Bible calls people who disobey God – *sinners, transgressors, rebels* or *children of disobedience*. But why is it that all of us slip so easily into sinning? Why do we find it easier to disobey God than to obey Him?

❖ Sinful Nature

When Adam sinned everything changed. Sin is one of the most addictive things in the world and once Adam had sinned it was something he wanted to go on doing.

He was part of a created order that was made *"very good"*, as we have seen,[4] but his act of rebellion against God changed things. He could have accepted the law of God and have lived happily under its direction. But instead he chose to disobey and became subject to another ruling principle of life. He accepted the mastery of sin – as though sin was to be the king of his life – and became subject to what Paul calls *"the law of sin and death"* *(Romans 5:21; 6:16; 8:2)*.

In some way his nature was changed by that first wrong act, and that change of nature was passed down to his descendants. This is why Seth was born in Adam's own likeness, *"after his image"* *(Genesis 5:3)*. This is why the world became so wicked so quickly, before the time of the flood. And this is why our world is in such a godless and heedless state today. We are all born with that condition in which Adam found himself after he had become a sinner. From this it follows that sin is more than just an act, or acts, of disobedience against God. Sin is also a state of being – a condition of mind and heart into which we are born; a state that we now consider perfectly natural.

Everybody since Adam has been born with the feelings and tendencies that we consider natural – that's what human nature is all about. Everybody is born with a nature which is self-centred and self-serving. Even the best people who ever lived had those tendencies from birth. The challenge for them was to overcome those natural feelings and redirect their lives towards God, and it's exactly the same challenge that we too face. In a Psalm that revealed his innermost thoughts, King David once said this:

*"I know my transgressions, and **my sin is ever before me**. Against you, you only, have I sinned and done what*

---

[4] *Genesis 1:31.*

*is evil in your sight, so that you may be justified in your words and blameless in your judgement. Behold, **I was brought forth in iniquity, and in sin did my mother conceive me***" *(Psalm 51:3-5).*

He meant that from the time of his birth he had possessed a tendency to do wrong actions – to sin. That tendency was an inherent part of his nature. Both Old and New Testaments agree about this. Here are some other statements about the human condition, from other books of the Bible:

*"**The heart is deceitful above all things, and desperately sick**; who can understand it? I the* LORD *search the heart and test the mind, to give every man according to his ways, according to the fruit of his deeds"* (Jeremiah 17:9,10).*

*"Whatever goes into the mouth passes into the stomach and is expelled. But what comes out of the mouth proceeds from the heart, and this defiles a person. For **out of the heart come evil thoughts, murder, adultery, sexual immorality, theft, false witness, slander. These are what defile a person**"* (Matthew 15:17-20).*

*"We all once lived in the passions of our flesh, carrying out the **desires of the body and the mind**, and were by nature children of wrath, like the rest of mankind"* (Ephesians 2:3).*

*"You must no longer walk as the Gentiles do, in the **futility of their minds**. They are darkened in their understanding, alienated from the life of God because of the ignorance that is in them, due to their **hardness of heart**. They have become callous and have given themselves up to sensuality, greedy to practise every kind of impurity. But that is not the way you learned Christ! – assuming that you have heard about him and were taught in him, as the truth is in Jesus, to put off your old self, which belongs to your former manner of life and is corrupt through deceitful desires, and to be renewed in the spirit of your minds, and to put on the new self, created after the likeness of God in true righteousness and holiness"* (Ephesians 4:17-24).*

This is the sort of exercise you can do for yourself when you become familiar with the Bible. By regular reading, and then noting down verses about a particular topic that you are thinking about, you can soon build up a collection. It's then a matter of stopping and asking what the verses mean. And there is nothing more important to any of us than finding out about our natural condition.

These verses tell us that by nature we are in great difficulty. If sin gets the upper hand and controls our life, we are dead! But if we can find some other way of living and behaving, which makes us right with God, there is hope of something better. In that way we will be able to escape from sin and its deadly effect. It's as critical and as important as that.

❖ "All have Sinned"

We are not to blame in God's sight because we are born with human nature – that's not our fault, it's our misfortune. This is a very important distinction, and one we could easily overlook. By nature we all have thoughts and desires which are the product of what goes on inside our minds or hearts.[5] Those thoughts tempt us to do wrong, but they are not sinful until we accept them and decide that they are things we want to do. This is how the apostle James describes the way in which sin comes about:

> *"Let no one say when he is tempted, 'I am being tempted by God,' for God cannot be tempted with evil, and he himself tempts no one. But each person is tempted when he is **lured and enticed by his own desire**. Then desire when it has conceived gives birth to sin, and **sin when it is fully grown brings forth death**" (James 1:13-15).*

Notice the process that James describes. We are tempted when our natural desires seek to lure and entice us to do or accept something that we know is wrong. At that stage we can choose to resist and kill off the thought – which is how we overcome sin. But if we let the thought grow (and here James uses a word which could equally refer to a child growing inside his or her mother), then the thought becomes a real idea – something we really want to do. This then causes us to carry out the act – and we sin.

---

5 *The Bible uses both terms – "mind" and "heart" – to describe our innermost feelings.*

But there is another point to consider, the Bible also tells us that the desire to do something bad can be as bad as the bad deed itself. Jesus once said that it is just as bad to decide that you would like to do something wrong as it is to actually do it (Matthew 5:27,28). Both sinful ideas and deeds are fatal – James says that the end-product is death.

Every one of us, in lots of different ways and at many different times in our lives, has done wrong things: things that are against the law of God. Paul was writing about people in the First Century when he said that: *"all, both Jews and Greeks, are under the power of sin" (Romans 3:9)*, and that *"all have sinned and fall short of the glory of God" (3:22)*. Sadly, this is true of all following centuries too. For in all that time human nature has not changed; we too are made in Adam's image, after his likeness (1Corinthians 15:49). The desire to sin is like a disease which has been passed on from generation to generation, and without a cure we will all die, because of sin. That's why Paul could talk about *"sin"* and *"death"* in the same breath. The one always leads to the other, unless something is done to break the connection.

❖ Is Death the End?

None of this really matters, of course, if death is not such a serious condition. If it is the gateway to another life, if we have an immortal soul, then we can always make up for lost time later on, and try to put our lives right with God when we get there. But what if death really is the end of conscious existence and there is no second chance? What if it's only in this life that we have an opportunity to get ever-lasting life and, if we neglect this opportunity, we lose out on an eternity of joy in the age to come which God has promised? Again we need to collect a few Bible passages that will help us work out which of these two alternatives is the right one, or if there's something in-between.

We have to start in Eden because that's where the original death sentence was passed on Adam. He was told that his act of rebellion had triggered the sentence that God had warned him about. If he ate, he died; and now he had eaten, so God said:

"Because you have listened to the voice of your wife and have eaten of the tree of which I commanded you, 'You shall not eat of it,' cursed is the ground because of you; in

*pain you shall eat of it all the days of your life; thorns
and thistles it shall bring forth for you; and you shall eat
the plants of the field. **By the sweat of your face you
shall eat bread, till you return to the ground, for
out of it you were taken; for you are dust, and to
dust you shall return**" (Genesis 3:17-19).*

It was a three-fold sentence. From now on:

1 *the ground would be cursed;*

2 *life would be hard; and*

3 *it would end in death – Adam had come from dust and
to dust he would return.*

❖ Made of Dust and Breath

Adam was a creature made from dust.

*"The LORD God formed the man of dust from the ground
and breathed into his nostrils the breath of life, and the
man became a living creature" (Genesis 2:7).*

Now, when he breathed his last, his body would decompose and all that would be left would be a pile of dust. It's
true that today we aren't specially created as Adam was.
But when we die our bodies will decompose in just the
same way. We too, like our ancestors, are destined to
become dust when we die. But what about our life, our
spirit, our conscious existence, our soul, or whatever we
might choose to call it? Is there something else that will
survive?

Some Bible versions translate Genesis 2:7 rather differently, suggesting that man became *"a living soul"*. This has
led many people to believe that God created man and
woman with something special inside them, something that
was destined to survive after their death. This line of
thought led to the belief that the soul was immortal, and
that as everybody had one, nobody could ever really die.
Good people would live forever in Heaven after death; bad
people would suffer forever in Hell. As this seemed a bit
tough on those who were not all that bad, there developed
an idea that there could be in-between states as well –
called "purgatory" and "limbo".

If you read all through the Bible, notebook in hand, this
is what you will find. There is no mention of an "immortal
soul" anywhere in the Bible: it is a man-made idea. The

nearest you can get to that idea is what the serpent said to Eve, when he deceived her with the words: *"You will not surely die" (Genesis 3:4)*. Sadly, she was deceived by that lie, and many of her descendants have followed the same line of thinking in later generations.

Adam was made a *"living creature" (Genesis 2:7)*, and the very same phrase is used many times about the animals God made. *"Out of the ground the LORD God formed every beast of the field and every bird of the heavens and brought them to the man to see what he would call them. And whatever the man called every living creature, that was its name" (2:19)*. Man's existence was essentially the same as the animals that God made. What set man and woman apart was that God had made them with a capacity to become spiritual. They could develop characters and personalities that were modelled upon divine beings. So God gave them the companionship of angels, instructed them in heavenly things and encouraged them to take control of themselves and their environment.

They were challenged to choose the things that were best and noblest in life; but when they made their own wrong choices, they lost all that. Banished from the garden, they had to make their own way in life, and it was a much harder way than God would have arranged for them. They had to find a way back into God's favour and, graciously, God gave them several hundreds of years more in which to live – for Adam was *"930 years, and he died" (Genesis 5:5)*, as did all his descendants after him.

❖ Spirit

If *"soul"* means "creature", or sometimes just "life", what about the idea that we have a *"spirit"* inside us, a spark of the divine, something that will survive us? What was it, for example, that God breathed into Adam that energised and empowered him – the force the Bible calls *"the breath of life" (Genesis 2:7)*?

It's certainly the case that we can't exist without the breath of life; if we lose that energising force, we cease to exist. But that's equally so with the animals. An ancient observer of the human condition once said that *"a living dog is better than a dead lion" (Ecclesiastes 9:4)*. Everybody can understand what he meant for there is a huge difference between something which is alive and something which is dead. That life force makes all the difference. It enables a body to function and when it is gone the body is lifeless.

Life is a gift from God and that means that all living creatures – animal and human alike – are energized by God's power in some way. The apostle Paul once said that God *"gives to all mankind life and breath and everything"* *(Acts 17:25)*, and if God chooses to take that breath away we would die. What if He did that on a wide scale?

*"If he should set his heart to it and gather to himself his spirit and his breath, **all flesh would perish together, and man would return to dust"** (Job 34:14,15).*

What would then happen to the spirit – the life force that God had supplied? Scripture gives us that answer as well:

*"... the dust returns to the earth as it was, and **the spirit returns to God who gave it"** (Ecclesiastes 12:7).*

And what of the person who has lost that spirit, that breath of life from God?

*"When his breath departs he returns to the earth; **on that very day his plans perish"** (Psalm 146:4).*

❖ Unconsciousness

The *breath or spirit of life* is not something which is independent of man's body. It is the Bible's way of describing the vital force which keeps us alive and which leaves us when we die. This life-force that empowers us while we are alive returns to God at death. We are left lifeless. Every part of us, including our brains, will then be buried in the ground and will begin to decompose; or we will be burned and destroyed at once.

There is no conscious existence left. Our thought processes, our memories and our feelings all end then, as the Bible explains many times. Death is like a dreamless sleep; the end of our consciousness:

*"Turn, O LORD, deliver my life; save me for the sake of your steadfast love. For **in death there is no remembrance of you**; in Sheol (in the grave) who will give you praise?" (Psalm 6:5);*

*"Is your steadfast love declared in the grave, or your faithfulness in Abaddon (the place of destruction)? Are your wonders known **in the darkness,** or your right-*

eousness **in the land of forgetfulness?**" *(Psalm 88:11,12);*

"Sheol (the grave) does not thank you; **death does not praise you***; those who go down to the pit do not hope for your faithfulness. The living, the living, he thanks you, as I do this day" (Isaiah 38:18).*

All this would be fairly grim news if there was no alternative available. It does mean, however, that there is no need to create an elaborate scheme of reward in heaven and punishment in hell, with purgatory in-between. Those are pagan and not Bible ideas anyway. They were added to the original gospel because people were mistaken about the true condition of our existence. When the Bible uses the term *"hell"* it just means a place of destruction, usually the grave,[6] and you will never find any promise in the Bible about going to heaven after death. But you will find the Scripture saying of King David, who is described as being really close to God, that:

"David **slept with his fathers***, and was buried in the city of David" (1 Kings 2:10);*

"David is **not ascended into the heavens***" (Acts 2:34);*

"For David, after he had served his own generation by the will of God, **fell on sleep, and was laid unto his fathers, and saw corruption***" (Acts 13:36).*

❖ Waking Up from Sleep!

However this does not mean that David missed out on a future reward, as we shall see when we think about the things God promised David. The very language used is encouraging, for both Testaments use the term *"sleep"*, and those who are asleep can be awakened. This is the real promise of God to all His people in every age – that there will come such a time of awakening: the Bible calls it resurrection. There will come a time when God will bring back to consciousness those that He decides to awaken. Not everybody will be restored to consciousness; some people are

---

[6] *"Hell" is an old English word which simply means 'a covered place'. Hence it is used in the Bible to describe the grave – the covered place in which people are buried.*

dead and gone forever (Jeremiah 51:39,57). But many people will be called back to life:

> *"**Many of them that sleep in the dust of the earth
> shall awake**, some to everlasting life, and some to
> shame and everlasting contempt" (Daniel 12:2).*

We will explore more about this promise of resurrection
from the dead later, but first there is one more question we
need to look at.

❖ Why do we die?

You may feel that you can answer this question already
from what we have considered. Sin and Death are closely
connected, as we saw; we sin and so we die. But it's not
quite as easy as that when you start thinking about it. Lots
of people have never even heard about the law of God; they
live and die without even knowing there is a Bible, the
Word of God. If they don't know God's law, they cannot be
formally classed as "sinners". So why do they die?

They die because they are mortal: we all are. Unless we
do something to escape the effects of our natural condition
we shall all die, and will cease to exist forever. But Paul
says something else as well.

He explains that God has a way of calling everyone to
account, whether they have known His law or not. In the
second part of Romans chapter 2, he explains that God has
given men and women an inbuilt mechanism called "the
conscience" which introduces a measure of right and wrong
into everybody's life. People have long argued that a bad
deed is recognised as such the world over – that there are
some universal standards that determine what constitutes
good and bad behaviour. Paul calls that the law within
them, "written on their hearts", and says that everybody
should respond to these inner feelings and live properly
and decently in this life, whether they know the written law
of God or not. But, unless they find the gospel of salvation,
even people who have lived decently will die because they
are mortal, not immortal:

> *"For all who have sinned without the law will also perish
> without the law" (Romans 2:12).*

Notice here that the root problem is a lack of knowledge
about God and His gracious purpose. Those who "perish"
are those who know nothing about "the law" of God. Long

before, the inspired Psalmist had summed up the situation when he declared that: *"Man in his pomp yet without understanding is like the beasts that perish" (49:20).*

We do not live forever – and we have no immortal soul that does. Instead the Bible describes us as *"mortal"*, which means "liable to death". We are all born with a limited life expectancy which differs depending upon where we live in the world. After due time our body will wear out and we will die, as we say, "of natural causes". This is something the Bible recognises and records, for it contains the death notices of lots of people. It encourages us to face up to our mortality and do something about it:

*"Let not sin therefore reign in your **mortal** bodies, to make you obey their passions" (Romans 6:12);*

*"For this **perishable** body must put on the imperishable, and this **mortal** body must put on immortality. When the **perishable** puts on the imperishable, and the **mortal** puts on immortality, then shall come to pass the saying that is written: 'Death is swallowed up in victory'" (1 Corinthians 15:53,54);*

*"For we who live are always being given over to death for Jesus' sake, so that the life of Jesus also may be manifested in our **mortal** flesh" (2 Corinthians 4:11).*

Being mortal doesn't mean that we will die and never live again. It means that because we are mortal we have to do something about it if we want to become immortal. We are not immortal already. We are dying creatures, at risk of death from the time we are born. Indeed some die at birth, or are stillborn; others die at a very early age, from illness or accident. Some die in distressing and difficult situations; and yet others die in old age, some in very old age. The time factor varies, but the event is the same – we cease to breathe; the life goes out of us; we die.

What happened to Adam is important in helping us to understand our situation. When he sinned:

1 He became a mortal, dying creature, so it follows that all his descendants would be mortal too; and

2 He had become a sinner and something in his personality changed so that from then on sin would be natural for

him and his descendants – that's why we still talk about "human nature".

3 Because sin is so natural for us, we have all copied Adam's bad example and have become sinners.

*"Therefore, just as sin came into the world through one man (Adam), and death through sin, and so **death spread to all men because all sinned"** (Romans 5:12).*

Now the size of the human problem is clear – that we are all in danger of dying forever and of missing out on everything that God has in mind for His world and His people. So the apostle Paul explains just what God has done to make an escape plan for humanity. If you want to be in God's new world, there *is* a way that will enable you to be there.

Things to Read

📖 Isaiah 38, verses 9-19 will give you an insight into the thoughts of a faithful man of God – King Hezekah – when he was about to die. Notice how he describes life – as something that can easily be lost – and what he says about death.

📖 John 11:1-46 gives an account of Lazarus being raised from the dead. Notice the language that is used throughout and what everyone present believed to be the only solution to the problem of death.

Questions to Think About

5.1 King David is described as "asleep" and as seeing "corruption" (1 Kings 2:10; Acts 13:36). From the Psalms, can you find out what faithful men hoped would happen after death? (Psalm 16:8-11; 17:15; 49:12-15; 71:20)

5.2 What gives men and women a hope which animals do not have? What do we need to do to realise that hope? (Psalm 49:12,20; Hebrews 11:13,39-40)

5.3 What does the word *"soul"* mean when used in the Bible? (Genesis 2:7; 12:5; Exodus 1:5; Leviticus 4:2; Joshua 10:28; 1 Peter 3:20)

6
What do we know about God?

God made the world and everything that is in it. He made it in such a way that we see clear evidence of His design. He did this so that everyone could come to understand that there is a God and so that they would then seek to worship Him. He also revealed His purpose through people who were given special powers of communication, and we now have that complete revelation in the Bible. From that we can learn much more about God than the created world can teach us. We can find out what sort of God He is and what He is doing to get mankind out of the mess we are in.

✓ We are dying, but He lives forever;

✓ We are failures, but God is successful in everything He does;

✓ We are weak, but He is immensely powerful.

❖ Finding out about God

Just from looking at the world God has made we can understand that His power and ability are amazing. The world He made is so wonderfully designed. Think about the way a tree works. It sucks up goodness from the soil so that it can grow, produce leaves, flowers and fruit and, when that cycle of activity is finished, its products fall to the ground. They then provide nutrients for next year's growth, while the seeds land in places where other trees can begin to grow. In the process the tree provides wood, which can be used for a large number of useful purposes; fruit that can be eaten by man, birds or animals; and leaves that give shelter and shade. And the whole process looks beautiful – both when the leaves are growing and when they are changing colour and falling.

That's the sort of insight the natural world can give us, but what more does the Bible tell us about the God who made all things? What in particular does the apostle Paul say about God in his Letter to the Romans? If you were to take your notebook and read again the first three chapters of the letter you would collect this information:

Romans	What we learn about God
1:1	God has a gospel – *good news* for mankind
1:3	God has a Son, descended from David, who was born by His power
1:7	God loves the believers at Rome and sends them grace and peace because He is their Father
1:10	God's will controls everything
1:18	God is angry with people who pay no attention to Him and His ways
1:20	God is not visible to human eyes
1:20,23	God is Eternal and Immortal – He is without beginning or end, and His realm of existence is far above that of mankind
1:24,26,28	God has left the world alone for the time being, to let human society go its own godless way
2:5,11,16	There will, however, come a day when God's righteous judgement will be revealed, and then He will reward people as they deserve. He will be even-handed and fair in that judgement
3:3,4	God is faithful and true in all His ways; He can never be otherwise

3:21	God has opened a way whereby we can be counted "right" or "righteous" in His sight
3:25	God made this possible by providing His Son to die for mankind
3:29,30	He did this for both Jew and non-Jew, because there is only one God (and hence the God of all people)

You can easily check these findings for yourself by looking at the listed passages. As you understand more and more about the Bible you will come to appreciate that it is full of information like this. It is a book from God, but it is also a book about God and His gracious purpose – it's all about His good news for mankind. The very fact that He communicates with us in this way is a wonderful indication that He wants us to know about Him. He wants to share something with us. You wouldn't write a letter to someone unless you wanted to share something with, or get something from, the person who received it. It's the same with God. From the moment He revealed how the world was created, God began to explain why He made everything and what it is all about. And He did that with a specific purpose in mind.

From the very beginning, God is revealed as both **powerful** and **purposeful** – someone who knows what He is doing and has all the power needed to get it done. He only has to speak to make things happen and step-by-step He brings an ordered world into existence. Such is the power of His Word:

"For the word of the LORD is upright, and all his work is done in faithfulness. He loves righteousness and justice; the earth is full of the steadfast love of the LORD. ***By the word of the LORD the heavens were made, and by the breath of his mouth all their host*** *... Let all the earth fear the LORD; let all the inhabitants of the world stand in awe of him!* ***For he spoke, and it came to be; he commanded, and it stood firm"*** *(Psalm 33:4-9).*

The world we know came into existence in a wonderfully ordered way. When His creative work was completed man and woman stood side-by-side in God's new-made world and He told them of His purpose for them. His world was made to be awe-inspiring, as the Psalmist understood, but God's purpose involved more than the creature living in reverential fear of the Creator.

❖ The Holy One

God's Word of power was also a Word of instruction to Adam. He gave a Law by which both Adam and Eve were to live and He warned about the dangerous consequences of disobedience. This was the way in which God revealed Himself, in the second chapter of the Bible, as a moral God – One who is concerned about good and evil. It clearly matters very much to Him whether people do right or wrong. The seriousness with which God viewed this was very telling. For God is holy – set apart by His very nature from things that are unholy.[1] For example, the prophet Isaiah said this about the nature and character of Almighty God:

> "Thus says the One who is high and lifted up, who inhabits eternity, **whose name is Holy**: 'I dwell in the high and holy place, and also with him who is of a contrite and lowly spirit, to revive the spirit of the lowly, and to revive the heart of the contrite' " (Isaiah 57:15).

God is so much against sin and wickedness that –

➘ He warned Adam in the severest terms not to break His Law, and

➘ when that Law was broken He punished both Adam and Eve and excluded them from His presence;

➘ when mankind followed their way of disobedience, God destroyed that society, in the days of Noah, and

➘ rescued only a faithful few (and all this is recorded in just the first nine chapters of the Bible).

❖ Moral Purity

As the Bible continues we learn more clearly what God's holiness really means to us. It is a characteristic of His very

---

[1] It takes a while for that language – of "holiness" – to appear. The earliest occurrences are in the Book of Job, which is a book that belongs to early Bible times. But the idea of God's holiness is a very early one and the idea becomes very widely used.

existence: He is Holy[2] and can never be otherwise. It is because we are not holy that we cannot even see Him, or approach His presence. God has a level of moral purity which is far above us and our level of behaviour. Here are a few Bible verses that tell us more about God's standards of morality:

*"I will proclaim the name of the LORD; ascribe greatness to our God! The Rock, **his work is perfect, for all his ways are justice. A God of faithfulness and without iniquity, just and upright is he**" (Deuteronomy 32:3, 4);*

*"For **you are not a God who delights in wickedness; evil may not dwell with you**" (Psalm 5:4);*

*"**The LORD is upright**; he is my rock, and **there is no unrighteousness in him**" (Psalm 92:15);*

*"O LORD, you have ordained them as a judgement, and you, O Rock, have established them for reproof. **You who are of purer eyes than to see evil and cannot look at wrong**" (Habakkuk 1:12,13);*

*Let no one say when he is tempted, "I am being tempted by God," for **God cannot be tempted with evil**, and he himself tempts no one (James 1:13);*

*"This is the message we have heard from him and proclaim to you, that **God is light, and in him is no darkness at all**" (1 John 1:5).*

❖ Knowing God

We have just looked at one aspect of God's character, the aspect of His holiness, and we have seen that the idea is found right through Scripture. That is true about every aspect of His person. It's not just God's *holiness* that is depicted in His Word. The Bible is all about God – His gracious purpose and His loving and lovely character. For the Bible is a revelation from God, given us so that we can get to know Him. Then we can seek to establish a loving relationship with Him.

---

2 *The word "holy" means to be separate or sacred.*

69

It's like that in life with all the people we care about: the first thing in any relationship is getting to know one another. In personal relationships we get to know someone by talking about things which are of common interest, by watching how they behave in different circumstances and seeing how they relate to other people. When we cannot see the individual in question all that often, we might exchange letters or speak on the telephone. If the person is someone we admire but cannot communicate with, for whatever reason, we might have to be satisfied with reading about him or her, or hearing from others what they are really like.

God is beyond our immediate reach and is far above our normal way of thinking. He is God and we are men and women; He is immortal and we are mortal. He is in heaven and we are on earth; He is holy and we are sinful. There are so many things that separate us from Almighty God.

*"He who is the blessed and only Sovereign, the King of kings and Lord of lords, **who alone has immortality, who dwells in unapproachable light,** whom no one has ever seen or can see. To him be honour and eternal dominion. Amen" (1 Timothy 6:15,16);*

*"For my thoughts are not your thoughts, neither are your ways my ways, declares the LORD. For as the heavens are higher than the earth, **so are my ways higher than your ways and my thoughts than your thoughts"** (Isaiah 55:8,9).*

Just those two Scriptures make our position seem fairly hopeless, for the gulf that separates us appears to be unbridgeable. Yet a moment's thought will change that, for we are reading and learning about God in His Word. He is communicating with us and is telling us things we could never otherwise know. So He obviously wants us to know Him and is seeking to establish a relationship with us. That's amazing! The Creator of the Universe is reaching out to His creation, seeking a response. He exists on a much higher plane than us in every respect, but He invites us to find the way up to His level. That last passage from Isaiah, for example, is not just a statement about the difference that exists. God's thoughts are much above ours, but look at the setting or context of those words – something which is always important when reading and understanding the Bible.

70

"Seek the LORD while he may be found; call upon him while he is near; let the wicked forsake his way, and the unrighteous man his thoughts; let him return to the LORD, that he may have compassion on him, and to our God, for he will abundantly pardon. For my thoughts are not your thoughts, neither are your ways my ways, declares the LORD. For as the heavens are higher than the earth, so are my ways higher than your ways and my thoughts than your thoughts. For as the rain and the snow come down from heaven and do not return there but water the earth, making it bring forth and sprout, giving seed to the sower and bread to the eater, so shall my word be that goes out from my mouth; it shall not return to me empty, but it shall accomplish that which I purpose, and shall succeed in the thing for which I sent it" (Isaiah 55:6-11).

The God who is telling us about Himself in His Word – a Word which is both living and powerful, and which can certainly accomplish what God intends it to achieve – is a God who wants us to look for Him and find Him. Doing so requires a certain attitude of mind, says the prophet on God's behalf: we must be willing to put aside unworthy thoughts and sinful practices, and we must come to God as people who need His help. If we come in this way we can be confident that He is willing and able to give us all the help we need (Hebrews 11:6).

❖ God's Invitation

Over and over again, the Bible invites us to use our lives for their intended purpose – to spend time getting to know God, by reading His Word, understanding its message, and living according to God's guidance. We are promised that, if we do our part, God will most certainly fulfil His side of the arrangement. Here is a small selection of what is on offer:

"Ask, and it will be given to you; seek, and you will find; knock, and it will be opened to you. For everyone who asks receives, and the one who seeks finds, and to the one who knocks it will be opened. ... If you then, who are evil, know how to give good gifts to your children, how much more will your Father who is in heaven give good things to those who ask him!" (Matthew 7:7-11);

"If any of you lacks wisdom, let him ask God, who

71

gives generously to all without reproach, and it will be given him. But let him ask in faith, with no doubting, for the one who doubts is like a wave of the sea that is driven and tossed by the wind" (James 1:5,6);

"Come to me, all who labour and are heavy laden, and I will give you rest. Take my yoke upon you, and learn from me, for I am gentle and lowly in heart, and you will find rest for your souls. For my yoke is easy, and my burden is light" (Matthew 11:28-30).

God wants us to ask, seek and find – but we must be sincere in that quest if we are to succeed, and we must be prepared to persevere. This may be why the Bible is such a long and sometimes complicated book. God wants us to work through it to find out its true meaning and that meaning is only gradually revealed. If God had wanted to get His message across in a very brief and easily understood way, He could certainly have done that. Instead He has told us about His person and His purpose through the lives of other people – the people who feature in the 66 books of the Bible. The result is a unique record of personal quests to know more about God. In the process, we get a growing appreciation of God's purpose and its meaning for mankind, as more and more of God's intentions are made clear.

❖ Personal Testimony

It is not simply that the men and women of Bible times got to know God in one way or another. They have also left on record their personal appreciation of what that meant for them, so the Bible is like a set of testimonials or personal recommendations.

Take Moses for example. He had a remarkable opportunity to live in Egypt, which was the most developed country at that time, and to enjoy the best that Egyptian life could provide, for he was brought up in the Pharaoh's palace. But he gave all that up. He spent the greater part of his life either as a shepherd – preparing to rescue God's people out of slavery in Egypt – or as an unpaid leader of a rebellious and difficult group of people who were wandering across the Sinai Peninsula, on the way to the Promised Land. Why did he do it, and was it a wise choice?

"By faith Moses, when he was grown up, refused to be

called the son of Pharaoh's daughter, choosing rather to be mistreated with the people of God than to enjoy the fleeting pleasures of sin. He considered the reproach of Christ greater wealth than the treasures of Egypt, for he was looking to the reward" (Hebrews 11:24-26).

What impelled him to give Egypt up and to take his chance with the people of God? He got to know God and that made all the difference. Having been partly brought up in a Hebrew home he had been taught about God and the promises God had made to Abraham's descendants. Then, one day, Moses had a personal encounter which changed his life: an angel of God appeared to him in a bush which burned but was not consumed. Just looking at that phenomenon taught Moses that he was in the presence of someone who was far greater than himself.

"When forty years had passed, an angel appeared to him in the wilderness of Mount Sinai, in a flame of fire in a bush. When Moses saw it, he was amazed at the sight, and as he drew near to look, there came the voice of the Lord: 'I am the God of your fathers, the God of Abraham and of Isaac and of Jacob.' And Moses trembled and did not dare to look. Then the Lord said to him, 'Take off the sandals from your feet, for the place where you are standing is holy ground. I have surely seen the affliction of my people who are in Egypt, and have heard their groaning, and I have come down to deliver them. And now come, I will send you to Egypt ...'" (Acts 7:30-34).

The angel had come from God, with His authority – note that he spoke as if he were the LORD – and he identified God as *"the God of Abraham and of Isaac and of Jacob"*.[3] It's a marvellous thing that Almighty God is prepared to be associated with His people in this way. The angel was doing more than reminding Moses that He had made gracious promises in times past. Abraham, Isaac and Jacob were

---

[3] *Angels often represented God and spoke with His authority. It was said of the angel who led Israel through the wilderness: "Pay careful attention to him and obey his voice; do not rebel against him, for he will not pardon your transgression, for my name is in him" (Exodus 23:21). God was revealing or manifesting Himself through His representative and that idea runs right through the Bible until finally God revealed Himself through His Son (Hebrews 1:1; John 14:9; 1 Timothy 3:16). Ultimately God wants to be seen in the things we see and do, so that we too live as His representatives.*

now dead which meant, as we have seen already, that they no longer had any conscious existence. But the angel used the present, not the past, tense. He said *"I am the God of your fathers"*, not *"I was the God of your fathers"*. This vital distinction was explained by the Lord Jesus Christ himself when, in debate with his opponents, he proved the authority of Bible teaching about resurrection by referring to the precise wording used and, in so doing, shows us once again his view of Biblical inspiration:

> *"You are wrong, because you know neither the Scriptures nor the power of God. For when they rise from the dead, they neither marry nor are given in marriage, but are like angels in heaven. And as for the dead being raised, have you not read in the book of Moses,[4] in the passage about the bush, how God spoke to him, saying, 'I am the God of Abraham, and the God of Isaac, and the God of Jacob'? He is not God of the dead, but of the living. You are quite wrong" (Mark 12:24-27).*

❖ God's Name Declared

That declaration of God's association with the fathers of Israel was just the beginning of Moses' spiritual education. The angel proceeded to tell Moses what He wanted him to do and what sort of a God it was that He was to obey and He did this by declaring God's very special name.[5] This is what he said:

> *"God said to Moses, 'I am who I am.' And he said, 'Say this to the people of Israel, "I am has sent me to you."' God also said to Moses, 'Say this to the people of Israel, "The LORD, the God of your fathers, the God of Abraham, the God of Isaac, and the God of Jacob, has sent me to you." This is my name forever, and thus I am to be remembered throughout all generations" (Exodus 3:14,15).*

God has many ways of describing Himself – many titles

---

[4] *Notice that here Jesus refers to Exodus as "the book of Moses", thus endorsing his authorship of the second book of the Bible. That's typical of the way you pick up information all the time when reading the Bible, if you're looking out for it.*

[5] *The special name of God is sometimes known as the Memorial name of God, because God says: "This is my name forever, and thus I am to be remembered throughout all generations" (Exodus 3:15).*

which explain aspects of His person and purpose. He is the Almighty, the Holy One, the Most High and the Eternal. While some English translations of the Bible use just "God" or "Lord", the original languages have over twenty different ways of describing Him and sometimes the English equivalent loses something of the original force. Take the expression translated *"I AM WHO I AM"* in the Exodus passage. The Hebrew – which when transliterated reads *"eh'yeh asher eh'yeh"* – carries a range of meanings, as many Bible versions acknowledge. It also means *"I WILL BE WHO I WILL BE"*. It is God's way of declaring both that He is Eternal and that He is purposeful – He will accomplish what He intends to do. Of that there can be no doubt!

In this example God was rescuing a people for Himself, bringing them out of Egypt to be His people and by doing so was showing a new aspect of His character or personality. For the first time God declared the meaning of His Name, for although He has many titles, God has just one Name. That name, in the original Hebrew, is "Yahweh", sometimes rendered "Jehovah" in English translations, sometimes just "GOD" or "LORD" (using block capitals). It conveys the meaning of a Covenant God[6] who is both a Redeemer and a Deliverer, as the angel explained to Moses:

> *God spoke to Moses and said to him, "I am the LORD. I appeared to Abraham, to Isaac, and to Jacob, as God Almighty, but by my name the **LORD** [Hebrew: **Yahweh**] I did not make myself known to them. I also establ:shed my covenant with them to give them the land of Canaan, the land in which they lived as sojourners. Moreover, I have heard the groaning of the people of Israel whom the Egyptians hold as slaves, and I have **remembered my covenant**. Say therefore to the people of Israel, 'I am the LORD, and I will bring you out from under the burdens of the Egyptians, and I will deliver you from slavery to them, and I will **redeem you** with an outstretched arm and with great acts of judgement. I will take you to be my people, and I will be your God, and you shall know that I am the LORD your God, who has brought you out from under the burdens of the Egyptians. I will bring you into the land*

---

[6] *A "Covenant" is a solemn agreement made between various parties in such a way that it establishes a relationship according to which people live together.*

that I swore to give to Abraham, to Isaac, and to Jacob. I will give it to you for a possession. I am the LORD' " (Exodus 6:2-8).

This lengthy extract tells us a lot about the character of God as He now reveals Himself further:

✓ *He is the God of Abraham, Isaac and Jacob who was known to them as "God Almighty";*[7]

✓ *He made a covenant or agreement with those early believers, which included that they would inherit the land in which they then lived;*

✓ *God keeps His covenant promises, which is why He was acting now to rescue their descendants;*

✓ *He is a God of action and purpose – He was remembering, delivering, redeeming, bringing them out (of Egypt) and bringing them in (to Canaan), and giving them that land for a possession;*

✓ *He was doing all this because He is "the LORD" (Hebrew: Yahweh).*

Piecing all this together, we see that the big step forward in God's revelation is that He had never before taken action to rescue a people for Himself in accordance with His covenant promises, but He was about to do just that. No wonder the angel briefed Moses so carefully prior to the Exodus that was about to take place. Israel was invited to become God's people, an invitation it readily accepted, and so, after ten great plagues had smashed the opposition of the Pharaoh in Egypt, God indeed rescued His people from their slavery.

❖ More of God's Character Revealed

Another step in Moses' spiritual education took place when he led Israel out of Egypt, as God's appointed leader. He took them to Mount Sinai, where God gave them His Law to keep and formally agreed with the new nation of Israel how they were to behave as His chosen people. It was anything but a smooth journey. Only two named individuals out of the original generation actually made it through the

[7] *This in Hebrew is "El Shaddai", which means 'The Almighty' or 'The All-Providing One'.*

Wilderness into the Promised Land, because of the rebellious and unbelieving attitude of all the others.[8] God kept His side of the agreement but the people utterly failed to fulfil their undertakings, however enthusiastically they had made them.

During this time Moses became increasingly familiar with the attitudes and characteristics of the people for whom he now cared. He asked God for more insight and understanding. He wanted to know God better and asked if he could see Him, but God explained that could not be, *"He said, 'you cannot see my face, for man shall not see me and live'" (Exodus 33:20)*. But, to meet Moses' plea, God said that he would show Moses more about what He is like and, placing him in the cleft of a rock, He allowed Moses to see something of His glory and hear the following declaration:

> *"The* LORD *descended in the cloud and stood with him there, and proclaimed the name of the* LORD*. The* LORD *passed before him and proclaimed, 'The* LORD*, the* LORD*,* **a God merciful and gracious, slow to anger, and abounding in steadfast love and faithfulness, keeping steadfast love for thousands, forgiving iniquity and transgression and sin, but who will by no means clear the guilty,** *visiting the iniquity of the fathers on the children and the children's children, to the third and the fourth generation'" (Exodus 34:5-7).*

This is just the way that the Bible enlarges and amplifies our knowledge of God. As we get to know more about the sort of God we worship, He becomes more and more attractive and appealing to us. For now we learn that

✓ *God is merciful and gracious towards His people;*

✓ *long-suffering and patient;*

✓ *willing to forgive their faults – provided they acknowledge their guilt and come asking for forgiveness;*

✓ *determined to punish sin that continues unchecked (and, if need be, sinners);*

✓ *He does all this because He is abounding in love and kindness; for*

✓ *He is a faithful God who keeps His covenant promises.*

---

8 *The two named individuals were Joshua and Caleb (see Numbers 14:30), although it is possible that others from the tribe of Levi (the priestly tribe) also survived.*

It's little wonder that Moses responded to this further revelation of God's character by bowing his head towards the earth and worshipping Him.

❖ God of Love

Exodus is only the second book in the Bible and already so much has been declared about the God of the Bible. No wonder there are 66 books altogether – there is so much to learn about the God we want to worship. By the time we reach the New Testament God has revealed Himself as a Father, and the extent of His love for mankind is more fully disclosed. This is what one apostle wrote:

> "**God is love**. In this the love of God was made manifest among us, that God sent his only Son into the world, so that we might live through him. In this is love, not that we have loved God but that he loved us and sent his Son to be the propitiation for our sins. **Beloved, if God so loved us, we also ought to love one another.** No one has ever seen God; if we love one another, God abides in us and his love is perfected in us" (1 John 4:8-12).

Notice that God is still the same God – invisible and unreachable by mankind – but He is reaching out to us, especially through the love that He shows in Jesus. Now we are invited to know God by knowing Jesus, who declared himself to be the way to God. As we shall see, Jesus Christ is God's final and fullest revelation of what He is like, and the importance of understanding what God has shared with us is underlined in these words spoken by the Lord in prayer to his Father:

> "He lifted up his eyes to heaven, and said, 'Father, the hour has come; glorify your Son that the Son may glorify you, since you have given him authority over all flesh, to give eternal life to all whom you have given him. And **this is eternal life, that they know you the only true God, and Jesus Christ whom you have sent**'" (John 17:1-3).

Our eternal life depends upon knowing God and the Lord Jesus Christ and we can only know them by understanding what has been revealed to us in God's Word, the Bible. But what a joy it will be to know them better and to establish a relationship with them, and what a transformation this will make in our lives. Just as a new relationship can enhance and change our lives, so knowing Almighty God is bound to be a transforming experience. One of the prophets of God expressed it like this:

> *"Thus says the* LORD: *'Let not the wise man boast in his wisdom, let not the mighty man boast in his might, let not the rich man boast in his riches, but* **let him who boasts boast in this, that he understands and knows me, that I am the** LORD **who practises steadfast love, justice, and righteousness in the earth. For in these things I delight, declares the** LORD*'" (Jeremiah 9:23,24).*

Things to Read

📖 The two occasions when Moses encountered God are so significant that they are well worth reading. They are in Exodus chapters 3 and chapter 33 verse 18 to chapter 34 verse 9.

📖 Read about God's great love for us in 1 John chapter 3:11-24.

Questions to Think About

6.1 Psalm 90, which was written by Moses, tells us several things about God. Write down what those things are (but don't just copy out the verses)

6.2 What is the one thing the Bible insists upon with regard to the nature of God? What would be the one word you might choose to describe that aspect of His nature? (Deuteronomy 6:4-5; Isaiah 45:5-6 and John 17:3)

7

What do we know about Jesus?

Jesus Christ is God's final and fullest revelation of what He is like. But what exactly do we know about Jesus – especially about his person and purpose? How important is he in the purpose of God, and exactly what is the relationship between God and Jesus? These are big questions for us to think about but, as we have already seen, they are vital ones too. Jesus himself said that our eternal life depends upon our knowing God and himself; or, as he put it:

> "This is eternal life, that they know you the only true God, and Jesus Christ whom you have sent" (John 17:3).

We have been using the letter the apostle Paul wrote to the Romans as our starting-point in all these considerations. We will follow through Paul's explanation of what comprises the gospel of God when we have sorted out these preliminary and vital issues.

So, what do we learn from Romans about the person, nature and work of the Lord Jesus? This time we will look at the first eight chapters to see what Paul said about him. If you are reading the Letter with your notebook close at hand, you might want to do that exercise first and then compare your findings with this list.

> "Do your best to present yourself to God as one approved, a worker who has no need to be ashamed, rightly handling the word of truth" (2 Timothy 2:15)

Romans	What we learn about Jesus
1:1	Jesus is Paul's Lord and Master; he called him to be an apostle
1:2	He is Son of God; descended from David *"according to the flesh"* and declared to be God's Son by his resurrection
1:7	Both the Father and the Lord Jesus extend grace and peace
1:1,9	The gospel of God is also the gospel of His Son
2:16	God will judge mankind by Jesus Christ
3:22,24	If we have faith in Jesus we can be counted right with God, for Jesus brings redemption
5:6,8,10	Christ died for the ungodly – for us!
5:15-19	Where a man (Adam) brought death and destruction, another man (Jesus) has undone that damage
6:4	If we are united with Jesus – in his death and resurrection, by baptism – we can start a new life
6:9	The risen Lord Jesus is no longer subject to death
8:3	God has sent His own Son in the likeness of sinful flesh to enable us to fulfil the righteous requirements of the Law
8:34,39	Jesus was raised from the dead (by God) and now sits at God's right hand to intercede for us, for he too loves us!

This brief survey makes one thing evident: Jesus Christ is right at the centre of the purpose of God. He is an absolutely vital part of the gospel of God for it is through him, and only through him, that we can be reckoned to be "right with God". He can redeem us from sin and death because he has undone the damage Adam did to humanity. Sitting at God's right hand in heaven, having been raised from the dead by God, Jesus is now immortal and will intercede for us because he loves us.

❖ Jesus the Man

Three times when explaining the importance of the work of Jesus Paul refers to the way that Jesus was born and his resulting nature. Here are the passages:

> "Paul, a servant of Christ Jesus, called to be an apostle, set apart for the gospel of God, which he promised beforehand through his prophets in the holy Scriptures, concerning his Son, **who was descended from David according to the flesh** and was declared to be the Son of God in power according to the Spirit of holiness by his resurrection from the dead, Jesus Christ our Lord" (Romans 1:1-4);

> "Therefore, just as sin came into the world through one man, and death through sin, and so death spread to all men because all sinned ... For if many died through one man's trespass, much more have the grace of God and the free gift by the grace of that **one man Jesus Christ** abounded for many ... If, because of one man's trespass, death reigned through that one man, much more will those who receive the abundance of grace and the free gift of righteousness reign in life through **the one man Jesus Christ**" (5:12-17);

> "For God has done what the law, weakened by the flesh, could not do. **By sending his own Son in the likeness of sinful flesh** and for sin, he condemned sin in the flesh, in order that the righteous requirement of the law might be fulfilled in us" (8:3,4).

There are some very important points being made here, though they may not be immediately obvious. First Paul explains that the Lord Jesus Christ was a member of the human race, descended from King David. Then he puts him side-by-side with Adam, for Jesus is the man who undid the trouble which Adam brought into the world. Where Adam failed, Jesus succeeded. It was the righteousness of Jesus that cancelled out the effects of Adam's unrighteousness. Thus sin was condemned in the very place where it had been most effective – *"in the flesh"* (this phrase is another way of saying "within human nature"). Jesus was obedient to his Father in everything, so that where Adam had failed he succeeded. This contrast between Adam and Jesus is highlighted by Paul in Romans chapter 5, as we shall see. But there are important points for us to understand at this stage:

1. This great reversal of human fortune was made possible because God sent His Son and then raised him from the dead to sit at His own right hand, in power and great glory.

2. Jesus was a man, not a God who had come in human form, for he was tempted but obeyed, and he died, being mortal not immortal.[1]

3. He obeyed, suffered and died for us, to save us from sin and to show us how to live in a way which is right with God.

❖ Descended from David

Why do you think the first thing Paul says about Jesus is that he was descended from David, rather than from Adam? The clue is in that opening verse of Romans where the apostle says that he was: *"set apart for the gospel of God, which he promised beforehand through his prophets in the holy Scriptures, concerning his Son, who was descended from David according to the flesh"*. A prophet once told

---

[1] *It was a pagan teaching that immortal gods could become man and live among mortals and some people have still got those beliefs about the coming of Jesus into the world. The Bible does not teach that, for God is immortal (and can therefore never die); He is sinless (and could therefore never be tempted to sin); and if He had appeared on earth in person no one would have survived the experience (see 1 Timothy 6:16; Exodus 33:20). Jesus did not live in heaven before he came into existence on earth, for he inherited from his mother Mary those characteristics that made him a descendant both of Adam and of King David. God knew that he would be born in course of time, so in that sense he existed in the mind of God. But he did not come into being until he was born of Mary, and thus became the "offspring" of the woman (Genesis 3:15).*

David that one day he would have a mighty descendant who would rule over his kingdom for ever. Paul was announcing that Jesus was that long-awaited one, whose coming had been prophesied.

We have seen already that the life of Jesus was wonderfully portrayed in advance by the prophets of God, hundreds of years before his birth fulfilled those detailed predictions.[2] This ability to forecast future events with absolute accuracy is one of the evidences that God exists and that His Word is absolutely true. We looked at some of those predictions but there are far more than we considered.[3] The coming of Jesus – the Old Testament Messiah – is a vitally important aspect of God's gracious purpose.

The very first promise that God made to mankind concerned the coming of a Saviour and Deliverer who would rescue mankind from sin and death (Genesis 3:15). As time passed more and more promises were made about this Coming One. Abraham was told that this Saviour would bring a blessing to all nations (Genesis 22:17,18); Moses was told that he would be *"a prophet like you" (Deuteronomy 18:18);* Joshua had the very same name as Jesus, and he took Israel into the promised Land.[4] And when kings ruled in Israel, from about 1000 B.C. onwards, God's promises were enlarged accordingly.

King David was a man who was much loved by God,[5] and he reigned over the nation of Israel which then constituted God's kingdom on earth.[6] Because it was God's kingdom, not his own, David had no right to expect that his family would continue as rulers. None of his predecessor's children had succeeded to the throne. King Saul and his three sons had all died in battle and, as he was Israel's very first king, there was no clear understanding about a kingly line. It must have left everyone feeling very uncertain about things, especially about any long-term plans they might

---

[2] *In Chapter 2, pages 17-21*

[3] *You might, for example, want to read Isaiah chapter 53, in which the saving work of the promised Messiah is described in detail, some 700 years before Jesus was born.*

[4] *"Joshua" is Hebrew; "Jesus" is Greek – both names mean "God is Saviour".*

[5] *God once said of David: "'I have found in David the son of Jesse a man after my heart, who will do all my will'" (Acts 13:22).*

[6] *There is much more about the Kingdom of God in Chapter 20.*

have had for the kingdom.

God met those concerns by making David some long-term promises and by setting out what he and his descendants needed to do, if they wanted to continue as His appointed kings. We will have occasion to look in more detail at these promises later, when we investigate Bible teaching about the Kingdom of God and Israel's role in the purpose of God. For our present purposes we need to notice just one aspect of what David was promised, though you will find it helpful to read the whole of 2 Samuel Chapter 7, if you are not already familiar with it. Here is the part we are looking at now:

> *"When your days are fulfilled and you lie down with your fathers,* **I will raise up your offspring after you, who shall come from your body,** *and I will establish his kingdom. He shall build a house for my name, and I will establish the throne of his kingdom forever.* **I will be to him a father, and he shall be to me a son.** *When he commits iniquity, I will discipline him with the rod of men, with the stripes of the sons of men, but my steadfast love will not depart from him, as I took it from Saul, whom I put away from before you. And your house and your kingdom shall be made sure forever before me. Your throne shall be established forever"* (2 Samuel 7:12-16).

David's descendant – and the language is very particular in saying *"who shall come from your body"* – was the one who would ensure the continuance of the kingdom. There was to be one very important descendant – a special son. After David's days (about 1000 years later as it turned out), that son was indeed born, *"descended from David" (Romans 1:3)*, and he was also God's own Son. David had many other descendants before that, of course, and a succession of them ruled as kings in Jerusalem for more than 350 years.

Many of the kings who reigned on David's throne were very sinful and were disciplined by God. Eventually the kingdom of God came to an end when the last king – a man named Zedekiah – was removed from the throne. A period of over 600 years followed during which time Israel had no king at all. Their only hope of political independence was what the prophets had foretold: the coming of a Saviour and Deliverer. For, when the kingdom was coming to an end, the prophet Ezekiel had said that it would be no more, until the coming of a promised Deliverer who would reign as King:

> *"Thus says the Lord GOD: Remove the turban and take off the crown. Things shall not remain as they are. Exalt that which is low, and bring low that which is exalted. A ruin, ruin, ruin I will make it.[7] **This also shall not be, until he comes, the one to whom judgement belongs, and I will give it to him"** (Ezekiel 21:26,27).*

So, when the apostle began his letter to the Romans by announcing that Jesus was descended from King David, *"according to the flesh"*, he was saying that the long-awaited Deliverer had come. For, in the same sentence, Paul said both that he was David's descendant and that he was *"Son of God"*. Jesus was declared to be the Son of God by his resurrection from the dead – a sort of second birth, after which he was given immortal life by God.

This does not mean that Jesus only became the Son of God when he was raised by God from the dead. Scripture makes it clear that Jesus was God's Son from the moment he was born (see Luke 1:35). What becomes clear is that God took several opportunities to announce the fact that Jesus was His Son, and that He was pleased with the way that Jesus was behaving. He said so at his baptism (Matthew 3:17), at the transfiguration (17:5) and, as Paul now comments, the resurrection from the dead was the final seal of God's approval. He was *"declared to be the Son of God in power ... by the resurrection from the dead"* (Romans 1:4).

❖ Descended from Adam

The phrase *"according to the flesh"* tells us rather more than the fact that King David was a member of the family tree to which Jesus also belonged. That is true enough, as the genealogy of Jesus demonstrates.[8] But when Matthew records the ancestors of Jesus he starts, much like Paul, with this statement:

---

[7] *The kingdom that had existed in Israel was to be brought to an end. King Zedekiah was the last of Israel's kings to reign from Jerusalem. His reign ended in 586 B.C. when Jerusalem was captured by the Babylonians and its inhabitants were deported to Babylon.*

[8] *Jesus has two family trees (one in Matthew chapter 1:1-16; the other in Luke chapter 3).*

"The book of the genealogy of Jesus Christ, the son of **David***, the son of* **Abraham***" (Matthew 1:1).*

His particular emphasis, for he was writing especially for Jews, was to show that Jesus was the long-awaited descendant of both Abraham and David – the one about whom those great promises had been made. Matthew is thus content to take the family tree as far back as Abraham, the father of the Jewish race, but no further. Luke, who wrote for different readers, probably for Gentile ones, takes the family tree right back to its very origins, ending with:

"the son of Noah, the son of Lamech, the son of Methuselah, the son of Enoch, the son of Jared, the son of Mahalaleel, the son of Cainan, the son of Enos, the son of Seth, the son of **Adam***, the son of God" (Luke 3:36-38).*

God formed Adam from the dust of the ground and breathed the spirit of life into him. Jesus was born, *"according to the flesh,"* of the virgin Mary, and that very expression carries a lot of meaning. Paul has a lot to say about what it means to be born in that way. Later in his letter to Rome, he will say these things:

"While we were living **in the flesh***, our sinful passions, aroused by the law, were at work in our members to bear fruit for death ... For I know that nothing good dwells* **in me, that is, in my flesh***. For I have the desire to do what is right, but not the ability to carry it out. For I do not do the good I want, but the evil I do not want is what I keep on doing ... So then, I myself serve the law of God with my mind, but* **with my flesh** *I serve the law of sin ... For those who live* **according to the flesh** *set their minds on the* **things of the flesh***, but those who live according to the Spirit set their minds on the things of the Spirit. To set the mind* **on the flesh** *is death, but to set the mind on the Spirit is life and peace. For the mind that is set* **on the flesh** *is hostile to God, for it does not submit to God's law; indeed, it cannot. Those who are* **in the flesh** *cannot please God" (Romans 7:5,18-19,25; 8:5-8).*

This is a remarkable condemnation of human nature. The apostle confirms what we considered earlier, that human nature was perverted after Adam's sin.[9] It is now

---

[9] *In Chapter 5, pages 54-57.*

naturally inclined away from God. In our lives we seek to please ourselves first and foremost. As Paul now expresses it, *"we set (our) minds on the things of the flesh"* and are by nature *"hostile to God"* because we do not want to submit to His righteous Law. It requires a personal decision and a change of will before we can change direction and seek the things of God. The apostle Paul calls this new direction living *"according to the Spirit"* (Romans 8:4,5).[10]

❖ Born "according to the flesh"

Consider the huge implications of what the Spirit-guided writer meant when, at the start of this letter, Paul said that the Lord Jesus Christ was born *"according to the flesh"* (Romans 1:3). For his language to be consistent throughout the letter, he must have been saying that Jesus was born with the very same nature we have. It is the nature we have inherited from our forefather Adam. So Jesus also shared:

➤ instincts and feelings which tempted him to please himself rather than his Father; and hence

➤ a natural inclination not to want to obey God.

Not only does Paul tell us this – it is the consistent teaching of the New Testament. When Jesus was born he inherited our nature and fully shared our problems, both from within and without. Here is some of this teaching; the first quotation is especially emphatic:

> *"Since therefore the children share in flesh and blood, **he himself likewise partook of the same things**, that through death he might destroy the one who has the power of death, that is, the devil, and deliver all those who through fear of death were subject to lifelong slavery. For surely it is not angels that he helps, but he helps the offspring of Abraham. Therefore he **had to be made like his brothers in every respect**, so that he might become a merciful and faithful high priest in the service of God, to make propitiation for the sins of the people. For because **he himself has suffered when tempted**, he is able to help those who are being tempted" (Hebrews 2:14-18);*

---

10 *See Chapter 15, pages 219-224, where life "according to the Spirit" is considered in detail.*

*"For we do not have a high priest who is unable to sympathize with our weaknesses, but one **who in every respect has been tempted as we are, yet without sin**" (Hebrews 4:15);*

*"He came to his own, and his own people did not receive him. But to all who did receive him, who believed in his name, he gave the right to become children of God, who were born, **not of blood nor of the will of the flesh nor of the will of man, but of God**. And the Word became flesh and dwelt among us" (John 1:11-14);*

*"If anyone loves the world, the love of the Father is not in him. For all that is in the world – **the desires of the flesh and the desires of the eyes and pride in possessions** – is not from the Father but is from the world. And the world is passing away along with its desires, but whoever does the will of God abides forever ... every spirit that confesses that **Jesus Christ has come in the flesh** is from God, and every spirit that does not confess Jesus is not from God" (1 John 2:15-17; 4:2-3).*

When you take stock of what these Scriptures are really saying, it is clear that Jesus was born with the very same feelings and desires we experience. It had to be like that if he was to experience exactly what we feel and yet overcome those feelings. Further you will notice that people who teach that Jesus did not share our nature are *"not from God"* – a strong statement by the apostle John that warns us of the importance of understanding the right things about God's purpose.

❖ Tempted but not Overcome

There is an important distinction, however, that we need to understand at this stage. We have seen that Scripture describes the Lord Jesus as a man – just as Adam was. The contrast between the two of them is central to Paul's argument in Romans chapter 5 and elsewhere:

*"If, because of one man's trespass, death reigned **through that one man**, much more will those who receive the abundance of grace and the free gift of righteousness reign in life **through the one man Jesus Christ**" (Romans 5:17);*

*"For as in **Adam** all die, so also in **Christ** shall all be made alive ... The **first man Adam** became a living being; the **last Adam** became a life-giving spirit" (1 Corinthians 15:22,45).*

Paul does not say that Jesus assumed the form of mankind, or that he was a man for a temporary phase of his existence. He was and is a man. Even in his present existence in heaven, now that Jesus has been made immortal and has been glorified, he is still a man. Sitting at God's right hand he can now act as our go-between with God – our mediator. He is ideally suited for that role because he knows exactly what we are going through as we struggle against sin. And when he comes back to earth to judge the world on God's behalf, Jesus will still be a man – for that is his essential nature. It is the hallmark of everything that Jesus accomplished that although he shared our nature he overcame that nature and was not overcome by it, as everybody else had been. That may be why his favourite way of referring to himself was as *"Son of man"* : [11]

*"For there is one God, and there is one mediator between God and men, **the man Christ Jesus**" (1 Timothy 2:5);*

*"The **Son of Man** is going to come with his angels in the glory of his Father, and then he will repay each person according to what he has done. Truly, I say to you, there are some standing here who will not taste death until they see the **Son of Man** coming in his kingdom" (Matthew 16:27,28);*

*"The times of ignorance God overlooked, but now he commands all people everywhere to repent, because he has fixed a day on which he will judge the world in righteousness **by a man whom he has appointed**; and of this he has given assurance to all by raising him from the dead" (Acts 17:31).*

The remarkable and wonderful thing that happened when Jesus was born and lived on earth is that, although he was tempted and tried in just the same way we are, he never once sinned. This is the vital difference that we need to be quite clear about. When we are tempted to do wrong things, by thoughts that naturally occur to us, the thought

---

[11] *The expression "Son of man" occurs 84 times in the gospels.*

itself is not wrong. Jesus himself said that happens naturally: it is part of the human condition. We sin when we give way to those thoughts and let the ideas develop unchecked, until they become things that we want to do.

We have already considered this, but two of the Scriptures we looked at then will remind us that temptation is not sin: [12]

*"What comes out of the mouth proceeds from the heart, and this defiles a person. For **out of the heart come evil thoughts**, murder, adultery, sexual immorality, theft, false witness, slander. These are what defile a person"* (Matthew 15:17-20);

*"Let no one say when he is tempted, 'I am being tempted by God,' for God cannot be tempted with evil, and he himself tempts no one. But each person is tempted when he is lured and enticed by his own desire. Then **desire when it has conceived gives birth to sin, and sin when it is fully grown brings forth death"** (James 1:13-15).*

❖ Sinless Son of God

Jesus was tempted and tried by all sorts of things, sometimes even by his disciples when they wanted him to avoid the cross and find an easier way. He had powers and opportunities open to him that do not trouble us,[13] and he was pushed to limits of suffering and sorrow that we do not experience, and that helped his spiritual development.[14] Notwithstanding all that, the marvellous thing is that Jesus never once broke God's law in thought, word or deed. You can hear the note of wonder in the Scriptures that record that remarkable achievement:

"For we do not have a high priest who is unable to sympathize with our weaknesses, but one who in every

---

[12] *See also Chapter 5, page 56.*

[13] *Jesus was given the Holy Spirit – the power of God – without limitation (John 3:34) and had resources available to him, that he could have used to serve himself, that we have no access to. Thus his temptations were more challenging than any we will ever face. Even so he overcame.*

[14] *Several Scriptures (like the one from Hebrews 5:7-9 quoted on page 92) explain that Jesus progressed during his life on earth. Step by step he advanced towards perfect obedience, never once failing in the process.*

respect has been tempted as we are, **yet without sin**" (Hebrews 4:15);

"In the days of his flesh, Jesus offered up prayers and supplications, with loud cries and tears, to him who was able to save him from death, and he was heard because of his reverence. Although he was a son, **he learned obedience through what he suffered. And being made perfect,** he became the source of eternal salvation to all who obey him" (Hebrews 5:7-9);

"Christ also suffered for you, leaving you an example, so that you might follow in his steps. **He committed no sin, neither was deceit found in his mouth.** When he was reviled, he did not revile in return; when he suffered, he did not threaten, but continued entrusting himself to him who judges justly" (1 Peter 2:21-23);

"For our sake he made him to be sin **who knew no sin,** so that in him we might become the righteousness of God" (2 Corinthians 5:21);

"Everyone who makes a practice of sinning also practises lawlessness; sin is lawlessness. You know that he appeared to take away sins, and **in him there is no sin**" (1 John 3:5).

❖ "Not my will"

That Jesus overcame temptation is one of the wonders of the Word of God and we should be both appreciative and grateful. It was no easy accomplishment; far from it! If we ever think that Jesus was not really tempted, but only appeared to be struggling against sin, think about his inner struggle in the Garden of Gethsemane. It was in a garden setting – in Eden – that Adam had failed. Now the man whom God had sent to undo all the resulting harm was to be found in a garden in earnest prayer to his Father.

"When he came to the place, he said to them, 'Pray that you may not enter into temptation.' And he withdrew from them about a stone's throw, and knelt down and prayed, saying, 'Father, if you are willing, remove this cup from me. Nevertheless, **not my will, but yours, be done.**' And there appeared to him an angel from heaven,

92

strengthening him. And being in an agony he prayed more earnestly; and his sweat became like great drops of blood falling down to the ground" (Luke 22:40-44).

It clearly took an act of will on the part of the Lord Jesus to go through everything that he knew faced him. Remember that, unlike us, his life had been mapped out in advance,[15] and thus he had a detailed picture of what was coming – the suffering, shame, public humiliation, separation from God, his betrayal, the estrangement of his disciples and much more. No wonder he was *"in agony";* but how marvellous that he was willing to endure all that for us. Someone had come, at long last, who was willing to set his own will aside so that he might accomplish all that his Father wanted. It was a vital turning point in the history of the human race; again one that had been anticipated in the Old Testament Scriptures.

❖ Willing and Obedient

A thousand years before Jesus was born, King David had been inspired by God to write these words about a coming Deliverer:

> *"Sacrifice and offering you have not desired, but you have given me an open ear. Burnt offering and sin offering you have not required. Then I said, 'Behold, I have come; in the scroll of the book it is written of me:* **I desire to do your will, O my God; your law is within my heart"'** *(Psalm 40:6-8).*

To have God's law in the heart is to want to do God's will more than you want to please yourself. David had himself been a man after God's own heart, but he had been unable to let God's will rule his life at all times, and on one occasion he failed very badly indeed. So David was not writing about himself or his achievements. He was predicting that the time would come when someone would be born who would read the Scriptures, identify fully with what was described there, and then willingly comply with all that was required. It would mean setting aside human free-will to become God's servant, precisely what the prophet Isaiah wrote about in four prophecies known as the four "Servant Songs" (to be found in Isaiah chapters 42, 49, 50 and 53).

---

[15] *Chapter 2, pages 17-19*

We have already reviewed some of the things the writer to the Hebrews said about the wonderful achievements of Jesus, earlier in this chapter. He notes what David had written, in Psalm 40, and shows that Jesus entirely fulfilled those requirements. First he explains that it was Jesus who read the Psalm and saw it applied to him:

> **"When Christ came into the world, he said**, *'Sacrifices and offerings you have not desired, but a body have you prepared for me ..."' (Hebrews 10:5).*

If you are reading carefully, you will notice that the Psalmist wrote *"you have given me an open ear"* and the New Testament citation of that Psalm reads *"a body have you prepared for me"*. The first is in the original Hebrew and the second has been translated into Greek, hence the difference. Jews and Greeks had their own special ways of describing a servant or a slave. For the Jew it was someone who was always listening out for the Master's command.[16] When the Greeks described slaves, however, they thought of them as mere bodies, available to serve them.[17]

Jesus fully accepted that his role was to be a servant or slave of God – even though he was His only Son! (John 3:16); the more he read about his destiny in the Scriptures, the more willing he was to do the will of God. Having quoted the passage from the Psalm, the writer then explains the consequences of such perfect and unselfish obedience. A man has perfectly obeyed God as an act of total obedience and, in so doing, has fulfilled the law of God absolutely. So, he explains:

> *"When he said above, 'You have neither desired nor taken pleasure in sacrifices and offerings and burnt offerings and sin offerings' (these are offered according to the law), then he added, 'Behold, I have come to do your will.'* **He abolishes the first in order to establish the second. And by that will we have been sanctified through the offering of the body of Jesus Christ once for all"** *(Hebrews 10:8-10).*

---

[16] *For example, in one of the Servant Songs: "The LORD God has opened my ear, and I was not rebellious" (Isaiah 50:5).*

[17] *Revelation 18:13 uses the same Greek word to describe slaves, and then explains what is meant – "cattle and sheep, horses and chariots, and slaves (lit: bodies), that is, human souls".*

The perfect obedience of Jesus has made possible the removal of the requirements of the law, which had proved impossible to keep because of human weakness, and its replacement by a new order of things. The wonder of it is that through the willingness of Jesus to be God's Servant and to obey Him in every respect, it became possible for us to be counted right with God. That's something we need to look at more closely in the next chapter.

❖ Rewarded for Obedience

There is one other Scripture to consider which also talks about Jesus fulfilling the role of a Servant, for it adds a new thought to our considerations so far. Again it is the apostle Paul who writes:

*"Have this mind among yourselves, which is yours in Christ Jesus, who, though he was in the form of God, did not count equality with God a thing to be grasped, **but made himself nothing, taking the form of a servant, being born in the likeness of men.** And being found in human form, **he humbled himself by becoming obedient to the point of death, even death on a cross. Therefore God has highly exalted him** and bestowed on him the name that is above every name, so that at the name of Jesus every knee should bow, in heaven and on earth and under the earth, and every tongue confess that Jesus Christ is Lord, to the glory of God the Father"* (Philippians 2:5-11).

Jesus perfectly obeyed everything his Father asked of him, including dying on the Cross, in a painful and shameful way. There was nothing automatic or pre-arranged about this. As we have seen, Jesus understood what he was being asked to do and did it, completely and willingly. He was the Son of God and might have expected, or even demanded, some recognition of that remarkable status. Instead he set any such claims aside and did his Father's will. Because of that God raised him from the dead, rewarded him with the gift of immortality, and raised him to glory at His right hand in heaven. Jesus was exalted above all others *because* he was faithful and obedient.

Now every one of us should bow the knee before Jesus and acknowledge him as *"Lord"*, to the glory of God the Father. How carefully Scripture distinguishes between Father and Son and their respective roles, but what a blend of divine activity we see as Father and Son work together to accomplish the great purpose of redeeming mankind. It is that work accomplished by Father and Son, in perfect union, which the apostle Paul now begins to consider as he writes to the believers at Rome.

Things to Read

📖   Matthew 26:26-46 contains a description of the agony that Jesus suffered in the Garden of Gethsemane and his wonderful self-control. It shows that it was a real struggle for him to overcome his natural inclinations so that he would obey his Father in all things.

📖   Isaiah chapter 53 is one of the four Servant Songs recorded by the prophet. It tells of the suffering that Jesus would endure and how he would be saved out of it (see verse 12).

Questions to Think About

7.1   For Jesus to have been tempted in every way that we are tempted he must have had the same nature as us. What does the Bible say about our natural tendencies and feelings? (Jeremiah 17:9,10; Mark 7:18-23; Galatians 5:19-21; James 1:13-16)

7.2   What was Jesus given by God as a reward for his faithful obedience? (Acts 2:32-36; Matthew 28:18; Philippians 2:9-11; Revelation 5:11-12)

"For to this you have been called, because Christ also suffered for you, leaving you an example, so that you might follow in his steps. He committed no sin, neither was deceit found in his mouth" (1 Peter 2:21-22).

8
Father and Son Together

The last two chapters have dealt with some basic facts about the nature and work of both the Father and the Son. When seeking to understand the Bible we must allow it to instruct us by bringing Scriptures together and letting them explain one another. For though we are looking at 66 different books, written over a long period of time, they have one message because they are the product of one mind, that of Almighty God Himself.

Since the Bible was written, church creeds that were formulated hundreds of years later have caused confusion by introducing words and phrases which have no Biblical basis. The Bible never says that Father and Son are 'co-equal' and 'co-eternal'. It never talks about 'confounding the Persons' or 'dividing the Substance'. Terms like 'Unity in Trinity' and 'Trinity in Unity' are completely unbiblical and are foreign to the language of both Testaments. For the Doctrine of the Trinity is a human idea, not a scriptural one.

When we let the Bible speak for itself we find that the true position is wonderfully clear. The important thing is that Bible teaching gives proper recognition to all that both Father and Son have worked together to achieve. This gives the Lord Jesus the honour that is properly due to him – which the man-made Doctrine of the Trinity denies him – and it gives God the glory that is truly due to His great name. First we will consider the problem facing both mankind and Almighty God. Then we will see the wonderful solution He made possible by the gift of His Son.[1]

❖ The Problem Addressed

Mankind was in a death trap! Since Adam rebelled and

---

[1] *We should never underestimate the love that God showed to mankind when He decided to cause His Son to be born of Mary. Scripture recognises it as the greatest possible act of love that God could ever have shown (John 3:16; 1 John 4:9-10; 2 Corinthians 9:15).*

started mankind on its downward path, into sin and ending in death, there had seemed to be no escape. Even the best of endeavours had proved inadequate, until at last this sentence could be passed upon all men:

"That every mouth may be stopped, and the whole world may be held accountable to God. For by works of the law no human being will be justified in his sight, since through the law comes knowledge of sin" (Romans 3:19,20).

This was the dilemma – God had given mankind a law, in which He had defined what was "right" in His sight and what was "wrong", but nobody had been able to keep it.[2] So the law had ended up condemning everybody to death. Elsewhere he calls it a "ministry of death, carved in letters on stone" (2 Corinthians 3:7).[3] God was right but everybody else was wrong. He was Holy; mankind was "Guilty" when measured by that standard.

God is holy and righteous in all His ways – He is the *"High and Lofty One who inhabits eternity, whose name is Holy"*. [4] God defines and declares what is right and what is wrong. Once that position has been stated, God never changes or alters His position; for God cannot be unrighteous. Scripture says that *"God is not man, that he should lie, or a son of man, that he should change his mind" (Numbers 23:19).*

So what was to be done about it? How could God forgive men and women the wrongs they had committed in His sight without compromising His holiness? He could not just say "That's all right! I forgive you". That would indicate that He had changed his attitude towards sin and that it wasn't really so bad after all.[5]

This is what God did to uphold the standard of His holiness and yet enable Him to forgive sinful mankind. He

---

[2] *At first the law was just one commandment – if Adam sinned he would die. That is called the "law of sin and death" (Romans 8:2) and it became a ruling principle. If you sin you will die. Later, to demonstrate what God's requirements really were in detail, or what holiness meant in practice, God gave Moses a code of conduct contained in both the Ten Commandments and a set of regulations. This law is known as the "Law of Moses" (John 7:23).*

[3] *This expression refers to the Ten Commandments which were written on two tablets of stone.*

[4] *Isaiah 57:15.*

acted in such a way that He both displayed:

⬎ the meaning of absolute goodness and, in stark contrast,

⬎ the awfulness of sin.

In this chapter we will concentrate on the first demonstration – the display of God's righteousness through the life of His Son. This is how Paul expresses that development:

> *"By works of the law no human being will be justified in his sight, since through the law comes knowledge of sin. But now the righteousness of God has been manifested apart from the law, although the Law and the Prophets bear witness to it – the righteousness of God through faith in Jesus Christ for all who believe" (Romans 3:20-22).*

Can you see what this very important passage is saying? God is shown to be right in a way which is quite different from the way in which the law showed rightness or righteousness. Jesus came to show mankind what "right" really means. And, in the way he was killed, the people who killed him showed what "wrong" really means. So the coming of Jesus showed, as never before, the difference between right and wrong. This is such an important point. It is right at the centre of the apostle's argument and we need to spend a while thinking about it.

❖ God's Righteousness Demonstrated

We have seen already how God's law spelled out His standards and what they meant in everyday terms. If people lived accordingly they would have happy and wholesome lives. But nobody ever did, and it seemed that nobody ever could be consistently good. Everybody did something wrong. So there was never a practical, living demonstration of godliness. People knew how to live if they wanted to please God, but they couldn't do it.

Paul now explains that God, in His great love and deter-

---

5 *Imagine what it would be like if a human government first said that they would execute any murderers, but later changed their position and said that they would forgive murderers. It would send out the signal that murder wasn't so bad after all. As a result, people would probably regard murder as something that they could risk doing. If they were caught they would be forgiven!*

mination to save sinners from sin and death, found a way of showing people godliness in action. He arranged for people to see what He was truly like, although they could not see Him. In demonstrating His holiness and righteousness, God also declared how lovely and attractive a life of moral purity and freedom from sin really is.

And there was another reason for this demonstration. God cannot lower His standards or compromise His holiness. In revealing more about Himself God would show that He was absolutely right to condemn sin. And He would invite people to agree with Him about that. Here's Paul again on this very theme:

> *"Now **the righteousness of God has been manifested apart from the law** ... **the righteousness of God through faith in Jesus Christ for all who believe** ... **This was to show God's righteousness**, because in his divine forbearance he had passed over former sins. **It was to show his righteousness** at the present time, so that he might be **just and the justifier** of the one who has faith in Jesus" (Romans 3:21-26).*

Note the last phrase in particular. God wanted to pardon sinners and to declare them "not guilty"; in Paul's terminology, He wanted to be their *"justifier"*. But He could not do that by being unjust Himself. Instead He showed His righteousness in a way that left no doubt about His attitude to sin and its awful consequences. God sent Jesus into the world so that right-minded men and women could see that God was right to condemn sin and determine to follow Him. God knew that human nature would show itself in its true colours when confronted by someone who lived an utterly selfless and wholly God-centred life. That was precisely what happened.

❖ Godliness on Display

When Jesus lived on earth his quality of life exposed the failings and shortcomings of the people he lived alongside. Many people found that sort of life deeply attractive and began to follow him. Others were deeply disturbed by it, especially the religious authorities – people who were supposed to be showing their fellow men how best to live. While some people came to love Jesus, the hatred of others grew and grew until at last they determined to kill him.

So the coming of Jesus demonstrated the righteousness of God in two quite different ways.

◥ The lovely life that Jesus lived demonstrated the very essence of the life of God – what godliness was really like and why God was right to seek to destroy sin;

◥ The shocking reaction of the men who hated Jesus, plotted his death, and had him cruelly executed by crucifixion, showed in the starkest terms what human nature is really like, and thus why God is absolutely right to seek to destroy sin. Sin was shown up as *"sinful beyond measure" (Romans 7:13)*.

The way Jesus lived, and the things he said and did, demonstrate what a life of purity and godliness is really like. The people among whom he lived had never experienced anything like it. They had heard about God's grace and truth, but they had never seen it in action in quite this way. The *"glory of God"* had been something wonderful but hidden.[6] Now it was openly displayed, being lived out in the circumstances of everyday life. A man from Nazareth, a carpenter, had come to show mankind just what godliness was really like. The life that God required was being lived out in the streets of first century Israel.

*"The Word became flesh and dwelt among us, and **we have seen his glory, glory as of the only Son from the Father, full of grace and truth** ... And from his fullness we have all received, grace upon grace. For the law was given through Moses; **grace and truth came through Jesus Christ**. No one has ever seen God ... **he has made him known"** (John 1:14-18);* [7]

---

[6] *God had revealed Himself on occasions as the "God of glory" and His glory appeared in the Tabernacle and Temple, when He was enthroned upon the mercy seat (Leviticus 16:2). But only the high priest ever encountered God in that way and then only on one day each year.*

[7] *John 1:18 in the ESV illustrates a problem that is sometimes encountered when the translators allow their own prejudices to influence the way they translate the Greek text. The ESV says of Jesus: "No one has ever seen God; the only God, who is at the Father's side, he has made him known". The RSV, for example, translates the same text like this: "No one has ever seen God; the only Son, who is in the bosom of the Father, he has made him known". As we can see from the rest of Scripture, that is a rendering that is much more in harmony with what the Bible teaches elsewhere.*

*"**I am the way, and the truth, and the life**. No one comes to the Father except through me. If you had known me, you would have known my Father also.From now on you do know him and have seen him."* Philip said to him, *'Lord, show us the Father, and it is enough for us.'* Jesus said to him, *'**Have I been with you so long, and you still do not know me**, Philip? **Whoever has seen me has seen the Father**. How can you say, "Show us the Father"? Do you not believe that I am in the Father and the Father is in me? The words that I say to you I do not speak on my own authority, but the Father who dwells in me does his works. Believe me that **I am in the Father and the Father is in me**, or else believe on account of the works themselves"'* (John 14:6-11).

In that first quotation John told his readers that God's method of communication had now taken on a different and quite wonderful form. God had previously communicated through the spoken and written Word, which had told mankind of His gracious plan and purpose. That was the Word which first brought the world into existence (John 1:1; Genesis 1:1; Psalm 33:6,9). Since then, the same Word had communicated God's purpose to mankind through the Jewish fathers and the prophets. But now the method of communication was different:

⭢ *"The Word became flesh and dwelt among us, and we have seen his glory"* (John 1:14; Hebrews 1:1).

⭢ Nobody can see God (Colossians 1:15; 1 Timothy 1:17), for He is invisible, but Jesus has *"made him known"* as never before.

❖ God's Living Word

Jesus said to Philip that he was the way to God – the way that leads through truth to life. He explained that if Philip thought about the life he had witnessed over the years in which he had been a close follower of Jesus, he would realise that he had seen a living demonstration of what God was like. Jesus and the Father were so close in purpose and intention that to see one was to glimpse the other. Jesus had perfectly demonstrated the family likeness. Because he was wholly dedicated to doing what his Father wanted, the Father had done His work through the works of Jesus. So, Jesus said:

*"**He whom God has sent utters the words of God**, for he gives the Spirit without measure" (John 3:34);*

*"Jesus answered them, '**My teaching is not mine, but his who sent me**. If anyone's will is to do God's will, he will know whether **the teaching is from God** or whether I am speaking on my own authority. The one who speaks on his own authority seeks his own glory, but the one who seeks the glory of him who sent him is true, and in him there is no falsehood'" (7:16-18);*

*"'He who sent me is true, and **I declare to the world what I have heard from him**.' They did not understand that he had been speaking to them about the Father. So Jesus said to them, 'When you have lifted up the Son of Man, then you will know that I am he, and that **I do nothing on my own authority, but speak just as the Father taught me**. And he who sent me is with me. He has not left me alone, for I always do the things that are pleasing to him'" (8:26-29);*

*"**I have not spoken on my own authority, but the Father who sent me has himself given me a commandment – what to say and what to speak**. And I know that his commandment is eternal life. **What I say, therefore, I say as the Father has told me**" (12:49,50).*

All these are sayings found in the gospel of John, the very apostle who explained that God was communicating with mankind in a very special way when *"the Word became flesh"*. In recording them, John reminded his readers that Jesus communicated God's message both by the things that he said and by the way that he lived. As another inspired writer expresses it:

*"Long ago, at many times and in many ways, God spoke to our fathers by the prophets, but in these last days **he has spoken to us by his Son**" (Hebrews 1:1,2).*

❖ Father and Son

All this was something that Father and Son did together but that was not understood by those who conspired to have Jesus crucified. Perhaps that was because they did not want to understand it. Jesus explained to them that he

103

had not come on his own authority; that he did not speak his own thoughts, but those given him by God; he appealed to them to listen to what God was saying through him. They simply charged him with blasphemy, claiming that he was making himself equal with God. Here's one example of that charge:

> "This was why the Jews were persecuting Jesus, because he was doing these things on the Sabbath. But Jesus answered them, 'My Father is working until now, and I am working.' **This was why the Jews were seeking all the more to kill him, because not only was he breaking the Sabbath, but he was even calling God his own Father, making himself equal with God.** So Jesus said to them, 'Truly, truly, I say to you, **the Son can do nothing of his own accord, but only what he sees the Father doing.** For whatever the Father does, that the Son does likewise. For the Father loves the Son and shows him all that he himself is doing'" (John 5:16-20).

Jesus was claiming to be God's Son but the people thought he was claiming equality with God, which Jesus strongly denied. They were very jealous for God's sovereignty and very protective of His position. To understand why this was, we need to appreciate how insistent their Scriptures were about the uniqueness and unity of God. Here are a few examples:

> "The LORD is God; **there is no other besides him** ... know therefore today, and lay it to your heart, that the LORD is God in heaven above and on the earth beneath; **there is no other**" (Deuteronomy 4:35-39);

> "Hear, O Israel: The LORD our God, the LORD is one. You shall love the LORD your God with all your heart and with all your soul and with all your might" (6:4,5);

> "See now that I, even I, am he, and **there is no god beside me**; I kill and I make alive; I wound and I heal; and there is none that can deliver out of my hand" (32:39);

> "**Before me no god was formed, nor shall there be any after me.** I, I am the LORD, and besides me there is no saviour" (Isaiah 43:10,11);

"Thus says the LORD, the King of Israel and his Redeemer, the LORD of hosts: 'I am the first and I am the last; besides me there is no god. Who is like me? Let him proclaim it. Let him declare and set it before me'" (44:6,7);

"I am the LORD, and there is no other, besides me there is no God; I equip you, though you do not know me, that people may know, from the rising of the sun and from the west, that there is none besides me; I am the LORD, and there is no other. I form light and create darkness, I make well-being and create calamity, I am the LORD, who does all these things" (45:5-7);

"There is no other god besides me, a righteous God and a Saviour; there is none besides me. Turn to me and be saved, all the ends of the earth! For I am God, and there is no other" (45:21,22).

Given this emphasis it is no surprise that the Jewish leaders were jealous guardians of the unity of God, something they still insist on to this day. If the Lord Jesus had been claiming equality with God, his claim would have been a direct challenge to those Scriptures. But he was not. Over and over again Jesus protested that he was not equal with God. What he said was that God was his Father, and that he was God's Son.

❖ Only Begotten Son

As the Son of God, Jesus was unique. God had never begotten a Son before and will never do so again. Jesus was born of the virgin Mary and had no human father. Mary was told:

"Behold, you will conceive in your womb and bear a son, and you shall call his name Jesus. He will be great and will be called the Son of the Most High ... And Mary said to the angel, 'How will this be, since I am a virgin?' And the angel answered her, 'The Holy Spirit will come upon you, and the power of the Most High will overshadow you; therefore the child to be born will be called holy – the Son of God'" (Luke 1:31-35).

This was the long-awaited breakthrough promised by God through the prophet Isaiah, who had said that a virgin would bear a special child:

*"Behold, **the virgin shall conceive and bear a son**, and shall call his name Immanuel" (7:14).*

By fathering a Son who would live on earth among men and women, God drew near to mankind in a very special way, one which had never happened before. This is why Jesus was given the name *"Immanuel"*, which means 'God with us'. That is the same point the New Testament makes about his coming:

*"The Word became flesh and dwelt among us, and we have seen his glory, glory as of **the only Son from the Father**, full of grace and truth" (John 1:14);*

*"God so loved the world, that **he gave his only Son**, that whoever believes in him should not perish but have eternal life. For God did not send **his Son** into the world to condemn the world, but in order that the world might be saved through him. Whoever believes in him is not condemned, but whoever does not believe is condemned already, because he has not believed in the name of **the only Son of God**" (John 3:16-18);*

*"In this the love of God was made manifest among us, that **God sent his only Son into the world**, so that we might live through him. In this is love, not that we have loved God but that **he loved us and sent his Son**" (1 John 4:9).*

The coming of God's Son was a remarkable development in His plan of salvation. He initiated it. Unless God had caused His Son to be born on earth there would have been no hope for mankind. For there was no prospect of anyone else being able to live a righteous life and by so doing declare that God was right about all that mankind had done, or had failed to do. God's law had always been broken, even by people who tried to keep it. Now someone had come who would keep the law and, in doing so, would redeem people who would otherwise have been condemned.

*"When the fullness of time had come, **God sent forth his Son, born of woman**, born under the law, to redeem those who were under the law, so that we might receive adoption as sons" (Galatians 4:4).*

❖ Son not Father

Today some people regard the statement that Jesus was God's Son as of less importance than it really is. They believe Jesus to be part of a triune godhead, of the same substance as the Father, co-equal and co-eternal. But Jesus made no such claims. He said that he had been sent by God; he had not come of himself. He did not claim to be equal with his Father. He was His Father's Son, and God was his God as much as He was anybody else's. How could Jesus have expressed the position more clearly? We saw earlier in this chapter how the Jews thought he was claiming to be equal with God, and looked at part of his reply. Now look at the full reply, and see how insistent Jesus is:

> *"This was why the Jews were seeking all the more to kill -him, because not only was he breaking the Sabbath, but he was even calling God his own Father, making himself equal with God. So Jesus said to them, 'Truly, truly, I say to you, **the Son can do nothing of his own accord, but only what he sees the Father doing. For whatever the Father does, that the Son does likewise. For the Father loves the Son and shows him all that he himself is doing.** And greater works than these will he show him, so that you may marvel. For as the Father raises the dead and gives them life, so also the Son gives life to whom he will. **The Father judges no one, but has given all judgement to the Son, that all may honour the Son, just as they honour the Father. Whoever does not honour the Son does not honour the Father who sent him'"** (John 5:18-23).*

That pattern is repeated often, for Jesus regularly explained the superiority of his Father in every respect.

> *"**I can do nothing on my own.** As I hear, I judge, and my judgement is just, because I seek not my own will but the will of him who sent me. If I alone bear witness about myself, my testimony is not deemed true. **There is another who bears witness about me, and I know that the testimony that he bears about me is true** ... The testimony that I have is greater than that of John (the Baptist). For the works that the Father has given me to accomplish, the very works that I am doing, bear witness about me that **the Father has sent me. And the Father who sent me has himself borne witness about me"** (John 5:30-37);*

107

*"Jesus said to them, 'When you have lifted up the Son of Man, then you will know that I am he, and that **I do nothing on my own authority, but speak just as the Father taught me. And he who sent me is with me.** He has not left me alone, for I always do the things that are pleasing to him'" (8:28,29);*

*"You heard me say to you, 'I am going away, and I will come to you.' If you loved me, you would have rejoiced, because I am going to the Father, for **the Father is greater than I** ... but **I do as the Father has commanded me**, so that the world may know that I love the Father" (14:28-31);*

*"In the days of his flesh, Jesus offered up prayers and supplications, with loud cries and tears, **to him who was able to save him from death, and he was heard because of his reverence. Although he was a son, he learned obedience through what he suffered**. And being made perfect, he became the source of eternal salvation to all who obey him, being designated **by God** a high priest after the order of Melchizedek" (Hebrews 5:7-10);*

*"About the ninth hour Jesus cried out with a loud voice, saying, 'Eli, Eli, lema sabachthani?' that is, **'My God, my God, why have you forsaken me?'**" (Matthew 27:46);*

*"Jesus said to her, 'Do not cling to me, for I have not yet ascended to the Father; but go to my brothers and say to them, **"I am ascending to my Father and your Father, to my God and your God."'** Mary Magdalene went and announced to the disciples, 'I have seen the Lord'" (John 20:17,18).*

❖ God the Father

The New Testament is just as insistent as the Old that there is only one God. But it also rejoices in the fact that God now has a Son, the Lord Jesus Christ. They are seen as distinct, and the Lord Jesus Christ is still declared to be subordinate to His Father. It wasn't that he *was* inferior only when he was on earth, and became equal when in heaven with God, as people who believe in the Trinity suppose. That wrong thinking makes nonsense of Scriptural

108

teaching like this, all these verses having been written *after* Jesus ascended to heaven:

*"We know that 'an idol has no real existence,' and that **"there is no God but one"** (1 Corinthians 8:4);*

*"You were called to the one hope that belongs to your call – one Lord, one faith, one baptism, **one God and Father of all, who is over all and through all and in all"** (1 Corinthians 4:4-6);*

"To the only God, our Saviour, through Jesus Christ our Lord, *be glory, majesty, dominion, and authority, before all time and now and forever. Amen" (Jude 25);*

*"I want you to understand that the head of every man is Christ, the head of a wife is her husband, and **the head of Christ is God"** (1 Corinthians 11:3);*

"Then comes the end, when he delivers the kingdom to God the Father *after destroying every rule and every authority and power. For he must reign until he has put all his enemies under his feet. The last enemy to be destroyed is death. For 'God has put all things in subjection under his feet.' But when it says, 'all things are put in subjection,' it is plain that he is excepted who put all things in subjection under him. **When all things are subjected to him, then the Son himself will also be subjected to him who put all things in subjection under him, that God may be all in all"** (1 Corinthians 15:24-28).*

None of these Scriptures detract from the work of the Lord Jesus when, for our sins, he suffered and died. Far from it! The New Testament agrees entirely with the Old in describing the supremacy of God. It highly exalts Jesus for the work that he accomplished together with his Father. Have you ever thought about that? If Jesus was part of an eternal godhead, his mission to earth was really bound to succeed – it couldn't be otherwise. But if he first came into existence on earth, there was no certainty about the success of his mission. It depended upon him and his willingness to do his Father's will. So how greatly we should honour the Son for all that he has accomplished on our behalf.

God the Father	The Lord Jesus Christ – His Son
Immortal and Eternal – He can never die	Born mortal – He could die, and did, for us
Holy and Righteous – *"God cannot be tempted with evil" (James 1:13)*	*"In every respect has been tempted as we are, yet without sin" (Hebrews 4:15)*
Self-existent: *"from everlasting to everlasting" (Psalm 90:2)*	Born of a virgin: *"when the fullness of time had come, God sent forth his Son, born of woman" (Galatians 4:4)*
Nobody can see the invisible God and live (Exodus 33:20), *"who alone has immortality, who dwells in unapproachable light, whom no one has ever seen or can see" (1 Timothy 6:16)*	Jesus showed mankind what God is like by living according to God's laws and thus displaying His character – the family likeness (John 14:9)
God is *"the only true God" (John 17:3)*	Jesus Christ is His Son, whom He sent into the world (John 17:3)
God told Jesus what to say and do; Jesus willingly obeyed (John 8:26-29)	God asked Jesus to die as a sacrifice; Jesus willingly obeyed

*"Sacrifice and offering you have not desired, but you have given me an open ear. Burnt offering and sin offering you have not required. Then I said, **"Behold, I have come; in the scroll of the book it is written of me: I desire to do your will, O my God; your law is within my heart"** (Psalm 40:6-8).*

❖ Willing Obedience

That last point is crucial to our appreciation of what Father and Son have done to save mankind from sin and death. God needed someone who would undo the harm done by a wilfully disobedient man – Adam. But there was no-one able to live a sinless life. So God caused a Son to be born and asked him to surrender his life in total obedience. This Jesus did. He did not have to do it; he chose to do it, and that is an important difference. It was his life of willing obedience that undid the harm first done by Adam. Because of this great accomplishment we should highly honour the Lord Jesus and greatly exalt him.

> *"I am the good shepherd. I know my own and my own know me, just as the Father knows me and I know the Father; and I lay down my life for the sheep. And I have other sheep that are not of this fold. I must bring them also, and they will listen to my voice. So there will be one flock, one shepherd. **For this reason the Father loves me, because I lay down my life that I may take it up again. No one takes it from me, but I lay it down of my own accord. I have authority to lay it down, and I have authority to take it up again. This charge I have received from my Father**" (John 10:14-18);*

> *"Though he was in the form of God, (he) did not count equality with God a thing to be grasped, but made himself nothing, taking the form of a servant, being born in the likeness of men. And being found in human form, **he humbled himself by becoming obedient to the point of death, even death on a cross. Therefore God has highly exalted him and bestowed on him the name that is above every name, so that at the name of Jesus every knee should bow, in heaven and on earth and under the earth, and every tongue confess that Jesus Christ is Lord, to the glory of God the Father**" (Philippians 2:6-11).*

Things to Read

A lot of Scripture has been referred to in this chapter and it is important to make sure that the extracts quoted properly reflect the teaching of the entire passage. Pick those that especially interest you and look at them in their context in the Bible.

Try reading the whole of John chapter 5 or Philippians chapter 2 to get the sense of how Jesus challenged his adversaries, and how the apostles explained their understanding of how Father and Son worked together to achieve our salvation.

Questions to Think About

8.1 Jesus said that he and his Father were one. Look at that saying (in John 10:30) to understand just what Jesus was claiming. Then compare it with John 17:11,21-23. What do those Scriptures teach?

8.2 When the apostle John said that the Word was with God in the beginning (John 1:1-3), what was he telling his readers about Jesus? Was he saying that Jesus existed at the beginning; or that God had a plan and purpose from the beginning which would eventually result in the birth of God's only begotten Son? Give your reasons for whichever option you think is right. (Compare John 1:1-14 with Psalm 33: 6-9; Proverbs 8:1-32 and Hebrews 1:1)

9

Why did Jesus have to Die?

Careful Bible reading shows how a verse in one chapter of Romans fits in with the rest of Scripture to reveal a hugely important truth – the reason for the death of the Lord Jesus Christ. This is something that really matters to us because the Bible insists that Jesus died for our sins. The fundamental problem that faces all of us is that of sin and its inescapable consequence death.

Here is the verse from Romans that will start our exploration into the reason for the death of Jesus:

*"There is no distinction: for all have sinned and fall short of the glory of God, and are justified by his grace as a gift, through the redemption that is in Christ Jesus, **whom God put forward as a propitiation by his blood, to be received by faith. This was to show God's right- eousness, because in his divine forbearance he had passed over former sins**" (Romans 3:22-25).*

The words shown in bold text comprise verse 25 but it is important to look at a verse in its setting or context. It's easy to take a verse out of its context to support a point of view. However, to see what the Bible *really* teaches, you have to look at each verse in its own context, as part of the overall argument.

❖ "Redemption in Christ Jesus"

Verses 24-26 are so full of information that we need to slow down and think hard about what they are saying. This is another thing to note about Bible reading. Sometimes you need to read an entire book or several chapters at a stretch to get the flow of the argument. At other times you need to slow right down and look carefully at every word.

We are going to do that now, first by looking at these verses overall and then, in the next two chapters, by examining in more detail the way we can receive God's salvation, through the death of Jesus. We have already learned that a step-by-step approach can help us to unlock things, so let's try that again.[1]

Verses	Teaching
3:19-20	No one could keep God's commandments, so God's Law serves the purpose of showing us how wrong we are. But keeping God's law can't make us right with God, because we just can't keep it perfectly;[2]
3:21	God has found another way of declaring that He is against Sin in all its aspects, without in any way lowering His standards or seeming to compromise with sin. This new way – which is outside the scope of the law that God gave through Moses – was anticipated in the Law and the Prophets;[3]
3:22	It requires men and women to believe in Jesus Christ, so that they can be counted "right" with God, or "just" in His holy sight.
3:23-24	This righteousness is not something we can achieve by ourselves, it comes about as God's free gift (an act of His "grace" or divine favour).
3:25	God can redeem (or rescue) mankind from the power of sin and death because of what Jesus has done. God gave Jesus to redeem us. If we want to be saved we must do something as well – we must believe these things and act upon them.

---

[1] *Here is another chance for you to write down the key points in this argument and then compare your list with the summary that follows, if you want to develop your analytical skills. But it's not compulsory!*

[2] *The Bible term for being right with God is "righteous" and the term Paul uses for being found "Not Guilty" in God's law court is "justified".*

[3] *We should therefore find some indications in the Law itself that it would eventually fail to achieve the object of bringing people to God and that another arrangement would be needed, and those pointers are indeed to be found there, as the Letter to the Hebrews explains in some detail.*

❖ God's Right – We're Wrong!

Here's one further technique we can use to get things crystal clear in our minds. Those various points can be summarised in just a few key statements, as follows:

✓ God is right about everything – His law is righteous; His acts and attitudes are perfect.

✓ When we break God's law we are shown up as sinners, and we are in the wrong.

✓ God's wants to put us in the right, but He can't do that by putting Himself in the wrong. So He has chosen another way to show right from wrong: He gave His Son to die on our behalf.

✓ If we recognise the rightness of God, by accepting the death of Jesus on our behalf, we can be forgiven.

These are vitally important issues. God wants to save mankind from sin, for He is against sin in all its forms, and always will be. That is the sort of God He is and always must be, as we saw earlier.[4] Just as God cannot lie and cannot sin, He cannot compromise His righteousness – He has always been "right" or "righteous" and He always will be. But now there is a way of forgiveness made possible by God's great love for us and by the full and willing cooperation of the Lord Jesus, God's only begotten Son.

❖ God's Law of Love

The law defined God's righteousness in a particular way by explaining what was best and worst for Israel as a nation.[5] It defined what was "right" and "wrong", being based upon two key principles:

↘ Those who sought to keep the law should put God at the centre of their lives. They should love Him first and foremost and thus be willing to do whatever He asked of them; and

---

[4] *Chapter 6 pages 68-69.*

[5] *The Law also introduced principles of hygiene and social justice which were far in advance of the times, but here we are concentrating on the way the Law showed right from wrong.*

↘ They should put others before themselves and care for them as much as they cared for themselves.

Those key principles were explained by the Lord Jesus when, on one occasion, he was asked which was the greatest commandment in the law.[6] His answer was:

> *"You shall love the Lord your God with all your heart and with all your soul and with all your mind. This is the great and first commandment. And a second is like it: You shall love your neighbour as yourself. On these two commandments depend all the Law and the Prophets"* (Matthew 22:37-40).

Keeping the law was a way of demonstrating love for God and for other people. Breaking the law was a failure to love and live acceptably before God. Yet when we fail to love, that never diminishes God's love for us. His love is like that of a mother for her children: she still loves them even when they don't seem to show any love back. So it was that God wanted, and still wants, to save sinners from sin and to rescue them from death, but He could not do that by compromising His righteousness.

God couldn't ignore sin and its awful effects. To do so would be like declaring that a life of sin wasn't that bad after all. God is absolute perfection, total goodness, and complete purity of being. The Bible shows this whenever it describes His character. He is light, with no darkness in it; He is the God of truth, and so He cannot lie.[7] God is right and can never compromise about what is right and wrong:

> *"Are you not from everlasting, O LORD my God, my Holy One? ...* ***You who are of purer eyes than to see evil and cannot look at wrong"*** *(Habakkuk 1:12,13).*[8]

❖ Sin and Sinfulness Exposed

We have seen already that when Jesus lived on earth the righteousness of God was shown by the way he lived every

---

[6] *Jesus said the two key principles are to be found in Deuteronomy 6:4-5 and Leviticus 19:18 – to love God and to love one's neighbour. Love is therefore the overriding principle.*

[7] *See 1 John 1:5; Isaiah 65:16 and Titus 1:2.*

[8] *This verse does not say that God cannot pass judgement upon what is wrong; it says that He cannot do anything wrong. Any form of wrongdoing would be contrary to His holiness and righteousness.*

day. He demonstrated the character of God, which is why some people marvelled at the loveliness of his behaviour and the wonderful words he spoke.[9] But this demonstration of righteousness in action was not to everyone's taste: his enemies hated him for it. For Jesus showed them up for what they truly were. They were playing at being holy without really facing up the demands of holiness.[10]

It often happens in Scripture, as in life, that you come to appreciate the qualities of one person by seeing the deficiencies of someone else. King David, for example, was appreciated as a good king because his predecessor King Saul had been awful. In the same way, Jesus is seen to be so much better than people like Judas Iscariot, who betrayed him. The best and the worst are presented side-by-side as a deliberate contrast to one another. The lovely life that Jesus lived was cruelly brought to an end by the wicked scheming of men who should have acted so much better. The apostle John makes that point many times in his account of the life of Jesus, starting with the comment that Jesus was the light of the world and his opponents preferred darkness to light.[11] He describes the way that Jesus raised Lazarus from the dead, and immediately mentions the scheming of those who opposed Jesus, saying that now they not only wanted to kill Jesus, but Lazarus as well![12]

Their evil thoughts and plans eventually came to fruition when Jesus was cruelly put to death on the cross. This act was the clearest possible demonstration that sin was sinful. If you want to know what sin is really like, look at what it did to Jesus. If you want to know whether God was right to condemn sin – look at the cross of Christ. That is what Paul was saying when he declared that God's righteousness was shown by what happened to Jesus. In his life and in his death, Jesus showed how right God is to hate sin, how dangerous and deadly sin is to us, and how important it is that we should try to live in a way which is right with God. The apostle Peter made precisely the same point when he explained the meaning of the death of Jesus on the day of

---

[9] *See, for example, John 6:68 and 7:46.*

[10] *Jesus called his opponents "hypocrites" a word which really means 'play-actors' (see Matthew 23:13-29).*

[11] *John 3:19-21.*

[12] *John 11:45-53; 12:9-10.*

117

Pentecost:

> *"Men of Israel, hear these words: Jesus of Nazareth, a man attested to you by God with mighty works and wonders and signs that God did through him in your midst, as you yourselves know –* **this Jesus, delivered up according to the definite plan and foreknowledge of God,** *you crucified and killed by the hands of lawless men"* (Acts 2:22,23).

❖ God's Purposeful Plan

Notice that Peter assures the population of Jerusalem that nothing had gone wrong with God's purpose. Everything that happened was according to His *"definite plan and foreknowledge"*. It had to be like this: there was no other way. From the very beginning God had instructed mankind about the dangers of Sin.

⬎ There was that one law in Eden, about not eating from the fruit of the tree.

⬎ Then there was a more detailed code of laws given to Israel through Moses, which spelled out right from wrong.

⬎ God had required sacrifices in which an animal or animals had to be offered to show that a life must be surrendered before sin could be forgiven.[13]

⬎ In both the Tabernacle and the Temple, worshippers were kept at a distance from the things that were holy, to show that there was a great difference between the holiness of God and the natural sinfulness of people.

⬎ God had then instituted a Priesthood which was given a limited right of approach into His presence, to show that there was a way into His favour and fellowship, a way which required sacrifice and the shedding of blood.

⬎ He arranged Feasts to commemorate and celebrate certain key events. For example, the Feast of Passover

---

13 *The shedding of blood (resulting from the taking of a life) was an important element in the instruction that God gave by the institution of sacrifice (see Leviticus 17:11 and Hebrews 9:22).*

118

reminded Israel that they were delivered from slavery because of the shed blood of a lamb.[14]

These various arrangements served at least two purposes. First, they showed the difference between right and wrong – between God and mankind. Second, they indicated that there was a way to find favour with God – a way into His presence. If you could keep the law; find an acceptable sacrifice; become a priest, or celebrate the prescribed feast, you could get near to God. Or if someone could do that for you, then that would open up a new way of approach into the presence of God. The great news given us in the New Testament is that Jesus has done all these things for us.

✓ Jesus kept the law of God absolutely, never once being in breach of its demands;

✓ He offered himself as a sacrifice for sins and surrendered his own life for us;

✓ By living with us he showed us what godliness is like in practice;

✓ He became a Priest who acts as a go-between for us;

✓ He fulfilled what the Feasts pointed forward to, by delivering us from bondage[15] and gaining access into the presence of God and making reconciliation for our sins.[16]

❖ **"Propitiation"**

Sometimes the Bible uses words with a very particular meaning which we don't often use. One verse in Romans chapter 3 contains such a word. Here is the verse again, in which the apostle says about the death of the Lord Jesus:

---

[14] *The Passover clearly pointed forward to the work of Jesus, as the New Testament makes clear (John 1:29, 1 Corinthians 5:7 and 1 Peter 1:18-20).*

[15] *The Feast of the Passover (details in Exodus 12) was, in particular, a feast that was associated with Israel's freedom from slavery in Egypt.*

[16] *The Letter to the Hebrews carefully explains the way in which Jesus was the fulfilment of those things that had been included in the Old Testament. Jesus himself said that he was the Way into the Father's presence (John 14:6).*

*"... whom God put forward as **a propitiation by his
blood**, to be received by faith. This was to show God's
righteousness, because in his divine forbearance he had
passed over former sins" (3:25).*

When Jesus died on Calvary his life was given and his
blood was shed. The apostle John carefully records both
those happenings. Blood as a *physical substance* has no
special significance or importance in Scripture. Because it
carries the life force around a body, blood is seen to be a
powerful **symbol of life**, which belongs to God, not to us.[17]
This was why God instructed the Jews not to eat blood. So,
when we read about the shed blood of Jesus, we should
think about the wonderful life he lived and the marvellous
way in which he chose to lay down that life for us.

Paul says that God put Jesus forward *"as a propitiation
by his blood"* and we need to work out just what that
means. Notice that our Bible reading has narrowed down
from one verse to just one word, and a difficult word at
that. If we were to look it up in a dictionary, we would be
told that "propitiation" means:

✓   winning somebody's favour; or

✓   appeasing or conciliating somebody of something.

It's about making amends or putting something right
that was previously wrong. But what does it mean in the
Bible? The Bible can act as its own interpreter. If the same
Greek word is used elsewhere in the Bible that is going to
give us more help than anything. For how a word is used
elsewhere in the Bible is the best possible way of finding
out what it really means.

Of course the way the word is translated into English
also helps and sometimes different translations may throw
light upon a difficult verse, even those versions which are
more paraphrases than translations. Here is the same
verse in a few different versions:

*"God presented him as **a sacrifice of atonement**,
through faith in his blood. He did this to demonstrate his
justice, because in his forbearance he had left the sins*

---

17 *Noah was commanded: "You shall not eat flesh with its life, that is, its
blood" (Genesis 9:4) and later that was included in the Law of Moses
(Leviticus 17:11,14).*

committed beforehand unpunished" (New International Version);

*"God appointed him as **a sacrifice for reconciliation**, through faith, by the shedding of his blood, and so showed his justness ..." (New Jerusalem Bible);*

*"**God offered him**, so that by his blood he should become the means by which people's sins are forgiven through their faith in him" (Today's English Version: The Good News Bible);*

*"Whom God put forward [before the eyes of all] **as a mercy seat and propitiation by his blood** [the cleansing and life-giving sacrifice of atonement and reconciliation, to be received] through faith ..." (Amplified Bible);*

*"Whom God put forward as **a sacrifice of atonement (or: a place of atonement)** by his blood, effective through faith ..." (New Revised Standard Version).*

❖ Sacrifice for Reconciliation

God wanted to forgive sinners but could not do that unless His righteous demands had been met. He had condemned sin and sinners to death and there was no going back on that judicial sentence unless someone achieved 'atonement' or 'reconciliation' for others. This is what God and Jesus did.

Notice that Paul says it was God who 'presented', 'appointed', 'offered' or 'put forward' His Son. If God had not taken the initiative, there would have been no Jesus. It was a wonderful act of divine love and mercy that the Father caused a Son to be born and that had him live in our world, subject to all its evil and malice. It must have been painful to stand by while His Son was cruelly treated and publicly executed. God knew from the outset what would happen; yet He graciously and marvellously provided His Son.

Jesus voluntarily laid down his life as a sacrifice '*of atonement*', or '*for reconciliation*': giving his life so that we can have life. Jesus died as our representative so that we can live. In his death he showed even more clearly than he had done in his life that sin is exceedingly sinful and he showed, as never before, how wonderful love is. For the gift

121

of Jesus was an act of unsurpassed love on the part of both Father and Son. They worked together to achieve the salvation that the death of Jesus has made possible for us.

Without this statement of God's position with regard to sin, the only alternative would have been to punish sinners, as God had said would happen. You sin – you die and remain in the grave for ever! But in His great mercy, God had forgiven people in the past in anticipation of the work that would be accomplished through Jesus. In His divine forbearance *"he had passed over former sins" (Romans 3:25)*. The death of Jesus put things right retrospectively. It was to be effective both for the future and for the past. We shall learn more about the significance of this sacrifice as Paul develops the argument in Romans, especially as it affects us and what we must do to gain advantage from it. For the moment we note that the death of Christ made it possible for God to forgive without in any way compromising His holiness.

❖ Place of Atonement

The word *"propitiation"* can be translated in many different ways, as we have seen. But does it occur anywhere else in Scripture and, if so, what do we learn from that? To find that out either you need a very helpful cross-reference in the margin of your Bible or a way of tracing the occurrences of Greek or Hebrew words.[18] This is what we would discover in this particular case.

The Greek word here translated *"propitiation"* only occurs in one other place in the New Testament, and that is in Hebrews 9:5 which reads:

> *"Above the Box were the winged creatures representing God's presence, with their wings spread over **the place where sins were forgiven**. But now is not the time to explain everything in detail".*[19]

The Box of which the apostle speaks is the Ark of the Covenant which was found in the Most Holy Place in the Temple. This Box was the very symbol of the glorious pres-

---

18 *These Bible aids are called analytical concordances: they list the occurrences of English words and then show how the same original word (in Hebrew for the Old and Greek for the New Testament) is translated differently in English.*

19 *This quotation is from the Good News Bible (Today's English Version)*

ence of God and it was into this Most Holy Place that the high priest went just once each year, with the blood of sacrifices, to make atonement for the nation. He sprinkled that blood on the mercy seat beneath the cherubim, whose wings were spread out above it, and there God met with His people through the ministrations of the high priest.

This Mercy Seat – the lid of the Ark of the Covenant – was *"the place where sins were forgiven"*. Both this phrase, in Hebrews 9:5 and the word *"propitiation"* in Romans 3:25 are translations of the same Greek word. However, Hebrews adds the important thought that the death of Jesus makes it possible for us to meet with God. Once we were far away from Him, separated by His holiness and righteousness because of our sin. But the work of Father and Son has closed that gap. As Paul wrote elsewhere:

> *"Now, in union with Christ Jesus, you who used to be far away have been **brought near by the blood of Christ**. For Christ himself has **brought us peace** by making Jews and Gentiles one people ... Christ came and preached the Good News of peace to all – to you Gentiles, who were far away from God, and to the Jews, who were near to him. It is through Christ that all of us, Jews and Gentiles, **are able to come in the one Spirit into the presence of the Father"** (Ephesians 2:13-18).*

❖ No Longer Angry

God is angry with the wicked every day and the time will soon come when that anger is shown towards men and women in our world, because it has forsaken Him. We saw that in Romans 1:18 and 2:5. But God's anger can be turned away from us and we can receive His love and mercy instead. His anger derives from his constant and unchangeable opposition to sin in all its forms: that is His absolute position. But once Christ died to demonstrate that God is totally right to oppose sin, the forgiveness of our sins became possible.

If we agree with God about the awfulness of sin and accept that He is right then we too can declare the righteousness of God. He can then justify, or reckon us right in His sight, and that is precisely the point that Paul now proceeds to make. In these last few chapters we have looked at the way in which Almighty God and His Son, the Lord Jesus Christ, have been working together to make it possible to overcome the problem of sin and death that confronts all of us. We have found that this can mean an enormous amount to us, if we want it to. Now we have to turn our attention to what we are supposed to do about it, for that is what the apostle begins to explain.

Things to Read

As we have been thinking about the high priest going into the presence of God, you might want to read Leviticus chapter 16 and the New Testament explanation given in Hebrews chapter 9:1-15 of how this was fulfilled by Jesus.

The death of the Lord Jesus is vividly portrayed in all four gospels. Try Luke's account (Luke 23:27-56).

Questions to Think About

9.1 Jesus willingly offered himself as a sacrifice for sins; nobody forced him or compelled him to lay down his life. What should that mean for us? (John 10:17-18; Luke 22:42; Romans 12:1-2)

9.2 If Jesus gave his life for us, what should we be willing to do for him? (Galatians 2:20)

10

How we can be
Justified by Faith

Paul has established a lot of things in the opening three chapter of his Letter to the Romans especially about the purpose and work of God the Father and Jesus Christ His Son. When things were hopeless for mankind God acted by causing His Son to be born. Jesus was born as a man among men and women to show us how to live and especially to demonstrate that God was absolutely right to condemn sin. Jesus showed sin up for what it is – wilful disobedience to God's law, that should stop now!

The problem is that we can't stop because sin has a hold on us. This is partly because our nature prompts us to disobey God so that it is natural for us to want to please ourselves. When we do that, we find that we get into a pattern of disobedience which is extremely addictive. We like pleasing ourselves!

So how do we break the cycle and strike out in a different direction? How can we become acceptable to God and be forgiven for all the past misdeeds and bad things we have already done? This is the vital truth Paul now explains to the readers of his letter. He shows that God offers us a way of salvation which relies more on the things we *believe* than on the things we *do.* The things we do are important by way of confirming what we believe but, by themselves, they can never save us. We can never be acceptable to God by our actions alone.

❖ "Just and the Justifier"

We have already established that everyone without exception has disobeyed God's law. Everybody was "guilty" in His holy sight because everyone had broken His law (Romans 3:19,23). God provided Jesus so that men and women could be declared "Not guilty". He did this by working with Jesus to show us what righteousness is really like. How lovely and how appealing it is when somebody lives completely free of the power of sin, as only Jesus ever has. And how awful sin is: for sinners put that lovely man to death in a cruel and humiliating way.

God had to be shown to be *just* – to be right in the way He has gone about things in every respect. But He also wanted to save as many as possible, by *justifying* or *forgiving* them. God showed how serious He is about destroying sin by providing a Son and then asking him to die as a sacrifice for sin. Jesus did this willingly, as an act of submission and total obedience. So the death of Christ demonstrated both:

✓ the gracious kindness and love of God and the Lord Jesus, and

✓ the awfulness of sin (the terrible excesses to which sinners will go).

The death of the Lord Jesus Christ accomplished two things, as Paul explains:

> *"This was to show God's righteousness, because in his divine forbearance he had passed over former sins. It was to show his righteousness at the present time, so that he might be [1] just and [2] the justifier of the one who has faith in Jesus"* (Romans 3:25,26).

God has to be just in His dealings – He cannot be otherwise. It is impossible for God to deal with matters in an unjust way. But He could have shown His justice in some way less favourable to mankind. For example, He could have destroyed the world that He created: the wickedness of man certainly deserved that. But because God is also loving and merciful, He is at present giving all men and women the opportunity to repent of their sins.[1] When a person is truly repentant their attitude allows God both to be *"just and the justifier of the one who has faith in Jesus"*.

❖ **Having Faith**

'Faith' is another Scriptural term with a quite specific meaning. Nowadays people use the word loosely to mean all sorts of different things; they talk about having faith in something when they really mean 'hoping for the best'. When the Bible uses that term it means quite specifically 'believing in God and in His promises'. One whole chapter of

---

[1] *"Repentance" is a Scriptural term that means 'turning away from sin and turning towards God'.*

the Letter to the Hebrews is taken up with key information about people who believed God.[2] In it the writer explains what a difference faith made to their lives because it affected the choices they made and the things they did. He describes faith as something that gave them assurance and conviction (Hebrews 11:1). Then he demonstrates what it meant for people like this:

God's People	What their faith required of them
Noah	"Being warned by God concerning events as yet unseen, in reverent fear constructed an ark for the saving of his household. By this he condemned the world and became an heir of the righteousness that comes by faith" (11:7)
Abraham	"Obeyed when he was called to go out to a place that he was to receive as an inheritance. And he went out, not knowing where he was going. By faith he went to live in the land of promise, as in a foreign land, living in tents with Isaac and Jacob, heirs with him of the same promise" (11:8,9)
Moses	"Refused to be called the son of Pharaoh's daughter, choosing rather to be mistreated with the people of God than to enjoy the fleeting pleasures of sin. He considered the reproach of Christ greater wealth than the treasures of Egypt, for he was looking to the reward (11:24-26)

The important thing about these three faithful people, and something that is true of all those who get mentioned in this chapter, is that they believed in something specific. And what they believed was just as important as the way they believed it. If you were asked "Do you have Noah's faith?" you might think the questioner was asking: 'Do you have enough trust and confidence in God to do something

---

[2] *In Sripture the word "faith" and the word "believe" are translations of the same Greek word. They both mean the same thing.*

about your own salvation?' But the real question is, 'Do you believe, as Noah did, that God is about to destroy our society, and will you find a safe hiding place in that day?' In other words, what we believe is a vital part of living by faith. Only then can we consider how much we believe those things.

❖ God's Coming Judgement

The apostle Peter said that God doesn't *want* people destroyed. Because of His long patience, He is waiting for them to respond to His gracious invitation to be saved from sin.[3] But Peter also said that such waiting time is limited and that eventually judgement will come. Paul says exactly the same: a day of God's wrath and anger is coming when the world will be called to account and the present evil age of human rule will come to an end. In its place God will establish His new society – a world ruled over by the Lord Jesus Christ. Here are a few Scriptures that explain God's intention and which warn us of the importance of doing something about it:

> "Do you suppose ... that you will escape the judgement of God? Or do you presume on the riches of his kindness and forbearance and patience, not knowing that God's kindness is meant to lead you to repentance? But because of your hard and impenitent heart you are storing up wrath for yourself on the day of wrath when God's righteous judgement will be revealed. He will render to each one according to his works: **to those who by patience in well-doing seek for glory and honour and immortality, he will give eternal life;** but for those who are self-seeking and do not obey the truth, but obey unrighteousness, there will be wrath and fury. There will be tribulation and distress for every human being who does evil, the Jew first and also the Greek, but **glory and honour and peace for everyone who does good, the Jew first and also the Greek**" (Romans 2:3-10);

> "We will all stand before the judgement seat of God; for it is written, 'As I live, says the Lord, every knee shall bow to me, and every tongue shall confess to God.' So then

---

[3] *2 Peter 3:9-11.*

each of us will give an account of himself to God."
(14:10-12);

*"Just as it was in the days of Noah, so will it be in the days of the Son of Man. They were eating and drinking and marrying and being given in marriage, until the day when Noah entered the ark, and the flood came and destroyed them all ... so will it be on the day when the Son of Man is revealed ... **Whoever seeks to preserve his life will lose it, but whoever loses his life will keep it"** (Luke 17:26-33);*

*"The times of ignorance God overlooked, but **now he commands all people everywhere to repent,** because he has fixed a day on which he will judge the world in righteousness by a man whom he has appointed; and of this he has given assurance to all by raising him from the dead" (Acts 17:30,31).*

❖ "What must I do?"

Just by collecting those verses we can see some of the things we must do if we want to be saved from God's wrath when His judgements fall.

↘ Seek for glory, honour and immortality – another reminder in passing that we are, in fact, mortal beings who need to become immortal;

↘ Patiently try to do the things that are right in God's sight and stop doing the things He tells us are wrong;

↘ Live in awareness of the fact that one day we will have to give an account of ourselves to God;

↘ Be willing to give up things in this life, so that we can obtain the life to come;

↘ Repent of our wrong way of life and become focused on God, His purpose and His Word.

One thing is very clear: we can never live a good enough life to satisfy the righteous requirements of God's Law. Try as we might, we cannot earn eternal life by the things we do. Our lives are just not deserving of glory, honour and immortality. Eternal life has to be a gift of God's grace, as

Paul confirms:

> *"When you were slaves of sin, you were free in regard to righteousness. But what fruit were you getting at that time from the things of which you are now ashamed? The end of those things is death. But now that you have been set free from sin and have become slaves of God, the fruit you get leads to sanctification and its end, eternal life.* **For the wages of sin is death, but the free gift of God is eternal life in Christ Jesus our Lord"** *(Romans 6:20-23).*

We all deserve to die because of the way we live, but God offers us eternal life as a free gift of His grace. Paul argues that we will want to live better lives to show God how much we appreciate His gift. But how is it that God will give us eternal life in the first place? What do we have to do to become eligible? We have to believe God or, to put it in Bible terminology: we need *faith* if we are to be justified.

❖ Justified by Faith

This is something the apostle Paul taught over and over again, and it is quite understandable that he should put it right at the centre of his teaching. He had been brought up to understand that you were saved by keeping the commands of the Law that God had given through Moses. He believed that obedience was the key, and that meant keeping the sabbath law and the feasts, making the required offerings, and observing the meticulous rules and regulations which governed a Jew's everyday life. By Paul's day those rules were a mixture of commandments that God had given and others that men had added. They had been interpreted by various Jewish teachers in a way which made them a lot more complicated than God had intended. But Jews were expected to keep all of them, complicated or not!

Putting all those things together produced a way of life which Paul described as *"a law of works"* (Romans 3:27). The principle was that if you could keep the various laws you would get eternal life; but if you failed to keep them you got nothing! The more he had thought about it and the more earnestly he had tried to earn eternal life, the more he had realised what a failure he was. He describes his eventual sense of utter frustration later in the letter (in Romans chapter 7). Then, one day, everything became clear – blindingly clear!

On the way to Damascus to arrest and imprison some people who believed in Jesus, Saul the Pharisee met the risen Lord Jesus Christ. It was a vision in which Jesus appeared to him, brighter than the midday sun. The account of Saul's conversion is to be found three times in the Acts of the Apostles – it's that important! For Saul, who later took the Latin name Paul, it turned his life upside down. The things he had thought right were suddenly seen to be wrong; and those things that he had once despised, he now came to accept as true. The works that he had been doing – persecuting, arresting, imprisoning and executing those who believed in Jesus – now condemned him. He had thought he would be saved by those works. Now he realised that he would be condemned by them and that realisation stayed with him for the rest of his life. Writing to Timothy, over twenty years after his conversion, Paul said:

> *"I thank him who has given me strength, Christ Jesus our Lord, because **he judged me faithful**, appointing me to his service, though formerly I was a blasphemer, persecutor, and insolent opponent. But I received mercy because I had acted ignorantly in unbelief, and **the grace of our Lord overflowed for me with the faith and love that are in Christ Jesus**. The saying is trustworthy and deserving of full acceptance, that Christ Jesus came into the world to save sinners, of whom I am the foremost. But I received mercy for this reason, that in me, as the foremost, Jesus Christ might display his perfect patience **as an example to those who were to believe in him for eternal life**. To the King of ages, immortal, invisible, the only God, be honour and glory forever and ever. Amen"* (1 Timothy 1:12-17).

It came as a shock to Paul, blinded as he was by the glory of the risen Christ, to be told what it was he was to do (Acts 9:6): *"Rise and be baptized and wash away your sins, calling on his name" (Acts 22:16)*. That was all he had to do to be justified in God's sight – to believe in the Lord Jesus Christ and to be baptized into his saving name. No feasts, no sacrifices, no tithes, no priests – all the things that he had before reckoned as vital were now seen to have become unnecessary. Belief in Jesus and in the promises of God had swept them all away.

Paul's personal appreciation of salvation influenced his preaching. He made it a key part of his presentation of the gospel that we are saved by faith and not works. It is what we believe and who we believe in that is crucial to our salvation. Paul became an avid preacher of the gospel straight away, wanting to testify to Jesus in Damascus, to persuade the Jewish community there (Acts 9:19-22). What he preached there is only briefly mentioned – that Jesus is the Son of God and the Christ (the Messiah). When longer accounts of his teaching are given, and in his letters, like that to the Romans, you can easily see the same theme developed further.

It's time we did some work in Romans again. If you read through the first ten chapters, notebook at the ready, see what sort of list you can compile to show what Paul says there about justification by faith.[4] Then compare your findings with this table:

"Therefore, since we have been justified by faith, we have peace with God through our Lord Jesus Christ. Through him we have also obtained access by faith into this grace in which we stand, and we rejoice in hope of the glory of God"
(Romans 5:1,2)

---

[4] *If you have a concordance which lists Bible words and gives the various references where they appear, you could search for "faith", "believe" or "belief". But, useful though that is, in getting to understand a Bible book, you can't beat reading it through over and over again.*

Romans	Justification by Faith
1:16,17	*"the gospel ... is the power of God for salvation to everyone who **believes**, to the Jew first and also to the Greek. For in it the righteousness of God is revealed from faith for faith, as it is written, '**The righteous shall live by faith**' "*
3:21-24	*"now the righteousness of God has been manifested apart from the law ... **the righteousness of God through faith in Jesus Christ for all who believe**. For there is no distinction: for all have sinned and fall short of the glory of God, and are justified by his grace as a gift, through the redemption that is in Christ Jesus"*
4:5	*"to the one who does not work but trusts him who justifies the ungodly, **his faith is counted as righteousness**"*
4:9	*"**faith was counted to Abraham as righteousness** ... the righteousness that he had by faith while he was still uncircumcised"*
4:13	*"the promise to Abraham and his offspring that he would be heir of the world did not come through the law but **through the righteousness of faith**"*
5:1,2	*"Therefore, since we have been **justified by faith**, we have peace with God through our Lord Jesus Christ. Through him we have also obtained access **by faith** into this grace in which we stand, and we rejoice in hope of the glory of God"*
9:30-32	*"Gentiles who did not pursue righteousness have attained it, that is, a **righteousness that is by faith**; but ... Israel who pursued a law that would lead to righteousness did not succeed in reaching that law. Why? Because **they did not pursue it by faith**, but as if it were based on works"*
10:9,10	*"if you confess with your mouth that Jesus is Lord and **believe** in your heart that God raised him from the dead, you will be saved. For with the heart **one believes and is justified**, and with the mouth one confesses and is saved"*
10:17	*"**faith comes from hearing**, and hearing through the word of Christ"*

This is not a comprehensive list as there are other references to faith in Romans. But it gives an overall impression of how important the theme is in Paul's thinking. We cannot earn salvation; instead we are entirely dependent on God's mercy and kindness towards us. The gift of eternal life is His to give as He sees fit and the marvellous thing is that God wants to give it to us. He cannot do so, however, unless we accept that He was and is right in His attitude towards sin, and we need to show that we accept that by confessing it to Him.

That confession is made public by baptism into the saving name of Jesus – something Paul explains in detail in Romans chapter 6 – and it has to follow a proper understanding of the gospel. For if we are to be justified by the things that we believe, clearly we have to understand those things first.

❖ Understanding the Gospel

There is a pattern in the Acts of the Apostles which shows us what "justification by faith" meant in practice in first century days. When the gospel was preached by the apostles, people were taught about the purpose of God, centred in the work of the Lord Jesus. There are several accounts of talks that were given, in Jerusalem, Asia and Europe, usually either by Peter or Paul. They were the two leading apostles, for Jews and Gentiles respectively. You can examine those talks for yourself by reading Acts chapters 2, 3, 7, 13 or 17.

Jewish listeners were very well acquainted with the Old Testament Scriptures, so it was customary to demonstrate how Jesus had fulfilled the promises made in those Scriptures. However, it was all new to most Gentile listeners; so a rather different approach was appropriate when preaching to them. Paul made it his practice to start his preaching at the Jewish synagogue in the towns he visited, if there was one. But he usually got a better response from Gentiles.

As Romans 9:30-32 says (in the table we have compiled above), Jews were often insistent on working their way into God's Kingdom. They did not want to abandon the past and to believe new things. Yet faith would only come if they heard the Word of God and listened to what it had to say about Jesus Christ. This is equally true for us. Here's a quick analysis of one of Paul's Bible Talks, this one given in a place called Antioch, in modern Turkey, in a Jewish synagogue. You can read the full text in Acts chapter 13.

1 God chose the nation of Israel when they were in Egypt so He rescued them from there and brought them to the land of Canaan as an inheritance (13:16-20);

2 He then gave them judges and later kings – the second king being David who was *"a man after my heart, who will do all my will"* (13:21-22);

3 Jesus is the long-promised descendant of King David, whose coming was announced by John the Baptist (13:23-25);

4 Now the message of salvation that Jesus preached has come to you. It was not understood by the people of Jerusalem which was why Jesus was executed, just as the Scriptures had predicted (13:26-29);

5 God raised Jesus from the dead and he then appeared to many people. We are witnesses of what happened and bring you the good news that *"what God promised to the fathers, this he has fulfilled to us their children by raising Jesus"* (13:30-33);

6 All that happened is in fulfilment of the Scriptures – Psalm 2:7, Isaiah 55:3 and Psalm 16:10 (these are the Scriptures Paul quoted). Jesus fulfilled them. King David is now dead and his body has corrupted away; not so Jesus (13:33-37);

7 *"Let it be known to you therefore, brothers, that **through this man forgiveness of sins is proclaimed to you, and by him everyone who believes is freed from everything** from which you could not be freed by the law of Moses"* (13:39);

8 Take care that you understand these things, because the Scriptures warn that Jews might not believe the great work that God is doing in their midst (13:40,41). (This warning was taken from Habakkuk 1:5.)

❖ Check Your Own Understanding

The benefit of a summary like this is that you can see at a glance the sort of things that were taught in the first century – things that comprised the original gospel taught by the apostles. That list is fairly typical of the message then being preached to a Jewish audience. It comprises:

❖ a selection of Old Testament predictions – both good things and bad;

❖ an explanation that these things had been fulfilled by the life, death and resurrection of the Lord Jesus; and

❖ a challenge to believe and receive forgiveness of sins: an appeal to be justified by faith, not by works.

The original hearers of that message found it very disturbing, as you will see if you read the chapter, and it can be equally challenging for us as we learn to understand the Bible message for ourselves. Here are a few questions for you to consider. Do you know –

a Why God chose Israel as His special nation and whether or not the Jews are still important in the purpose of God?

b Why King David is so important in God's purpose that the New Testament begins with an immediate reference back to him and to Abraham (Matthew 1:1)?

c What the Scriptures say about David's special descendant?

d What God promised *"to the fathers"* about the work that Jesus would accomplish?

e Why Psalm 2 talks about all the nations of the earth fighting against God's resurrected Son?

f How King David, a man after God's own heart, who *"fell asleep and was laid with his fathers and saw corruption",* is going to inherit eternal life?

g If forgiveness comes as a result of belief, what exactly do we have to believe in order to be saved?

❖ Beliefs Matter

This book will look at all those issues as we work our way through to a fuller understanding of the gospel. For the moment the key thing to note is that there was a lot of teaching and understanding involved in first century Christianity. Saying that we believe in Jesus, or having a general conviction that God loves us are not enough for salvation - though those two things are important. Read right through the Acts of the Apostles and you will find that the content of the message was very important indeed. The apostles reasoned and explained from the Scriptures, backing up their explanations by reference to their own experience and knowledge of the teaching of Jesus. Here's just one chapter which shows the apostle Paul's method of approach:

> *"He **reasoned** in the synagogue every Sabbath, and **tried to persuade** Jews and Greeks ... And they came to Ephesus, and he left them there, but he himself went into the synagogue and **reasoned** with the Jews ... he powerfully **refuted** the Jews in public, showing by the Scriptures that the Christ was Jesus" (Acts 18:4,19,28).*

If you want to check that pattern out for yourself, look at Acts 17:2-3,17; 24:25; 26:22-23; 28:23. All the time the apostles were seeking to persuade and instruct from the Scriptures because the message they were preaching mattered and the Bible was the authority they used. And when the apostle wrote to the early churches themselves, as in the Letter to the Romans, he explained again what it was that he believed. That's why he was giving such a carefully reasoned statement of his faith to the believers in Rome – because this is the faith that saves!

In the letter to the Galatians we read of people who had been converted by Paul but who had changed their beliefs and accepted a more Jewish-based understanding, in which they would keep some elements of the law as well as believing in Jesus. Paul wrote to them in very strong language indeed, challenging them in these terms:

> *"I am astonished that you are so quickly deserting him who called you in the grace of Christ and are turning to a different gospel – **not that there is another one, but there are some who trouble you and want to distort the gospel of Christ**. But even if we or an angel from*

heaven should preach to you a gospel contrary to the one we preached to you, let him be accursed. As we have said before, so now I say again: **If anyone is preaching to you a gospel contrary to the one you received, let him be accursed** *... For I would have you know, brothers, that the gospel that was preached by me is* **not man's gospel**. *For I did not receive it from any man, nor was I taught it, but I received it through a revelation of Jesus Christ" (Galatians 1:6-12).*

For Paul there was only one gospel: only one message about the purpose of God. Anything else was hopeless because it was man-made – "man's gospel". He knew only one way to obtain God's favour for, as he explained elsewhere:

"I ... urge you to walk in a manner worthy of the calling to which you have been called, with all humility and gentleness, with patience, bearing with one another in love, eager to maintain the unity of the Spirit in the bond of peace. **There is one body and one Spirit – just as you were called to the one hope that belongs to your call – one Lord, one faith, one baptism, one God and Father of all, who is over all and through all and in all**" *(Ephesians 4:1-6).*

Paul mentions seven things we must understand if we want to be right with God. These all concern the **ONE FAITH**:

1   **One Body** – one true Christian community;

2   **One Spirit** – one Divine power;

3   **One True Hope** – all other hopes and aspirations are delusions;

4   **One Lord Jesus Christ**;

5   **One True and saving Faith**;

6   **One Baptism** – by immersion undertaken after understanding the one faith;

7   **One God and Father of all** – who is supreme and sovereign.

❖ Belief and Baptism

That *"one faith"* is the faith the apostles preached and it necessitates a proper understanding of those things that have been revealed by God, as we are finding out. God requires belief and baptism. Paul writes about both those things in chapters 4 to 6 of the Letter to the Romans, so we will see in more detail what they involved. These two go together as the New Testament demonstrates very clearly:

"And he (Jesus) said to them, 'Go into all the world and proclaim the gospel to the whole creation. **Whoever believes and is baptized will be saved**, *but whoever does not believe will be condemned'"* (Mark 16:15,16);

"Go therefore and make disciples of all nations, **baptizing** *them in the name of the Father and of the Son and of the Holy Spirit,* **teaching** *them to observe all that I have commanded you. And behold, I am with you always, to the end of the age"* (Matthew 28:19,20);

"When they **believed** *Philip as he preached good news about the kingdom of God and the name of Jesus Christ, they were* **baptized***, both men and women. Even Simon himself* **believed***, and after being* **baptized** *he continued with Philip"* (Acts 8:12,13);

"And many of the Corinthians **hearing** *Paul* **believed** *and were* **baptized***"* (Acts 18:8).

What they heard and then believed is what the New Testament is all about. They heard and believed the gospel, which comprises *"good news about the kingdom of God and the name of Jesus Christ"*. We will learn more about both those aspects of God's good news as our investigation proceeds.

Things to Read

📖 The Acts of the Apostles gives us an insight into First Century Christianity.

📖 Read some more of the Bible Talks that were being given – in Acts chapters 3 and 17. See how different the approach is when the first audience is Jewish and the second is Gentile.

📖 Read about the baptism of a man who had become familiar with the Old Testament Scriptures and who came to understand that he needed to be baptised (Acts 8:26-40).

Questions to Think About

10.1 Jesus was once asked whether few or many would be saved. What do you think his answer teaches us? (Luke 13:23-27; Matthew 7:13-14; 19:16-26)

10.2 A very good living man named Cornelius wanted to be saved from sin. What was he required to do, or was his good living good enough for God? (Acts 10:34-48)

11
What is the Faith that Saves?

When Paul spoke to the Jewish people of Antioch and explained the Good News from God some of the things he said make us pause for thought. Asking questions as you read the Bible is a very helpful way of identifying what you know and what you don't. Write down any questions you might have and you may get help from other people in due course or you may find that, as you continue to read, the answers will come from other Scriptures.

Here are some of the questions identified earlier when we thought about what the apostle taught. We asked:

a Why God chose Israel as His special nation and whether or not the Jews are still important in the purpose of God?

b Why King David is so important in God's purpose that the New Testament begins with an immediate reference back to him and to Abraham (Matthew 1:1)?

c What the Scriptures say about David's special descendant?

d What God promised *"to the fathers"* about the work that Jesus would accomplish?

e If forgiveness comes as a result of what we believe, what exactly do we have to believe to be saved?

We can now begin to find answers to all these questions; for Paul has reached the point in his Letter to the Romans when he tells us more about faith. In doing so he concentrates upon just two Old Testament characters – Abraham and King David.

❖ Faithful Abraham

Abraham is the father of the Jewish nation. His son was named Isaac. Isaac had a son named Jacob who, in turn, had twelve sons; the families of those sons became the twelve tribes of the nation of Israel. But there is something even more important about Abraham. At a time when the earth was given over to idol worship, Abraham responded to God's call and left the city where he was living to go somewhere that God would show him. He responded because he was willing to believe God and to put his trust in Him. It was a remarkable act of faith:

> *"**By faith** Abraham obeyed when he was called to go out to a place that he was to receive as an inheritance. And he went out, not knowing where he was going. **By faith** he went to live in the land of promise, as in a foreign land, living in tents with Isaac and Jacob, heirs with him of the same promise. For he was looking forward to the city that has foundations, whose designer and builder is God" (Hebrews 11:8-10).*

This response made Abraham a pioneer in spiritual matters. He did not live for the present but for the future and he became confident that God would give him and his descendants a lasting and deep-rooted inheritance, described here as *"the city that has foundations"*.

In Romans chapter 4, Paul calls Abraham *"the father of all who believe"*, *"the father of us all"*, and *"the father of many nations"* (4:11,16,17). He looks at several episodes in Abraham's life – the times when God made promises to Abraham, which he believed implicitly; his circumcision; and the long period when he and Sarah got older and older and waited for the child that God had promised them.

❖ Life of Faith

You can read Abraham's entire life story from the end of Genesis chapter 11 to chapter 25 (just fifteen chapters in all) and it is a very worthwhile exercise. If you do so you will follow Abraham's journeying from Ur of the Chaldees (in modern Iraq) to Haran (now in Syria) and then to Canaan (now known as Israel). He came with his family and some servants, together with flocks and herds, and they settled into a nomadic life as shepherds, grazing wherever there was common land available and moving on from time to time. Over the years he had several wives, as was customary at that time, and as his family grew so life became more complicated for him. He lived at the time when God expressed His displeasure by destroying Sodom and Gomorrah, two cities which had become extremely immoral and totally godless, and Abraham witnessed that.

Abraham is described as *"a friend of God"*[1] and we need to concentrate on that aspect of his life. How did he become right with God? Was it because he left Ur although he did not know where the journey would end? Was he God's friend because of the things he did? Paul says emphatically that was not the case.

> *"What then shall we say was gained by Abraham, our forefather according to the flesh? For if Abraham was justified by works, he has something to boast about, but not before God. For what does the Scripture say? 'Abraham believed God, and it was counted to him as righteousness.' Now to the one who works, his wages are not counted as a gift but as his due. And to the one who does not work but trusts him who justifies the ungodly, his faith is counted as righteousness"* (Romans 4:1-5).

Abraham's faith was a saving faith: one that Paul says all the faithful should share. So what exactly did Abraham believe and why does that matter to us? We have seen already that what we believe is important and the apostle Peter tells us why that is when he said:

> *"His divine power has granted to us all things that pertain to life and godliness, through the knowledge of him who called us to his own glory and excellence, by which he has granted to us his precious and very great promises, so that through them you may become partakers of the divine nature, having escaped from the corruption that is in the world because of sinful desire. For this very reason, make every effort to supplement your faith with virtue, and virtue with knowledge, and knowledge with self-control, and self-control with steadfastness, and steadfastness with godliness, and godliness with brotherly affection, and brotherly affection with love. For if these qualities are yours and are increasing, they keep you from being ineffective or unfruitful in the knowledge of our Lord Jesus Christ"* (2 Peter 1:3-8).

---

[1] *2 Chronicles 20:7; Isaiah 41:8 and James 2:23.*

❖ Precious Promises

This is another of those Scriptures which needs to be analysed carefully, because it tells us a lot about saving faith. Do your own analysis if you wish and then compare it with the points listed below. Peter is saying that:

1   God has given us everything we need to find eternal life and to become godly.

2   We can achieve those things by getting to know God and the Lord Jesus Christ (you may remember that we saw that same truth expressed by the Lord Jesus in John 17:3).

3   God has called us – just as He once called Abraham – and has given us *"precious and very great promises"*.

4   These promises are the means whereby we *"become partakers of the divine nature"*. The promises themselves are an important part of the process of perfection, because they change our desires and affections towards the things of God and away from our naturally sinful desires.

5   It follows that it matters very much what we believe. Only the promises of God can have that transforming effect; man-made promises will not suffice.

6   Belief in those divine promises constitutes saving faith and such knowledge-based faith is to be the beginning of a life of virtue, self-control, steadfastness, godliness, brotherly affection and love. What we know about God and the Lord Jesus will affect the way we live and those qualities will increase in us the more we know and the closer we get to them both.

7   We are not, however, saved by the things we *do* but by the things that we *believe* – for we are saved or 'justified' by *faith*.

It is exactly the same for us as it was for Abraham. *"Abraham believed God, and it was counted to him as righteousness"*, and if we believe God we too can be counted as 'righteous'. We have seen already that what we believe is as important as how we believe it; now let's examine what precisely Abraham believed.

144

❖ Seven Great Promises

Abraham was given seven sets of promises by God which are the very basis of the New Testament gospel, for the gospel was preached to Abraham as well as to us (Galatians 3:8). These promises are listed below together with their references so that you can look them up and read them in full.

Genesis	No:	Promise	New Testament Reference
12:1-3	1	I will show you a land and make of you a great nation, and I will bless you and make your name great, so that you will be a blessing. I will bless those who bless you, and him who dishonours you I will curse, and in you all the families of the earth shall be blessed.	Galatians 3:8
12:7	2	To your offspring I will give this land of Canaan.	
13:14-17	3	All the land that you see around you I will give to you and to your offspring forever. I will make your offspring very numerous, like the dust of the earth.	
15:5,6	4	I will make your offspring numerous like the stars of heaven. Abraham "believed the Lord, and he counted it to him as righteousness."	Romans 4:18 Galatians 3:6 James 2:23
15:13-16	5	Your offspring shall be strangers in someone else's land for 400 years, but they will eventually be given freedom with great possessions, and I will judge that nation that made them servants.	Acts 7:6,7
17:1-8	6	I make a covenant with you and you will be the father of many nations; I will establish that covenant with you and with your offspring as an everlasting one and I will give you and your offspring all the land of Canaan for an everlasting possession and I will be your God and their God.	Romans 4:17 Acts 7:5

Genesis No:		Promise	New Testament Reference
22:15-18	7	By myself I have sworn, declares the Lord ... I will surely bless you, and I will surely multiply your offspring as the stars of heaven and as the sand that is on the seashore. And your off-spring shall possess the gate of his enemies, and in your offspring shall all the nations of the earth be blessed, because you have obeyed my voice.	Acts 3:25 Hebrews 6:13,14 Hebrews 11:12 Galatians 3:16

Do these promises coincide with your own beliefs about what constitutes the gospel of salvation? If not, you will see the full benefit of going yourself to the Scriptures to see exactly what God really promises, not what you might have thought was on offer. Look up the New Testament references too, if you want to be sure that these promises are regarded as really important.

Now it is time to summarise what these promises mean:

1 Abraham was shown **the land of Canaan** before he was told that it **was to be given** (1) to his offspring and then (2) **to him and his offspring.** Yet he never received any of that land, not even enough to put his foot on (as Stephen comments in Acts 7:5).

2 He was told that **his offspring would become a great nation**, as numerous as the dust of the earth. This was fulfilled when his descendants were rescued by God from Egypt, having been 400 years in a land which was not theirs[2]. Exodus 12:40 specifically refers to this promise (No. 5 in the above table) when describing the birth of the new nation of Israel. Its people were the descendants of Abraham, through Isaac and Jacob.

3 Abraham was also told that his offspring would be like the stars of heaven; that God would make an everlasting

[2] *It appears that the descendants of Abraham were in Egypt for 400 years but the Scripture may mean that they had been strangers in Canaan and then Egypt for that period of time.*

covenant with them and be their God, and that they would be the ones who would inherit the land where Abraham lived. He would thus be the *"father of many nations"*, an expression which Paul interprets, in Romans chapter 4, to mean that **Abraham would be the *"father of all who believe"*** – believers throughout the ages.

4   **Abraham would have one special descendant**[3] who would take control of everything, including ruling over his enemies.[4] This descendant would bring a blessing for all generations – the greatest of all blessings being **the forgiveness of sins and the way of salvation**: of becoming 'right with God'.

❖ Abraham's Special Offspring

Although Abraham's descendants would include both those who were naturally descended from him as well as those who imitated his faithful example – the *"dust of the earth"* and the *"stars of heaven"* appearing to describe both fleshly and spiritual descendants – one of his offspring would be special. It is significant that the last and greatest of the seven sets of promises speaks of the offspring in the singular, for Abraham was promised that *"your offspring shall possess the gate of **his** enemies, and in your offspring shall all the nations of the earth be blessed"* (Genesis 22:18).

The English word *"offspring"*, or *"seed"* as it is translated in other versions, can refer to many descendants or just to one descendant, and that translation faithfully reflects the meaning of the underlying Hebrew word. It becomes a matter of interpretation when looking at the earlier promises to know whether the promise is about one or many descendants. Fortunately we are not left simply to our own deductions in this matter, but are guided by the New Testament writers – another example of how Scripture

---

3 *See the next section, which shows how the New Testament interprets these promises to refer to one special offspring, or descendant.*

4 *'Possessing the gates' in ancient days meant taking control of the city.*

interprets Scripture.[5]

❖ Only One Hope

Here are explanations of two key parts of Genesis 22. If you read that chapter you will find that God tested Abraham by asking him to offer Isaac – his long-awaited son – as a sacrifice. Abraham had been willing to do this, believing that God would then have raised him from the dead (as Hebrews 11:17-19 explains). This supreme act of faithful obedience brought Abraham the seventh and greatest set of promises, accompanied by an oath – *"By myself have I sworn"* – the promise and the oath making the outcome doubly certain. This is how the writer to the Hebrews explains the significance of it:

> *"For when God made a promise to Abraham, since he had no one greater by whom to swear, he swore by himself, saying, 'Surely I will bless you and multiply you.' And thus Abraham, having patiently waited, obtained the promise. For people swear by something greater than themselves, and in all their disputes an oath is final for confirmation. So when God desired to show more convincingly to **the heirs of the promise** the unchangeable character of his purpose, he guaranteed it with an oath, so that by two unchangeable things, in which it is impossible for God to lie, we who have fled for refuge might have strong encouragement to hold fast to the hope set before us" (Hebrews 6:13-18).*

The promises of God were seen as something very precious which had to be passed on from generation to generation. For between them they comprised *"the hope"*. There are not many different hopes – there is only the *"one hope that belongs to your call"* (Ephesians 4:4). The true hope of the gospel is centred in the Lord Jesus Christ, who declared himself *"the way, and the truth, and the life" (John 14:6)*. There are not many truths, just the one; not many

---

[5] *If you want to follow this up, here are some suggestions. Genesis 12:1-3,7 can refer to one special descendant or to many; 13:14-17 refers to many (Abraham's natural descendants); 15:5-6 refers to many (Abraham's spiritual descendants); 15:13-16 has specific reference to Israel's national experience; 17-1-8 refers to many (Abraham's spiritual descendants – whether Jews or Gentiles) and 22:15-18 refers to many and to one (there would be numerous descendants of Abraham (stars and sand), but one would be quite special.*

ways, just the one way that leads to life for all who find it and walk in that direction.

The apostle Paul wrote to the Galatians in very strong terms telling them how wrong they were to follow a different gospel from the one he had taught.[6] He went on to explain in detail about the things they should believe if they wanted the faith that saves. He explained that before God gave Israel the law through Moses, He had already given promises to Abraham and the fathers. Now, he explained, the law had been fulfilled by the work of the Lord Jesus but the promises remained to be fulfilled. Believing those promises was now the way to obtain God's favour. In Paul's own words:

> "Know then that it is those **of faith** who are the sons of Abraham. And the Scripture, foreseeing that God would justify the Gentiles **by faith**, preached the gospel beforehand to Abraham, saying, 'In you shall all the nations be blessed.' [Genesis 12:3] So then, those who are **of faith** are blessed along with Abraham, the man of faith" (Galatians 3:7-9).

The apostle then turns his attention to the full meaning of the seventh promise,[7] the one which was confirmed with an oath, sworn by the very existence of God, and this is what he says:

> "Now the promises were made to Abraham and to his **offspring**. It does not say, 'And to offsprings,' referring to many, but referring to **one**, 'And to your **offspring**,' who is **Christ**" (Galatians 3:16).

This inspired explanation confirms what we have anticipated when looking at Genesis chapter 22 – that Abraham was promised one special descendant who would fulfil the promises. It is clear from something the Lord Jesus once said that Abraham understood that himself.[8] This faithful man knew that one day, a descendant would be born in his family line who would be able to *"possess the gate of his enemies"*, and in whom *"all the nations of the earth"* would be blessed. The setting of that promise gives the clue to his understanding for it is full of significance.

---

[6] *See Chapter 10, pages 137-138.*

[7] *The seventh promise is in Genesis 22:15-18.*

[8] *John 8:56.*

❖ The Only Son

As Paul says in Romans chapter 4, Abraham waited a long time for the birth of Isaac, the son he and Sarah had been promised. When at last he was born they were both well past the age when a natural birth could have occurred. It was a miracle: the result of their long-standing faith. Abraham had never given up hope, although he was approaching 100 years old and Sarah had been childless all her life. His faith was truly remarkable.

"He did not weaken in faith when he considered his own body, which was as good as dead (since he was about a hundred years old), or when he considered the barrenness of Sarah's womb. No distrust made him waver concerning the promise of God, but he grew strong in his faith as he gave glory to God, fully convinced that God was able to do what he had promised. That is why his faith was 'counted to him as righteousness'" (Romans 4:19-22).

Then, one day, God asked Abraham to go to Mount Moriah (where Jerusalem would later be built) and offer his son – his only son – as a sacrifice.[9] It was a remarkable and wonderful foreshadowing of what God Himself would do. Years later He gave His only Son to be sacrificed in the same vicinity and the chapter is full of allusions to this future sacrifice. Abraham and Isaac were spared the actual sacrifice. Instead the angel who restrained Abraham explained that one day God would make the necessary provision – a sacrifice for the sins of the world.

"Abraham lifted up his eyes and looked, and behold, behind him was a ram, caught in a thicket by his horns. And Abraham went and took the ram and offered it up as a burnt offering instead of his son. So Abraham called the name of that place, 'The LORD will provide'; as it is said to this day, 'On the mount of the LORD it shall be provided'" (Genesis 22:13,14).

---

[9] *The record says three times that Isaac was Abraham's only son (see Genesis 22:2,12 and 16), so that we can see the parallel between God offering His only begotten son some 2000 years later. Ishmael had already been born, of course, but he is not counted here because he was not born to Sarah, but to one of Abraham's concubines. Paul later makes that very distinction in Galatians chapter 4, where he contrasts the child of the servant with the child of the freeborn Sarah.*

This was another of those forward-looking promises. God's Son would be the one whom God would provide to make the promises possible and to bring a blessing for mankind. Thus Abraham came to look forward to that day which he needed as much as any of us. That's what the Lord Jesus meant when he said:

"Your father Abraham rejoiced that he would see my day. He saw it and was glad" (John 8:56).

This does not mean Jesus existed in the time of Abraham, for he did not. It means that Abraham looked forward to the time when God would send His only-begotten Son, born of Mary, in the family line of Abraham. This is one reason why the New Testament begins with the words:

*"The book of the genealogy of Jesus Christ, the son of David, **the son of Abraham**" (Matthew 1:1).*

❖ David's Covenant Promises

A thousand years after Abraham some of the promises made to him had been fulfilled. His descendants constituted a nation that now occupied the land in which he had lived. They had been formed into that nation after many years when they had been strangers in Egypt. They had come out of that land with great possessions, being delivered from there by God's miraculous power. Led out by Moses, they had conquered the land of Canaan under Joshua's leadership and eventually God had given them kings to rule over them. David was the second such ruler and it was under his direction that Israel occupied the very place that had featured in the Genesis 22 account. God had asked Abraham and Isaac to go there and it was then He had given them that seventh and greatest promise – the one about a descendant who would come and bring a blessing for all nations.

In David's time the area of Mount Moriah was further developed and became part of the city of Jerusalem, which David had captured from its previous occupants. It then became Israel's capital city. Jewish links with it thus go back about 1000 years before Christ, some 3000 years in all. In this very place, God later made great promises to David, promises that built upon what Abraham had been told would happen.

It started when David said that he would like to build God a temple – a permanent place of worship instead of the tent that was then in use. David was a warrior and God wanted to establish a temple which would be a House of Peace, so He said that it would not be appropriate for David to build Him such a dwelling. Instead God said that He would do something for David and his descendants. If you want to do a similar exercise with this set of promises, as for those given to Abraham, now is the time to read 2 Samuel chapter 7, write down the important points about what God would do, and then compare your findings with the list below.

Here are the crucial parts of this agreement which God made with David, such a solemn and binding agreement that it is later referred to as a covenant of promise:

> *"Thus says the* LORD: *Would you build me a house to dwell in? ... I took you from the pasture, from following the sheep, that you should be prince over my people Israel. And I have been with you wherever you went and have cut off all your enemies from before you. And I will make for you a great name, like the name of the great ones of the earth. And I will appoint a place for my people Israel ... And I will give you rest from all your enemies. Moreover, the* LORD *declares to you that the* LORD *will make you a house.* **When your days are fulfilled and you lie down with your fathers, I will raise up your offspring after you, who shall come from your body, and I will establish his kingdom. He shall build a house for my name, and I will establish the throne of his kingdom forever. I will be to him a father, and he shall be to me a son.** *When he commits iniquity, I will discipline him with the rod of men, with the stripes of the sons of men, but my steadfast love will not depart from him ... And your house and your kingdom shall be made sure forever before me. Your throne shall be established forever " (2 Samuel 7:5-16).*

❖ Working it Out

These few verses contain many different promises. With Abraham the promises were spread out over several years; with King David they came all together, which makes our analysis a little easier. This is what we are being told:

1   God had made David the king over His people Israel –
    notice that this nation is therefore something special,
    because they are God's people. We need to look at that
    in a bit more detail later.

2   God had helped David to overcome his enemies and
    would continue to work with him to establish him as a
    great king.

3   He would also work with his chosen nation, Israel, to
    keep them secure and at peace; they would have rest
    from all their enemies.

4   David would have a dynasty – *"the house of David"* –
    which would succeed him; this was later confirmed to
    mean that there would be a line of kings descended
    from David who would reign on the throne in Jerusalem
    (see, for example, 2 Kings 8:19; 19:34).

5   After David's death, God would raise up a descendant
    of David who would be of his family line – *"who shall
    come from your body"* – and God would establish his
    kingdom. This was a promise, similar to that which
    Abraham received, about one special descendant, as
    the following details make clear.

6   This descendant would build a house for God. The word
    "house" can mean a temple or a group of people who
    are related together, or both.

7   His kingdom would last forever.

8   God would be His Father and he would be God's Son.

9   Should this Son commit iniquity he would be chas-
    tened, but God's steadfast love would not depart from
    him.

10 David's house and David's kingdom would be made
    sure forever before God.[10]

This ten-point plan refers to a dynasty which is unique,
for it has to do with the Kingdom of God. David had been
chosen to be a king for God, over God's people not over his
own subjects, and David's throne is later referred to as *"the*

---

[10] *Some versions translate 2 Samuel 7:16 as follows – "And thine house
and thy kingdom shall be established for ever before thee: thy throne shall
be established for ever" (KJV). Rendered like this, the verse promises David
that he will be present when his special descendant reigns as King, and the
verse then teaches bodily resurrection to a new life on earth in God's
Kingdom.*

throne of the LORD". He ruled on God's behalf and only because of God's approval, and it would be the same for all his successors. God would work with them as He had worked with David to establish them, give them success in terms of peace, safety and security. If they remained faithful to God, they and the nation they governed would prosper. If the king or the nation broke God's law and lost faith, however, they would be disciplined and chastened.

❖ David's Special Offspring

There were to be many kings who would reign on David's throne at Jerusalem – 22 altogether and they reigned for a total of over 400 years. We will examine the Kingdom of God in more detail in the next chapter. For the moment, notice that some kings of the house of David fulfilled parts of this great set of promises. For example, King Solomon, David's immediate successor, built a temple in Jerusalem; the one David had wanted to build for God. There were many kings who received help from God to ensure that the nation dwelt safely and securely, but all of them committed iniquity in one way or another; even David himself fell into that category.[11] It would take a very special descendant indeed who could avoid that. Yet such a descendant was intended in the purpose of God, one who would be qualified to establish the kingdom forever.

David thought a lot about these promises that God had made to him, both straightaway and over a longer period. His immediate reaction was an appreciation that what God had promised was not going to be easily achieved, for he said:

> *"Who am I, O Lord GOD, and what is my house, that you have brought me thus far? And yet this was a small thing in your eyes, O Lord GOD. **You have spoken also of your servant's house for a great while to come**, and this is instruction for mankind, O Lord GOD!"* (2 Samuel 7:18,19).

He understood that the promises that God had made would take time to accomplish, but that mankind needed to take notice of and be instructed by them. The conviction that the offspring of whom God had spoken could not come

---

[11] *This was what the prophecy had foreseen: that they would "commit iniquity" and would be disciplined accordingly (2 Samuel 7:14).*

without help from God stayed with David all through his life for among his last sayings was this phrase:

> *"When one rules justly over men, ruling in the fear of God, he dawns on them like the morning light, like the sun shining forth on a cloudless morning, like rain that makes grass to sprout from the earth. For does not my house stand so with God?* **For he has made with me an everlasting covenant, ordered in all things and secure.** *For will he not cause to prosper all my help and my desire?" (2 Samuel 23:3-5).*

Unless God caused these things to prosper, David recognised that they could not be accomplished. Mere humanity could not achieve such an outcome; for David's special descendant would be both son of David and Son of God. This is such a great idea that it deserves more detailed consideration when we are thinking about the Kingdom of God. For the moment take note of two things about this dual parentage:

1 It is one of the first things the apostle Paul mentioned when writing to the Romans – *"The gospel of God, which he promised beforehand through his prophets in the holy Scriptures, concerning his Son, who was descended from David according to the flesh and was declared to be the Son of God in power according to the Spirit of holiness by his resurrection from the dead, Jesus Christ our Lord"* (Romans 1:1-4; see also Acts 13:22,23).

2 It is something the Lord Jesus pointed out to his opponents when they challenged him about the claims he made – that the Messiah had to be both David's descendant and God's own Son:

> *"'What do you think about the Christ? Whose son is he?' They said to him, 'The son of David.' He said to them, 'How is it then that David, in the Spirit, calls him Lord, saying, "The Lord said to my Lord, Sit at my right hand, until I put your enemies under your feet"? If then David calls him Lord, how is he his son?' And no one was able to answer him a word, nor from that day did anyone dare to ask him any more questions" (Matthew 22:42-46).*

The Lord's point was quite clear although his opponents did not want to face up to it. The Messiah would have dual

155

parentage. He would be descended from David's line – through Mary – but he would also be God's own Son. Because of this he would have a status higher even than David, who was one of Israel's greatest kings.

❖ Summary

We have seen that these promises made to Abraham and David are an essential part of the gospel, which is centred in the Lord Jesus Christ. They foretell the coming of a special descendant who would accomplish many things and bring great blessings to mankind. In particular he would overcome all his enemies and reign as king forever, over God's people and on God's throne.

Abraham gave birth to a son – Isaac – as God had promised and in due course a nation came into existence; all of its people were descended from Abraham, through Isaac and Jacob. They occupied the land of promise but they did not occupy it forever and no king came from among them who could keep God's law perfectly. A few hundred years after the time of David the kingdom of Israel ceased altogether and it has never been reconstituted. But the faith that saves requires us to understand that the promises of God have not failed; they are merely awaiting their fulfilment when the coming king reigns on David's throne.

"He has granted to us his precious and very great promises, so that through them you may become partakers of the divine nature, having escaped from the corruption that is in the world because of sinful desire" (2 Peter 1:4)

Things to Read

📖 The promises God made to Abraham are so important they deserve to be read in their original setting (Genesis 12:1-3; 12:7; 13:14-17; 15:5,6; 15:13-16; 17:1-8; 22:15-18).

📖 Using the Table on pages 145 and 146, look up the New Testament references that are listed to see for yourself how those promises are interpreted and applied there.

Questions to Think About

11.1 In a couple of sentences explain why God chose Israel as His special nation and whether or not it is now important in the purpose of God?

11.2 Can you make a list of the things the special offspring or descendant will accomplish? (Genesis 22:15-18 and 2 Samuel 7:12-16)

12

Jesus Christ – the Promised King

Having introduced us to Abraham and David the apostle Paul now writes about Adam. In particular he contrasts his failure in Eden with the success of the Lord Jesus Christ. His argument is all about rulership and dominion. It leads naturally on from what he has said about the promises made to Abraham and David and the need for people to believe them and live accordingly. We must all trust in God if we are to be delivered from sin and death. But why did it all go wrong and how can it be put right?

❖ Where Adam Failed

If we approach Romans chapter 5, as we have looked at previous chapters – by analysing exactly what Paul says, thinking about it and then looking at other Scriptures for help and further guidance – we shall have a useful starting point. You might want to try that exercise yourself and then see how your findings compare with those listed below.

Paul goes right back to the start of God's dealings with mankind and makes this diagnosis of the underlying sickness which afflicts us all. This is what he says about Adam's failure and its results:

✓ *"Sin came into the world through one man, and death through sin, and so death spread to all men because all sinned" (Romans 5:12);*

✓ *"Death reigned from Adam to Moses, even over those whose sinning was not like the transgression of Adam" (5:14);*

✓ *"Many died through one man's trespass ...the judgement following one trespass brought condemnation" (5:15,16);*

✓ *"Because of one man's trespass, death reigned through that one man" (5:17);*

✓ *"One trespass led to condemnation for all men" (5:18);*

✓ *"By the one man's disobedience the many were made sinners" (5:19);*

✓ *"Sin reigned in death" (5:21).*

The key point here is that Adam was given the opportunity to keep God's law – not to eat of the forbidden fruit – and he chose to disobey. Or, to express it in a different way, he was given the opportunity to *conquer* those desires and to *rule* over his wrong thoughts, but he gave in to the temptation and was conquered by desire instead. Notice that Paul uses the language of rulership when he says that: *"Death reigned from Adam to Moses", "death reigned through that one man"* and *"Sin reigned in death".*

In Paul's analysis, sin and death got the upper hand and men and women have become subjects or slaves in the kingdom of sin and death. Notice the terminology, which is very significant. Paul does not talk about the Devil or Satan taking control – he talks about the problem of sin and death. We will look at the subject of the Devil and Satan in a later chapter.[1] For the moment we need to understand exactly what point the apostle is making.

❖ The Kingdom in Eden

God created Adam and Eve and settled them into an ideal environment, where everything was *"very good"* (Genesis 1:31). It wasn't perfect because that term would imply that nothing could ever go wrong. God wanted them to have the opportunity to choose between right and wrong. This gave them a way in which they could, if they wished, show their appreciation of all that God had given them and demonstrate their love for Him, if that was how they felt about their Creator. So God asked them to live faithfully. He told them that disobedience would bring severe consequences and invited them to take charge of His world by first ruling over themselves and their desires. They were to have dominion and thus rule as king and queen over God's new world:

> *"God said, 'Let us make man in our image, after our likeness. And **let them have dominion** over the fish of the sea and over the birds of the heavens and over the live-*

---

[1] *See Chapter 24.*

stock and over all the earth and over every creeping thing that creeps on the earth.' So God created man in his own image, in the image of God he created him; male and female he created them. And God blessed them. And God said to them, 'Be fruitful and multiply and fill the earth and **subdue it and have dominion** *over the fish of the sea and over the birds of the heavens and over every living thing that moves on the earth'" (Genesis 1:26-28).*

God made them in His image, a term which does not mean physical resemblance, for there are physical differences between men and women. Being made in the divine likeness meant that they were able to reflect the very characteristics of God Himself and of the angels that lived with Him. They could become a godly man and woman.

But first they had to *"have dominion"* and *"subdue"* any thoughts or desires that might be put to them. In the state in which they had been created no such thoughts were likely to occur to them from within[2], so God made and then introduced a creature that might have such thoughts. He was different from the other creatures God had made, for he had animal cunning in abundance.

❖ Enter the Serpent!

The inspired record says this about the creature: *"Now the serpent was more crafty than any other beast of the field that the* LORD *God had made" (Genesis 3:1).*[3] The serpent became a tempter in this ideal garden setting. It suggested to Eve that God had not really meant what He said about the forbidden fruit, but that it might benefit them: *"God knows that when you eat of it your eyes will be opened, and you will be like God, knowing good and evil" (3:5).* That suggestion awakened desire in Eve that had not been there before. She looked, liked what she saw, wanted it and wanted the wisdom that it might bring, so she took the

---

[2] *Now it is natural for us to think evil thoughts (see Mark 7:21), but that verse describes our situation after the fall of man. Adam and Eve were created "very good" and they would have had no such inner tendencies at the time.*

[3] *Because the record says that the serpent was made "more crafty" than the beasts of the field, we can deduce that he had more than his share of what we now call "animal cunning". He was a very perceptive beast and he took his natural characteristics too far, in that he even questioned what God had said. Notice that he was a beast of the field, not a supernatural being.*

fruit and ate it.

In the New Testament the apostle Paul confirms what is apparent from the Genesis record – that Eve was deceived by the serpent's suggestions and did not fully realise what she was doing when she ate the fruit (1 Timothy 2:14). In that very verse, he also explained that Adam was not deceived. When Eve offered the fruit to Adam he knew exactly what the choice was: to obey God or to disobey Him. He chose to disobey, perhaps so that he would not be separated from Eve. If so it was an act of love towards her, it was an act which showed that Adam's love for Eve was greater than his love for God.

All three of the culprits were held accountable – the serpent as well. Any idea that the serpent was not really a creature, or that it is another way of describing a supernatural devil, or Satan, quite clearly fails.[4] God regarded the serpent as responsible for challenging His commandment and for tempting the woman to disobey:

> "Because you have done this, cursed are you above all livestock and above all beasts of the field; on your belly you shall go, and dust you shall eat all the days of your life. **I will put enmity between you and the woman, and between your offspring and her offspring; he shall bruise your head, and you shall bruise his heel**" (Genesis 3:14,15).

❖ Eve's Special Offspring

The sentence that God passed on the serpent meant that all its natural offspring, whether serpents or snakes, would in future slither on their bellies. In doing so they would be crawling in the dust of the earth and there is a spiritual lesson to be learned from this. The serpent was the first being to challenge the truth of God's Word and to question His law. So the Bible makes the serpent an example or a symbol of all those in later times who would also question

---

[4] *There is no reference to either the Devil or Satan in any of the first five books of the Bible. The earliest occurrence of that terminology is in the Book of Job. The subject as a whole is considered in Chapter 24.*

what God has said.[5]

Eve, however, was to have one special descendant –
someone who would be born of a woman but who would
not have a human father. The Bible describes the coming
child very carefully as *"her offspring"* (Genesis 3:15) and
people might have wondered just how that could be. How
could a child be born without a human father? It required a
miracle for that to happen for God was to be the Father and
Mary (descended from Eve) would be the mother. Through
Mary, Jesus would inherit all the characteristics of the
human race. He would be born mortal and would feel just
like us, including being tempted just as we are.

This prediction – about the woman's offspring – is the
very first promise of the gospel. It is perfectly in line with
what was later promised to Abraham and David about a
special offspring who would be born to their family. The offspring would be the Lord Jesus Christ. Here the three

Gospel Promise

Eve	"I will put enmity between you [serpent] and the woman, and between your offspring and her offspring; he shall bruise your head, and you shall bruise his heel" (Genesis 3:15);
Abraham	"Your offspring shall possess the gate of his enemies, and in your offspring shall all the nations of the earth be blessed" (Genesis 22:17,18);
David	"I will raise up your offspring after you, who shall come from your body, and I will establish his kingdom. He shall build a house for my name, and I will establish the throne of his kingdom forever. I will be to him a father, and he shall be to me a son" (2 Samuel 7:12-14).

---

[5] *In the New Testament, the opponents of John the Baptist and of Jesus are
described respectively as "vipers" (Matthew 3:7), "serpents" and a "brood of
vipers" (Matthew 23:33).*

promises are shown side-by-side:

All these promises are about rulership and dominion. Eve was promised that one would come – the offspring of a woman – who would crush to death all things that oppose God and are contrary to His will. But the promised one would be bruised in the process. That's something that both Old and New Testaments comment on as God's purpose unfolds:

*"When the fullness of time had come, **God sent forth his Son, born of woman, born under the law**, to redeem those who were under the law, so that we might receive adoption as sons" (Galatians 4:4,5);*

*"He **was wounded for our transgressions; he was crushed for our iniquities**; upon him was the chastisement that brought us peace, and with his stripes we are healed" (Isaiah 53:5);*

*"Such persons do not serve our Lord Christ, but their own appetites, and by smooth talk and flattery they deceive the hearts of the naive. For your obedience is known to all, so that I rejoice over you, but I want you to be wise as to what is good and innocent as to what is evil. **The God of peace will soon crush Satan under your feet**" (Romans 16:18-20).*

In that last passage the apostle Paul is evidently looking back to what happened in Eden, when the serpent deceived Eve with "smooth talk". He assures his readers that all such deception will end when the opponents of God are crushed under their feet, when all the present wrongs are put right.[6]

❖ Absolute Self-Control

Jesus was completely dominant over self and selfish desire; there was never a time when he lost control or when he allowed wrong thinking or foolish desire to get the upper hand. His obedience to the will of God His Father was absolutely outstanding. Whatever his nature prompted him

---

6 *When Jesus was confronted by opponents and deceivers during his preaching work – people who were acting like serpents and vipers – he was always able to get the better of them in discussion. (See, for example, Matthew 22:23-33.) This was a foretaste of how things will be when Jesus returns to subdue all his enemies (see Psalm 2:9-12).*

to do, and he had exactly the same feelings that we have, he never once yielded to those inner desires. He had come to do His Father's will and, as we saw, he did so perfectly.[7] He was obedient, where Adam was not and, faced with much greater temptations than those which Adam faced,

Adam	Jesus
"many died through one man's trespass"	"much more have the grace of God and the free gift by the grace of that one man Jesus Christ abounded for many" (5:15)
"the judgement following one trespass brought condemnation"	"the free gift following many trespasses brought justification" (5:16)
"because of one man's trespass, death reigned through that one man"	"much more will those who receive the abundance of grace and the free gift of righteousness reign in life through the one man Jesus Christ" (5:17)
"one trespass led to condemnation for all men"	"one act of righteousness leads to justification and life for all men" (5:18)
"as by the one man's disobedience the many were made sinners"	"by the one man's obedience the many will be made righteous" (5:19)
"as sin reigned in death..."	"... grace also might reign through righteousness leading to eternal life through Jesus Christ our Lord" (5:21)

Jesus prevailed.

This obedience was a vital part of God's purpose. The consequences of Adam's sin could only be reversed by a man who showed perfect obedience to God's commandments. Paul highlights that comparison in Romans chapter 5, where the differences between Adam and Jesus stand

---

[7] Chapter 7 pages 89-95

out clearly.

Where Adam failed the Lord Jesus Christ succeeded and what Adam lost the Lord regained, both for himself and for all his followers. Adam's life could be summed up as one of trespass, disobedience, condemnation and death. That of Jesus was one of obedience, righteousness, grace and life. The one lost control of himself and with it the prospect of ruling over God's creation; the other gained control and was given that dominion by God. Adam was deposed and evicted from God's presence, but Jesus was exalted and enthroned. This comparison is in Paul's mind when he says this of the differences between Adam and Jesus, both of whom were God's special creation:

> *"Have this mind among yourselves, which is yours in Christ Jesus, who, though he was in the form of God, did not count equality with God a thing to be grasped, but made himself nothing, taking the form of a servant, being born in the likeness of men. And being found in human form, he humbled himself by becoming obedient to the point of death, even death on a cross. Therefore God has highly exalted him and bestowed on him the name that is above every name, so that at the name of Jesus every knee should bow, in heaven and on earth and under the earth, and every tongue confess that Jesus Christ is Lord, to the glory of God the Father" (Philippians 2:5-11).*

Notice the careful comparisons made between Adam and the Lord Jesus:

❧ *Both were "in the form of God", made in His image;*

❧ *Adam wanted to be equal with God; Jesus had no such aspirations – he just wanted to do his Father's will, first and foremost;*

❧ *Both were born in "human form" [8] and came to a personal realisation that God had created them and that He wanted something of them; [9]*

---

[8] *It is a very important New Testament teaching that Jesus shared the same nature that we possess. He came "in the flesh" (1 John 4:2) and had the very same nature that we share (Hebrews 2:14).*

[9] *See Psalm 40:7-8.*

⟩ *Adam exalted himself – by putting self first – and was abased by God. Jesus humbled himself – by putting God's will uppermost at all times – and he was exalted by God;*

⟩ *Adam was disobedient in one thing – he ate the forbidden fruit; Jesus was obedient unto death, "even death on a cross" – an act of supreme self-sacrifice;*

⟩ *Adam was banished from the place where he should have had dominion – he lost his kingdom. Jesus was highly exalted by God because of his obedience and now we should bow the knee before him. Shortly everyone in both heaven and earth will acknowledge the Lord Jesus Christ as King, "to the glory of God the Father".*

❖ Jesus Christ the King

This passage of Scripture, with its careful and deliberate contrast between Adam and Jesus, explains that Jesus is the successor to Adam, and there are several others which make the same point. Sometimes the contrast is quite subtle; you have to be looking for it. The Bible often functions at that level, by giving little pointers in the right direction, but expecting us to be alert to its indications. This is why we can find new things as we read it time and time again and it is one of the reasons why the Bible is such a fascinating book. Here are a couple of examples where you can see the contrast for yourself:

> *"I will crush his foes before him and strike down those who hate him. My faithfulness and my steadfast love shall be with him, and in my name shall his horn be exalted. I will set his hand on the sea and his right hand on the rivers. He shall cry to me, 'You are my Father, my God, and the Rock of my salvation.' And **I will make him the firstborn, the highest of the kings of the earth. My steadfast love I will keep for him forever, and my covenant will stand firm for him. I will establish his offspring forever and his throne as the days of the heavens**" (Psalm 89:23-29);*

> *"He is the image of the invisible God, the firstborn of all creation. For by him all things were created, in heaven and on earth, visible and invisible, whether thrones or*

dominions or rulers or authorities – all things were creat-
*ed through him and for him. And **he is before all***
things, and in him all things hold together. And he
*is **the head of the body, the church. He is the begin-***
ning, the firstborn from the dead, that in everything
***he might be preeminent"** (Colossians 1:15-18).*

In both these passages Jesus is described as God's
"firstborn", a term that means the one who is pre-eminent
or exalted above all. It does not describe the time when he
was born, but the position to which God has exalted him. It
is true that Jesus was the first person ever to rise from the
dead to an endless life and in that sense he is the first in
time as well. But the key point being made, when Jesus is
spoken of as *"firstborn,"* is that he is above and beyond all
others in the purpose of God.[10]

Jesus came into existence when he was born of Mary in
Bethlehem, for he was the offspring of the woman as well
as Son of God. Both Mary and Almighty God contributed
something to his make-up, just as both our parents make
us the unique people we are. Jesus inherited characteristics from both his Father and mother. As we have seen
before,[11] the marvellous thing is that Jesus completely subjected and controlled those human tendencies he inherited
from his mother and lived to do his Father's will. That was
the great victory he accomplished and that is the way in
which he reigned over sin, in the flesh, and overcame its
power and allure. Nobody has ever done that either before
or after Jesus. It is the hallmark of his great victory over
sin and wickedness, in all its forms.

❖ Jesus Christ Above All

Once we realise that Jesus is pre-eminent in the purpose of
God, lots of other Scriptures fit into place. From the
moment that Adam sinned, God began to implement His
plan to recover and restore mankind. He knows everything.
So God knew that man would sin and had already decided
how He would restore the position. He would intervene to
rescue mankind. The birth and destiny of His Son was
known about from the time of Creation; that's how things

---

[10] *One of the clearest verses to establish this is Psalm 89:27, where God*
says of the coming King, descended from David's line: "And I will make him
the firstborn, the highest of the kings of the earth".
[11] *Chapter 7, pages 89-95.*

are with God! The marvel of it all is that He was still prepared to go ahead with Creation, knowing what would be involved for Him and for His Son. He did so because He loves mankind and wants men and women to find true happiness and fulfilment.

Adam and Eve were quite changed by their experience of rebellion and disobedience and their previous harmonious existence was shattered. The record says of them that: *"the eyes of both were opened, and they knew that they were naked. And they sewed fig leaves together and made themselves loincloths" (Genesis 3:7)*. When challenged about their wrongdoing Adam and Eve set about blaming each other, and must have looked a sorry pair in their fig-leaf outfits.

God took pity on them and made them a proper covering, one that required the sacrifice of an animal, or animals.[12] In this way He demonstrated that the proper covering for sin, one that was acceptable in His sight, would require a sacrifice for sin. Jesus was already in His mind, for the inspired record says of the Lord Jesus Christ that he was *"the Lamb that was slain" (Revelation 13:8)* and *"the Lamb of God, who takes away the sin of the world!" (John 1:29)*.

❖ Did Jesus Pre-Exist?

There are several other Scriptures some people use to suggest that Jesus existed with God from the beginning of creation. Properly understood they actually teach that Jesus was:

✓ In the mind of God from the beginning, and

✓ Supreme above all others in the purpose and love of God.

Here are a few of those passages, with some explanatory comment where necessary:

---

12 *"the LORD God made clothes out of animal skins for Adam and his wife, and he clothed them" (Genesis 3:21)*.

"In the beginning was the Word,[13] *and the Word was with God, and the Word was God. He was in the beginning with God. All things were made through him, and without him was not any thing made that was made ... And the Word became flesh and dwelt among us, and we have seen his glory, glory as of the only Son from the Father, full of grace and truth" (John 1:1-3,14).*

The apostle John often uses language like this to describe the plan and purpose of God. He calls this purpose *"the Word"*. This purpose, which was in the mind of God, is pictured for us as though it were a person. The Old Testament often uses figurative language to describe the purpose or the wisdom of God (see, for example, Proverbs 8:12-31 or Psalm 147:15). It's a figure of speech known as *'personification'* – when an abstract idea, like wisdom, is pictured as though it were a person. That is what the Scriptures employ here to make the plan of God that much more vivid.

God had a plan in mind, says John, and His all-powerful Word was ready for action, as once it had been when He created the world. This time, however, it was a new creation that God brought into existence – *"the only Son from the Father" (John 1:14)*, a phrase which is also translated as *"the only begotten of the Father"*. Some other expressions by John in his gospel account harmonise with this use of language, for John records these words of Jesus, who had come to make a new start possible between God and mankind:

"God so loved the world, that he gave his only Son, that whoever believes in him should not perish but have eternal life. For God did not send his Son into the world to condemn the world, but in order that the world might be saved through him" (John 3:16,17);

"He who comes from above is above all. He who is of the earth belongs to the earth and speaks in an earthly way. He who comes from heaven is above all. He bears witness to what he has seen and heard, yet no one receives

---

[13] *Note that John does not say "In the beginning was Jesus". His teaching is that from the very beginning God had a purpose in mind, for the Greek word "logos" (here translated "Word") has that very idea. The Greeks thought that the 'logos' was the very plan and purpose behind everything, and John says that it was God's plan.*

his testimony. Whoever receives his testimony sets his seal to this, that God is true. For he whom God has sent utters the words of God, for he gives the Spirit without measure. The Father loves the Son and has given all things into his hand" (3:31-35);

"I am the living bread that came down from heaven. If anyone eats of this bread, he will live forever. And the bread that I will give for the life of the world is my flesh" (6:51);

"He said to them, 'You are from below; I am from above. You are of this world; I am not of this world ...When you have lifted up the Son of Man, then you will know that I am he, and that I do nothing on my own authority, but speak just as the Father taught me. And he who sent me is with me. He has not left me alone, for I always do the things that are pleasing to him'" (8:23,28-29);

"The Father himself loves you, because you have loved me and have believed that I came from God. I came from the Father and have come into the world, and now I am leaving the world and going to the Father" (16:27,28).

The key teaching in all these verses is that Jesus did not choose to come because he was already living in heaven and God sent him down to the earth. He came into existence by an act of God when he was born by the operation of God's Holy Spirit power. That was a direct result of divine action and intervention; and he had come to do his Father's will, to speak His words, to perform His acts and to demonstrate His power at work.

Jesus was sent by God, in just the same way that God sent John the Baptist: *"There was a man sent from God, whose name was John" (John 1:6).* This does not mean that John the Baptist had lived in heaven before he was born on earth, but that he was someone who was sent by God to do a particular task. God initiated his work, then caused him to be born on earth (to aged parents), so that he could go and proclaim the coming of Jesus.[14]

---

14 *You can read about the birth of John the Baptist in chapter 1 of Luke's account of the gospel.*

One further example may help. When Jesus said: *"I am the living bread that came down from heaven. If anyone eats of this bread, he will live forever. And the bread that I will give for the life of the world is my flesh" (6:51),* he likened his coming to the provision of manna in the wilderness (see John 6:31).[15] God, not Moses, had fed the children of Israel in the wilderness of Sinai by providing manna, which had formed upon the ground like frost (Exodus 16:14). This was not bread which literally descended from heaven. It originated in heaven because God caused it to be formed on earth, and God is in heaven. In just the same way, Jesus was formed on earth when God caused him to be born of Mary. He did not physically descend from heaven but, like the manna, he came into existence on earth when God made that happen (see Luke 1:35).

Everything Jesus would do was known about in advance by God, who knows all, even before a thing happens.[16] In what he said, Jesus was therefore taking no note of his own achievements and accomplishments; instead he was magnifying his Father. Make no mistake! If God had not taken the initiative and had caused him to be born, there would have been no Jesus.

❖ Father and Son at Work

John records many of the sayings of Jesus about the unity of purpose that existed between himself and His Father. They were working together for our salvation, but always it was the Father's work and purpose that was being done.

*"Jesus answered them, '**My Father is working until now, and I am working**.' This was why the Jews were*

---

[15] *"Our fathers ate the manna in the wilderness; as it is written,'He gave them bread from heaven to eat.' Jesus then said to them, 'Truly, truly, I say to you, it was not Moses who gave you the bread from heaven, but my Father gives you the true bread from heaven. For the bread of God is he who comes down from heaven and gives life to the world.' They said to him, 'Sir, give us this bread always.' Jesus said to them, 'I am the bread of life'"* (John 6:31-35).

[16] God knows everything in advance. Thus he could say to the prophet Jeremiah: *"Before I formed you in the womb I knew you, and before you were born I consecrated you; I appointed you a prophet to the nations"* (Jeremiah 1:5)..This does not mean that Jeremiah was living in heaven before being born, but that God had a purpose he was to fulfil and that had been formed before even the prophet was born.

*seeking all the more to kill him, because not only was he
breaking the Sabbath, but he was even calling God his
own Father, making himself equal with God" (John 5:17);*

**"We must work the works of him who sent me while
it is day;** *night is coming, when no one can work" (9:4);*

**"The words that I say to you I do not speak on my
own authority, but the Father who dwells in me
does his works.** *Believe me that I am in the Father and
the Father is in me, or else believe on account of the
works themselves" (14:10,11);*

**"The works that I do in my Father's name bear wit-
ness about me,** *but you do not believe because you are
not part of my flock. My sheep hear my voice, and I know
them, and they follow me. I give them eternal life, and
they will never perish, and no one will snatch them out of
my hand.* **My Father, who has given them to me, is
greater than all,** *and no one is able to snatch them out
of the Father's hand.* **I and the Father are one"** *(10:25-
30).*[17]

This joint enterprise was misunderstood by those who
heard Jesus, just as it is sometimes misunderstood today.
Jesus continually deferred to his Father, and he explained
over and over that he was not acting on his own authority,
or doing things by himself. He was using the power that
God had given him, and was working together with his
heavenly Father. Yet, perversely, his opponents saw his
actions as a claim to equality with God.

❖ Unity or Trinity?

Nowadays there are people who look at these very verses
and consider that Jesus was equal with his Father – 'one
and indivisible' as the Doctrine of the Trinity puts it – and
they see these verses as proof that Jesus was claiming to
be part of a triune godhead. The man-made notion of a
Trinity is completely non-Biblical and gives quite the wrong

---

[17] *This was a passage we looked at in Question 8.1. See page 456
(Answers). We saw that the oneness of Jesus with his Father was one of
purpose and intention; he was one with his Father in the work he had come
to do and wanted his followers to share the same aims and ambitions in life
(John 17:20-21).*

understanding of what Father and Son accomplished together.

✗ *The Language is unscriptural. The word "Trinity" never appears in the Bible, far less phrases like "one God in Trinity, and Trinity in Unity ... confounding the Persons: nor dividing the Substance ... the Glory equal, the Majesty co-eternal ... The Father uncreate, the Son uncreate: and the Holy Ghost uncreate", and so on.*

✗ *Such language comes from the Athanasian Creed which was formulated in a church council during the fourth or fifth century after Christ – that's 200-300 years after the New Testament was completed.*

✗ *This formula ignores what we have found to be the crucial comparison between Jesus and his predecessor Adam. It was vital that as a man had brought about the problem facing mankind, a man had to bring about the solution, albeit a man who was working in perfect harmony with his heavenly Father.*

❖ Adam and Jesus

We will give the last word in this chapter to the apostle Paul, who showed, in Romans chapter 5, the contrast between Adam's dismal failure and the glorious success of the Lord Jesus Christ. He makes that comparison again in another of his letters, chapter 15 of the First Letter to the Corinthians; and as he does so he tells us more about the nature and work of Jesus. Here are the key verses, though you may want to read the whole chapter to follow his entire argument:

> *"Christ has been raised from the dead, the firstfruits of those who have fallen asleep. **For as by a man came death, by a man has come also the resurrection of the dead. For as in Adam all die, so also in Christ shall all be made alive.** But each in his own order: Christ the firstfruits, then at his coming those who belong to Christ. Then comes the end, when he delivers the kingdom to God the Father after destroying every rule and every authority and power. **For he must reign until he has put all his enemies under his feet. The last enemy to be destroyed is death. For 'God has put all***

things in subjection under his feet.' But when it says, 'all things are put in subjection,' it is plain that he is excepted who put all things in subjection under him. When all things are subjected to him, then the Son himself will also be subjected to him who put all things in subjection under him, that God may be all in all" (1 Corinthians 15:20-28);

"Thus it is written, 'The first man Adam became a living being'; the last Adam became a life-giving spirit. But it is not the spiritual that is first but the natural, and then the spiritual. The first man was from the earth, a man of dust; the second man is from heaven. As was the man of dust, so also are those who are of the dust, and as is the man of heaven, so also are those who are of heaven. Just as we have borne the image of the man of dust, we shall also bear the image of the man of heaven" (15:45-49).

These are the points the inspired apostle makes here:

✓ *Adam brought death to all. Those who are descended from him are mortal, and have nothing immortal about them. We are born "in Adam", as Paul expresses it.*

✓ *Jesus brings life for all those who are reborn of him – who are "in Christ".*

✓ *That life will come when Jesus comes again – "at his coming", when he will rule for God and will destroy "every rule and every authority and power" which opposes God, just as Adam should have done.*

✓ *Jesus will then reverse the death sentence that now prevails and will destroy death by conferring eternal life on those who are the subjects of his kingdom.*

✓ *When, by his kingly rule, Jesus has subdued all opposition, he will hand over the rulership of that kingdom to his Father, "that God may be all in all", or 'everything to everyone' as one translation renders the Greek words.*

✓ *Adam lived for himself. Jesus will give life to others.*

174

✓ *Adam was made from dust and filled his mind with earthly things; Jesus put aside all such earthly things and filled his mind with heavenly thoughts.*

✓ *We have been made in Adam's image and have been subject to all the problems that result. Being mortal we die and being prone to sin we too fall. We shall however be made in the image of the Lord Jesus Christ when he gives us the gift of eternal life.*

This analysis raises issues we have not yet considered, but the Bible works like that. One passage confirms things we have already come across but also tells us new things. In this way it enlarges our understanding and encourages us to read and find out yet more about the purpose of God – the coming of Jesus; the Kingdom over which he will reign and the resurrection of the dead. 1 Corinthians chapter 15 is all about that – and the way in which we can become like Jesus, to *"share his image"* as Paul expresses it.

All that will come if we follow the apostle Paul's reasoned explanation in Romans as we have being doing. He is unfolding the gospel for us, in his own way, and there are other vital topics that he deals with first. God has a gracious purpose for mankind which is centred in the Lord Jesus Christ. Some people will benefit enormously from that purpose, but who and why? How can God forgive some people their sins, give them eternal life and make them like the Lord Jesus Christ?

Understanding that is our next challenge.

Things to Read

📖 If you are not familiar with what happened in the Garden of Eden then Genesis chapter 3 is a really helpful chapter to read.

📖 1 Corinthians chapter 15 gives a slightly different comparison between Adam and Jesus from that in Romans chapter 5, as we have seen. It's all about the hope of resurrection from the dead and makes encouraging reading, for it gives us real hope of life after death.

Questions to Think About

12.1 Put in your own words, in just two or three sentences, just what Paul is saying in Romans chapter 5 about Adam's failure and Jesus' success. Why does it matter so much to us?

12.2 Why is it so important that Jesus was descended from Mary, rather than having lived in heaven before being conveyed somehow to earth?

"But as for you, continue in what you have learned and have firmly believed, knowing from whom you learned it and how from childhood you have been acquainted with the sacred writings, which are able to make you wise for salvation through faith in Christ Jesus"
(2 Timothy 3:14,15)

13
How can We become like Jesus?

Adam failed dismally to obey the commands of God and to become perfect. The Lord Jesus Christ triumphed marvellously over all the temptations that confronted him. The Bible invites us to become like Jesus. We are made in Adam's image which means that we are naturally inclined to sin and must eventually die: that's the inheritance Adam passed on to all mankind. We can, however, be changed to become like the Lord Jesus Christ. He achieved what God meant for mankind and reflects the character and likeness of Almighty God his Father. So when the Bible promises that we can become like Jesus it is offering us the wonderful prospect of becoming godly or godlike in all our ways.

This is what is on offer from God, because of the saving work of the Father and Son:

*"See what kind of love the Father has given to us, that we should be called children of God; and so we are. The reason why the world does not know us is that it did not know him. Beloved, we are God's children now, and what we will be has not yet appeared; but **we know that when he appears we will be like him, because we shall see him as he is**"* (1 John 3:1,2);

*"And not only the creation, but we ourselves, who have the firstfruits of the Spirit, groan inwardly as **we wait eagerly for adoption as sons, the redemption of our bodies**"* (Romans 8:23);

*"Just as we have borne the image of the man of dust, **we shall also bear the image of the man of heaven**"* (1 Corinthians 15:49);

*"Our citizenship is in heaven, and from it we await a Saviour, the Lord Jesus Christ, **who will transform our lowly body to be like his glorious body**, by the power that enables him even to subject all things to himself"* (Philippians 3:20,21).

❖ Jesus in the Image of God

When God created man it was His intention that he should reflect the divine image. He wanted mankind to live in such a way that they would reflect His values, character and attributes. That intention was captured in the declaration: *"Let us make man in our image, after our likeness. And let them have dominion" (Genesis 1:26).* But, as we have seen,[1] mankind spoiled God's intention and chose a different path which we have all followed. Today people want to do it their way, not God's.

Jesus recaptured God's original intention by choosing the path of perfect obedience. He lived as God would have us all live: in perfect harmony with his Father, in complete agreement and total obedience to his Father's will. The result was that the life of God was portrayed on earth in His Son, who could say: *"Whoever has seen me has seen the Father" (John 14:9).* That did not mean that Jesus *was* the Father. He went on to make that clear by explaining that he and his Father were working together, and that both the words he spoke and the things that he did were done jointly.[2]

We have looked at the great work accomplished by both the Father and the Son in earlier chapters. They were working together to achieve a new start for mankind. This would be a new creation, one in which mankind would have control over everything that challenges the will of God and in which God and His glory would be supreme. This is how the writer to the Hebrews sums up what God has done through Jesus:

> *"Long ago, at many times and in many ways, God spoke to our fathers by the prophets, but in these last days he has spoken to us by his Son, whom **he appointed the heir of all things, through whom also he created the world**. He is the radiance of the glory of God and the exact imprint of his nature, and he upholds the universe by the word of his power. After making purification for*

---

[1] *In Chapter 4, pages 42-44*

[2] *"Do you not believe that I am in the Father and the Father is in me? The words that I say to you I do not speak on my own authority, but the Father who dwells in me does his works. Believe me that I am in the Father and the Father is in me, or else believe on account of the works themselves" (John 14:10,11).*

sins, he sat down at the right hand of the Majesty on high, having become as much superior to angels as the name he has inherited is more excellent than theirs" (Hebrews 1:1-4).

Once again you will notice that we are told lots of different things in one tightly-packed passage and we are now able to unpack it for ourselves. We learn that:

✓ Through Jesus, God communicated with mankind as never before: God *"has spoken to us by his Son";*

✓ God has appointed Jesus *"the heir of all things"*; this is a reward that Jesus has received from his Father for his perfect obedience (see also Philippians 2:9);

✓ Jesus reflected the glory of God in the way he lived. His life showed people what God is like – the original Greek has the sense of the impression made by a seal in wax to leave a perfect imprint;

✓ God created *"the world to come"* through, or because of, the Lord Jesus Christ – they worked together to make it possible for men and women like us to inhabit a new society; [3]

✓ Jesus has become superior to the angels because he has received from God a status and position which is greater even than theirs: they are God's servants but he is God's Son.

✓ He made *"purification for sins"* in order that he might bring *"many sons to glory"* (Hebrews 2:10), namely all those who have been purified and who thus become members of God's family, by adoption.

❖ Purification for Sins

We have reached the point in Romans where Paul explains how we can become members of God's family. In Chapter 4 he showed the vital importance of faith and we have

---

[3] *We know that it is the "world to come" that is in the writer's mind because he says so in Hebrews 2:5: "Now it was not to angels that God subjected the world to come, of which we are speaking".*

explored what constitutes a saving faith by examining both what Abraham and David believed and how the Lord Jesus Christ is central to the fulfilment of those promises.

He is the promised offspring – promised to Eve, Abraham and David – and he alone can undo the harm that Adam's disobedience inflicted on mankind. But how does the work that Jesus accomplished change our position before God? Apart from believing the right things, what else must we do, if anything? This is what Paul says at the start of his detailed comparison of Adam and Jesus:

> *"Therefore, since we have been **justified by faith**, we have peace with God through our Lord Jesus Christ. Through him we have also **obtained access** by faith into this grace in which we stand, and we **rejoice in hope** of the glory of God" (Romans 5:1,2).*

Faith makes a huge difference to our relationship with God. Without it we are regarded as unrighteous: enemies of God, with no access into His presence and no hope. That is the very opposite of what Paul says we can have when we are *"justified by faith"*. In another letter he explains that without the work of God in Christ we were: *"by nature children of wrath, like the rest of mankind ... separated from Christ, alienated from the commonwealth of Israel and strangers to the covenants of promise, having no hope and without God in the world" (Ephesians 2:3,12).* The death of Jesus makes all the difference in the world, for it makes possible *"purification for sins"*. But how and why is that possible?

❖ Christ Died for Us

Our journey through Romans has already shown us that the death of Jesus on the cross declared that God was right to condemn sin, because the cross shows us how awful sin really is. If sin took Jesus to the cross we should have nothing to do with it! But we cannot conquer sin ourselves and desperately need God's help. So God has taken action. A quick search through Romans will soon highlight some of the things God has done for us, as follows:

↘ *"God put forward (Jesus) as a propitiation by his blood, to be received by faith" (3:23);* [4]

↘ *"at the right time Christ died for the ungodly" (5:6);*

➥ *"while we were still sinners, Christ died for us"* (5:8);

➥ *"we have now been justified by his blood"* (5:9);

➥ *"we were reconciled to God by the death of his Son"* (5:10);

➥ *"we have now received reconciliation"* (5:11).

Wonderful things have been done by God and the Lord Jesus Christ to make it possible for us to be saved and to become like Jesus. We couldn't do it but they could. That's the very contrast that Paul makes:

*"For while we were still weak, **at the right time Christ died for the ungodly**. For one will scarcely die for a righteous person – though perhaps for a good person one would dare even to die – but God shows his love for us in that while we were still sinners, **Christ died for us**. Since, therefore, we have now been **justified by his blood**, much more shall we be saved by him from the wrath of God. For if while we were enemies we were reconciled to God by **the death of his Son**, much more, now that we are reconciled, shall we be saved by his life. More than that, we also rejoice in God through our Lord Jesus Christ, through whom **we have now received reconciliation**"* (Romans 5:6-11).

On the one hand mankind is described as *"ungodly"*, *"sinners"* in need of salvation and *"enemies"* who are opposed to God's will and ways. On the other hand, Jesus has *"died for the ungodly"*, so that we might be *"justified by his blood"* and be *"saved by him"*. He now lives so that we might be *"saved by his life"* because, through him, we can be *"reconciled"* to God. This is a huge contrast between what we deserve and what God will do for us.

A little later in Romans Paul adds one further helpful detail about what exactly it was that God accomplished for us through Christ. Here it is:

*"God has done what the law, weakened by the flesh, could not do. **By sending his own Son in the likeness***

---

4 *We have seen already that the death of Jesus on the cross was something that God required as a means of turning away His wrath (Chapter 9, pages 119-124).*

of sinful flesh and for sin[5] *he condemned sin in the flesh"* (8:3).

❖ Sin Condemned!

Father and Son worked together. God sent His own Son – He took the initiative and the Lord Jesus Christ fully cooperated in what was required of him. He died for the ungodly, unworthy and undeserving, just as we are, and the shedding of his blood brought reconciliation. Jesus came with our nature,[6] but he never once yielded to its promptings. This is why Paul describes him as coming *"in the likeness of sinful flesh"*: he was made like us but he was unlike us, too, in that he was perfectly obedient to God in everything.

Having lived a sinless life, Jesus then voluntarily gave his life as a sacrifice *"for sin"*. He died that we might have life and in the process, Paul explains, he condemned sin. That which had condemned all mankind was now condemned itself! Sin was shown up for what it really is – terrible, wicked and evil. There just aren't enough words to describe the awfulness of sin when you think about what happened to Jesus.

That condemnation was made by Jesus *"in the flesh"*. Although tempted just as we are to commit sin, he had always resisted that temptation and thus had both conquered sin and shown it up for the wicked and evil thing it is. Now, in his death, Jesus showed ultimate obedience to his Father and completely overcame any tendency to sin within his nature. In that way he was free from sin but, because he died as a sacrifice for sin, his death brought freedom for us as well. He died for us.

❖ The Blood of Jesus Christ

Twice in this explanation of what God accomplished in the death of Jesus we are told about the importance of the shed blood of the Lord Jesus. God put forward the Lord Jesus *"as a propitiation **by his blood**, to be received by faith"* (3:25) and we can now be *"justified **by his blood**"* (5:9) and thus be saved from the wrath of God. There are

---

[5] *An alternative translation, which many versions offer, and which the ESV puts in the margin, is that Jesus died "as a sin offering".*
[6] *Chapter 7, pages 82-89.*

182

several other references in the New Testament to the shed blood of the Lord Jesus[7] and we may wonder what this language tells us about the meaning of the death of Jesus. Is there anything special about his blood, or is it just a way of referring to his sacrificial death? There are many references to the offering of the *body*[8] of Christ or to his *death*[9] for us, so the *blood* as such has no special significance. But it carries an important meaning even so.

From Eden onwards, when animals were killed to make a covering for the sins of Adam and Eve, God made an arrangement which allowed people to approach Him by offering animal sacrifices. This was done from early times (for example in Genesis 8:20 and 12:7) and an important principle was established early on that the blood represented life (Genesis 9:4). In time this principle became fundamental to the law which God gave to Moses. This is detailed in the books of Exodus to Deuteronomy in the Old Testament and it comprised a way of life for the nation of Israel which embodied spiritual principles. This was one of them:

> *"If any one of the house of Israel or of the strangers who sojourn among them eats any blood, I will set my face against that person who eats blood and will cut him off from among his people. For **the life of the flesh is in the blood, and I have given it for you on the altar to make atonement for your souls, for it is the blood that makes atonement by the life**" (Leviticus 17:10,11).*

❖ A Life Given

This principle was demonstrated in the clearest way when a person drew near to worship God and seek forgiveness by coming, as the law required, with an animal sacrifice. The worshipper had to place hands on the animal to identify with the offering saying, in effect, that he or she was really the guilty party and that their sin deserved death. The death of the animal thus represented what should really happen to them, were it not for God's forgiveness of sin.

---

[7] *For example, Ephesians 2:13; Hebrews 9:14;10:10;13:12,20;1 Peter 1:2,19 and 1 John 1:7.*

[8] *Ephesians 2:16; Colossians 1:21; Hebrews 10:5,10; 1 Peter 2:24.*

[9] *Romans 5:10; Hebrews 2:9,14; 9:15; 1 Corinthians 11:26.*

Their life was in effect forfeit but, in figurative terms, it was then given back to them. They were allowed to live, though the animal was dead, and thus they could see that they had been forgiven.

One weakness in this arrangement was, of course, that the animal was likely to be an unwilling participant and could not represent the worshipper in any other way than in its death, being an animal not a person. As the animal had no moral sense, or spiritual feelings, it was also a fairly poor representative of the worshipper.

But those sacrifices served another purpose. They point-

*"For since the law has but a shadow of the good things to come instead of the true form of these realities, **it can never, by the same sacrifices that are continually offered every year, make perfect those who draw near.** Otherwise, would they not have ceased to be offered, since the worshippers, having once been cleansed, would no longer have any consciousness of sin?" (Hebrews 10:1,2)*

ed forward to the sacrifice of the Lord Jesus Christ, as the writer to the Hebrews makes very clear. He wrote to Jewish believers who had been brought up with animal sacrifices and who must many times have made such offerings many times. Now he explained the full significance of those sacrifices and what they had been leading up to.

One man had come who willingly offered himself as a sacrifice on behalf of others. Jesus was willing to die for the ungodly so that men and women can be justified by his blood. In that way he would make reconciliation possible between God and man by bridging the moral gap. It would be a once-for-all sacrifice, for it would be available for everyone who wanted to come to God through him, whether Jew or Gentile. And, because Jesus was raised from the dead, the one who made the offering would also be available to act as a mediator or priest, to bring worshippers right into the presence of God. Hebrews, chapters 9 and 10, explains this in detail and here are some key verses:

> *"Christ has entered, not into holy places made with hands, which are copies of the true things, but into heaven itself, now to appear in the presence of God on our behalf. Nor was it to offer himself repeatedly, as the high priest enters the holy places every year with blood not his own, for then he would have had to suffer repeatedly since the foundation of the world. But as it is,* **he has appeared once for all at the end of the ages to put away sin by the sacrifice of himself.** *And just as it is appointed for man to die once, and after that comes judgement, so* **Christ, having been offered once to bear the sins of many,** *will appear a second time, not to deal with sin but to save those who are eagerly waiting for him" (Hebrews 9:24-28).*

Paul says the same thing in Romans when describing the way in which Jesus was a *"sin offering"*. He says of the sacrifice on the cross that: *"the death he died he died to sin,* **once for all***"* (Romans 6:10). Notice that Paul says two things here:

1 *Jesus made an offering which would never need to be repeated, and that*

2 *He died to sin.*

That second point means that when the body of Jesus was dead upon the cross he would never again be subject to the temptations that came from within or from any that might come from without. Sin had no more influence over the Lord Jesus from the time that he died, any more than it does over any other lifeless being. When God raised His Son from the dead it was so that he could experience a sinless life in heaven where he is described as being:

> *"**Holy, innocent, unstained, separated from sinners, and exalted above the heavens**. He has no need, like those high priests, to offer sacrifices daily, first for his own sins and then for those of the people, since he did this once for all when he offered up himself. For the law appoints men in their weakness as high priests, but the word of the oath, which came later than the law, appoints a Son who has been made perfect forever" (Hebrews 7:26-28).*

❖ A Life Recovered

The sacrifice of Jesus was not, as some people suggest, a payment that had to be made – a life for a life. There was no Devil demanding the blood of Christ before he would allow God to forgive mankind, or anything like that. Such an idea is not only unbiblical; it is preposterous! The death of Jesus was God's way of giving men and women like us an opportunity to identify with what was being declared about right and wrong.

Where Adam and Eve got things wrong, by deciding that it was right to do what they wanted to do, the Lord Jesus came to put matters right. He redefined what is right and what is wrong. Here are the attributes that Jesus declared to be acceptable to God, a declaration he made by the way he lived and died. And these are the things that he declared unworthy and unacceptable to God:

Right	Wrong
"love, joy, peace, patience, kindness, goodness, faithfulness, gentleness, self-control"	*"Sexual immorality, impurity, sensuality, idolatry, sorcery, enmity, strife, jealousy, fits of anger, rivalries, dissensions, divisions, envy, drunkenness, orgies, and things like these"*

These two sets of characteristics are defined as *"the fruit of the Spirit"* and the *"works of the flesh"*, in Galatians 5:19-23, and they summarise the difference between right and wrong as Jesus defined them in his life. He always did those things that pleased the Father. Those who opposed him during his life on earth fully expressed the works of the flesh in the way they lived, schemed and worked to see him killed. They were as perverse and devious in their dealings as he was straight and open in all his ways.

Because Jesus lived in this way and died still blameless and faultless, God restored his life by raising him from the dead. Jesus did not conquer death unaided: how could he? He was dead and therefore unconscious. The Scriptures insist that God raised His Son from the dead[10] that He might give him eternal life:

> "*Men of Israel, hear these words: Jesus of Nazareth, a man attested to you by God with mighty works and wonders and signs that God did through him in your midst, as you yourselves know – this Jesus, delivered up according to the definite plan and foreknowledge of God, you crucified and killed by the hands of lawless men. God raised him up, loosing the pangs of death, because it was not possible for him to be held by it ... This Jesus God raised up, and of that we all are witnesses*" *(Acts 2:22-24,32).*

It was part of the divine purpose that Jesus should suffer and die before entering into glory at God's right hand in heaven. For God knew that recovering the human race would need more that just a death, even the death of a perfect man. He knew that mankind would need on-going help if they were to be able to find eternal life. So he raised Jesus from the dead.[11]

❖ Not a 'Substitute'

Of course if the death of Jesus was some sort of a payment[12] – his life instead of ours – it would have been impossible for God to have raised Jesus from the dead. That would have been like paying back some money you owed and then stealing it back again! The Bible never suggests that Jesus died instead of us, or as a substitute for us. Instead it says that he died on our behalf – *"for us".*

---

[10] *Acts 3:15; 4:10; 10:40; 13:30,33,34,37; 17:31; Rom.4:24; 6:4;8:11; 10:9; 1 Corinthians 6:14; 15:15; 2 Corinthians 4:14; Galatians 1:1; Ephesians 1:20; Col. 2:12; 1 Thessalonians.1:10; Hebrews 13:20; 1 Peter 1:21.*

[11] *This why Paul can say that we have been saved by his life, as well as by his death (Romans 5:10). God raised Jesus because he had been sinless, and therefore it would have been wrong to leave him dead (Psalm 16.8-11}, but the result has made all the difference for us, as well as for Jesus.*

[12] *Some people believe that a price had to be paid to rescue sinners from an angry God, who would only forgive them if someone took the blame. If that was so then it would be Jesus who saves us from God. That can't be right!*

*"God shows his love **for us** in that while we were still sinners, Christ died for us" (Romans 5:8);*

*"If God is for us, who can be against us? He who did not spare his own Son but gave him up **for us** all, how will he not also with him graciously give us all things?" (8:31,32);*

*"Walk in love, as Christ loved us and gave himself up **for us**, a fragrant offering and sacrifice to God" (Ephesians 5:2);*

*"For God has not destined us for wrath, but to obtain salvation through our Lord Jesus Christ, who died **for us** so that whether we are awake or asleep we might live with him" (1 Thessalonians 5:9,10).*

Jesus died for us, so that we can live with him, and now he lives for us. It is a vital part of the gospel message that Jesus Christ is now alive and is sitting at the right hand of God in heaven, waiting for the time when he will be sent again to earth, this time to rule as king. But while he waits, he is able to help us in our attempts to become like him. He died for us and now he lives for us.

*"For if while we were enemies we were reconciled to God by the death of his Son, much more, now that we are reconciled, shall we be **saved by his life**" (Romans 5:10);*

*"Christ Jesus is the one who died – **more than that, who was raised – who is at the right hand of God, who indeed is interceding for us**. Who shall separate us from the love of Christ? Shall tribulation, or distress, or persecution, or famine, or nakedness, or danger, or sword?" (8:34,35);*

*"He is able to save to the uttermost those who draw near to God through him, since **he always lives to make intercession for them** ... For Christ has entered, not into holy places made with hands, which are copies of the true things, but into heaven itself, **now to appear in the presence of God on our behalf**" (Hebrews 7:25; 9:24).*

❖ Jesus the Great High Priest

Jesus lives in heaven today as our God-given go-between. The role he now fulfils is a vital part of his atoning and reconciling work; without it we would still be unable to be right with God. So the saving work of the Father and the Son continues.

> *"It is pleasing in the sight of God our Saviour, who desires all people to be saved and to come to the knowledge of the truth. For **there is one God, and there is one mediator between God and men, the man Christ Jesus**, who gave himself as a ransom for all" (1 Timothy 2:3-6);*

> *"How much more will the blood of Christ, who through the eternal Spirit offered himself without blemish to God, purify our conscience from dead works to serve the living God. Therefore **he is the mediator of a new covenant, so that those who are called may receive the promised eternal inheritance**, since a death has occurred that redeems them from the transgressions committed under the first covenant" (Hebrews 9:14,15).*

It follows that we need no other mediator or intercessor – no priests or any other intermediaries. There are people who pray to 'saints' to intercede on their behalf or to the Virgin Mary, as though any of those were alive today. Scripture informs us that they are all asleep in the unconsciousness of the grave that awaits all of us. But Jesus is alive and active on our behalf. Each one of us is able to approach God through the Lord Jesus Christ; indeed we are encouraged to do so. We are now told to approach God in the name of the Lord Jesus Christ, but notice the preconditions: those things that we must do to be acceptable to God:

> *"Therefore, brothers, since we have confidence to enter the holy places by the blood of Jesus, by the new and living way that he opened for us through the curtain, that is, through his flesh, and since **we have a great priest over the house of God**, let us draw near with a true heart in full assurance of faith, with our hearts sprinkled clean from an evil conscience and our bodies washed with pure water. Let us hold fast the confession of our hope without wavering, for he who promised is faithful" (Hebrews 10:19-23).*

❖ Spiritual Checklist

Here is some more analysis for us, for this passage gives us a lot of careful advice: [13]

✓ The writer addresses his readers as *"brothers"*, which means they are members of the family of God and are related to the Lord Jesus Christ (see Hebrews 2:10,11);

✓ They are approaching God *"by the blood of Jesus"*. This means that they are somehow associated with the great sacrifice that was made by Jesus;

✓ This approach is by the only available way – *"the new and living way"*; clearly there is no other way of approach except this one;

✓ Jesus is the one who will guide the worshipper through into God's presence, for he is the *"great priest"* over God's house;

✓ Faith – belief in the promises of God and trust in Him – is the vital key, as we have worked out. But it needs to be *"full assurance of faith"*, just as we need to have *"a true heart"*, for we must be honest and sincere in our approach to God.

Now notice how all these things are brought together:

1 *Our hearts must be sprinkled clean from an evil conscience;*

2 *Our bodies must be washed with pure water, and*

3 *We must confess our hope in God without wavering.*

The apostle is writing about Christian baptism and is telling his readers that this is the way God has appointed for anyone and everyone to approach Him. We must take advantage of the saving work that has been accomplished for us in the death and resurrection of Christ. And baptism is the only way we can do that.

❖ Christian Baptism

It is precisely this way of approaching God that the apostle Paul writes about in his Letter to the Romans. Chapter 6, which is where we have now reached, is all about the

[13] *If you want to work through this yourself first, and then compare your findings with the list that follows, go ahead!*

meaning of baptism. If we want to be like Jesus when he comes again, we have to identify with him now and associate ourselves with the experiences he went through. We'll be looking at what baptism comprised in first century days in the next chapter, but here is an extract of what Paul said about the way in which we can follow Jesus now and thus start to live a new life with him, one that is right with God.

> *"What shall we say then? Are we to continue in sin that grace may abound? By no means! How can we who died to sin still live in it? Do you not know that all of us who have been **baptized into Christ Jesus** were **baptized** into his death? We were buried therefore with him by **baptism** into death, in order that, just as Christ was raised from the dead by the glory of the Father, we too might walk in newness of life. For if we have been united with him in a death like his, we shall certainly be united with him in a resurrection like his ... Now if we have died with Christ, we believe that we will also live with him"* (Romans 6:1-5,8).

To be baptized into Christ is to be baptized into his death. In the waters of baptism a believer goes under the water as though a burial was taking place and comes out of the water as though it were a resurrection. This act thus symbolises an association with Jesus, much as worshippers in Old Testament times would have placed their hands on a sacrifice to signify that *they* should really have died, not the animal. Baptism is designed to do the same thing – to help us identify with the saving work of both Father and Son for us.

It also marks a clean break with our old life, the one we declare we want to put to death and leave behind. Henceforth the baptized believer will be seeking to live with Jesus, so that we can *"live with him"*, both now and in the age to come. Baptism is the beginning of the road for all those who want to walk along the *"new and living way"* that leads to the kingdom of God. It is the first step, and a vital one at that, into a new life with the Lord Jesus. It is also the way that God has ordained whereby we enter into His family and become adopted children, brothers and sisters of the Lord Jesus Christ.

"See what kind of love the Father has given to us, that we should be called children of God; and so we are. The reason why the world does not know us is that it did not know him. Beloved, we are God's children now, and what we will be has not yet appeared; but we know that when he appears we will be like him, because we shall see him as he is" (1 John 3:1,2).

Things to Read

📖 If you want to read a little more about the work of Jesus as both sacrifice and priest, then read Hebrews chapters 9 and 10.

📖 In this chapter we have been thinking again about the death of Jesus. This was a real and terrible event and you may want to read another of the gospel accounts. Try Mark chapter 15.

Questions to Think About

13.1 If we want to be like Jesus in the future, should we try to live like him now? How can we do this in our everyday lives? (Philippians 2:1-5; Colossians 3:1-6; John 15:12-15)

13.2 What has to happen before our present human nature can be changed to be like that of the Lord Jesus Christ – for ever free from sin and death? (1 Corinthians 15:51-58)

14

What Exactly is Christian Baptism?

We have discovered that if we want to become like the Lord Jesus Christ, starting to live like him now and becoming wholly like him when he comes again, we have to be baptised. We have also worked out that we need to have a saving faith if we are to become right with God, being *justified by faith*.

The apostle Paul spends the whole of Romans chapter 6 describing what baptism is intended to achieve, just as in chapter 4 he explained the importance of saving faith. Our search to understand the Bible has already demonstrated the importance of analysing a particular passage and then being able to see that teaching within the framework of the Bible as a whole, allowing Scripture to interpret Scripture. So let's put those techniques to work again.

❖ Romans 6

What exactly does Paul tell us about baptism in this chapter? Try reading it yourself and jotting down the things you discover, then compare that with the list below.

1 Making a clean break with sin requires that we must have *"died to sin"* (6:2);

2 We do this in symbol when we are baptized into Christ, for in that way we are *"baptized into his death"* – burial in water is the way in which, in symbol, we are *"buried therefore with him by baptism into death"* (6:4);

3 Baptism marks the end of the old life and the start of a new life for it symbolises more than just a death. It means that *"just as Christ was raised from the dead by the glory of the Father, we too might walk in newness of life"* (6:4);

4 It is therefore an act of union and unity with both Father and Son (6:5) and a declaration that we no longer want

to be *"enslaved to sin"* (6:6), but want to be *"free from sin"* (6:7);

5 It is a work of faith – *"if we have died with Christ, we believe that we will also live with him"* (6:8), based on our knowledge of *"the standard of teaching to which you were committed"* (6:17); [1]

6 It requires a complete change of mind and attitude from that with which we are born – a willingness to *"obey from the heart the things"* we learn about from God's Word (6:11,17,19);

7 It marks a change of allegiance and loyalty as befits those who become God's children. For, from baptism on, believers are to *"present yourselves to God as those who have been brought from death to life, and your members to God as instruments for righteousness"* (6:13);

8 This means a new start in life now – a new quality of life with God now, and in the age to come *"the free gift of God is eternal life in Christ Jesus our Lord"* (6:23).

❖ First Century Practice

If baptism really is as important as Paul reckons in this chapter, and he clearly believes it to be so, we should find that it is the universal practice of all First Century believers. If we see what they said about it and what they did, then we will be able to base our practices on a firm foundation of original faith. There were examples of people coming through water to a new life in the Old Testament, notably Noah and his family coming through the flood. Israel escaping from Egypt through the Red Sea; and there are occasions when the priests had to be washed all over before entering into consecrated service.[2] But it is the New

---

[1] *Notice that Paul's reference to a "standard of teaching to which you were committed" is very much the same as the 'saving faith' we were considering in Chapter 11. Some people say, quite wrongly, that if you have faith, that is enough for God: you don't need any works to save you. But the Bible teaches that faith without works is a dead faith (James 2:17).*

[2] *There are New Testament references to both the Flood and the Crossing of the Red Sea as a prototype of Christian baptism (see 1 Corinthians 10:1-4 and 1 Peter 3:20,21).*

Testament that initiates baptism to mark a new start for Jews and Gentiles alike.

❖ John the Baptist

Right at the start of the New Testament, in the gospel accounts, we read of a man who was *"sent from God" (John 1:6)*. John the Baptist was of the priestly line and could have ministered at the temple in Jerusalem. Instead he lived in the wilderness and appealed to the faithful in Israel to come out to him and be baptized in the River Jordan. It is the first thing that Mark records in his account of the gospel:

> *"The beginning of the gospel of Jesus Christ, the Son of God. As it is written in Isaiah the prophet, Behold, I send my messenger before your face, who will prepare your way, the voice of one crying in the wilderness: 'Prepare the way of the Lord, make his paths straight.'* **John appeared, baptizing in the wilderness and proclaiming a baptism of repentance for the forgiveness of sins. And all the country of Judea and all Jerusalem were going out to him and were being baptized by him in the river Jordan, confessing their sins"** *(Mark 1:1-5)*.

John had come, just as the prophets had foretold (Malachi 3:1 and Isaiah 40:3 being the two Scriptures quoted), as a forerunner of the Messiah, the Lord Jesus Christ. His message was that the people of Israel needed *"forgiveness of sins"* and that was a huge challenge to the existing religious system. They had their magnificent temple in Jerusalem, an extensive priesthood, sacrifices were offered continually and all the feasts were kept. But they needed something different and John invited them to repent and be baptized.

Repentance is an act of turning away from sin and going in the opposite direction. As we have seen, we are born with a natural tendency to go our own way, not in God's direction. Repentance means turning around and going towards Him – just like point 6 in our analysis of Romans chapter 6. Watch for it and you will see that repentance often accompanies baptism; the two go together. The very first message that Jesus preached when he began his ministry was: *"Repent, for the kingdom of heaven is at hand."* *(Matthew 4:17)*.

195

People flocked to hear John's message and to be baptized in the River Jordan, for his was a challenging message, to live lives that were right in the sight of God and to wash away their sins by immersion in the Jordan. We know that he practised immersion in water because of an incidental comment in the gospel of John, where we are told that: *"John also was baptizing at Aenon near Salim, because water was plentiful there, and people were coming and being baptized" (John 3:23).*

It is always the case in the New Testament that people who were baptized were immersed; sprinkling or pouring water on an infant or an adult were not practised at that time and have no Scriptural basis whatsoever. There is one other significant detail that confirms that John took those being baptized into the River Jordan, rather than just standing on the riverbank.

❖ Jesus was Baptized

One day the Lord Jesus came to the Jordan to be baptized by his cousin John. We do not really know how much contact they had over the years. The families lived miles apart, but they might have met at the various feasts in Jerusalem or on family occasions. John knew enough about Jesus to stand in awe of him, for he protested that, if anyone was to be baptized, it should be him, not Jesus, which caused Jesus to say something which is relevant to all of us:

"Then Jesus came from Galilee to the Jordan to John, to be baptized by him. John would have prevented him, saying, 'I need to be baptized by you, and do you come to me?' But Jesus answered him, 'Let it be so now, for thus it is fitting for us to fulfil all righteousness.' Then he consented. And when Jesus was baptized, immediately he went up from the water, and behold, the heavens were opened to him, and he saw the Spirit of God descending like a dove and coming to rest on him; and behold, a voice from heaven said, 'This is my beloved Son, with whom I am well pleased'" (Matthew 3:13-17).

Clearly what Jesus had done was pleasing to God, as the voice from heaven made clear. The physical event is carefully recorded in that the Lord went *"up from the water"* afterwards, so he had evidently been in the Jordan, not on the riverbank, when John baptized him. But the crucial saying for us is this. Jesus said that baptism is something we all need if we are to *"fulfil all righteousness"*. It was something for *"us"*, not just for him, and if he needed it – with such a wonderful character – how much more do we?

Jesus had no sins which needed forgiveness of course and therefore no need to repent, but he was keen to do anything and everything that showed his willing obedience. God was initiating a new means of approach to Himself, through baptism, so Jesus was baptized as well to show us that way. In doing so, he endorsed John's work and his methods by encouraging others to be baptized, for the record says that:

> *"Jesus and his disciples went into the Judean country-side, and he remained there with them and was baptizing ... Now when Jesus learned that the Pharisees had heard that Jesus was making and baptizing more disciples than John (although Jesus himself did not baptize, but only his disciples), he left Judea and departed again for Galilee"* (John 3:22; 4:1-3).

John's work was coming to an end and that of Jesus was beginning, for John was soon to be imprisoned and later executed. As opposition to the Lord's ministry also began to grow and as he neared the time when he must die as a sacrifice for sin, the Lord used one phrase which indicates how he viewed baptism – as an act of dying to self and pledging to live wholly to God. He said:

> *"I have a baptism to be baptized with, and how great is my distress until it is accomplished!"* (Luke 12:50).

For him the death on the cross would be what his baptism had pointed forward to. In the Jordan he had publicly pledged to die to self and now, in Jerusalem, he would literally fulfil that pledge. And he would not be alone when that happened.

❖ Dying with Christ

Paul used symbolic language when he said, in Romans 6, that *"we have died with Christ"* in the waters of baptism. But one man literally died with Christ; he was the thief who was crucified with him and who made a remarkable confession of faith in the most challenging circumstances.

Some people say that the thief on the cross demonstrates that you don't have to be baptized to be saved because, they say, he wasn't baptized. In reality nobody knows whether he was or not. He may well have been baptized earlier by John or by the disciples of Jesus and the indications are that he probably had been, for he knew and believed a huge amount about the person and work of Jesus. But that is not the real point here.

This man actually died alongside Christ – the only man ever to have died like this. Hence his death was like an act of baptism in itself. It was also accompanied by repentance and by a most remarkable declaration of what he believed, at a time when many of the followers of Jesus had lost their faith or seriously doubted that Jesus really was the Messiah.

Think about the things this man said to his companion about Jesus and bear in mind that every utterance would have taken tremendous effort given his physical position on the cross:

> *"One of the criminals who were hanged railed at him, saying, 'Are you not the Christ? Save yourself and us!' But the other rebuked him, saying, 'Do you not fear God, since you are under the same sentence of condemnation? And we indeed justly, for we are receiving the due reward of our deeds; but this man has done nothing wrong.' And he said, 'Jesus, remember me when you come into your kingdom.' And he said to him, 'Truly, I say to you, today you will be with me in Paradise'" (Luke 23:39-43).*

You should be practised enough by now to be able to pick out the key statements he made, to see their importance:

✓ *He feared God;*

✓ *He accepted that his death was deserved, that it was a just outcome for his life of sin, whatever that entailed;*

✓ *He knew that Jesus was sinless – that "he has done nothing wrong", itself a clear indication that he had encountered Jesus before or had enquired about him;*

✓ *He petitioned Jesus to remember him when he came into his kingdom, so he believed Jesus to be a king, he knew about the coming kingdom of God, and*

✓ *He believed that Jesus would yet reign as king, although Jesus was then dying on a cross. So the thief also believed in resurrection.*

That was a truly remarkable confession at such a time, one that was wholly deserving of the assurance the Lord Jesus now gave him, that he would indeed be in his kingdom – *"in Paradise"*. That statement of Jesus has sometimes caused some confusion in that Jesus was in the grave for three days and nights before his resurrection, so how could the thief and Jesus be together that day? Because the word *"Paradise"* just means a garden,[3] some people think that Jesus was just saying to the thief that they would both be in a garden somewhere later that day, buried together! That really is a desperate interpretation. But what do the words really mean?

Bible translators have done an excellent job on the whole and we are really fortunate nowadays to have such a range of different versions available, even though we only need one version to understand the Bible for ourselves. Almost any of the available translations will be satisfactory if we apply a disciplined approach to our Bible reading and thinking. This, however, is one of those places where some translators have slipped up through not understanding the real importance of what Jesus said; for the punctuation they insert in the English rendering is misleading. There is no punctuation in the original Greek, so its placement is a matter of interpretation. Here's how the saying of Jesus *should* read, for it was a most solemn and binding promise:

"Truly, I say to you today, you will be with me in Paradise".

Just before he died, Moses sought to impress upon his listeners the importance of what God was doing with them and the seriousness of their calling as the people of God. Time and again be emphasized what he was saying by

---

3 *"Paradise" is a word of Persian origin which was first used to describe the parks and gardens of Persian kings. In the Greek translation of the Old Testament it was the word used for the Garden of Eden, and other such fertile places (Genesis 2:8; Nehemiah 2:8; Ecclesiastes 2:5).*

using the word *"today"*, or *"this day"*. Here's just one example, but the footnote gives many more for you to follow up:

> *"If you act corruptly by making a carved image in the form of anything, and by doing what is evil in the sight of the* LORD *your God, so as to provoke him to anger,* **I call heaven and earth to witness against you today**,[4] *that you will soon utterly perish from the land that you are going over the Jordan to possess" (Deuteronomy 4:25,26).*

Jesus was using the same sort of language when he stressed to the repentant thief that indeed it was the case *("I say to you today")* that he will be there in God's Kingdom after Jesus has raised him from the dead. There was no doubt about that whatsoever!

❖ What Jesus Taught

On two occasions the Lord Jesus spoke about the vital need of those who wanted salvation to submit to the act of baptism. One night a member of the Jewish establishment visited him and acknowledged that the miraculous works Jesus was doing showed that he came from God and was working with God. Jesus responded by challenging this learned man in these terms:

> *"'Truly, truly, I say to you,* **unless one is born again he cannot see the kingdom of God.'** *Nicodemus said to him, 'How can a man be born when he is old? Can he enter a second time into his mother's womb and be born?'* *Jesus answered,* **'Truly, truly, I say to you, unless one is born of water and the Spirit, he cannot enter the kingdom of God.** *That which is born of the flesh is flesh, and that which is born of the Spirit is spirit. Do not marvel that I said to you, "You must be born again." The wind blows where it wishes, and you hear its sound, but you do not know where it comes from or where it goes. So it is with everyone who is born of the Spirit'" (John 3:3-8).*

It was terminology that was not entirely new to Nicodemus. As a member of the Jewish Council he knew only too well that when a Gentile was being admitted into the Jewish faith he had to submit to ritual washing by immersion in water. The Rabbis said that the result was

---

[4] *Deuteronomy 4:8,39,40; 5:1,3; 6:6; 7:1; 8:11,19; 9:3; 10:13; 11:2 and lots more.*

that he emerged like a new-born babe! Now he was being told that to enter the kingdom of God everybody needed to be reborn in two ways:

↘ *There must be a rebirth by water – this means baptism by immersion, for we have already seen how Paul in Romans 6 describes the outcome as the start of a new life in Christ;*

↘ *There must be a spiritual renewal – birth of the Spirit – the transformation of a person's life from within, to accompany the outward act. We shall look at that in more detail as we advance in our study of Romans.*

Nicodemus did not abandon his position or his Jewish beliefs there and then, although he became a secret follower of Jesus and, in due course, made his position public.[5] So he was evidently impressed with the insight Jesus gave him that night.

It was the risen Christ who charged his disciples to go and baptize in these words:

"*All authority in heaven and on earth has been given to me. Go therefore and make disciples of all nations, **baptizing them in the name of the Father and of the Son and of the Holy Spirit**, teaching them to observe all that I have commanded you*" *(Matthew 28:18-20);* [6]

---

5 *See John 19:39. Nicodemus and Joseph of Arimathea were both members of the Jewish Sanhedrin (the Jews' ruling council) and they made their position clear, as followers of Jesus, after he had been crucified, by attending to his burial.*

6 *The "name of the Father and of the Son and of the Holy Spirit" is not a Trinitarian formula, for we have seen that to be unscriptural, but a reminder that this way of salvation is the result of the work of Father and Son, made possible by God's Holy Spirit power. It is always the case that the forgiveness of sins comes as a gift of God (e.g. Acts 2:38; 13:38; Ephesians 4:32; Romans 3:25 – "his divine forbearance"). There is an interesting link with Romans 1:4, where we read that God (the Father of Jesus) declared Jesus to be His Son by raising him from the dead by the exercise of His power (the Holy Spirit). Again, it is the Father and Son who are working together, and God who is empowering His Son.*

"And he said to them, 'Go into all the world and proclaim the gospel to the whole creation. ***Whoever believes and is baptized will be saved,*** *but whoever does not believe will be condemned'" (Mark 16:15,16).*

Notice the important references to *"teaching"* and *"believing"* – both things that have to come before baptism, for whenever a baptism takes place it is always preceded by teaching.

❖ "What Shall We Do?"

Within a few weeks of the death and resurrection of the Lord Jesus Christ his followers were out on the streets of Jerusalem doing what he commanded. They preached the great news that Jesus was alive, that his death had been a gracious act of God, as well as a demonstration of human wickedness, and that it was now possible to come to God through him.

The apostle Peter was one of the foremost preachers and two of his early messages can be read in summary form in Acts chapters 2 and 3. Peter explained that Jesus Christ – the promised offspring of Eve, Abraham and David – had made available the long-awaited blessing for all nations:

*"All the prophets who have spoken, from Samuel and those who came after him, also proclaimed these days. You are the sons of the prophets and of the covenant that God made with your fathers, saying to Abraham, '****And in your offspring shall all the families of the earth be blessed.****' God, having raised up his servant, sent him to you first, to bless you by turning every one of you from your wickedness" (Acts 3:24-26).*

They could be turned away from their sins, which is what they would earnestly desire if they had truly repented of their previous conduct, and could be blessed with life, instead of being under the curse of sin and death. But what must they do to be saved? That cry, in one form or another, is to be heard several times through the Acts of the Apostles. For example, when Peter had preached in Jerusalem that was what the crowd asked him:

*"Now when they heard this they were cut to the heart, and said to Peter and the rest of the apostles, '****Brothers, what shall we do?****' And Peter said to them, '****Repent and be baptized every one of you in the name of****"*

202

Jesus Christ for the forgiveness of your sins, and you will receive the gift of the Holy Spirit.[7] *For the promise is for you and for your children and for all who are far off, everyone whom the Lord our God calls to himself.' And with many other words he bore witness and continued to exhort them, saying, 'Save yourselves from this crooked generation.'* **So those who received his word were baptized,** *and there were added that day about three thousand souls" (Acts 2:37-41).*

First he instructed them about the purpose of God centred in the Lord Jesus, then he encouraged his hearers to repent and be baptized. And they were. It was a remarkable response to the teaching of Jesus, a huge encouragement to the apostles, and it is also deeply instructive for us. Believers' baptism is the only true way into the Christian church and it must be a response to a saving faith, one based on proper understanding of what the Bible teaches. We can never be good enough to gain entry into the Kingdom of God. As Jesus said to Nicodemus, we all need to be born again.

❖ Not Good Enough

There were lots of good people in New Testament times, as we count goodness, people who had made the worship of God a major preoccupation. There was Cornelius, for example, a Roman centurion who was: *"a devout man who feared God with all his household, gave alms generously to the people, and prayed continually to God"* (Acts 10:2). He needed instruction in the things of God, so Peter was sent to help him, after which he and *"all who heard the word"* were baptized (Acts 10:44-48).[8]

There was an Ethiopian, a Jewish proselyte, who was so keen on the Word of God that he was reading his Scriptures in the chariot as he made his way back home from Jerusalem. The apostle Philip further instructed him, after which the record says:

"As they were going along the road they came to some water, and the eunuch said, 'See, here is water! What

---

[7] *We have not yet looked at the Holy Spirit as a topic but Paul has a lot to say about it in Romans chapter 8, so we will look again at this at that time.*

[8] *If you answered Question 10.2 (see pages 140 and 457) you will have looked at the Cornelius incident already.*

*prevents me from being baptized?' And he commanded the chariot to stop, and **they both went down into the water**, Philip and the eunuch, and he baptized him" (Acts 8:36-38).*

There was a jailor in Philippi who once imprisoned the apostle Paul and his companion Silas only to discover that it was the best thing he had ever done! That night an earthquake occurred and the prisoners who could have escaped chose not to. That so impressed the jailor that he:

*"Called for lights and rushed in, and trembling with fear he fell down before Paul and Silas. Then he brought them out and said, **'Sirs, what must I do to be saved?'** And they said, **'Believe in the Lord Jesus**, and you will be saved, you and your household.' And they spoke the word of the Lord to him and to all who were in his house. And he took them the same hour of the night and washed their wounds; **and he was baptized at once, he and all his family**. Then he brought them up into his house and set food before them. And he rejoiced along with his entire household that he had believed in God" (Acts 16:29-34).*

His household would have consisted of slaves and servants as well as members of his family. The inspired writer Luke paints a very happy picture of a company of adults being taught *"the word of the Lord"* and then being baptized. When Paul left Philippi he left at least one household of believers behind.

❖ Saul the Pharisee

One man's conversion is so important to the development of First Century Christianity that it appears three times in the Acts account. He was a good man, according to his understanding. Much later he catalogued his spiritual credentials and reckoned that he had unrivalled qualifications as a conscientious servant of God.[9] It looks as if he had a very promising career before him as an influential Jew in Jerusalem. But he discovered on the road to Damascus that he was by no means good enough for God. Mistakenly

---

[9] *"Circumcised on the eighth day, of the people of Israel, of the tribe of Benjamin, a Hebrew of Hebrews; as to the law, a Pharisee; as to zeal, a persecutor of the church; as to righteousness, under the law blameless" (Philippians 3:5,6).*

he was persecuting the followers of the Lord Jesus, believing them to be blasphemers. Then he encountered the risen Christ:

> *"Suddenly a light from heaven flashed around him. And falling to the ground he heard a voice saying to him, 'Saul, Saul, why are you persecuting me?' And he said, 'Who are you, Lord?' And he said, 'I am Jesus, whom you are persecuting. But rise and enter the city, and you will be told what you are to do'"* (Acts 9:3-6).

He discovered in the most dramatic fashion that his beliefs were utterly mistaken and that he was in fact working against God, not working for Him. He was persecuting the followers of God's Son! What a mistake to make. And what a complete turnaround was needed if he was to please God. Turn around he most certainly did. Saul the Pharisee became Paul the apostle – one of the most ardent and dedicated followers of the Lord Jesus. And his understanding increased in leaps and bounds, as we have seen from our study of his Letter to the Romans. But a change of belief was not enough, even for a man as gifted and knowledgeable as the apostle. The immediate follow-up to his experience near Damascus was that he asked:

> *"I said, **'What shall I do, Lord?'** And the Lord said to me, 'Rise, and go into Damascus, and **there you will be told all that is appointed for you to do'** ".*

The answer was not long coming, for God sent a believer named Ananias to see him, who said:

> *"The God of our fathers appointed you to know his will, to see the Righteous One and to hear a voice from his mouth; for you will be a witness for him to everyone of what you have seen and heard. And now why do you wait? **Rise and be baptized and wash away your sins, calling on his name"** (Acts 22:10-16).*

It was the same for Paul as it is for each one of us; there is no alternative if we want to enter the kingdom of God. Repentance, Belief and Baptism are the three key requirements for every believer. Without the first two the third is not acceptable to God. There is an incident recorded in the Book of Acts of several people who had been baptized by John the Baptist, perhaps at an early stage in his ministry. It is clear from the record that their knowledge of the gospel was partial – they knew nothing about the Holy Spirit for example.

They were further instructed in the gospel and were baptized again (see Acts 19:1-7). That incident shows that sometimes, if the understanding is inadequate at baptism, a believer should be baptized again, this time with a proper belief. But usually someone should only be baptized once, for to repeat this symbolic death with Christ would make it look as though he needed to die over and over again, and that most certainly is not required. Jesus died *"once for all".*[10]

❖ Consistent New Testament Teaching

It is quite understandable, given his dramatic turnaround from Judaism to Christianity, that the apostle Paul should see baptism as an absolute essential. For him it was the way – the only way – in which his sins could be washed away and his failings be blotted out.[11] But it is not just a removing of sin; it is a conferring of something hugely important. Baptism gives us entry into the family of God.

Paul explains this by first reviewing the fact that without the way of salvation, now opened up by the Father, we would all be prisoners of sin and death. Then he shows how two keys open that prison door to give us release and, marvellously, we are liberated to become children of God and heirs of His gracious promises – all because of belief and baptism:

> *"The Scripture imprisoned everything under sin, so that the promise by faith in Jesus Christ might be given to those who believe. Now before faith came, we were held captive under the law, imprisoned until the coming faith would be revealed. So then, the law was our guardian until Christ came, in order that we might be justified by faith. But now that faith has come, we are no longer under a guardian, for in Christ Jesus you are all sons of God, through faith. For as many of you as were baptized into Christ have put on Christ. There is neither Jew nor Greek, there is neither slave nor free, there*

---

10 *See Hebrews 6:4-6.*

11 *The language of 'washing away our sins' is used in Acts 22:16, 1 Corinthians 6:11, Hebrews 10:22 and Colossians 2, verses 12-14, where Paul again describes baptism as 'burial in water' and then says it is effective for blotting out the record of our debt.*

*is neither male nor female, for you are all one in Christ Jesus. **And if you are Christ's, then you are Abraham's offspring, heirs according to promise"** (Galatians 3:22-29).*

This is the passage in Galatians that we looked at earlier,[12] when we followed Paul's reasoning that Abraham was promised one special offspring, not many, and that the Lord Jesus Christ was that promised descendant (Galatians 3:16). His complete argument is that the Israelites were given a law by which to live, but the people were unable to keep it. Instead of giving them a chance to serve God by demonstrating their obedience, that law imprisoned them. It showed them every day that they were failures before God and made them increasingly dependent upon His mercy and grace. Unless He forgave them, they had no hope of becoming right with him. But, says the apostle, there was still hope because of the promises God had made to Abraham which came before the law given through Moses – more than 400 years before. And it was a designed strategy.

God wanted His people to realise their dependence upon Him and their need of His forgiveness which He was willing to give, provided they came to Him in the way He had prescribed. That way required (a) a saving faith and (b) baptism into Christ – these are the things *we* have to do, which we have encountered time and time again as we have been getting to understand the Bible. But now Paul adds a further thought, which has to do with what we *get*. It's an idea we haven't come across before:

*"And if you are Christ's, **then you are Abraham's offspring, heirs according to promise"** (Galatians 3:29).*

Do you remember that Abraham was promised many offspring – as many as the stars of heaven in number? They would be a heavenly or a spiritual family descended from him. By faith and baptism we can become part of that number, members of the family of God and spiritual descendants of Abraham. He will become our spiritual father:

*"That is why it depends on faith, in order that the promise may rest on grace and be guaranteed to **all his off-***

---

[12] *Chapter 11 page 149.*

spring – *not only to the adherent of the law but also to* **the one who shares the faith of Abraham, who is the father of us all, as it is written, 'I have made you the father of many nations'"** *(Romans 4:16,17).*

So Christian baptism – believer's baptism – is the way in which we become heirs of the promises of God, related to the faithful of old who also lived by faith; and we are united with the Lord Jesus, both in his death and in his resurrection. It is the way to start a new life now, and it leads to eternal life in the kingdom of God.

Things to Read

📖 Read Acts chapter 9 to find out about the conversion of Saul the Pharisee. As he became Paul the apostle, the writer of the Letter to the Romans, it will give you a good insight into the transformation that came about.

📖 Galatians chapter 3 ends by explaining that baptism makes us heirs with Abraham through the Lord Jesus Christ. The whole chapter is well worth reading as it shows the big difference between the Law of Moses and the promises of God, which had already been given to Abraham.

Questions to Think About

14.1 What does the apostle Peter say about baptism in 1 Peter 3:18-22? How important does he reckon baptism to be?

14.2 Can you find any Bible examples of infants being baptized or christened? What does that teach us? At what age should we be baptized? Why do you think this is so?

15

What happens after Baptism?

Baptism changes our relationship with God because it unites us with Him. Through our union with Jesus Christ, our position in His sight is totally changed. Without a relationship with God we are lost. With it we are found!

The apostle Paul, writing to the believers in Ephesus, started by telling them how different their life had been before they accepted the gospel of salvation, before they believed and were baptized. To see the full force of his argument it's a good thing to tabulate the two states, so you can see the difference side-by-side. You can do this exercise for yourself by reading Ephesians chapter 2 and identifying the two descriptions, then comparing your findings with this:

Before you found Christ	After you accepted the gospel
"You were dead in the trespasses and sins in which you once walked, following the course of this world, following the prince of the power of the air, the spirit that is now at work in the sons of disobedience – among whom we all once lived in the passions of our flesh, carrying out the desires of the body and the mind, and were by nature children of wrath, like the rest of mankind" (Ephesians 2:1-3) [1]	*"God ... made us alive together with Christ – by grace you have been saved – and raised us up with him and seated us with him in the heavenly places in Christ Jesus, so that in the coming ages he might show the immeasurable riches of his grace in kindness toward us in Christ Jesus. For by grace you have been saved through faith. And this is not your own doing; it is the gift of God" (2:4-8)*

[1] *We will look at what the Bible says about the way we are tempted later – by things which are both internal and external. For the moment, note that the apostle puts two thoughts together and that the second explains the first. He says that by nature we followed "the prince of the power of the air", and then he explains what that means when he says it was "the spirit that is now at work in the sons of disobedience".*

209

Before you found Christ	After you accepted the gospel
"You were at that time separated from Christ, alienated from the commonwealth of Israel and strangers to the covenants of promise, having no hope and without God in the world" (2:12)	*"You are no longer strangers and aliens, but you are fellow citizens with the saints and members of the household of God, built on the foundation of the apostles and prophets, Christ Jesus himself being the cornerstone, in whom the whole structure, being joined together, grows into a holy temple in the Lord. In him you also are being built together into a dwelling place for God by the Spirit" (2:19-21)* [2]

This shows how great the difference is between someone who is baptized and someone who is not. Without belief and baptism, which result in God's gracious forgiveness of our sins, we are cut off from all aspects of His purpose. However religious we are and however well behaved, being good is never good enough. There is only one way of salvation.

But what about any change within us? Does anything happen to the way we feel, and how does this fit in with the birth of the Spirit, that Jesus spoke about to Nicodemus? [3] That is what the apostle Paul now writes about in his Letter to the Romans – which we are using as our guide to the gospel of salvation.

❖ You are Dead – So Die!

Chapter 6 of Romans is all about the way we should live after baptism. As we have seen, baptism is a burial in water, an association with both the death and the resurrection of the Lord Jesus. In symbol we end our old life – life

---

[2] *Here's another interesting comparison which will help us in understanding what is meant by life in the Spirit. Once we followed the "spirit that is now at work in the sons of disobedience" (which means that we lived just as we pleased without any thought for the law of God and what was required of us), but after baptism we have a different spirit – God's spirit.*

[3] *See Chapter 14 pages 200-201.*

"in Adam" – and begin a new life – life *"in Christ"*. There are two quite separate aspects to this change that must take place: one that takes place now, and one that will take place at the return of Jesus to earth. It's important to understand these two phases:

1. Living *"in Christ"* means that we must be spiritually renewed. That was mentioned in chapter 14. What Paul now explains is that this change does not happen automatically. We do not come out of the waters of baptism as different people with another nature, one which is entirely free from sin. We have to be born again, and we have to live differently.

2. If we begin a new life in Christ at our baptism – if we are spiritually born again – then we will be completely changed one day, by God's power, when we are made like the Lord Jesus Christ.[4] At the second coming of Christ those who are found acceptable will be changed to have an immortal and sinless nature. We will then be reborn by God's Holy Spirit power and will have a spiritual body.[5] Here's the apostle Paul in another of his letters:

> *"Behold! I tell you a mystery. We shall not all sleep, but **we shall all be changed, in a moment, in the twinkling of an eye, at the last trumpet**. For the trumpet will sound, and the dead will be raised imperishable, and we shall be changed. **For this perishable body must put on the imperishable, and this mortal body must put on immortality**" (1 Corinthians 15:51-53).*

When that change takes place those privileged to enter the kingdom of God will have been reborn in two ways – by water (through their baptism) and by the Spirit (when their bodies are made immortal by God's power). But what happens in the meantime?

❖ Challenged to Live

What the apostle Paul concentrates upon in Romans chapters 6 to 8 is the challenge that faces us when we have been baptized into Christ. That is why we are now looking

---

[4] *Chapter 13 was all about that.*

[5] *Paul talks about a "spiritual body" in 1 Corinthians 15, verses 42-49.*

at those three chapters together. In them Paul explores the change that must take place in the baptized believer's life. It is clear that baptism is an important step for everyone but, from what Paul now says, we can see what an absolutely vital one it is if we want to become part of God's eternal purpose by:

✓ *joining His family,*

✓ *becoming part of Abraham's spiritual offspring, and*

✓ *sharing the inheritance that God gives to all His children.*

Here's the recurring theme. *'If you have died in symbol in the waters of baptism'*, says the apostle, *'make sure that you consider yourself dead to sin in all its tempting guises'.* Or, in the inspired words of the record in Romans chapter 6:

> "One who has died has been set free from sin. Now if we have died with Christ, we believe that we will also live with him. We know that Christ being raised from the dead will never die again; death no longer has dominion over him. For the death he died he died to sin, once for all, but the life he lives he lives to God. **So you also must consider yourselves dead to sin and alive to God in Christ Jesus**" (6:7-11);

> "**Let not sin therefore reign in your mortal bodies, to make you obey their passions.** Do not present your members to sin as instruments for unrighteousness, but **present yourselves to God as those who have been brought from death to life, and your members to God as instruments for righteousness**" (6:12-13);

> "I am speaking in human terms, because of your natural limitations. For just as you once presented your members as slaves to impurity and to lawlessness leading to more lawlessness, so now **present your members as slaves to righteousness leading to sanctification**" (6:19);

> "Now that you have been set free from sin and have **become slaves of God**, the fruit you get leads to sanctification and its end, eternal life" (6:22).

212

Paul is dealing here with the change that has to take place inside the baptized believer. Baptism is the outward act when we make public our desire to change the way we live, when we resolve that we want to live with the Lord Jesus Christ, as a member of the family of God. We all have to work with God and the Lord Jesus to make that change happen inside. Paul's words are all about the inner transformation that must take place if we are to make our baptism meaningful all through our lives.

It would be a strange thing indeed if all we had to do to become God's children was to work out what to believe, say that we believed it, be immersed in water, but then carry on living just as we had before – regardless of God and Jesus. That would be like someone who was taught to drive, learning the rules that apply to all road users, passing a driving test and then driving regardless of everyone else and oblivious of the highway code. Some people do live like that; but not necessarily for very long!

❖ Picture Language

There were no cars or driving tests in the time of the apostle. So, to help us understand just what has to change inside our minds, the apostle uses three different examples to describe what the change feels like, things that we can all relate to. We have seen one of these pictures already when he described the change that must take place as though we had become God's obedient slaves.

❖ *Slaves (6:14-23)*

In the ancient world a slave was owned by his master. He had no time off for himself and no rights of his own; he was his master's property. Notice however that Paul does not say that God has acquired us and *made* us His own; he urges us to *give* ourselves to God – to become His slaves. He wants us to surrender our liberty in God's service. Just as Jesus was God's servant, so the apostle urges us to give our time, energy, talent and all that we have in the service of the One who has purchased us for Himself. We can serve God by devoting ourselves to those things that have to do with righteousness and holiness.

That's a powerful thought but also a very demanding one, so the apostle tempers it by using two other pictures in the next two chapters.

❖ *Marriage (7:1-6)*

We may not be able to identify with Roman slaves, unless we take the trouble to find something out about them, but we can readily understand Paul's next point of comparison. Before baptism, he explains, we are like people who are very unhappily married, to a companion that is making life so miserable that we just want to die. Now, he says, that is just what happens in baptism – we die to the old relationship and are free to marry again, this time in a happy and fulfilling relationship:

> "Likewise, my brothers, you also have died to the law through the body of Christ, **so that you may belong to another,** to him who has been raised from the dead, in order that we may bear fruit for God. For while we were living in the flesh, our sinful passions, aroused by the law, were at work in our members to bear fruit for death. But now we are released from the law, having died to that which held us captive, so that we serve not under the old written code but in the new life of the Spirit" (Romans 7:4-6).

This change of partners would have had a special meaning to any Jewish readers who had been living with God under an Old Covenant relationship, trying to keep the Law of Moses. But it is also true for us all who were under "the law of sin and death", as Paul describes the ruling principle by which we all live and die 'in the flesh' (Romans 8:8).

The helpful thing about this picture of a new relationship in Christ is that we can all understand how readily someone would want to make the change from an unhappy existence into a new life with a loving and caring partner. People change when they get married and learn to live together; that's what makes marriage such an exciting and enjoyable experience. But they change because they want to please their partner and because they learn together how best to live in a way which shows their love for one another. The change is not something they have to do; it's something they *want* to do, because of love.

That's how it is with baptism. We do change after we have accepted the Lord Jesus Christ as our partner for life. The idea that we are married to him is an idea the apostle uses again (Ephesians 5:22-33) and it is a Bible-long theme that those who establish a relationship with God are as though they were married to Him.[6] It makes this new relationship sound wonderfully close to both Father and Son, when we seek to live *"in the new life of the Spirit"* (7:6).

❖ *God's Children (8:14-29)*

The third picture Paul uses is one we have all experienced because we are all somebody's children. He uses the idea of the family to help us realise that when we are baptized into Christ we become God's children, members of his family and brothers and sisters in Christ. God has begotten only one Son, the Lord Jesus Christ, but in association with him through baptism we are adopted into the same family:

> *"So then, brothers, we are debtors, not to the flesh, to live according to the flesh. For if you live according to the flesh you will die, but if by the Spirit you put to death the deeds of the body, you will live.* **For all who are led by the Spirit of God are sons of God.** *For you did not receive the spirit of slavery to fall back into fear, but* **you have received the Spirit of adoption as sons, by whom we cry, 'Abba! Father!' The Spirit himself bears witness with our spirit that we are children of God, and if children, then heirs** – *heirs of God and fellow heirs with Christ, provided we suffer with him in order that we may also be glorified with him"* (8:12-17).

Notice that here Paul takes the trouble to mention that we should not think of ourselves as slaves who have been bought by a Master. If our minds are properly attuned to what God is doing with us and in us, we will realise that God has adopted us as His children. We too become His sons and daughters. By saying that we can address God as *"Abba! Father"*, the apostle tells us just how special this new relationship really is, for the language is that which a child would use when speaking to his or her father. A modern equivalent would be "Daddy"; it's that close a relationship that is on offer.

❖ **"Led by the Spirit of God"**

We haven't yet looked at what the Bible means by the Spirit of God, or the Holy Spirit as it is sometimes described. We

---

[6] *For the idea of the nation of Israel being 'married' to God see, for example, Isaiah 54:5.*

have reached that point in the Letter to the Romans where Paul begins to talk a lot about it, so we need to begin to think about what it means.[7] So far in the letter Paul has only made three references to the Spirit, as follows:

1 *"... his Son, who was descended from David according to the flesh and was declared to be the Son of God in power according to **the Spirit of holiness** by his resurrection from the dead, Jesus Christ our Lord" (Romans 1:3,4);*

2 *"God is my witness, whom **I serve with my spirit** in the gospel of his Son" (1:9);*

3 *"A Jew is one inwardly, and circumcision is a matter of the heart, **by the Spirit, not by the letter**. His praise is not from man but from God" (2:29).*

These three references give us a helpful starting-off point, because the word translated *"spirit"* in both Old and New Testaments has a range of different meanings. Sometimes it relates to us and sometimes to God or to the Lord Jesus. We'll take them one at a time:

✓ *Romans 1:3,4*

God raised the Lord Jesus from the dead by using His power and might. That is made very clear in a series of verses you might want to look up.[8]

As in many other places in Scripture, the Holy Spirit is declared to be the power of God in action – you could say it describes "God at work". But you will notice that Paul called it the *"Spirit of holiness"* in Romans 1:4, not only because God is holy and this is His power, but because the power of God was being specially directed to achieve holiness. God raised His Son from the dead so that His great plan of salvation would be made available to mankind, who could thereby become holy and right-

---

[7] *The next chapter will explore the subject by looking right across Scripture to get a fuller picture about God's Holy Spirit.*

[8] *Acts 2:24,32; 3:15; 4:10-12; 5:30-32; 13:33-35; 17:31; 2Corinthians 13:4; Ephesians 1:19-23.. One of the most helpful verses is: "He was crucified in weakness, but lives by the power of God. For we also are weak in him, but in dealing with you we will live with him by the power of God" (2 Corinthians 13:4).*

216

eous in His sight.

✓ *Romans 1:9*

When Paul said that he serves God with *"my spirit"*, he meant that he was using *his* mind and all *his* faculties – what you could call *"the inner man"* – to do the best he could for God. He was not just using his body in service but everything he possessed. The Bible talks a lot about the spirit of man, both to describe the life-force we have, which comes from God, and the way our mind and affections operate, for good or ill.

✓ *Romans 2:29*

We have not yet looked at the special role of the Jew in the purpose of God, except to note that Abraham's offspring were to be a special nation. Here Paul is saying that what makes someone special in the sight of God is not what has been done to him outwardly but what happens to him or her inside.[9] In the same way, it was not the outward code of laws given by God which was meant to make the Jews special. It was their response to that law which would have changed their thinking first and then their doing. Here *"the Spirit"* means that inward change that God wants to achieve in the hearts and minds of His people. It is something to be achieved by a change in the way we think and feel.

❖ The Inner Man

Chapters 7 and 8 of Romans are all about the fundamental change that needs to take place within a baptized believer. God wants us to be holy within and then to live in a way which *shows* the change that has come about inside our hearts and minds. That can't happen overnight; it is a process that takes a while to achieve and with which we need God's help. Paul says that his life after baptism start-

---

[9] *Circumcision is an act which requires a small piece of flesh to be cut off. It was designed by God as one way that would mark out the Jews as different from other nations. The act had an important lesson to teach about the need to cut off fleshly thoughts and desires, but Israel concentrated instead on the physical distinction and sneered at those who were 'the uncircumcised' heathen.*

ed with quite a struggle inside himself. It was as though he was at war inside!

Romans chapter 7 describes this struggle. Nothing worthwhile is ever achieved without effort and our nature, inherited from Adam, is not inclined towards God, but is in opposition to His will. Mankind has become so accustomed to having its own way that changing direction takes some doing. This is how Paul described the change then taking place in his own life:

> "We know that the law is spiritual, but I am of the flesh, sold under sin. I do not understand my own actions. For I do not do what I want, but I do the very thing I hate. Now if I do what I do not want, I agree with the law, that it is good. So now it is no longer I who do it, but **sin that dwells within me**. For I know that **nothing good dwells in me, that is, in my flesh**. For I have the desire to do what is right, but not the ability to carry it out. For I do not do the good I want, but the evil I do not want is what I keep on doing. Now if I do what I do not want, it is no longer I who do it, but sin that dwells within me. So I find it to be a law that when I want to do right, evil lies close at hand. **For I delight in the law of God, in my inner being, but I see in my members another law waging war against the law of my mind and making me captive to the law of sin that dwells in my members**. Wretched man that I am! Who will deliver me from this body of death?" (Romans 7:14-24).

This is another of those fact-filled passages that requires some careful analysis and you may be surprised by what you discover.

Paul describes his nature in several different ways:

✓ "of the flesh, sold under sin"
✓ "sin that dwells within me"
✓ "nothing good dwells in me, that is, in my flesh"
✓ "sin that dwells within me"
✓ "the law of sin that dwells in my members"
✓ "this body of death." [10]

---

[10] *Notice that the real enemy against which Paul is struggling is his nature. The struggle comes from inside him, not from outside.*

❯ He sees another principle at work, however, which he describes as *"the law of my mind"*. His own desire is to do God's will; to do what is right, to do good, to obey the law of God.

❯ The apostle asks for deliverance from this wretched state.

❯ Nowhere does the apostle talk about the Devil or Satan as the problem he has to overcome. Indeed, there is no reference to the Devil at all in the Letter to the Romans, and only one mention of Satan, which we have already considered.[11] The problem of sin is deep-rooted in the human condition.[12]

❖ Holiness Within

Paul is not left in the wretched state he has just described and neither is any baptized believer. God has a plan and purpose which achieves what it sets out to accomplish. He wants people to be like the Lord Jesus Christ, and that means being holy and without fault in His presence. It's not going to be an overnight transformation because becoming holy takes time and ultimately it requires a change of nature. For look at the end result: God *"is able to keep you from stumbling and to present you blameless before the presence of his glory with great joy" (Jude 1:24).*

How can it be done? How does the process of achieving holiness change the way we think, feel and behave? That is what the apostle now explains in Romans chapter 8.

The transformation starts with forgiveness and with our realisation that once we have been baptized, and have a saving faith by which we live, the sacrifice of Christ releases us from the power of sin.[13] This is a terrific thing to realise and appreciate. It means that instead of being condemned criminals in the sight of God, we are forgiven sinners who have a living and abiding relationship with Him. This realisation leads to a remarkable change of mind as, over time, we come to understand more and more about

---

[11] *Chapter 12, page 163.*

[12] *As we shall see in Chapter 24 of this book, the Devil and Satan are terms that describe, in pictorial language, all forms of opposition to God. But the real problem is Sin.*

[13] *We looked at Romans 8:3 in Chapter 13, pages 181-182.*

God's purpose and the great love that God and Jesus have towards us. The outcome is a growing confidence that the God who has begun to work with us will continue until He has completed that work.[14]

These are some of the comments the apostle made as he pondered the change that he knew was taking place in him, and you can still hear the wonder and amazement he felt as he contemplated it:

> *"There is therefore now **no condemnation** for those who are in Christ Jesus. For the law of the Spirit of life has **set you free** in Christ Jesus from the law of sin and death"* *(8:1,2);*

> *"For those who live according to the flesh set their minds on the things of the flesh, but **those who live according to the Spirit set their minds on the things of the Spirit.** To set the mind on the flesh is death, but to set the mind on the Spirit is life and peace"* *(8:5,6);*

> *"Anyone who does not have the Spirit of Christ does not belong to him. But **if Christ is in you**, although the body is dead because of sin, **the Spirit is life because of righteousness**. If the Spirit of him who raised Jesus from the dead dwells in you, he who raised Christ Jesus from the dead will also give life to your mortal bodies through his Spirit who dwells in you"* *(8:9-11);*

> *"And we know that **for those who love God all things work together for good,** for those who are called according to his purpose"* *(8:28);*

> *"If God is for us, who can be against us? He who did not spare his own Son but gave him up for us all, how will he not also with him graciously give us all things? Who shall bring any charge against God's elect? It is God who justifies. Who is to condemn? **Christ Jesus is the one who died – more than that, who was raised – who is at the right hand of God, who indeed is interceding for***

---

[14] *Much as we would all like to become perfect overnight, it does take time. The apostle James encourages us to stick to the things we believe, even when life is tough, by saying: "The testing of your faith produces steadfastness. And let steadfastness have its full effect, that you may be perfect and complete, lacking in nothing" (James 1:3).*

*us. Who shall separate us from the love of Christ? Shall tribulation, or distress, or persecution, or famine, or nakedness, or danger, or sword? … No, in all these things we are more than conquerors through him who loved us. For I am sure that neither death nor life, nor angels nor rulers, nor things present nor things to come, nor powers, nor height nor depth, **nor anything else in all creation, will be able to separate us from the love of God in Christ Jesus our Lord"** (8:31-39).*

❖ Living "according to the Spirit"

These are extracts from the chapter and you may want to read all of what Paul said, although we will be looking at some other parts later. We noted earlier that the apostle referred to the Spirit just three times in the early chapters. His use of that term now increases dramatically and he uses it in a lot of different ways. His theme is the change that comes about within the believer as a result of a saving faith and baptism into the name of Jesus. Previously he has explained how we can be baptized *"into Christ"*, now he wants to tell us how Christ can be formed in us – how we can start to live the way he did.

Here are the different terms Paul uses when describing what the believer's new life is like:

✓ **"in Christ Jesus"** *(8:1,2)*
✓ *"the law of the Spirit of life" (8:2)*
✓ *"walk ... according to the Spirit" (8:4)*
✓ *"the Spirit" (8:5)*
✓ *"set the mind on the Spirit" (8:6)*
✓ *"in the Spirit" (8:9)*
✓ *"the Spirit of God dwells in you" (8:9,14)*
✓ *"the Spirit of Christ" (8:9)*
✓ **"Christ in you"** *(8:10)*
✓ *"the Spirit of him who raised Jesus from the dead" (8:11)*
✓ *"by the Spirit" (8:13)*
✓ not *"the spirit of slavery" (8:15)* but *"the Spirit of adopt -ion" (8:15)*
✓ *"our spirit" (8:16)*
✓ *"the firstfruits of the Spirit" (8:23)*
✓ *"the mind of the Spirit" (8:27)*
✓ *"the Spirit intercedes" (8:27)*
✓ *"the Holy Spirit" (9:1)*

At first glance this might appear a confusing selection of different terms, but we have learned how helpful it can be to analyse our findings and thus understand them better. Stand back from the detail and ask yourself what it is that Paul is writing about. He is writing about *the new life in Christ*. His theme is: What does it feel like inside when a person has been baptized into Christ and has changed his or her relationship with God?

❖ Being Spiritually Minded

We have seen that the first reaction is to wonder how to overcome temptation and how to be successful living as a Christian. 'Not by personal achievement' the apostle concludes (in chapter 7); it will result in despair if we try to 'go it alone'. We have to become spiritually minded:

> *"Walk not according to the flesh but according to the Spirit. For those who live according to the flesh set their* **minds** *on the things of the flesh, but those who live according to the Spirit set their* **minds** *on the things of the Spirit. To set the* **mind** *on the flesh is death, but to set the* **mind** *on the Spirit is life and peace. For the* **mind** *that is set on the flesh is hostile to God, for it does not submit to God's law; indeed, it cannot. Those who are in the flesh cannot please God" (Romans 8:4-8).*

The things we think about are crucial in our journey to God's kingdom. We have to turn from the things that naturally attract us and develop new appetites and desires for the things that please God. We are *"in Christ"* because we have been baptized; now we want Christ *"in us."* Note those two different phrases in the above list, which have been picked out in bold type.

So how do we achieve that? By being *"born of the Spirit"* – spiritual rebirth, that's how! The *"law of the Spirit of life"* (8:3) is the gospel and when we understand and believe the gospel we begin to *"walk according to the Spirit"*, *"set our minds on the Spirit"*, let the *"Spirit of God dwell in us"*.

The gospel is *"the power of God for salvation to everyone who believes"* (Romans 1:20) and when that power begins to work in someone's mind it begins to change their understanding and to alter the direction their lives take. Paul said that they had *"become obedient from the heart to the standard of teaching to which you were committed"* (6:17). This means that the gospel must start to change the way

222

we feel about things as well. Baptism cleanses the conscience and purifies our innermost feelings and desires. It starts the process of making our life a fit dwelling place for God and the Lord Jesus Christ.[15]

❖ God at Work

Letting Scripture interpret Scripture, as we have learned to do, we find the same apostle explaining the same things when writing to the believers in Ephesus, a city in the Roman province of Asia Minor. He assured them that they would not have to live as Christians by themselves, without any help from God, but that the Father would continue to work with them to achieve their salvation. This is what he said:

> *"I do not cease to give thanks for you, remembering you in my prayers, that the God of our Lord Jesus Christ, the Father of glory, may give you **a spirit of wisdom and of revelation in the knowledge of him**, having the eyes of your hearts **enlightened**, that you may know what is the **hope** to which he has called you, what are the riches of his glorious inheritance in the saints, and what is the immeasurable greatness of his power toward us who believe, according to the working of his great might that he worked in Christ when he raised him from the dead and seated him at his right hand in the heavenly places"* (Ephesians 1:16-20).

The key idea here for us is that God will help us to overcome through wisdom and knowledge. He has given us His Word so that we can be enlightened, and can increasingly understand the hope that we have been given. God will work together with us on this joint enterprise and we will be companying with the Lord Jesus Christ as we tread the path to God's Kingdom. We have our part to do, but we are not without help and our helper wields all the power that is necessary to bring us to salvation. This power is the same power that first achieved the salvation and exaltation of the Lord Jesus – the power of resurrection: the power of God directed to achieve holiness.

> *"Therefore, my beloved, as you have always obeyed, so now, not only as in my presence but much more in my*

---

absence, **work out your own salvation with fear and trembling, for it is God who works in you, both to will and to work for his good pleasure**" *(Philippians 2:12,13).*

This work of God will reach its final phase when, at the coming of Jesus, the power of God will be openly revealed and the mortal bodies of baptized believers will be changed to spiritual bodies, like that of the Lord Jesus Christ. In the same letter to the Philippians, the apostle considers that time:

"We await a Saviour, the Lord Jesus Christ, who will transform our lowly body to be like his glorious body, **by the power that enables him even to subject all things to himself**" *(3:20,21).*

All this is what the apostle is writing about in Romans chapter 8, including that transformation which he there calls *"the revealing of the sons of God"* and *"the redemption of our bodies"* (8:19,23). We will return to that subject in a later chapter, but first we need to look a little more at the subject of God's Holy Spirit, and the way it works in other ways as well.

Things to Read

📖 As we have been thinking about Romans chapter 8, and will be returning to it later, reading that chapter, or reading it again, should be really helpful.

📖 If you didn't read Ephesians chapter 2 at the start of this chapter, read it now, and notice the careful comparison the apostle makes between how things were without Christ and how they can be once we accept him as our Lord and Saviour.

Questions to think About

15.1 What does Paul mean in Romans chapter 8 when he contrasts living *"in the flesh"* with living *"in the Spirit"*? (8:1-11)

15.2 What did Jesus mean when he told Nicodemus (in John chapter 3) that he must be *"born again"*? Was he referring to baptism or to something else as well?

16
Who or what is the Holy Spirit?

The apostle Paul says a lot in his letter to the Romans about the Spirit and it is always helpful to compare one part of the Scriptures with another. So if we look a little further afield we will get an even clearer view of what the Holy Spirit is and does.

Nowadays some people talk a lot about the Spirit, sometimes saying that unless you have been "baptized in the Spirit", or have "Spirit Gifts", like the ability to speak in tongues or powers of healing, you are not a real Christian. But is that sort of talk right?

❖ Let the Bible Speak!

One of our key principles has been to let the Bible instruct us and we are not going to abandon that approach now. Even so, you might be surprised by what we are about to discover. How many times do you think we read about the Holy Spirit in the Old Testament? The really surprising thing is that there are only *three* such occurrences and here they are:

1   *"Cast me not away from your presence, and take not your **Holy Spirit** from me" (Psalm 51:11);*

2, 3   *"In all their affliction he was afflicted, and the angel of his presence saved them; in his love and in his pity he redeemed them; he lifted them up and carried them all the days of old. But they rebelled and grieved his **Holy Spirit**; therefore he turned to be their enemy, and himself fought against them. Then he remembered the days of old, of Moses and his people. Where is he who brought them up out of the sea with the shepherds of his flock? Where is he who put in the midst of them his **Holy Spirit**, who caused his glorious arm to go at the right hand of Moses? ..." (Isaiah 63:9-12).*

225

❖ What does it mean?

The very first occurrence, in Psalm 51, is part of a prayer by King David in which he wholeheartedly repents of what he had done: first taking someone else's wife as his own and then arranging for her husband's murder! In that psalm, which was later set to music and used as part of the temple worship, the king deeply repents of the wrong he has done. He had been so close to God and much in His favour, including being a prophet through whom God spoke.[1] He very much wanted to be forgiven, to have his fellowship with God restored, and to have that previous relationship restored, including being God's prophet once again.

We can see this more clearly if we look at the accompanying verses. It is always best to look at a passage in its setting, or context, to get the right meaning. Pulling out a verse here or there can lead to misunderstanding. So here is David's full request to God:

*"Create in me a clean heart, O God, and **renew a right spirit within me**. Cast me not away from your presence, and **take not your Holy Spirit from me**. Restore to me the joy of your salvation, and **uphold me with a willing spirit"** (Psalm 51:10-12).*

This is really helpful in understanding about the Spirit, because it shows us that the word has a wide range of meaning. David is asking:

1   That God will cleanse him of his sin and purge his conscience – for as an adulterer and murderer he could have had no peace of mind and must have felt alienated from God. He calls that having *"a right spirit"*; we might say that *he wanted to be right with God again* in the way he both thought and felt;

2   As we anticipated, David wanted *to continue as one of God's prophets* and be empowered by that Holy Spirit

---

[1] *At the end of his life David says this about the privilege of being God's spokesperson: "The Spirit of the Lord speaks by me; his word is on my tongue. The God of Israel has spoken; the Rock of Israel has said to me ..." (2 Samuel 23:2,3). And the New Testament also recognises David's inspired words as Scripture, "... which the Holy Spirit spoke beforehand by the mouth of David" (Acts 1:16).*

that enabled men and women to be God's spokes-
persons; 2

3   David wanted more than just to feel right with God and
     become his spokesman again; he wanted God to help
     him recapture that positive delight in doing His will that
     he had earlier enjoyed – *he wanted to be a willing ser-*
     vant who rejoiced in God's salvation, not just someone
     who was afraid to step out of line for fear of the conse-
     quences.

But why does King David call the ability God had given
him to speak as a prophet God's *Holy* Spirit, when that
term had never been used before and David would never
use it again? 3 It was because he had come to realise how
sinful he was and how holy God is. So he was praying that
a *holy* God would still continue to use him as part of His
great purpose, and God responded graciously to that prayer
and continued to be close to David all through the rest of
his life – despite the two great sins he had committed.

So when David called God's Spirit his *"Holy Spirit"*, he
was thinking about God's power being directed to achieve
holiness. He wasn't holy: he knew that he was a sinner.
But he recognised that God is holy and that everything He
does will be holy and eventually leads to holiness.

❖ What about Isaiah?

The prophet Isaiah was not concerned directly about his
own sinfulness but about the sinfulness of God's people
Israel, both in the past and in the present. The work that
God had given him to do as a prophet involved trying to get
the people among whom he lived to change their ways and
want to be holy, like God.

In the verses we looked at (Isaiah 63:9-12), the prophet
is reviewing Israel's history right back at the time when
they came out of Egypt, as recorded in the Book of Exodus.
His theme is the wonderful mercy of God which He shows
regardless of human response. He had rescued Israel even

---

2 *"For no prophecy was ever produced by the will of man, but men spoke*
from God as they were carried along by the Holy Spirit" (2 Peter 1:21). It is
clear that the possession of such a privileged gift gave the prophets a
remarkable sense of the presence of God in their lives, which is what David
is also asking for.

3 *Remember that the term only occurs 3 times in all of the Old Testament.*

though He knew they would not be obedient and faithful; but His foreknowledge didn't mean that God was indifferent to their response. He wanted them to be obedient and He was really grieved when they became rebellious and mean-minded.

God had given the children of Israel a powerful angel to lead them through the wilderness of Sinai into the Promised Land. God's angels are not 'flesh and blood' like us; they are spirit creatures, as several Scriptures teach us.[4] That means they belong to another and higher order of beings, for they are God's servants who dwell in His presence. Angels are holy and wholesome in every respect. So, in Israel's wilderness journey, the angel of God's presence was there to guide, guard and preserve them all the way to their journey's end. But instead of living according to God's holy law, the Israelites *"rebelled and grieved"* God's representative, who is here twice described as *"God's Holy Spirit"*.

The angel is described in this way because the people of Israel were anything but holy – they were rebellious. Yet the angel was totally obedient to God's will. He was holy; they were not and, as a result, that entire generation perished in the wilderness. So, once again, the term "Holy Spirit" is used to contrast the wickedness of people with the holiness of God.

❖ **God at Work**

So, on the three occasions when God's Spirit is described as the "Holy Spirit" in the Old Testament Scriptures it refers to:

✓ God working through a prophet, or

✓ God working through an angel.

In both cases the deliberate comparison is between people who are sinful and God who is holy and righteous in all His ways. He cannot be anything else; that's how He always

---

[4] *The key thing to remember about God's angels is that Scripture says they are His messengers, spirit-beings who live forever, and they are so free from sin that they dwell in the presence of Almighty God. The New Testament says they are "ministering spirits sent out to serve for the sake of those who are to inherit salvation" (Hebrews 1:14). So the very idea that an angel, or angels, could sin and be cast out of heaven is completely wrong and a great insult to the angels.*

is and always will be. Everything God does is done by His Spirit, for this is how God works, but when that activity is specifically designed to achieve holiness, or when God's character is considered side-by-side with human rebellion, then God's Spirit is termed His Holy Spirit. That expression comes just 3 times in the Old Testament, as we have seen, but more than 90 times in the New, where the whole emphasis changes. For the New Testament is very much concerned about the way in which God can help individuals achieve personal holiness.

That doesn't mean that God is not interested in holiness in the Old Testament, or that His power was then usually directed towards ordinary and not extraordinary things. What it shows is that God's work was of a different order when He caused His Son to be born. Let's see if we can work that out by studying the things that God did by His Spirit in the Old Testament first. Then we will look at what happens with the birth of Jesus and in the lives of those who followed him.

❖ Old Testament Usage

Again, if you would like to track down the relevant Old Testament references for yourself, you can build a table of different activities. Or, if you prefer, you can just jot down the references from the following table and look those passages up to see what God's Spirit was doing at different times, then compare your conclusions with those suggested. Remember, this book is all about how we can understand the Bible for ourselves.

Usually, when building a table like this, we would list the passages in the order they appear in the Bible. This time we have listed the passages to show the way that Spirit activity in the past accomplished several things of a quite different nature. So the table is constructed to trace the way in which one thing led to another, as God made the physical world, gave life to people, and then directed His power to show people how they could become holy, like Him.

Verse	God's Activity
Genesis 1:2	*"The earth was without form and void, and darkness was over the face of the deep. And the Spirit of God was hovering over the face of the waters"* – God was active in creation by His Spirit.
Job 33:4	*"The Spirit of God has made me, and the breath of the Almighty gives me life"*. God breathed into Adam the breath (or spirit) of life and man became a living being (Genesis 2:7). So, our very life is a gift from God.
1 Samuel 10:1	*"The Spirit of God rushed upon him, and he prophesied among them"*. Many times the Spirit of God, or just *"the Spirit"* is said to have given prophetic or other powers to people (e.g. Numbers 11:25; 24:2; 2 Chronicles 15:1; Ezekiel 2:2; 11:5,24; Micah 3:8).
Exodus 31:3	*"I have filled him with the Spirit of God, with ability and intelligence, with knowledge and all craftsmanship"*. This passage refers to special abilities which were given to craftsmen who were to build God's dwelling place – the Tabernacle. Many other passages describe the way that special gifts were given by God – gifts such as wisdom, administrative skill, judgement and even physical power (see Numbers 11:25; Deuteronomy 34:9; Judges 14:19). These were Spirit gifts.
Isaiah 11:2,3	*"The Spirit of the Lord shall rest upon him, the Spirit of wisdom and understanding, the Spirit of counsel and might, the Spirit of knowledge and the fear of the Lord. And his delight shall be in the fear of the Lord"*. This passage tells us that the coming king – the Messiah – will be empowered by God so that he will be a wise counsellor and a very gifted ruler (see also Isaiah 61:1).[5]

It's clear from these verses that God was active in a whole range of different ways to do with the creation and maintenance of His world, and its various creatures. His Spirit power first brought life into being and, to this day, it is God who gives the gift of life to humans and animals alike. We have already noted that *"God gives to all mankind life and breath and everything" (Acts 17:25)*, and that if God takes that life away, we are all dead![6]

❖ Range of Meanings

Very often when the word *"spirit"* is used it refers to the life-force that is in man or woman, either physically, mentally or emotionally. We read about a great lady who was breathless with amazement – Scripture says *"there was no more spirit in her" (1 Kings 10:5 RSV)*;[7] about an Egyptian king who woke up in the morning troubled in spirit (Genesis 41:8); and about a father who was overjoyed in spirit when he knew that his long-lost son was in fact alive (Genesis 45:27). This is an important development in the use of the word, for it shows us that God created life and sustains it, by His Spirit, but that life is more than mere existence.

Life is a power or force that enables us to think, feel, love, hate, be happy and be sad. The *"spirit of man"* is a term that describes his existence and his awareness; it refers as much to his being alive as to his mental and moral development.

The passages we have looked at, both those in the table and the three Old Testament references to God's Holy Spirit, give us some idea of the range of meaning the word "spirit" possesses. It helps us realise that, in the Old Testament, the language is very much concerned with:

✓ the way God was working with the earth He created,

✓ the people He had brought into existence,

---

[5] *The passage from Isaiah chapter 61 is the one the Lord Jesus read in the synagogue at Nazareth when he went on to say that "Today this Scripture has been fulfilled in your hearing" (Luke 4:21).*

[6] *Chapter 5, pages 58-61.*

[7] *The English Standard version says "there was no more breath in her", for the same Hebrew word can be translated as "spirit" or "breath".*

✓ the message He conveyed to them through prophets, and by promises, and

✓ the reaction or response of men and women.

How people responded to God's Spirit in *their* spirit was an all-important matter. They had *existence*, but would they find life as it was really meant to be lived – life with God? That's a question that is just as relevant for us, living so much later than Old Testament times.

❖ Is the Holy Spirit a Person?

There are people who believe that the Holy Spirit is a part of the Trinity and that it is as much a person as are the Father and the Son. People feel very strongly indeed about this and even go so far as to say that those who come to different conclusions are not even Christians. Church creeds, formulated hundreds of years later than the Bible, declared the Trinity to be "orthodox doctrine," and made belief in it a requirement for salvation, so far as the established church is concerned. The real question, of course, is: 'What does the Bible teach about the Holy Spirit, and does it say that the Holy Spirit is a Person or something else?'

The very first place where we read about God's Spirit should help us answer that. Here it is, in the opening verses of the Bible:

*"In the beginning, God created the heavens and the earth. The earth was without form and void, and darkness was over the face of the deep. And **the Spirit of God** was hovering over the face of the waters. And God said, 'Let there be light,' and there was light" (Genesis 1:1-3).*

God created the world by His Spirit, for when God spoke He directed His power to fulfil His purpose. Look at these Scriptures which describe what happened in slightly different ways. None of them suggests that God's Holy Spirit is a person:

*"By the **word of the LORD** the heavens were made, and by the breath of his mouth all their host ... For **he spoke, and it came to be**; he commanded, and it stood firm" (Psalm 33:6,9);*

*"It is I who **by my great power** and my outstretched arm have made the earth, with the men and animals that are on the earth, and I give it to whomever it seems right to me" (Jeremiah 27:5);* [8]

*"It is he who made the earth **by his power**, who established the world **by his wisdom**, and **by his understanding** stretched out the heavens" (Jeremiah 10:12);*

*"For his invisible attributes, namely, **his eternal power and divine nature**, have been clearly perceived, ever since the creation of the world, in the things that have been made" (Romans 1:20).*

❖ A Power not a Person

God made the world by the exercise of His *great power*, according to His *wisdom* and understanding, by His *Spirit*. These are different ways of saying the same thing. Everything that God does is by His Spirit, for that is the language used in Scripture to describe God's almighty power. So the Holy Spirit is not a person but a power – God's power – by which great things are accomplished.

That power gives us *"life and breath and everything"* (Acts 17:25) including special, revealed knowledge of the purpose of God, because it is by His Spirit that God communicates:

*"**The Spirit of the LORD speaks by me; his word is on my tongue**" (2 Samuel 23:2);*

*"Many years you bore with them and warned them **by your Spirit** through your prophets. Yet they would not give ear" (Nehemiah 9:30);*

*"They made their hearts diamond-hard lest they should hear the law and the words that the LORD of hosts had sent **by his Spirit** through the former prophets" (Zechariah 7:12).*

---

[8] *See also Jeremiah 32:17; 51:15, where the same terms are used.*

❖ The Holy Spirit and Jesus

So far we have seen what the Old Testament says about God's power at work. But will all this change when we get to the New Testament, where the term is much more frequent? Will we find the meaning to be different here? People who only read the New Testament fail to understand that Bible ideas carry through from the Old to the New. God's purpose and ways never change: they progress. So a good understanding of the Old Testament really helps us with the New.

Let's put that to the test by looking at the first three occurrences of the term "Holy Spirit" in the New Testament.

1,2   *"Now the birth of Jesus Christ took place in this way. When his mother Mary had been betrothed to Joseph, before they came together she was found to be with child from the **Holy Spirit** ... Joseph, son of David, do not fear to take Mary as your wife, for that which is conceived in her is from the **Holy Spirit**"* (Matthew 1:18-20);

3   *"I baptize you with water for repentance, but he who is coming after me is mightier than I, whose sandals I am not worthy to carry. He will baptize you with the **Holy Spirit** and with fire"* (Matthew 3:11).

God's power was at work again, not now to create the world, but to redeem or rescue it. Things were in such a bad state that only God could save the situation. So He caused a Son to be born to Mary, by the exercise of His Spirit. This is how the gospel writer Luke describes what she was told about the birth of Jesus:

*"The **Holy Spirit** will come upon you, and **the power of the Most High** will overshadow you; therefore the child to be born will be called holy—the Son of God"* (Luke 1:35).

So it was that the power of God brought the Lord Jesus into being and that same power was later given to Jesus at his baptism, and by that power he was able both to do miracles and to declare the words of God.

*"**The Holy Spirit descended on him** in bodily form, like a dove; and a voice came from heaven, 'You are my beloved Son; with you I am well pleased' ... And Jesus,*

full of the Holy Spirit, returned from the Jordan and was **led by the Spirit in the wilderness**" *(Luke 3:22; 4:1);*

"God anointed Jesus of Nazareth with the Holy Spirit and with power. *He went about doing good and healing all who were oppressed by the devil, for God was with him" (Acts 10:38);*

"For he whom God has sent **utters the words of God, for he gives the Spirit without measure**" *(John 3:34).*

❖ Jesus exercising God's Power

Everything Jesus did was by the exercise of God's power. He said so over and over again, in case people thought that what he was doing and saying was just for himself and by himself:

"The testimony that I have is greater than that of John. **For the works that the Father has given me to accomplish, the very works that I am doing,** *bear witness about me that* **the Father has sent me**" *(John 5:36);*

"It is the Spirit who gives life; the flesh is of no avail. **The words that I have spoken to you are spirit and life**" *(6:63);*

"Do you not believe that I am in the Father and the Father is in me? **The words that I say to you I do not speak on my own authority, but the Father who dwells in me does his works.** *Believe me that I am in the Father and the Father is in me, or else believe on account of the works themselves" (14:10,11).*

Both Father and Son were working together to accomplish our salvation. The Father had created the Lord Jesus Christ and had empowered him to accomplish His purpose. The Son was willing and eager to cooperate with what his Father wanted. Theirs was a perfect unity: they were at one and, as we have seen, they want us to be equally united with them in purpose and in resolve.[9]

---

[9] *See John 17:18-23 for the clearest possible statement that Jesus and his Father shared a complete unity of purpose, and that they want us to be part of that same relationship.*

The exercise of God's power in accordance with His great love for us is designed to bring us to perfection, just as it first achieved that for the Lord Jesus. For the same power that had created and enabled Jesus to do and say wonderful things would later raise him from the dead. And that very power is also at work to achieve all that God purposes for His children in all ages. For everything that God does is by the power of His Holy Spirit.[10]

❖ Holy Spirit in Action

When we reviewed the working of God's Spirit in the Old Testament, we noted that God's power was directed to achieve several different things. In the table we compiled on page 230 they were:

No	Verse	God's Activity
1	Genesis 1:2	God was active in **Creation** by His Spirit.
2	Job 33:4	Our very **life is a gift** from God.
3	1 Samuel 10:1	The Spirit gives **prophetic or other powers** to people.
4	Exodus 31:3	**Special abilities** were given to craftsmen who were to build God's dwelling place – the Tabernacle – and other gifts were given by God, such as wisdom and administrative skill.
5	Isaiah 11:2,3	The coming king – **the Messiah – was to be empowered by God** so that he would be a wise counsellor and a much gifted ruler.

Now we can see why the language has changed in the New Testament. It is to concentrate our attention on God's

[10] *We considered this in Chapter 15 pages 224-227.*

eventual intention of make His people holy and righteous in His sight. He means to fill the new-made world with people who are like Him, who are adopted as His sons and daughters. So it follows that each of the activities listed above is also appropriate in the New Testament, but on a higher level, as follows:

1   God is now in the process of undertaking a **new creation**, in that He is inviting men and women to prepare for the new world that will come into existence when the Lord Jesus Christ returns to earth as King. That new creation begins for us at baptism: *"If anyone is in Christ, he is a new creation. The old has passed away; behold, the new has come"* (2 Corinthians 5:17), and it will be completed when the Lord Jesus returns to establish a new world order. Then he will say: *"Behold, I am making all things new"* (Revelation 21:5).

2   Everybody living today has been given the precious **gift of life** by God and thus has the opportunity to find out about God's purpose and love towards us. Our mortal existence is bound to end in death, but if we choose **God's offer of eternal life** we can be part of that new creation when Jesus reigns as God's appointed king: *"For the wages of sin is death, but the free gift of God is eternal life in Christ Jesus our Lord"* (Romans 6:23). Paul urges all his readers to live *"according to the Spirit"* and to *"set their minds on the things of the Spirit"* (Romans 8:5). He is encouraging them, and us, to make the most of God's offer of life.

3   The way to find out about eternal life is by reading and understanding the **Scriptures** that have come from God by the exercise of those **prophetic powers** that were granted to people in times past. The full purpose of God has now been revealed and we are told that we should beware of any suggestion to the contrary. For the New Testament ends with the words: *"I warn everyone who hears the words of the prophecy of this book: if anyone adds to them, God will add to him the plagues described in this book"* (Revelation 22:18).

4   The completion of the Scriptures and the establishment of Christianity in the first century was achieved by God-given **special abilities and powers**, called *"gifts of the*

Holy Spirit" (Hebrews 2:4). In Old Testament times these were provided so that a dwelling place for God would be established. This was a physical habitation, first a tabernacle and then a temple. In the New Testament scriptures it is a spiritual abode that God wants established. He wants to dwell in His people (Ephesians 2:21-22). So, to show that the gospel was true and to help those who were given the responsibility of preaching and teaching, God gave certain people special gifts which would last until the Christian community, in which God would dwell, had been established.

5   Jesus exercised the **Holy Spirit powers of the Messiah** during his life on earth and will do so again when he returns in that same power to establish and rule over the Kingdom of God.

❖ Gifts of the Holy Spirit

The special powers that were given to the apostles were for a specific reason and for a limited time. There had been other such occasions in the history of redemption, such as when Moses led God's people out of Egypt, attended by remarkable miracles; when the tabernacle was being built in the wilderness and when the prophets Elijah and Elisha made God's final appeal to the northern tribes.[11] In all those cases the divinely granted powers served their purpose and were then withdrawn.

It was the same in first century times. God gave special powers to selected people so that they could demonstrate that they were His representatives, teaching the true gospel. But it was also made clear that when the gospel had been fully recorded, those special powers or gifts would cease. They would then have fulfilled their purpose.

❖ Purpose

"These signs will accompany those who believe: in my name they will cast out demons; they will speak in new tongues; they will pick up serpents with their hands; and if they drink any deadly poison, it will not hurt them; they will lay their hands on the sick, and they will recover

---

[11] *The Exodus from Egypt is described in Exodus chapters 1-15; the building of the Tabernacle is in Exodus chapters 25-40; the Spirit-gifted work of Elijah and Elisha feature in 1 Kings chapter 17 to 2 Kings chapter 13.*

... And they went out and preached everywhere, while **the Lord worked with them and confirmed the message by accompanying signs"** *(Mark 16:17-20);*

"How shall we escape if we neglect such a great salvation? It was declared at first by the Lord, and it was attested to us by those who heard, while **God also bore witness by signs and wonders and various miracles and by gifts of the Holy Spirit distributed according to his will"** *(Hebrews 2:3,4);*

"He gave the apostles, the prophets, the evangelists, the pastors and teachers, **to equip the saints for the work of ministry, for building up the body of Christ ..."** *(Ephesians 4:11,12).*

❖ **Duration**

*"... **until we all attain to the unity of the faith and of the knowledge of the Son of God**, to mature manhood, to the measure of the stature of the fullness of Christ, so that we may no longer be children..."* *(Ephesians 4:13,14);*

"We know in part and we prophesy in part, but **when the perfect comes, the partial will pass away**. When I was a child, I spoke like a child, I thought like a child, I reasoned like a child. When I became a man, I gave up childish ways. For now we see in a mirror dimly, but then face to face. Now I know in part; then I shall know fully, even as I have been fully known"* *(1 Corinthians 13:9-12).*

Jesus made a wide range of Holy Spirit gifts available after his ascension to heaven, the most complete list being in the following passage:[12]

"To one is given through the Spirit the utterance of **wisdom**, *and to another the utterance of* **knowledge** *according to the same Spirit, to another* **faith** *by the same Spirit, to another* **gifts of healing** *by the one Spirit, to another the working of* **miracles**, *to another* **prophecy**, *to another the* **ability to distinguish between spirits**, *to another various* **kinds of tongues**, *to another the* **interpretation of tongues"** *(1 Corinthians 12:8-10).*

---

[12] *Similar lists are to be found in 1 Corinthians 12:28, Romans 12:3-8 and Ephesians 4:7-11.*

❖ Laying on of Hands

It is quite obvious from this list, and from the one in Mark 16 cited above, that the Holy Spirit gifts were just what were needed. By these the apostles could understand the gospel, preach it in different languages and perform 'signs and wonders.' These would help people understand that the message came from God. Just how that worked out for the apostles we can see by reading the accounts of their preaching and healing in the Acts of the Apostles.

One other detail we discover in the Acts is how the gifts were passed on as the gospel spread from city to city. The new believers were also in need of signs that would authenticate their ministry and the original apostles of Jesus were able to pass on the gifts by simply laying their hands on the new believers. Sometimes that necessitated a special trip from Jerusalem, or wherever they were then based, but it was the only way the gift could be transmitted. Here's one example:

> *"Now when the apostles at Jerusalem heard that Samaria had received the word of God, they sent to them Peter and John, who came down and prayed for them that they might receive the Holy Spirit, for he had not yet fallen on any of them, but they had only been baptized in the name of the Lord Jesus. Then* **they laid their hands on them and they received the Holy Spirit.** *Now when Simon saw that* **the Spirit was given through the laying on of the apostles' hands,** *he offered them money, saying, 'Give me this power also, so that anyone on whom I lay my hands may receive the Holy Spirit'" (Acts 8:14-19).*

Simon could see the way the power was transmitted and wanted that ability himself. He was told in no uncertain terms that he could not have that ability – far less buy it. You had to be one of the apostles of the Lord Jesus for that. The consequence of this was that when the apostles died out at the end of the first century, their powers died with them and the Gifts that had been conferred also disappeared with the passage of time.

As the first century faith became mature or fully grown up, the earlier need for signs and wonders was reduced. The New Testament Scriptures became available and were circulated to believers in different cities. Thus the plan and purpose of God became crystal-clear to all who read it, thought about it, and chose to follow the footsteps of those who had gone before. As Paul explains in his letter to the Ephesians, Jesus gave the gifts *"to equip the saints for the work of ministry, for building up the body of Christ ... until we all attain to the unity of the faith and of the knowledge of the Son of God, to mature manhood" (Ephesians 4:11-14)*.

❖ Was Anything Left?

The Holy Spirit gifts have passed. People who now claim to perform miracles of healing, or speak in tongues are not exercising God's power in the way it was demonstrated in first century times. They may be tapping into powers of persuasion like mass hysteria or auto-suggestion, but this is not the miraculous power of God at work as it was in New Testament times. You only have to read the Acts of the Apostles to see the difference; there the blind were given sight, the lame were made whole and even the dead were raised. What happened then was clearly supernatural.

But it would be equally wrong to say that everything to do with the Holy Spirit has gone today. God did so many things by that Spirit which we know about and benefit from today. He caused Jesus to be born, gave him power and understanding, raised him from the dead and exalted him to glory, gave him the gift of endless life. All those things have an on-going value for us, as we learn to come to God in prayer through Jesus Christ and discover that we have a mediator who can help us in our search for salvation.

We know about Jesus and indeed about all who have been part of God's plan of salvation because we read about them in the Bible, itself the product of God's Holy Spirit power. The Bible is a book of promises and those promises too are the product of the Holy Spirit. They make the Bible a living and powerful message from God – words of *"Spirit and life"* (John 6:63). The Bible can change the way we think, feel and act, if we let it – it's that powerful:

↘ *The gospel of salvation is the **"law of the spirit of life"** (Romans 8:3);*[13]

↘ *"We also thank God constantly for this, that when you received the word of God, which you heard from us, you accepted it not as the word of men but as what it really is, **the word of God, which is at work in you believers"** (1 Thessalonians 2:13);*

↘ *We are **"born again,** not of perishable seed but of imperishable, **through the living and abiding word of God;** for ... the word of the Lord remains forever." And **this word is the good news that was preached to you"** (1 Peter 1:23-25);*

↘ *"Every good gift and every perfect gift is from above, coming down from the Father of lights with whom there is no variation or shadow due to change. **Of his own will he brought us forth by the word of truth,** that we should be a kind of firstfruits of his creation" (James 1:17,18).*

This is the new life – the life of the Spirit – that we have been reading and thinking about in Romans chapter 8. And after this digression, to look at the meaning of the Spirit of God and the Holy Spirit, we need to pick up the apostle's argument once more to see what else he has to say about the gospel of salvation.

Things to Read

📖   It would be helpful to see how God gave special Holy Spirit powers to craftsmen in Old Testament times to enable them to build Him a dwelling place called "The Tabernacle". Read Exodus chapter 35 and onwards if you want to learn a little more about the dwelling place that God specified.

---

[13] *It is what the Holy Spirit has promised to believers by way of remission of sins and a new life in Christ which led the apostle Peter to say, on the Day of Pentecost: "Repent and be baptized every one of you in the name of Jesus Christ for the forgiveness of your sins, and you will receive the gift of the Holy Spirit. For the promise is for you and for your children and for all who are far off, everyone whom the Lord our God calls to himself" (Acts 2:38,39). He was referring to God's gift of salvation, by faith.*

242

📖 Now read 1 Corinthians chapters 12 and 13 to see a similar pattern in the early church, where gifts were given to get a different sort of dwelling place established – a community of believers.

Questions to Think About

16.1 Summarise some of the different meanings the word *"spirit"* can have in the Bible and explain in just one sentence what the term *"Holy Spirit"* is specifically referring to. (Genesis 1:1-3; 41:8; Numbers 14:24; Job 34:14; Ecclesiastes 3:21; 2 Samuel 23:2; 2 Peter 1:21; Acts 2:1-4)

16.2 How was the gift of the Holy Spirit transmitted from believer to believer in first century days and why was it therefore bound to come to an end by the beginning of the next century? (Acts 8:18; 1 Timothy 4:14; Hebrews 6:2)

"When they believed Philip as he preached good news about the kingdom of God and the name of Jesus Christ, they were baptized, both men and women" (Acts 8:12).

17
How do I become Immortal?

Adam was created with a nature that would have been made immortal if he had been obedient, but everything went wrong. The result was that he and his wife became subject to death and all their descendants, including all of us, are mortal. It's natural for us to sin, because we are born with a tendency in that direction, and it's therefore inevitable that we will die, sooner or later, because sin kills. The only thing we don't know is *when* that fate will overtake us. Will it be sooner or later? We can't be sure!

We came to this understanding as we worked through Romans and followed the apostle Paul's explanation about why we are all subject to sin and are all destined to die. Then he added that there was a prospect of eternal life: God is willing to give us life that would last for ever and the life which is on offer is not just everlasting life but a wonderful life in complete harmony with God. We can become members of the family of God, adopted children, who have a wonderfully close and meaningful relationship with Almighty God.

Here are just two Scriptures to remind us of the progress we make in our spiritual journey by learning to understand the Bible for ourselves:

*"Now that you have been set free from sin and have become slaves of God, the fruit you get leads to sanctification and its end, eternal life. For the wages of sin is death, but **the free gift of God is eternal life in Christ Jesus our Lord**" (Romans 6:22,23);*

*"For if you live according to the flesh you will die, but if by the Spirit you put to death the deeds of the body, you will live. For all who are led by the Spirit of God are sons of God. For you did not receive the spirit of slavery to fall back into fear, but **you have received the Spirit of adoption as sons, by whom we cry, "Abba! Father!" The Spirit himself bears witness with our spirit***

244

that we are children of God" (Romans 8:13-16).

The baptism of a true believer is the first step towards becoming immortal. It starts our new life – life with God and the Lord Jesus Christ. Paul calls this new relationship *"life according to the Spirit" (Romans 8:4)* and we have discovered that means life:

✓ with meaning and purpose; which is

✓ in conformity with the Word of God, and is

✓ in line with the gracious promises God has made for all those who become *"heirs of God and fellow heirs with Christ" (Romans 8:17).*

❖ God's Gift to Us

When you think about it, the Bible is like an ancient map which shows us just where to go to find an immense treasure. Jesus once told a parable about a man who came across buried riches as he was digging in the field, as a result of which he sold everything he had to buy that field and make the treasure his own.[1] You may have found this book and are reading it out of curiosity. If so you are like that man; for you have stumbled across an inheritance that can be yours, if you are prepared to do what is needed. Or you may have been keenly looking for the way to find eternal life. Either way you might have realised by now that the gift of immortality is the most wonderful offer from God. But how does it come about? How can we get it for ourselves?

Baptism starts the process because it requires us to make a formal declaration that we want a new life. That life then continues as we start to change the way we think – that's the crucial next step. Paul describes it in lots of different ways, as we have seen. He:

✓ calls it life *"according to the Spirit" (8:4)*;

✓ says that we should *"set the mind on the Spirit" (8:6)*;

✓ tells us to live *"in the Spirit" (8:9),* or *"by the Spirit" (8:13)*;

✓ says we are to have the Spirit dwell in us (8:9,14), and

---

[1] *Matthew 13:44.*

✓   urges us to cultivate *"the mind of the Spirit" (8:27)*.[2]

❖ "In Adam" or "In Christ"?

What Paul is really saying is this. We were born *"in Adam"* and we have now started a new life *"in Christ Jesus" (Romans 8:1,2)*. This change of status is the difference between eternal life and eternal death for, as Paul says in another letter:

> *"As in Adam all die, so also in Christ shall all be made alive" (1 Corinthians 15:22)*.

This is a bit like changing families. It's as if you had been adopted by someone else and left the home where you had lived all your life so far, by going to live with another family. How would you feel inside about such a change? It's that feeling inside us that Paul is considering – the change that should take place in our minds. He reminds us that we haven't been taken into the new household as a slave but as an adopted son or daughter. Notice his actual words:

> *"All who are led by the Spirit of God are sons of God. For you did not receive the spirit of slavery to fall back into fear, but you have received **the Spirit of adoption as sons**, by whom we cry, 'Abba! Father!'" (Romans 8:14,15)*.

Instead of saying "you have been adopted as sons", he says we have received the *"spirit of adoption as sons"* and he contrasts this with *"the spirit of slavery"*. In other words we shouldn't *feel* or *think* like a slave, but as a child of God; and one who has a very close and intimate relationship with his or her father. Paul's concern is about what's in our mind or spirit – what is happening inside us. He wants us to think right and feel right with God.

> *"For those who live according to the flesh set their **minds** on the things of the flesh, but those who live according to the Spirit set their **minds** on the things of the Spirit. To set the **mind** on the flesh is death, but to set the **mind** on the Spirit is life and peace. For the **mind** that is set on the flesh is hostile to God, for it does not submit to God's law; indeed, it cannot" (Romans 8:5-7)*.

---

[2] *Paul's use of the term "spirit" in Romans chapter 8 was examined more fully in chapter 15, pages 221-224.*

❖ Christ in Us

If we can learn to think like the Lord Jesus Christ and be motivated by those things that directed his life – by things that please God – it will be as though the life of Jesus was continuing on earth, inside us. That's what Paul means when he says this:

> *"Anyone who does not have the Spirit of Christ does not belong to him. But if **Christ is in you**, although the body is dead because of sin, the Spirit is life because of righteousness" (Romans 8:9,10).*

This is an exalted thought because, try as we might, none of us is going to be able to live as perfectly as Jesus lived. His was a life of total dedication and complete commitment. He never did or said anything wrong, nor did he break any of the laws of God. We cannot ever hope to achieve that standard, but when we try our best to live the life of Christ as members of the family of God, it is another vital step in the process of receiving immortality. For, if we want to become immortal like Jesus we must first learn to think like him, to love the things that he loved, and to follow the example that he left us. It was the apostle John who said this:

> *"See what kind of love the Father has given to us, that we should be called **children of God**; and so we are. The reason why the world does not know us is that it did not know him. Beloved, **we are God's children now**, and what we will be has not yet appeared; but we know that when he appears **we will be like him**, because we shall see him as he is. And everyone who thus hopes in him purifies himself as he is pure" (1 John 3:1-3).*

Just to want this outcome – to be like the Lord Jesus – is a purifying thought, it helps to transform us from Adam to Christ. It all starts in the mind. But it is not just left to us to do the best we can.

❖ God is for Us

In one of the most uplifting parts of the letter, Paul says that God is working with us to ensure our salvation. He has not left us on our own but works in many different ways to finish what He has begun in us. If we have become His children and now live with Him, He also lives with us.

That means that His great power and might are active to help us and that He will work with us. If we are related, through baptism, to the Lord Jesus he also is active on our behalf. For Scripture says that:

> *"He is able to save to the uttermost those who draw near to God through him, since he always lives to make intercession for them" (Hebrews 7:25).*

Neither God nor Jesus can do it all for us; we have to do our part. They will not take over our minds and think for us, nor will they manipulate our minds so that we think as they want. If God had wanted robots He would have created them. Instead He created men and women who can think for themselves. Thus God gave us the chance of showing our appreciation and affection by voluntarily choosing to do the things that please Him.

That's the choice we all now have and it's up to each of us whether we want to bother about God and His purpose, or not. He loves us, but nobody forces us to love Him in return; it's up to us. But if we are keen to show God that we care, and that we really want what is on offer, this is what He will do for us:

> *"**For those who love God all things work together for good, for those who are called according to his purpose ... If God is for us, who can be against us?** He who did not spare his own Son but gave him up for us all, how will he not also with him graciously give us all things? Who shall bring any charge against God's elect? It is God who justifies. Who is to condemn? Christ Jesus is the one who died – more than that, who was raised – who is at the right hand of God, who indeed is interceding for us. Who shall separate us from the love of Christ? ... In all these things **we are more than conquerors through him who loved us**. For I am sure that neither death nor life, nor angels nor rulers, nor things present nor things to come, nor powers, nor height nor depth, **nor anything else in all creation, will be able to separate us from the love of God in Christ Jesus our Lord"** (Romans 8:28-39).*

God can do more for us than we can even imagine and the Lord Jesus Christ will be at the right hand of God interceding for us, because he also loves us. Baptized believers are promised a life in fellowship with God and the Lord

Jesus, and this will be a loving and caring relationship, which is part of the process of being saved and being made holy. It starts in the mind, which has to be changed, and it requires constant recourse to the Word of God and prayer, so that the entire life changes direction.[3]

Paul says a lot more about this change in Romans chapters 12 to 16 – which is directly concerned with our behaviour and way of life. Here's just a glimpse of what he says there:

*"I appeal to you therefore, brothers, by the mercies of God, to present your bodies as a living sacrifice, holy and acceptable to God, which is your spiritual worship. Do not be conformed to this world, but **be transformed by the renewal of your mind, that by testing you may discern what is the will of God, what is good and acceptable and perfect"** (Romans 12:1,2).*

In this passage the apostle doesn't talk about *"the Spirit"*, but about having our minds transformed and renewed to understand the will of God. It's the same process that he described in Romans 8, just different language. His point in the earlier chapter is that we have to choose to live life on a higher plane – a spiritual one. Almighty God is a spirit being; so we must try to aspire to higher things – to *"the new life of the Spirit"* (Romans 7:6).

❖ Salvation from Sin

It follows that being saved is not something that happens overnight; it is a process that takes a lifetime. Baptism is certainly an event, and a crucially important one at that, but it is the beginning of a new journey not the end of the road. As Paul says in Romans:

*"I am not ashamed of the gospel, for it is the power of God **for salvation** to everyone who believes, to the Jew first and also to the Greek"* (Romans 1:16);

*"Since, therefore, we have now been justified by his blood, much more **shall we be saved** by him from the wrath of God"* (5:9);

---

[3] *Paul, in another letter, describes what God can do for us, when he says: "Now to him who is able to do far more abundantly than all that we ask or think, according to the power at work within us, to him be glory" (Ephesians 3:20,21).*

*"For if while we were enemies we were reconciled to God by the death of his Son, much more, now that we are reconciled, **shall we be saved by his life**" (5:10);*

*"For **in this hope we were saved**. Now hope that is seen is not hope. For who hopes for what he sees?" (8:24).*

When the Bible talks about *"hope"*, it means something real and powerful: a firmly-based hope which is rooted in the promises of God. In this context, the apostle describes how such a hope is destined to become a reality. He explains that God will confer the gift of immortality upon those people who live the life of the Spirit: all those who are related to God through the Lord Jesus Christ. He says that if they have tried to transform their minds in accordance with God's will, God will in due course transform their bodies as well and make them immortal.

This is what Paul says in Romans chapter 8 about that coming change. It can be seen most clearly in the form of a table, which is on the next page.

❖ The Redemption of our Bodies

The end of the process as Paul describes it leads to bodily transformation. What starts in the mind ends in a totally changed nature, one which is forever free from sin and death. We will then no longer live *"in the flesh"* but *"in the spirit"*; our bodies will become spiritual bodies, like those of the Lord Jesus and the angels in heaven. At the beginning of our thinking about the meaning of the Spirit we noted that the word has a wide range of meaning and now we can see the advantage of that. The process of becoming immor-

"All who are led by the Spirit of God are sons of God. For you did not receive the spirit of slavery to fall back into fear, but you have received the Spirit of adoption as sons, by whom we cry, 'Abba! Father!'" (Romans 8:14,15).

	Verse	Meaning
10	*"If Christ is in you, although the body is dead because of sin, the Spirit is life because of righteousness."*	In baptism we pledge to put to death our old way of life, because we want to end our life of sin, but we have hope of life because we have a new attitude of mind and heart.
11	*"If the Spirit of him who raised Jesus from the dead dwells in you, he who raised Christ Jesus from the dead will also give life to your mortal bodies through his Spirit who dwells in you."*	It is the same attitude that Jesus himself had (a spiritual one) and God, who raised Jesus from the dead, will raise us in due course, through that same power that has already begun to work in us and which lives in us.
13	*"For if you live according to the flesh you will die, but if by the Spirit you put to death the deeds of the body, you will live."*	That new attitude we possess – our new life from God – helps us to conquer the passions and feelings we have always had. We must put them to death every day if we want to live forever.
23	*"And not only the creation, but we ourselves, who have the firstfruits of the Spirit, groan inwardly as we wait eagerly for adoption as sons, the redemption of our bodies."*	This process of salvation which is taking place inside us is going eventually to lead to our redemption. It's a struggle now to overcome our lower nature and live Christ-like lives. However, if we genuinely try to do this as children of God, He will change us to be made like Christ at his return.

tal has to start in the mind and will eventually lead to bodily transformation. *'Life in the Spirit'* thus has these two senses:

1   a different mindset, and

2   a different bodily state.

But it is one process, not two: unless we have begun to live differently now, we cannot expect to live differently in the age to come. Paul says something else as well. He says that all creation is eagerly waiting for the time when it will be set free from all those things which now limit and restrain it.[4] At the time when God makes men and women free from sin and death, He is also due to change the way the world is constituted. Here's the actual passage:

> *"I consider that the sufferings of this present time are not worth comparing with the glory that is to be revealed to us. For the creation waits with eager longing for the revealing of the sons of God. For the creation was subjected to futility, not willingly, but because of him who subjected it, in hope that the creation itself will be set free from its bondage to decay and obtain the freedom of the glory of the children of God. For we know that the whole creation has been groaning together in the pains of childbirth until now. And not only the creation, but we ourselves, who have the firstfruits of the Spirit, groan inwardly as we wait eagerly for adoption as sons, the redemption of our bodies" (Romans 8:18-23).*

This is another of those passages where we need to jot down the various things we are told – try that exercise for yourself if you wish and then compare your list with this one. Paul says that:

↘   Now we suffer; but in the age to come things will be glorious. Scripture says that in that age *"all the earth shall be filled with the glory of the LORD"* (Numbers 14:21);

↘   When those who are members of God's family – the sons of God – are revealed to the world as the immortal occupants of the new age, the whole created order is to

---

[4] *This is an example of vivid picture language being used to make the point more graphic, a figure of speech known as personification. We will encounter that sort of language again when we come to think about the way the Bible describes sin in all its many different guises.*

be renewed. This is in line with other Scriptures that talk about the outpouring of God's Spirit power, which will then change both people and places (see Isaiah 32:15);

↘ God's created order has been damaged by the effects of sin and is now in *"bondage to decay"* – everything is in the process of deterioration and is on a downward path. This is happening as a result of Adam's sin when God cursed the ground, saying: *"Cursed is the ground because of you; in pain you shall eat of it all the days of your life; thorns and thistles it shall bring forth for you; and you shall eat the plants of the field"* *(Genesis 3:17,18);*

↘ At present all human life is subject to *"futility"* – it is useless to try to achieve anything lasting or fulfilling apart from God. This is part of God's plan, to direct our attention to Him and His gracious offer of salvation. He wants us to be set free from the present bondage of sin and death; [5]

↘ Present troubles in the world and in our personal lives are the birthpangs of a new age. They indicate that God's gracious purpose is nearing its fulfilment, when those who are His children will *"obtain the freedom of the glory of the children of God"*, which is a lovely and colourful way of saying that there are much better times ahead; [6]

↘ Our present bodies are to be changed and when that happens – when we are made immortal – all the sorrow and sadness we now experience will be taken away. In the new age it is said of those who walk in God's way that *"they shall obtain gladness and joy, and sorrow and sighing shall flee away"* *(Isaiah 35:9,10).*

---

[5] *King Solomon worked out that idea in detail in the Book of Ecclesiastes in which he observed: "Vanity of vanities, says the Preacher, vanity of vanities! All is vanity" (Ecclesiastes 1:2).*

[6] *When Paul says that the earth groans, that believers groan, and that even the Lord Jesus Christ groans (Romans 8:22-26), he is using the language of childbirth. Everyone is awaiting a new life in God's Kingdom and until that happens everyone has to endure a measure of suffering, in the sure knowledge that better times are coming. Jesus groans because he knows what we are going through and wants the best outcome for us.*

253

❖ Jesus the First-Begotten

The Lord Jesus was raised from the dead by the power of God's Spirit: he was *"declared to be the Son of God in power according to the Spirit of holiness by his resurrection from the dead" (Romans 1:4)*. That event began the Lord's new life with God, for whilst he had always lived in close communion with his Father, his mortality had separated them. Jesus was on earth but his Father was in heaven. Now, having become sinless and immortal, Jesus ascended to heaven to dwell at his Father's right hand. Father and Son continue to work together for our salvation, as they had done before, but now their work is of a different sort.

Jesus explained to his disciples while he was still with them that after his ascension he would still help them and be close to them, but his help would now be of a different kind entirely. As a resurrected and glorified Son the limitations of his earthly life would be removed.[7]

What happened to the Lord shows us what will happen to his followers. The great hope of life after death offered in the Bible is that of bodily resurrection from the dead. Over the years people have got confused about this because pagan teaching about an 'immortal soul' – which is not a Bible term or idea – became mixed up in their thinking with true Bible teaching. If all people lived forever anyway, or if their new life began in heaven immediately after death, what would be the point of the resurrection of the dead? So resurrection lost its true importance and became a sort of awkward Bible teaching. To this day at funerals, you can hear ministers and priests saying that the 'dear departed' has gone to be with God in heaven and then they take a reading from the Bible which says the dead will be raised. This is even more confusing when such people say how bad the sinful body was and how much better it is to live without it in heaven, while the Bible reading says that the body will be raised. No wonder people get confused!

❖ Death – the End

The clear teaching of the Bible, as we have already seen, is that when we die, we cease to exist. When God said to

---

[7] *The whole discourse is recorded in John chapters 14-16. In particular, Jesus promised to guide them into all truth, as the Scriptures were being completed (14:16,17,26; 16:13); to dwell with them (14:18,19); to help with their preaching (16:8,9) and with their prayers (16:23,24).*

Adam: *"By the sweat of your face you shall eat bread, till you return to the ground, for out of it you were taken; for you are dust, and to dust you shall return" (Genesis 3:19).* He was not promising him life in heaven after death, but the punishment of death in the dust of the ground. Death is a punishment not a reward: the end of life not a new beginning.[8]

For some people that will be the complete end, they will never exist again. The Bible says that unbelievers will *"perish"*; they will sleep forever in the unconscious state of death; they will never exist again. It's a strange thing, but people who have come to believe they are immortal seem to miss the clear warnings from God that, unless they do something about it, they will cease to exist. For Scripture says:

*"For God so loved the world, that he gave his only Son, that whoever believes in him should not **perish** but have eternal life" (John 3:16);*

*"For when he dies he will carry nothing away; his glory will not go down after him. For though, while he lives, he counts himself blessed, – and though you get praise when you do well for yourself – his soul will go to the generation of his fathers, who will **never again see light**. Man in his pomp yet without understanding is **like the beasts that perish**" (Psalm 49:17-20);*

*"One who wanders from the way of good sense will **rest in the assembly of the dead**" (Proverbs 21:16);*

*"**They are dead, they will not live**; they are shades, **they will not arise**; to that end you have visited them with **destruction** and **wiped out all remembrance of them**" (Isaiah 26:14);*

*"The gate is wide and the way is easy that leads to **destruction**, and those who enter by it are many" (Matthew 7:13);*

"Do not fear those who kill the body but cannot kill the

---

[8] *Chapter 4, page 45.*

*soul. **Rather fear him who can destroy both soul and body in hell**" (Matthew 10:28).*[9]

❖ Waking from Sleep

There is only one thing that can save us from extinction or total destruction, once we are dead, and that is resurrection. The Bible never promises us a dwelling place in heaven; quite the contrary. We read of the faithful of old that they *"slept with their fathers,"* [10] where *sleep* is an encouraging description, for we can be awakened from sleep. We are told that such faithful followers of God never obtained what He had promised them, but that they would enter into that inheritance when the faithful of all ages also received it. And we are told that they corrupted away in the grave.

Take King David as just one example of a faithful man who was pleasing to God, who was inspired to write many Psalms which talk about life and death. He is described as a man *"after God's own heart;"* so if anyone was going to survive death and go to heaven, King David would be a most likely candidate.[11] But this is what we are told by him and about him.

Ref	Writer	What was said?
Psalm 6:5	David	*"In death there is no remembrance of you; in Sheol who will give you praise?"*
Psalm 13:3	David	*"Consider and answer me, O LORD my God; light up my eyes, lest I sleep the sleep of death."* [12]

[9] *"Soul" has a wide range of meanings, just like "spirit". Here it means the inner life of a person as opposed to his or her physical existence – all those things like feelings and memories that make a person unique. There are those, Jesus says, who can kill you but God can recreate you, with the same personality and character traits that you had before. But God can also totally destroy you: so fear Him!*

[10] *For example: 1 Kings 11:21,43, where this expression is used both of King David and King Solomon..*

[11] *The phrase "after God's heart" (1 Samuel 13:14) means that King David would be someone who shared God's values and feelings and was thus very pleasing to Him.*

[12] *David used the language of sleep, but also prayed that God would wake him up from the sleep of death, as the verse indicates.*

Ref	Writer	What was said?
1 Kings 2:10	Inspired writer	*"Then David slept with his fathers and was buried in the city of David."*
Acts 2:29,34	Apostle Peter	*"Brothers, I may say to you with confidence about the patriarch David that he both died and was buried, and his tomb is with us to this day ... For David did not ascend into the heavens."* [13]
Acts 13:22,36	Apostle Paul	*"He raised up David to be their king, of whom he testified and said, 'I have found in David the son of Jesse a man after my heart, who will do all my will' ... David, after he had served the purpose of God in his own generation, fell asleep and was laid with his fathers and saw corruption."*
Hebrews 11:32, 39,40	Inspired writer	*"Time would fail me to tell of Gideon, Barak, Samson, Jephthah, of David and Samuel and the prophets ... all these, though commended through their faith, did not receive what was promised, since God had provided something better for us, that apart from us they should not be made perfect."*

This is the terminology used throughout Scripture – that of falling asleep in death and of being awakened from death by the resurrection of the dead. Here are just a few instances:

---

[13] *This is what Jesus taught as well when he said: "No one has ascended into heaven except he who descended from heaven, the Son of Man" (John 3:13).*

*"Many[14] of those who **sleep** in the dust of the earth shall **awake**, some to everlasting life, and some to shame and everlasting contempt" (Daniel 12:2);*

*"All were weeping and mourning for her, but (Jesus) said, 'Do not weep, for she is not dead but **sleeping**.' And they laughed at him, knowing that she was dead. But taking her by the hand he called, saying, 'Child, **arise**.' And her spirit returned, and she got up at once" (Luke 8:52-55);*

*"'Our friend Lazarus has **fallen asleep**, but I go to **awaken him**.' The disciples said to him, 'Lord, if he has fallen **asleep**, he will recover.' Now Jesus had spoken of his **death**, but they thought that he meant taking rest in **sleep**. Then Jesus told them plainly, 'Lazarus has **died**'" (John 11:11-14);*

*"And falling to his knees (Stephen) cried out with a loud voice, 'Lord, do not hold this sin against them.' And when he had said this, he **fell asleep**" (Acts 7:60);*

"If Christ has not been raised, your faith is futile and you are still in your sins. Then those also who have fallen asleep in Christ have perished" (1 Corinthians 15:17,18).

❖ The Great Awakening

When Jesus lived on earth he was able to awaken people from the sleep of death. Indeed, two of the passages listed above refer to miracles he performed when first he raised Jairus' daughter and then Lazarus. The very fact that Jesus raised these two people shows that he did not think they were better off dead, as they might well have been if it is true that at death we go immediately to heaven to be with God. He knew that death is a punishment and not a reward, and he was uniquely placed to be able to free people from the prison house of the grave. Jesus could do this because God his Father had given him that power. He explained that on one occasion in these words:

"Jesus said to them, 'Truly, truly, I say to you, the Son can do nothing of his own accord, but only what he sees the Father doing. For whatever the Father does, that the

---

[14] *Notice that it is "Many" who sleep who shall awake, not "All".*

Son does likewise. For the Father loves the Son and shows him all that he himself is doing. And greater works than these will he show him, so that you may marvel. For as the Father raises the dead and gives them life, so also the Son gives life to whom he will'" (John 5:19-21);

"For as the Father has life in himself, so he has granted the Son also to have life in himself ... Do not marvel at this, for an hour is coming when all who are in the tombs will hear his voice and come out, those who have done good to the resurrection of life, and those who have done evil to the resurrection of judgement" (5:26,28,29).

Note how careful the Lord Jesus is to distinguish between himself and his Father and to attribute glory and power to Him. That is typical of the way Jesus spoke of his Father, always stressing his own inferiority and thus magnifying God. Here he attributes to God the power to give life, but says that Jesus:

✓ has been given that power by God, and

✓ will exercise that power when he summons from death those who are responsible to judgement – those who have either done *"good"* or *"evil"* in God's sight.[15]

❖ Coming Conqueror

For this to happen, of course, it is necessary for the Lord Jesus to be back in the earth and that is something the Bible promises all the way through – that a conqueror would one day come to destroy the power of sin and death and thus set people free. Here is an example of that Bible-long theme, from the prophet Isaiah:

"On this mountain the LORD of hosts will make for all peoples a feast of rich food, a feast of well-aged wine, of rich food full of marrow, of aged wine well refined. And he will swallow up ... death forever; and the LORD God will wipe away tears from all faces, and the reproach of his people he will take away from all the earth, for the LORD has spoken. It will be said on that day, 'Behold, this is our God; we have waited for him, that he might save us. This is the

---

15 *Again it is clear that there are some people, who are not regarded as morally responsible to God, who will not be raised from the dead but will sleep on in the dust of the ground for ever. Such people will perish.*

LORD; *we have waited for him; let us be glad and rejoice in his salvation" (Isaiah 25:6-9);*[16]

"In the path of your judgements, O LORD, we wait for you; your name and remembrance are the desire of our soul" (26:8);

"Your dead shall live; their bodies shall rise. You who dwell in the dust, awake and sing for joy! For your dew is a dew of light, and the earth will give birth to the dead" (26:19).

These verses give us a glimpse of what resurrection will be like. The apostle Paul gives a detailed explanation in another of his letters which we need to look at in the next chapter.

Things to Read

Chapter 8 is probably the most difficult one in Romans, especially because it says such a lot about the Spirit of God in action. Now we have looked at that subject in some detail you may want to read the chapter again slowly and carefully. The more information there is in a passage of Scripture, the more benefit we get by looking carefully and prayerfully at what it is teaching.

Ephesians chapter 4 tells us a lot about God's Spirit. It starts off by explaining the way in which Spirit gifts were given in the first century and then tells us what we must do now, by renewing our minds and learning to live like Jesus. We need to learn what is true and then live according to that understanding.

Questions to Think About

17.1 John chapter 11 tells us about the resurrection of Lazarus. First Jesus explains what he believes about death and then what he can do about it. Look at the passage and summarize what you learn about death and resurrection. (John 11 verses 1-14; 21-26; 43-44)

---

[16] *The prophet is writing about the future of Jerusalem, which is the "mountain" in question. There is more about the future of Jerusalem in Chapters 20 and 21.*

17.2 What did God tell Adam would happen to him if he sinned? How was that happening going to be overcome as explained in the first promise God ever made to mankind? (Genesis 2:16-17; 3:14-21; 1 Corinthians 15:21-26)

"Many of those who sleep in the dust of the earth shall awake, some to everlasting life, and some to shame and everlasting contempt" *(Daniel 12:2).*

18

What happens at the Resurrection?

The resurrection of the dead is the true hope of life after death; there is no other hope of survival. If we are not raised from the dead we will continue forever in the unconscious state of death.

Some people think that we live forever anyway, because they say we have an immortal soul, but the Bible denies that. It tells us that we are mortal and urges us to find *the way of life*,[1] the only hope of salvation from sin and death. Others believe that we will come back after our death in some different form of existence, being reincarnated. The Bible insists that is not so, for it tells us starkly that:

> "*Just as it is **appointed for man to die once, and after that comes judgement**, so Christ, having been offered once to bear the sins of many, will appear a second time, not to deal with sin but to save those who are eagerly waiting for him*" (Hebrews 9:27,28).

The Lord Jesus Christ is coming again – the *"second time"* – and then we will have just one opportunity to be given immortal life, which is what the gift of life from God is all about. But what will the resurrection be like, who will be there, and what will happen afterwards?

❖ Mortal or Immortal?

We have seen already that mankind is described as *"mortal,"* not "immortal." This is made plain in the Letter to the Romans as it is everywhere in Scripture:

> "*Claiming to be wise, they became fools, and exchanged the glory of the immortal God for images resembling **mortal man** and birds and animals and reptiles*" (Romans 1:23);

---

[1] *The early believers seem to have called the gospel "the way" (see Acts 16:17; 18:25,26; 24:14; Romans 3:12,17). There was no other way to obtain immortality.*

*"Let not sin therefore reign in **your mortal bodies**, to make you obey their passions" (6:12);*

*"If the Spirit of him who raised Jesus from the dead dwells in you, he who raised Christ Jesus from the dead will also give life to **your mortal bodies** through his Spirit who dwells in you" (8:11).*

God alone possesses immortality, for He is described as: *"from everlasting to everlasting" (Psalm 90:2)* and as *"the King of ages, **immortal**, invisible, the only God" (1 Timothy 1:17)*. Of Almighty God it is said that He:

*"... alone has **immortality**, who dwells in unapproachable light, whom no one has ever seen or can see. To him be honour and eternal dominion. Amen" (1 Timothy 6:16).*

It was a huge gulf that separated God from mankind – He the immortal, invisible, all holy God and mankind mortal and sinful. However close a believer might come to establishing a lasting relationship with his or her Maker, death would end all that. That unconscious state would render a worshipper oblivious of everything. Hezekiah, a faithful king of Judah, once observed as he contemplated his own deliverance from death:

"In love you have delivered my life from the pit of destruction, for you have cast all my sins behind your back. For Sheol does not thank you; death does not praise you; those who go down to the pit do not hope for your faithfulness. The living, the living, he thanks you, as I do this day" (Isaiah 38:17-19).

❖ The Gulf Bridged

The great news, established by the resurrection of Jesus from the dead, is that the gulf has been crossed: a man has risen from the dead to be made immortal by God. That breakthrough has brought hope to all mankind, for what one man has done others might be able to share. Because Jesus lived, died and rose again for mankind, that marvellous event brings hope of immortality to all people who would otherwise perish at death and cease to exist. So immortality suddenly becomes attainable in a way it never has been before, because now there is a real hope of resurrection from the dead. Notice the excitement with which this was proclaimed:[2]

"Therefore do not be ashamed of the testimony about our Lord, nor of me his prisoner, but share in suffering for the gospel by the power of God, **who saved us and called us to a holy calling,** *not because of our works but because of his own purpose and grace, which he gave us in Christ Jesus before the ages began, and* **which now has been manifested through the appearing of our Saviour Christ Jesus, who abolished death and brought life and immortality to light through the gospel"** *(2 Timothy 1:8-10).*

The gospel has brought life and immortality to light, says the apostle, and that makes everything else both bearable and purposeful. Understanding what it teaches makes all the difference between dying without hope and having a real and living hope that will sustain us through anything and everything. Notice that this is the constant teaching of Scripture, as we noted earlier in Romans:

"When God's righteous judgement will be revealed ... He will render to each one according to his works: **to those who by patience in well-doing seek for glory and honour and immortality, he will give eternal life"** *(Romans 2:5-7).*

❖ Preaching the Resurrection

This message of hope spread like wildfire around the first century world. A man had been raised from the dead and, as a result, there was the hope of resurrection from the dead for everyone. If you were to work through the Acts of the Apostles, notebook in hand, to jot down the different occasions when that message was delivered you would find that it was a key teaching of first century believers. Here's just a sample of such passages:

"God raised him up, *loosing the pangs of death, because it was not possible for him to be held by it ...* **This Jesus God raised up,** *and of that we all are witnesses" (Acts 2:24,32);*

---

2 *When Paul wrote these words (in the last letter of his that we have recorded in the New Testament) he was facing death by execution, having been rearrested by the Roman authorities. But he could face that prospect and courageously declare that Jesus has abolished death, for he would die believing in the resurrection of the dead and for him his next conscious moment would be in the presence of his Lord. That is why he could say that for him to die was gain, not loss (Philippians 1:21).*

*"You killed the Author of life, whom **God raised from the dead**. To this we are witnesses ... **God, having raised up his servant**, sent him to you first, to bless you by turning every one of you from your wickedness" (3:15,26);*

*"They were teaching the people and proclaiming in Jesus **the resurrection from the dead**" (4:2);*

*"With great power the apostles were giving their testimony to **the resurrection of the Lord Jesus**, and great grace was upon them all" (4:33);*

*"**God raised him** on the third day and made him to appear" (10:40).*

The key thing about the preaching of the resurrection was that it was an event which *had* happened, something that could be checked, and which had been witnessed by a lot of people. Jesus had been crucified: there was no doubt about that – it was a public execution conducted by soldiers who were well-practised at that sort of death. The historic record is careful to note that his corpse had even been pierced by a spear, whereupon water (some watery body fluid) and blood had emerged. The witness who saw that adds this note:

"He who saw it has borne witness – his testimony is true, and he knows that he is telling the truth – that you also may believe" (John 19:35).

When the apostle Peter preached about the resurrection in Jerusalem he was only a short distance away from where it had all happened, and those who heard him could go and check things out for themselves. They could examine the tomb, talk to the witnesses and make their own judgement about the authenticity of everything that had happened. That's why the resurrection was, and is, such a powerful witness to the reality of God's rescue plan for man. Somebody once called it *"the best attested fact in human history."* [3] New Testament writings describe what happened in such a way that they stress the fact that it is a remarkable miracle well-attested by the surrounding events.

❖ Logical Reasoning

If you want to follow one of those arguments through for yourself, then read 1 Corinthians chapter 15, which is all about the resurrection. There the apostle first writes about the raising of the Lord Jesus Christ; then he reasons out the logical outcome – what that means for believers in every age. It's another letter written by the apostle Paul, like Romans, and he sets out step-by-step the following argument:

No	Verses in 1 Cor 15	Careful Argument
1	1-2	The gospel needs to be believed if we are to be saved
2	3-4	Christ's death, burial and resurrection was *"according to the Scriptures"*
3	5-10	There were many witnesses of what happened – more than 500
4	11	The resurrection is a vital part of the gospel to be believed
5	12-19	That Christ was raised is an absolutely vital part of the gospel; if he was not raised then everything we believe is in vain and our sins still count against us
6	20	*"But in fact Christ has been raised from the dead, the firstfruits of those who have fallen asleep"*
7	21-22	Adam brought death, but Christ brought life [4]

[3] *This was said by Professor Thomas Arnold of Rugby, a world-renowned historian.*

[4] *This is the same point Paul makes in Romans chapter 5 when he contrasts Adam and Jesus and shows how Jesus has reversed the result of Adam's sin (see Chapter 12, pages 165-166).*

No	1 Cor 15	Careful Argument
8	23-28	Everything will happen in an ordered sequence: Christ first, then his followers, at his coming; then Jesus will reign on earth and conquer all his enemies – death included. Eventually he will hand over the Kingdom to God his Father, that God *"may be all in all"* (v.28)
9	29-34	If these things are not true, why are people behaving as they are, and why am I in so much trouble because of what I believe and teach?
10	35-58	This is how things are going to work out ... (Here Paul gives a great deal of detail about the state of those who are resurrected and raised to glory)

This chapter contains an impressive piece of logical deduction in which the inspired apostle looks at the facts calmly and soberly. He concludes that, without the resurrection, he would have no hope of life whatsoever, nor would any who follow Jesus. Indeed, he reasons, they would have wasted their lives following a delusion rather than the truth from God. Contrast that reasoning with the muddled thinking of people who think you go to heaven at death. For them the resurrection is more of an embarrassment than anything else – the soul and body are combined again for no particular reason, in their scheme of things. But we have seen how wrong that way of thinking is. It is entirely the opposite of what the Bible teaches. As death is an unconscious state, resurrection is vitally necessary. Without it there is just no hope of life after death: we would remain forever unconscious in the grave.

❖ When will it Happen?

It's time to discover what the Bible says about the timing and detail of the forthcoming resurrection, since it is so important to all of us. Paul has already given an important pointer, which you will have picked up if you have read the whole of 1 Corinthians 15 already. Jesus has been raised as the *"firstfruits"* of all those who are to be raised *"at his coming"*. Here's a fuller extract:

> *"As in Adam all die, so also in Christ shall all be made alive. But each in his own order: Christ the firstfruits, then* **at his coming** *those who belong to Christ" (1 Corinthians 15:22,23).*

When Jesus comes again to earth he is going to raise many of the sleeping dead and call them forth to judgement. Until then all who die are still in the graves – their memories lost, their feelings gone, their identity known in detail only to God, who alone is able to recreate them as they once were. This is one reason why the coming again of the Lord Jesus Christ is so important to all those who believe in him and why it will be such a cause of concern to those who choose to reject him. Remember what Paul said early in Romans:

> *"Do you presume on the riches of his kindness and forbearance and patience, not knowing that God's kindness is meant to lead you to repentance? But because of your hard and impenitent heart* **you are storing up wrath for yourself on the day of wrath when God's righteous judgement will be revealed.** *He will render to each one according to his works: to those who by patience in well-doing seek for glory and honour and immortality, he will give eternal life; but* **for those who are self-seeking and do not obey the truth, but obey unrighteousness, there will be wrath and fury.** *There will be tribulation and distress for every human being who does evil" (Romans 2:4-9).*

It is the coming of Jesus that will bring all these things to a head; that will separate the *"good"* from the *"evil"*, as these passages confirm:

> *"An hour is coming when all who are in the tombs will* **hear his voice** *and come out, those who have done good to the resurrection of life, and those who have done evil to the resurrection of judgement" (John 5:28,29);*

> *"And this is the will of him who sent me, that I should lose nothing of all that he has given me, but raise it up on the last day. For this is the will of my Father, that everyone who looks on the Son and believes in him should have eternal life, and* **I will raise him up on the last day"** *(6:39,40);*

*"Jesus said to her, **'I am the resurrection and the life.*** *Whoever believes in me, though he die, yet shall he live'"* *(11:25);*

*"God raised him on the third day and made him to appear, not to all the people but to us who had been cho-sen by God as witnesses, who ate and drank with him after he rose from the dead. And he commanded us to preach to the people and to testify that **he is the one appointed by God to be judge of the living and the dead"** (Acts 10:40-42);*

*"Henceforth there is laid up for me **the crown of right-eousness**, which the Lord, the righteous judge, will award to me **on that Day**, and not only to me but also to all who have loved his appearing" (2 Timothy 4:8);*

*"Behold, I am coming soon, **bringing my recompense with me, to repay everyone for what he has done"** (Revelation 22:12).*

❖ Detailed Explanations

Two lengthy passages deal with this topic in some detail and recognise that when the Lord Jesus comes there will be some believers alive and others who have fallen asleep in death. Here is the first of them, in full:

"We do not want you to be uninformed, brothers, about those who are asleep, that you may not grieve as others do who have no hope. For since we believe that Jesus died and rose again, even so, through Jesus, God will bring with him those who have fallen asleep. For this we declare to you by a word from the Lord, that we who are alive, who are left until the coming of the Lord, will not precede those who have fallen asleep. For the Lord him-self will descend from heaven with a cry of command, with the voice of an archangel, and with the sound of the trumpet of God. And the dead in Christ will rise first. Then we who are alive, who are left, will be caught up together with them in the clouds to meet the Lord in the air, and so we will always be with the Lord. Therefore encourage one another with these words" (1 Thessalonians 4:13-18).

This is another of those passages where we can use our analytical skills and see just what we are being told. Here are some points that emerge:

🖎 Death is described as *"sleep"*, because it is an unconscious state in which everything has finished for the time being;

🖎 This passage is written to those who believe the gospel and is about their future expectations; it does not detail everything that will happen to everybody;

🖎 Paul received a specific revelation about this, which he calls "a word from the Lord";

🖎 Baptized believers who have died – those who are *"in Christ"* – will rise from the dead first; believers who are still alive will not precede them;

🖎 The Lord Jesus will return on the clouds of heaven and, with a cry of command and the last trumpet, he will raise the sleeping dead;

🖎 The resurrected dead and those baptized believers still alive will be caught up together to meet the Lord in the air as a preliminary to their being *"ever with the Lord"*. [5]

The second such passage is one we have already started to examine – the 'resurrection chapter' – 1 Corinthians chapter 15. Here is further detail that Scripture supplies:

"I tell you this, brothers: flesh and blood cannot inherit the kingdom of God, nor does the perishable inherit the imperishable. Behold! I tell you a mystery. We shall not all sleep, but we shall all be changed, in a moment, in the twinkling of an eye, at the last trumpet. For the trumpet will sound, and the dead will be raised imperishable, and we shall be changed. For this perishable body must put on the imperishable, and this mortal body must put on immortality" (15:50-53).

---

[5] *Going to meet Jesus means that we are due to return with him also. There is no reference here to the believers going to heaven with Jesus. You don't go to meet someone if you are going to their home – they come to meet you in those circumstances. The same terminology is used about believers who came to meet Paul when he was journeying to Rome (Acts 28:15).*

The added information is that there has to be a process of change and bodily transformation if we are to move from a *"perishable"* condition to one which is *"imperishable"*. Paul says that we must be changed from a *"mortal"* state to an *"immortal"* one. That will happen once the judgement has taken place, for when Jesus comes he is coming to judge the world and to declare people either "good" or "evil". In this passage the apostle is looking at the end product of the process of resurrection for all those believers who are found faithful and acceptable to Christ.

He does not here consider the fate of those who had stored up wrath for themselves: *"on the day of wrath when God's righteous judgement will be revealed"* (Romans 2:5). We shall need to give their fate a little thought later, but first we need to think about the meaning of judgement for all those who have accepted Christ as their Lord and Saviour, and have become baptized believers. Will they be judged?

❖ The Judgement Seat of Christ

If we started to reason this out for ourselves we might come to a lot of different conclusions. But those ideas would only be useful if they were true. We could all imagine that somebody who liked cooking might enjoy an eternity cooking in a heavenly kitchen. Or somebody who was a keen footballer could be pictured playing football forever. The real question is: what does the Bible teach? None of us has personal experience of life after death and the Bible strongly condemns the practice of consulting mediums and the teaching of spiritualism as something we should not do or get involved in.[6]

Instead we should be living in daily awareness of the fact that the time will soon come when we all have to appear before the judgement seat of the Lord Jesus Christ. This is what we are told about that coming experience:

> *"**God will bring every deed into judgement**, with every secret thing, whether good or evil"* (Ecclesiastes 12:14);

---

[6] *See, for example, Leviticus 19:31; 20:6,27; Deuteronomy 18:10,11; Isaiah 8:19; 19:3. People who practised as mediums in Old Testament days were so offensive to God, because they misrepresented Him and His teaching, that they were to be executed when they had been tracked down!*

*"Many of those who sleep in the dust of the earth shall awake, **some to everlasting life, and some to shame and everlasting contempt"** (Daniel 12:2);*

*"He commanded us to preach to the people and to testify that he is the one appointed by God to be **judge of the living and the dead"** (Acts 10:42);*

*"(God) has fixed a day on which he will **judge the world in righteousness** by a man whom he has appointed; and of this he has given assurance to all by raising him from the dead" (Acts 17:31);*

*"... on that day when, according to my gospel, **God judges the secrets of men by Christ Jesus"** (Romans 2:16);*

*"Why do you pass judgement on your brother? Or you, why do you despise your brother? **For we will all stand before the judgement seat of God"** (Romans 14:10);*

*"Therefore do not pronounce judgement before the time, **before the Lord comes**, who will bring to light the things now hidden in darkness and will disclose the purposes of the heart. Then each one will receive his commendation from God" (1 Corinthians 4:5);*

*"For we must all appear before **the judgement seat of Christ**, so that each one may receive what is due for what he has done in the body, whether good or evil" (2 Corinthians 5:10);*

*"I charge you in the presence of God and of Christ Jesus, **who is to judge the living and the dead, and by his appearing and his kingdom"** (2 Timothy 4:1);*

*"For it is time for **judgement to begin at the household of God**; and if it begins with us, what will be the outcome for those who do not obey the gospel of God?" (1 Peter 4:17).*

Collecting together verses like these, which talk about judgement, or the Judgement Seat of Christ, enables us to gather a lot of information from different parts of the Bible. It's a different technique from that of analysing one part of

272

Scripture, but it yields the same results once we have done the initial work. Cross-references can be helpful in accumulating the passages, and a concordance [7]can assist, but the key thing, once you have collected the information, is to look at what you have and draw proper conclusions from it, like this:

ꕷ God will judge the world through the Lord Jesus Christ, to whom He has delegated that task (Ecclesiastes 12:14; Acts 17:31; Romans 2:16 etc.);

ꕷ That judgement will be both of those living at his return and the resurrected dead (Acts 10:42; 2 Timothy 4:1);

ꕷ It will take place at the return to earth of the Lord Jesus Christ (1 Corinthians 4:5; 2 Timothy 4:1);

ꕷ The judgement will be righteous and will take account of the innermost thoughts and feelings of our hearts, as well as the things we have said and done (Ecclesiastes 12:14; Acts 17:31; Romans 2:16; 1 Corinthians 4:5; 2 Corinthians 5:10);

ꕷ Everybody who is accountable to God – who has done either *"good"* or *"evil"* in His sight – will appear before the judgement seat of Christ (Ecclesiastes 12:14; Romans 14:10; 2 Corinthians 5:10; 1 Peter 4:17); [8]

ꕷ The outcome of the judgement will be that some will receive the gift of everlasting life and others will not (Daniel 12:2; 1 Peter 4:17).

❖ Why a Judgement at all?

You may be wondering why there has to be a judgement at all. Why doesn't God just destroy sin and sinners outright and allow those who are acceptable to Him to become immortal? This isn't how God works, for everything He does

---

[7] *A Concordance is a listing of Bible verses according to a specific word. Some concordances give every occurrence of that word; others give just some of the occurrences.*

[8] *We have already seen (Chapter 17, pages 254-256) that some people will not be raised; clearly they will not be regarded by God as subject to His righteous judgement.*

is in accordance with His righteous character. He is just and holy, and can never compromise with sin. But He is also determined to show men and women the difference between right and wrong, between good and evil. God's judgement of the world will do that. At present there are people who appear to have "got away with it"; who have done very wrong things but who were never reprimanded for the error of their ways. They just died, like everybody else.

Take the case of those evil men in Jerusalem who tried Jesus on false charges and wrongly condemned him to death. They arranged with the Roman governor to have him executed and then visited him as he hung upon the cross, jeering and sneering. Do you think it right that they should never be held accountable for what they did? In fact we know, because Jesus has told us, that the time will come when they shall be raised to judgement, and we know the outcome:

> "He will say, 'I tell you, I do not know where you come from. Depart from me, all you workers of evil!' In that place there will be weeping and gnashing of teeth, when you see Abraham and Isaac and Jacob and all the prophets in the kingdom of God but you yourselves cast out'" (Luke 13:27,28).

❖ The Basis of Judgement

The basis of their judgement will be that they had every opportunity to learn from and follow the example of the Lord Jesus Christ, who lived and taught among them, and they not only rejected him, but they arranged to have him crucified. They are to see the risen Lord in all his glory, with those from all ages who acclaim him King and Lord, and then they are to be "cast out". Elsewhere we are told that the rejected will be cast into "outer darkness" (Matthew 22:13; 25:30).

As the judgement will affect all those who know enough about the purpose of God to be accounted good or evil in His sight, we need to be sure that we know the basis on which we could be judged. Imagine being summoned to the judgement seat of Christ and being presented with charges we knew nothing about and which we could then do nothing about! Fortunately, God doesn't work like that either. He always gives due notice to His creation of what His purpose is and what He wants people to do. And He always warns of the consequences of disobedience, whilst encouraging obedience by promising a happy outcome for those who follow His guidance in life.

Judgement will be based on our response to the offer of God as explained in His Word, the Bible. Those who saw the purpose of God at first hand, or who heard Jesus and the apostles preach, and saw the confirmatory signs and wonders, will have less excuse than others.

"Therefore we must pay much closer attention to what we have heard, lest we drift away from it. For since the message declared by angels proved to be reliable and every transgression or disobedience received a just retribution, **how shall we escape if we neglect such a great salvation? It was declared at first by the Lord, and it was attested to us by those who heard, while God also bore witness by signs and wonders and various miracles and by gifts of the Holy Spirit distributed according to his will"** *(Hebrews 2:1-4).*

That passage has especial relevance to all those who have witnessed miracles,[9] but the first sentence is relevant to people in every age. The basis of judgement will be our response to what God has revealed in His Word and what the Lord Jesus has said and done. Jesus said:

"I have come into the world as light, so that whoever believes in me may not remain in darkness. If anyone hears my words and does not keep them, I do not judge him; for I did not come to judge the world but to save the world. **The one who rejects me and does not receive my words has a judge; the word that I have spoken will judge him on the last day.** *For I have not spoken on my own authority, but the Father who sent me has himself given me a commandment – what to say and what to speak. And I know that his commandment is eternal life. What I say, therefore, I say as the Father has told me"* *(John 12:46-50).*

Everybody who hears the gospel, and understands it, encounters Jesus as he is portrayed in the Scriptures, and

---

[9] *God has been at work in the 20th and 21st centuries as well, and a major modern miracle has occurred – the return of the Jews to their ancient land. So we should bear in mind that the more we are privileged to see of God's outworking purpose, the more we should be responsive to His will.*

can decide whether or not to follow him. We might listen to his words and take note of what we are being asked to do, or we might decide not to bother. Or we may listen at first, but lose interest later. Whichever way we choose to respond to God's offer of salvation, we should be aware of the possible consequences of our decision. If called to give account of our actions, we could be in one of these two camps:

> *"... when the Lord Jesus is revealed from heaven with his mighty angels in flaming fire, inflicting vengeance on those who do not know God [10] and on those who do not obey the gospel of our Lord Jesus. (1)* **They will suffer the punishment of eternal destruction, away from the presence of the Lord and from the glory of his might, when he comes on that day** *(2)* **to be glorified in his saints, and to be marvelled at among all who have believed,** *because our testimony to you was believed" (2 Thessalonians 1:7-10).*

That's a stark set of alternatives. We could either be classed with those who do not know God and do not obey the gospel of our Lord Jesus, or with those who believe, obey, and are counted *"worthy of his calling"*. Once again you will note that it is knowledge of the gospel of salvation that makes us accountable at the coming of Jesus.

We are saved by faith, but that faith is expected to change our actions – hence Paul's reference to *"every work of faith"* in 2 Thessalonians 1 verse 11. Our thoughts, words and deeds demonstrate the quality and reality of our faith, though none of the things that we do can ever be enough to merit what God has in store for those who love Him.

We will be saved because of God's grace and mercy to us; but we are still expected to live in a way which shows that we really want to have a part in the world to come.[11]

The key thing is to get our life right with God now; then there will be nothing to worry about. Paul had done that and he was able to look forward with confidence knowing that the coming of Christ would mean the arrival of his reward – the gift of eternal life. Writing to Timothy on the eve of his execution he could say:

---

[10] *This has to be understood, in the light of what we have already seen, as referring to those who could have known God, and have established a relationship with Him, but who have chosen not to do that (see John 17:3).*

"The time of my departure has come. I have fought the good fight, I have finished the race, I have kept the faith. Henceforth there is laid up for me the crown of righteousness, which the Lord, the righteous judge, will award to me on that Day, and not only to me but also to all who have loved his appearing" (2 Timothy 4:6-8).

Things to Read

☐ The resurrection accounts of Jesus make fascinating reading and have convinced many unbelievers over the years that the only thing that fits all the facts is that Jesus must have risen bodily from the tomb. Try John chapter 20 or Luke chapter 24, or both.

☐ After ascending to heaven, Jesus wrote seven letters to various groups of believers. Read those letters in Revelation chapters 2 and 3 and then look at the two questions about them detailed below.

Questions to Think About

18.1 In the letters that Jesus wrote to the churches in Asia (Revelation chapters 2 and 3) he mentioned seven different rewards that would be available to those who are found acceptable to him when he returns. List those rewards. (Revelation 2:7,11,17,26-28; 3:5,12,20-21)

18.2 What do those believers have to do to inherit those rewards, and what are the dangers they have to overcome? (Revelation 2:1-3:22)

---

[11] *This important distinction can be seen by comparing Romans chapter 4 with James chapter 2, where some of the same people are referred to. Paul is insistent that we are saved by the things that we believe; James is equally insistent that faith, if it is the genuine thing, has to show itself by our actions. Otherwise, he says, it is not really a saving faith. That's also the meaning of Matthew 12:37.*

19
The Promised Reward

The resurrection leads to the judgement seat of Christ at his coming. To that judgement the resurrected dead will be summoned. Not everyone will be called to judgement and it is God who will decide who will be called to account and who will be left to perish. What matters is how people respond to the invitation that God makes, and the warnings that He gives, in His Word the Bible.

People who ignore God and who choose to be ungodly and unrighteous will be punished, as Paul made clear early on in his Letter to the Romans (see 1:18-21). There he referred to people who had every opportunity to learn about God but who didn't want to know. In this chapter we want to think about what happens to those who are accepted by God and are rewarded accordingly.

In exploring Paul's letter, we have now reached that chapter which is all about the believer's new life in Christ. It gives us encouragement to *"walk in the Spirit"* and to join all those who are waiting for the coming transformation. In the apostle's words:

> *"We know that the whole creation has been groaning together in the pains of childbirth until now. And not only the creation, but we ourselves, who have the firstfruits of the Spirit, groan inwardly as we wait eagerly for adoption as sons, the redemption of our bodies"* (Romans 8:22,23).

These are optimistic words to believers who were being encouraged to look forward expectantly to the coming transformation. Paul was not trying to frighten them by the thought of the judgement seat of Christ. On the contrary, he started this section of his letter by saying that they would have nothing to worry about if they lived in the right way – in faithful obedience to the things that God has revealed:

> *"There is therefore now no condemnation for those who are in Christ Jesus ... who walk not according to the*

flesh but according to the Spirit" (Romans 8:1-4).

So the judgement seat of Christ is not something to be frightened of, providing we are now living in a right relationship with God and are developing a spiritual attitude and manner of life. It is very much a matter of what we do now that determines what will happen then. In Romans chapter 9, Paul goes on to say that God has the perfect right to decide the outcome of everything at the coming of Jesus. For God is Sovereign: He is the Ruler over all.[1] He will express His anger towards those who deserve it and His mercy to those He chooses to favour.

❖ Sowing and Reaping

In another of his letters, Paul uses an image from farming to illustrate the way we need to prepare for the future when he says:

> *"Do not be deceived: God is not mocked, for **whatever one sows, that will he also reap.** For the one who sows to his own flesh will from the flesh reap corruption, but the one who sows to the Spirit will from the Spirit reap eternal life. And let us not grow weary of doing good, for in due season we will reap, if we do not give up" (Galatians 6:7-9).*

Again it's the choice between *"flesh"* and *"spirit"* – of either pleasing ourselves and living exactly as we want, or of living in a way which pleases God and gives Him glory. Notice that the outcomes are as stark as those we have seen from other passages of Scripture – we either end up with *"eternal life"* or our whole existence ends in *"corruption"*. The best outcome is obvious! What we do now determines what will happen then – it's a classic case of "cause and effect".

Jesus used the very same figure – of sowing and reaping – in his parables. In one he talks about a sower who cast his seed on all different sorts of ground which then responded according to its characteristics.[2] The path was too hard for the seed to take root; the stony

---

[1] *See, in particular, Romans 9:22-23.*

[2] *You can read the parable and the detailed explanation Jesus gives in Matthew chapter 13, verses 1-23.*

ground was too shallow; the weed-strewn ground was too much of a tangle; the good ground yielded the harvest. Another parable was about a farmer who had sown a field but his enemy came and sowed weeds in it: Jesus said that the good and the bad would have to be sorted out at harvest time.[3] He told another one about a man who planted seed and then watched it grow:

> *"The earth produces by itself, first the blade, then the ear, then the full grain in the ear. But when the grain is ripe, at once he puts in the sickle, because the harvest has come" (Mark 4:28,29).*

These parables all teach that things change over time, whether for good or bad, and that eventually there comes a time of reckoning when the quantity and quality of the crop can be determined. Jesus said explicitly that the harvest in his parables represented the end of the age (Matthew 13:39), so the idea of sowing and reaping as a parable of life "in Christ" had been well established before Paul used it. One key point of this particular theme is that changes take time to accomplish and it is not always apparent whether something that has started well will last the course. Grain goes through several stages before the growth cycle is complete – first the blade, then the ear and then the full grain which, when it has ripened, can be harvested. It is the same in our spiritual development. New ideas are sown in our minds and it takes a while before they take root and even longer before they are strong enough in our minds to change the way we behave.

❖ The Resurrection Harvest

The apostle Paul used the idea of fruit progressing and maturing over time, when he described what the resurrection body will be like. In the last chapter we looked at some of his careful reasoning in 1 Corinthians chapter 15 and you may have read the whole chapter at the time. If not, this is a good time to read it, for Paul sets himself this question to answer:

> *"Someone will ask, 'How are the dead raised? With what kind of body do they come?'" (1 Corinthians 15:35)*

He answers it by talking about the process of sowing

---

[3] *Matthew 13:24-30.*

and reaping and while doing so compares and contrasts the state we are in now with the condition that awaits all who are accounted worthy to be given the gift of eternal life:

"You foolish person! What you sow does not come to life unless it dies. And what you sow is not the body that is to be, but a bare kernel, perhaps of wheat or of some other grain. But God gives it a body as he has chosen, and to each kind of seed its own body" (15:36-38).

Seeing the two contrasting positions in the form of a table might make it clearer, but there is no real substitute for reading the passage.

1 Cor 15 verse:	How we are in this life	How we will be in the life to come
42	What is sown is perishable	... what is raised is imperishable
43	it is sown in dishonour ... in weakness	... it is raised in glory ... in power
44	It is sown a natural body	... it is raised a spiritual body
48	As was the man of dust (Adam), so also are those who are of the dust	... as is the man of heaven (Jesus), so also are those who are of heaven
49	as we have borne the image of the man of dust	... we shall also bear the image of the man of heaven
50-52	flesh and blood cannot inherit the kingdom of God, nor does the perishable inherit the imperishable	We shall not all sleep, but we shall all be changed, in a moment, in the twinkling of an eye, at the last trumpet. For the trumpet will sound, and the dead will be raised imperishable, and we shall be changed
53	this perishable body	... must put on the imperishable
53-54	and this mortal body	... must put on immortality

Paul is describing a process of change and development which results in an outcome very different from things at the present time. The perishable becomes imperishable; the natural becomes spiritual; the earthly becomes heavenly and the mortal becomes immortal. It will all come to fruition at the return to earth of Jesus Christ and the sounding of the last trumpet. Then, as we learned from 1 Thessalonians 4:13-18,[4] the dead who are raised and the living who remain will be caught up together to meet the Lord, before their appearance at the judgement seat, and the giving of immortality.

Take careful note of what we just did, as it is another step in understanding the Bible for yourself. We have just looked in detail at 1 Corinthians 15, verses 42-54, and have seen the contrast that Paul makes between the two states, before and after the resurrection process. Earlier we looked at 1 Thessalonians 4:13-18 in similar detail and listed our findings from that passage. Now we have just brought those two pieces of information together to get a more complete picture. That's how the Bible conveys God's message. It is not organised into topics, so that if you want to find out about life after death, for example, you just look up pages 25-35. You have to search out the full picture by reading it all and fitting what you have learned together, a bit like a jigsaw puzzle. That's why Jesus said:

*"**Ask**, and it will be given to you; **seek**, and you will find; **knock**, and it will be opened to you. For everyone who **asks** receives, and the one who **seeks** finds, and to the one who **knocks** it will be opened" (Matthew 7:7,8);* and

"He who has ears, let him hear" (Matthew 13:43).[5]

❖ God's Prerogative

Immortality is the most wonderful reward God can give us, provided we are to live forever in a happy and fulfilling environment. Nobody wants to live forever in misery and constant unhappiness. But who decides who will live and

---

[4] *Chapter 18, pages 269-270.*

[5] *This saying, which Jesus used quite a lot, means that if we really want to hear what Jesus has to say we need to listen really carefully and then think hard about what it means. The prophet Isaiah said something similar in Isaiah 55:1-5.*

who will die, and what right have they to make such vital and far-reaching decisions? That's the issue the apostle now addresses, as he continues with his Letter to the Romans, in chapter 9. First he refers to God's purpose with the nation of Israel and says that he is grief-stricken that they rejected Christ. But, he explains, they could never have been saved simply as a result of their natural descent from Abraham.

By nature we are all descended from Adam and we have already thought a lot about what that means – not only are we dying creatures, we are by nature inclined towards pleasing ourselves rather than God. We need a new nature: rebirth by water (in baptism) and by the Spirit (both in the development of a spiritual mind and eventually by resurrection to a new life in a 'spiritual body'). This has been the same all through history, including that of the nation of Israel. Although God made it a special nation,[6] it was necessary for the Jews to seek out God's salvation by believing His promises. This is how Paul explains it:

> *"It is not as though the word of God has failed. For not all who are descended from Israel belong to Israel, and not all are children of Abraham because they are his offspring, but 'Through Isaac shall your offspring be named.'* **This means that it is not the children of the flesh who are the children of God, but the children of the promise are counted as offspring"** *(Romans 9:6-8).*

He goes on to explain that, as salvation is God's free gift, one which nobody could ever earn, it is God's prerogative to decide who can inherit eternal life and who cannot. He uses the figure of a potter moulding clay and says that the clay has no right to complain to the potter what it becomes – whether a vase for public display or a pot for use only in the kitchen:

> *"Who are you, O man, to answer back to God? Will what is moulded say to its moulder, 'Why have you made me like this?' Has the potter no right over the clay, to make out of the same lump one vessel for honoured use and another for dishonourable use? What if God, desiring to show his wrath and to make known his power, has*

---

[6] *Romans 9:4,5.*

endured with much patience ves-
sels of wrath prepared for
destruction, in order to make
known the riches of his glory
for vessels of mercy, which he
has prepared beforehand for
glory?" (Romans 9:20-23).

There are some complicated
arguments here about those whom
God chooses and those He rejects
which need not trouble us at the moment. The key thing to
note is that God can do what He pleases because He is the
Creator, and has complete sovereignty over His creation. He
offers the same thing to all those who believe His promises
and choose to obey His commandments. Those who decline
will suffer *"destruction"*, while those who respond will be
rewarded with *"the riches of his glory"*.

❖ "The riches of his glory"

When we come across a new idea like this one – the glory
of God – we need a technique to work out what it means.
By far the best method is to let Scripture interpret
Scripture, rather than just looking to see what other people
think it means, and there are two helpful principles we can
apply.

✓ The first is to look at the immediate context, especially
  how the writer in question uses the word.

✓ The second is to track the development of the word or
  phrase through the Bible and see how it grows in meaning as different events are referred to.

Reading carefully, using cross-references in a Bible or
looking things up in a Concordance, will help with both
those things. For example, this is how the apostle uses that
expression in Romans:

Romans	Word Study: *"Glory"*
1:23	exchanged the **glory** of the immortal God for images resembling mortal man and birds and animals and reptiles
2:7,10	to those who by patience in well-doing seek for **glory** and honour and immortality, he will give eternal life; but glory and honour and peace for everyone who does good, the Jew first and also the Greek
3:23	all have sinned and fall short of the **glory** of God
5:2	Through him we have also obtained access by faith into this grace in which we stand, and we rejoice in hope of the glory of God
8:18	I consider that the sufferings of this present time are not worth comparing with the **glory** that is to be revealed to us
8:21	the creation itself will be set free from its bondage to decay and obtain the freedom of the **glory** of the children of God
9:23	in order to make known the riches of his glory for vessels of mercy, which he has prepared beforehand for **glory**
11:36	For from him and through him and to him are all things. To him be **glory** forever. Amen.
16:27	to the only wise God be **glory** for evermore through Jesus Christ! Amen.

From this it is clear that *"glory"* is quite an important idea in the apostle's thinking. It is:

⭲ **an attribute of the immortal God –**

> ⮫ God is glorious and majestic in all His ways – He is the *"God of glory"* (Romans 1:23; Acts 7:2);

⭲ **something that we should give to God –**

> ⮫ When we give God thanks and praise we are giving God glory and honour (Romans 16:27; Revelation 14:17);

⭲ **something He is going to share with His creation, when He makes them free and shares with them the riches of His glory –**

> ⮫ But how do we get to share in, or reflect, the glory of God in the way the apostle says will happen?

❖ **Sharing God's Glory**

From the immediate context in Romans we have narrowed down the question considerably. Using our second principle, we can now look at other parts of Scripture to find an answer. Here are some pointers:

1 God's creation displays His glory, for the Psalmist says: *"The heavens declare the **glory of God**, and the sky above proclaims his handiwork" (Psalm 19:1).* This is the equivalent of what we have already discovered in Romans, that *"his invisible attributes, namely, **his eternal power and divine nature**, have been clearly perceived, ever since the creation of the world, in the things that have been made" (Romans 1:20).*

2 When God rescued His people from Israel He showed them His glory in several different ways:

   a It was in the form of a devouring fire which appeared upon Mount Sinai (Exodus 24:17);

   b Sometimes the glory appeared in a cloud (Exodus 16:10);

   c Once Moses asked to be shown God's glory and was given an explanation – it was an expression of the nature and character of Almighty God.

286

❖ "Show me your Glory"

God had promised Moses that He would stay with His people and finish what He had started with them. So Moses asked if God would reveal something more about the sort of God He was, hence the request he made: *"Please show me your glory" (Exodus 33:8).* God explained that His nature is such that Moses could not behold Him and live, so He put Moses in a safe place and he heard this exposition of what the glory of God really meant:

> *"The* LORD *passed before him and proclaimed, 'The* LORD, *the* LORD, **a God merciful and gracious, slow to anger, and abounding in steadfast love and faithfulness, keeping steadfast love for thousands, forgiving iniquity and transgression and sin, but who will by no means clear the guilty, visiting the iniquity of the fathers on the children and the children's children, to the third and the fourth generation.'** *And Moses quickly bowed his head toward the earth and worshipped" (Exodus 34:6-8).*

This is a very important explanation of what God's glory really means for us. Those who are privileged to receive God's gift of immortality in the age to come are to be made like the Lord Jesus Christ – to *"bear the image of the man from heaven";* their bodies are to become *"spiritual", "imperishable"* and *"immortal"* (1 Corinthians 15:42-54).[7] But as they are also to be *"raised in glory",* and as God will make known to them *"the riches of his glory"* (Romans 9:23), we now know what that means.

The *character* of those who are to be raised to glory will be like that of Almighty God. By *nature,* they too will be merciful and gracious, patient, loving, faithful and forgiving. There is to be an inner transformation as well as a bodily one; a mental and moral one as well as a physical one. It is not only that death will have no power over them: henceforth they will be untroubled by sinful thoughts, temptations, or any inclinations of that sort. They will be equal to the angels and just as untouchable by sin.

From the very beginning God wanted a race of people who would be like that. He wanted a world that would be inhabited by people who would honour Him and who would

---

[7] *That is what we worked out in the table on page 281.*

share His values and virtues. It has taken a long time and a huge initiative on God's part to achieve that objective, but now the opportunity exists because of His saving work, accomplished through Jesus. This glorious outcome is possible and we can be part of it. This is what God has declared at various times as His purpose has been revealed step-by-step:

> *"But truly, as I live, and as **all the earth shall be filled with the glory of the** L*ORD *..." (Numbers 14:21);*

> *"Blessed be his glorious name forever; **may the whole earth be filled with his glory!**" (Psalm 72:19)*

> *"For thus says the* L*ORD, who created the heavens (he is God!), who formed the earth and made it (he established it; he did not create it empty, **he formed it to be inhabited!**): 'I am the Lord, and there is no other ... **In the LORD all the offspring of Israel shall be justified and shall glory**'" (Isaiah 45:18,25);*

> *"So they shall fear the name of the* L*ORD from the west, and his **glory** from the rising of the sun; for he will come like a rushing stream, which the wind of the* L*ORD drives. 'And **a Redeemer will come to Zion,** to those in Jacob who turn from transgression,' declares the* L*ORD" (Isaiah 59:19,20);*

> *"For **the earth will be filled with the knowledge of the glory of the** L*ORD *as the waters cover the sea" (Habakkuk 2:14);*

> *"After this I saw another angel coming down from heaven, having great authority, and **the earth was made bright with his glory**" (Revelation 18:1);*

> *"I heard a loud voice from the throne saying, 'Behold, **the dwelling place of God is with man. He will dwell with them, and they will be his people, and God himself will be with them as their God.** He will wipe away every tear from their eyes, and death shall be no more, neither shall there be mourning nor crying nor pain anymore, for the former things have passed away.' And he who was seated on the throne said,*

'Behold, I am making all things new'" (Revelation 21:3-5).

These passages combine to give us an overview of the purpose of God. He formed the earth with the intention of having it inhabited and will remake the earth into a glorious habitation for His people. That will require a lot of changes to the way things are now organised, not just to the political system but to the way people think and behave. That's why it's important for us to change now, so that we can be ready for all the changes that God will make when the Lord Jesus Christ returns to rule as king.[8]

❖ Earth not Heaven

People have become confused about their true nature, and no longer realise they are mortal. In the same way, there is widespread confusion about the place where God will give His promised reward to the faithful when they have been raised to glory. People just assume that the Bible promises heavenly bliss, without realising that the Bible describes that happy state as something that is coming from heaven to earth, when the Lord Jesus returns as king. Think about these verses:

*"For the evildoers shall be cut off, but those who wait for the LORD **shall inherit the land**. In just a little while, the wicked will be no more; though you look carefully at his place, he will not be there. But **the meek shall inherit the land** and delight themselves in abundant peace"* (Psalm 37:9-11);

*"The heavens are the LORD's heavens, but **the earth he has given to the children of man**"* (Psalm 115:16);

*"For the upright **will inhabit the land**, and those with integrity will remain in it, but the wicked will be cut off from the land, and the treacherous will be rooted out of it"* (Proverbs 2:21,22);

*"If the righteous is **repaid on earth**, how much more the wicked and the sinner!"* (Proverbs 11:31);

---

[8] *Notice that Isaiah 59:20 (referred to above) tells us where Jesus is coming to. The redeemer is coming to Zion (another name for Jerusalem) and Paul refers to that very prophecy in Romans 11:26 when he is describing the future role of the Jewish people in God's purpose (see Chapter 21).*

*"Blessed are the meek, **for they shall inherit the earth"** (Matthew 5:5);*

*"Our Father in heaven, hallowed be your name. **Your kingdom come, your will be done, on earth as it is in heaven"** (Matthew 6:9,10);*

*"In my Father's house are many rooms. If it were not so, would I have told you that I go to prepare a place for you? And if I go and prepare a place for you, **I will come again** and will take you to myself, **that where I am you may be also"** (John 14:2,3);*

*"The promise to Abraham and his offspring that he would be **heir of the world** did not come through the law but through the righteousness of faith" (Romans 4:13);*

*"Then I saw a new heaven and a new earth, for the first heaven and the first earth had passed away, and the sea was no more. And I saw the holy city, new Jerusalem, **coming down out of heaven from God**, prepared as a bride adorned for her husband. And I heard a loud voice from the throne saying, '**Behold, the dwelling place of God is with man. He will dwell with them**, and they will be his people, and God himself will be with them as their God'" (Revelation 21:1-3);*

*"You have made them a kingdom and priests to our God, and **they shall reign on the earth"** (Revelation 5:10).*

It is exactly this outcome that the apostle Paul has in mind when he says that the earth is awaiting its freedom, to realise its true potential. That will be achieved only when the resurrection of the dead takes place:

"We know that the whole creation has been groaning together in the pains of childbirth until now. And not only the creation, but we ourselves, who have the firstfruits of the Spirit, groan inwardly as we wait eagerly for adoption as sons, the redemption of our bodies" (Romans 8:22,23).

❖ God's Rescue Plan

The present problems that now confront people on earth –

including matters such as global warming, rising sea levels, changing climatic conditions and a polluted environment – are in fact the birthpangs of a new age. At a time just like this – when the earth is facing massive problems due to human mismanagement – God will intervene to rescue the position and to direct matters to a much happier outcome. He is going to fill the earth with His glory by sending His Son to earth to take control. The resurrection of the dead will then take place and those who are found faithful will be made immortal: thereafter they will live to give God glory and honour and praise and they will do so in every aspect of their new lives.

The Book of Revelation – the last book in the Bible – was given to explain what would happen up to and including the return of Jesus to earth. It announces at the beginning that it is:

> *"... from Jesus Christ the faithful witness, the firstborn of the dead, and the ruler of kings on earth. To him who loves us and has freed us from our sins by his blood and made us a kingdom, priests to his God and Father, to him be glory and dominion forever and ever. Amen.* **Behold, he is coming with the clouds, and every eye will see him, even those who pierced him, and all tribes of the earth will wail on account of him.** *Even so. Amen" (Revelation 1:5-7).*

Notice that there will be people who are sorry to see Jesus return. Indeed, we learn from other Scriptures that there will be those who challenge and oppose him when he comes. Jesus is coming to rescue the world and to save all those men and women who have prepared for that great event. It will be judgement time for the earth when mankind is called to account for the way in which God's earth has been despoiled and mismanaged.

> *"Then the seventh angel blew his trumpet,[9] and there were loud voices in heaven, saying,* **'The kingdom of the world has become the kingdom of our Lord and of his Christ, and he shall reign forever and ever.'** *And the twenty-four elders who sit on their thrones before God fell on their faces and worshiped God, say-*

---

[9] *This seventh trumpet is the last of seven trumpet blasts and thus equates to the "seventh" or "last trumpet" we have already encountered in 1 Corinthians 15:52 and 1 Thessalonians 4:16.*

*ing, 'We give thanks to you, Lord God Almighty, who is and who was, for **you have taken your great power and begun to reign.** The nations raged, but your wrath came, and **the time for the dead to be judged, and for rewarding your servants, the prophets and saints, and those who fear your name, both small and great, and for destroying the destroyers of the earth**'" (Revelation 11:15-18).*

❖ God's Kingdom is Coming

When Jesus comes to take control of the earth and to rule for God – when he comes to *"rule the world in righteousness"* – he will establish a new society on earth which Scripture calls the Kingdom of God. God's immortal saints will live in this kingdom, at peace with one another and with God. Lots of word pictures are given in the Scriptures about the sort of life that will then exist. It will be hugely advantageous for the nations of the world to have a righteous government ruled over by a just and upright king, who will care for them and protect them from all harm. This kingdom is to last for a thousand years at the end of which those who have lived as mortals in that age will themselves be subject to judgement and will be given the chance to become immortal.

We have already seen that the Lord Jesus Christ is to rule as the world's future King,[10] but we have not yet collected information about the sort of king he will be; what his kingdom will be like; and what powers he will exercise to ensure his rulership is both supreme and sublime. This is where regular Bible reading is really helpful, for it is not that easy to track down the many descriptions that exist just by looking for key words or phrases. We will look at that in the next chapter.

But there is one thing that may have been worrying you as we have considered the promised reward. Is it right to be thinking about a reward at all? Shouldn't we just follow the Lord Jesus and obey the commandments of God for their own sake, without any thought of what we get out of it, and just trust in the mercy and grace of God?

---

[10] *Chapter 12: "Jesus Christ – the Promised King"*

❖ God Rewards the Faithful

The disciples once asked Jesus outright what they would get for following him and he gave them an equally straight answer. Here's the exchange:

> *"Peter said in reply, 'See, we have left everything and followed you.* **What then will we have?**' *Jesus said to them, 'Truly, I say to you, in the new world, when the Son of Man will sit on his glorious throne, you who have followed me will also sit on twelve thrones, judging the twelve tribes of Israel. And everyone who has left houses or brothers or sisters or father or mother or children or lands, for my name's sake, will receive a hundredfold and will inherit eternal life'"* (Matthew 19:27-29).

Jesus was quite clear about it. If we make the effort in this life and do what is right in God's sight, there will be a hundredfold reward – God will give us back far more than we can ever give to Him. He has always worked on that principle. In early days He encouraged those who responded to His bidding by giving them a reward; for example:

✓ **Abraham** was a very wealthy man, and God told him that was a reward for his faithfulness (Genesis 15:1). At that time part of the reward God gave was material prosperity, but later the blessings on offer were seen to be spiritual blessings – the forgiveness of sins, a hope of new life, the companionship of other believers, and suchlike.

✓ The **Psalmist** said that for keeping God's commandments: *"there is great reward"* (19:11);

✓ The prophet **Isaiah** said that when the King comes, *"Behold, his reward is with him, and his recompense before him"* (40:10; 62:11);

✓ **Jesus** said that those who are persecuted in this life need not fear, for he will bring their reward at his Coming: *"Rejoice and be glad, for your reward is great in heaven, for so they persecuted the prophets who were before you"* (Matthew 5:12);

✓ The apostle **Paul** said: *"Whatever you do, work heartily, as for the Lord and not for men, knowing that from the Lord you will receive the inheritance as your reward. You are serving the Lord Christ"* (Colossians 3:23,24);

✓ The unnamed writer of the **Letter to the Hebrews** said this: *"without faith it is impossible to please him, for whoever would draw near to God must believe that he exists and that he rewards those who seek him"* (Hebrews 11:6).

So, whilst we have thought of the judgement seat of Christ as a place where the just will be separated from the unjust, where some will receive everlasting life and others *"shame and everlasting contempt" (Daniel 12:2)*, it is also to be considered as that time and place when God will reward believers in all ages who have faithfully followed His Word and have lived their lives accordingly. And the many pictures of the coming Kingdom of God are given so that we can look forward with keen expectation to that day when a king will reign once again at Jerusalem and God's kingdom will have been restored.

Things to Read

📖 It's time to look at some Scriptures about the coming Kingdom of God. Look at Isaiah chapters 2 and 11, to learn about the important position of Jerusalem in the future (as a centre of world government) and the qualities of the king who will reign from there.

📖 Read the account of the disciples asking Jesus about the reward they could expect in Mark chapter 10 and notice how Jesus said that there would be blessings and benefits for his followers both in this life and in the life to come.

Questions to Think About

19.1 If you ask people to show you where the Bible promises that you go to heaven when you die, the only passage they usually offer is John 14:1-6. Read the passage and then work out what it actually teaches.

19.2 What do you understand Psalm 146 to teach about life after death? Does it tell us anything about God's coming kingdom?

20

The Coming Kingdom of God

❖ When Jesus began to preach the gospel of salvation, having waited until he was thirty before beginning his ministry, his message concerned the Kingdom of God. He said: *"The time is fulfilled, and **the kingdom of God** is at hand; repent and believe in the gospel"* (Mark 1:15).

❖ When the Lord was instructing his followers how best to serve God, he summed up the first part of his talk in these words: *"But seek first **the kingdom of God** and his righteousness, and all these things will be added to you"* (Matthew 6:33).

❖ Later Jesus told Nicodemus that *"unless one is born of water and the Spirit, he cannot enter **the kingdom of God"** (John 3:5).

❖ When the apostle Philip was preaching in Samaria, where he baptized many new believers, the record says: *"When they believed Philip as he preached good news about **the kingdom of God** and the name of Jesus Christ, they were baptized, both men and women"* (Acts 8:12).

Clearly the Kingdom of God is one of the most important teachings of the New Testament and we need to give it some detailed attention, not least because the Bible gives us lots of different ideas about what God's kingdom is going to be like.

❖ Paradise Restored

The Garden of Eden, for example, is a description of what the world was like when God had a "king" ruling over His creation. He had asked Adam and Eve to *"have **dominion** over the fish of the sea and over the birds of the heavens and over the livestock and over all the earth and over every creeping thing that creeps on the earth"* (Genesis 1:26). If they had achieved that – had controlled themselves and had dominion or ruled over all that God had made – we would not be going through all the difficulties that confront us today. But, as we have seen, Adam lost control. It was not until the coming of the Lord Jesus Christ that control could be regained. Jesus was successful where Adam had failed – that's the teaching of Romans chapter 5.[1]

They lived in Paradise until Adam and Eve were banished and that was a glimpse into the sort of world that God had prepared for man and woman – a foretaste of what things will be like when Paradise is restored. You will recall that when the Lord Jesus indicated to the dying thief that he would indeed remember him when he came into his kingdom, he used these words: *"You will be with me in Paradise"* [2] *(Luke 23:43)*. This was a clear indication that the coming kingdom will indeed be as fertile and fruitful as the Garden of Eden. So it should come as no surprise that when the Lord Jesus gave a pictorial review of coming events he described the time when he will reign on earth in the following terms:

> *"The angel showed me the river of the water of life, bright as crystal, flowing from the throne of God and of the Lamb through the middle of the street of the city; also, on either side of the river, the **tree of life** with its twelve kinds of fruit, yielding its fruit each month. The leaves of the tree were for the healing of the nations. No longer will there be anything accursed, but the throne of God and of the Lamb will be in it, and his servants will worship him ... Blessed are those who wash their robes, so that they may have the right to the **tree of life** and that they may enter the city by the gates" (Revelation 22:1-3,14).*

This is the new state of affairs that will come from heaven to earth, just as Revelation chapter 21 describes it, and it is depicted as the Garden of Eden restored.[3] Just as there were rivers in Eden which flowed out to water the earth, and a tree of life, so those elements are included in this

---

[1] *Chapter 12 examined the contrast between Adam and Jesus Christ – the coming King.*

[2] *"Paradise" is a word that just means garden or park.*

[3] *"Depicted" means that Revelation uses picture language to describe what is coming, so it does not follow that everything will be exactly like this. But the symbols used are powerful ways of showing the coming transformation.*

description of a restored relationship with God. This time the arrangement will benefit the nations of the earth, who are now much in need of healing from generations of bondage to sin and death. Where it had been the case that the tree of life is unavailable, eternal life will become accessible to all whose sins are forgiven, because of their relationship with the Lord Jesus.

❖ Abundant Fruitfulness

God cursed the earth because of Adam's sin so that, to this day, it has not realised its original fruitfulness and fertility.[4] Paul depicted the earth, using picture language, as though it were groaning with frustration and in expectation, wanting to be free of its present limitations.[5] It would produce thorns and thistles, and mankind would have to work hard to earn a living from the soil. But in the coming age all that will change and there are many Scriptures that describe the abundant fruitfulness that will result from the coming of the king and the glories of his reign. If you bear in mind that Israel was largely an agricultural economy, you will realise why these descriptions would have meant so much to them. Here is a selection:[6]

> "May there be **abundance of grain** in the land; on the tops of the mountains may it wave; may its **fruit be like Lebanon**; and may people blossom in the cities like the grass of the field!" (Psalm 72:16);

> "The wilderness and the dry land shall be glad; **the desert shall rejoice and blossom like the crocus; it shall blossom abundantly** and rejoice with joy and singing. The glory of Lebanon shall be given to it, the majesty of Carmel and Sharon. They shall see the glory of the LORD, the majesty of our God" (Isaiah 35:1,2);

> "For the LORD comforts Zion; he comforts all her waste places and **makes her wilderness like Eden**, her

---

[4] *Genesis 3:17-19.*

[5] *"The creation itself will be set free from its bondage to decay and obtain the freedom of the glory of the children of God. For we know that the whole creation has been groaning together in the pains of childbirth until now" (Romans 8:21,22).*

[6] *See also Isaiah 29:17; 32:15; 41:18; 45:8; 55:13; 65:21; Hosea 14:5-7; Joel 3:18-20 and Zechariah 8:12.*

desert like the garden of the LORD; joy and gladness will be found in her, thanksgiving and the voice of song" (Isaiah 51:3);

"Instead of the thorn shall come up the cypress; instead of the brier shall come up the myrtle; and it shall make a name for the LORD, an everlasting sign that shall not be cut off" (55:13);

"But you, O mountains of Israel, shall shoot forth your branches and yield your fruit to my people Israel, for they will soon come home ... **I will make the fruit of the tree and the increase of the field abundant,** *that you may never again suffer the disgrace of famine among the nations ... And they will say, 'This land that was desolate has become* **like the garden of Eden,** *and the waste and desolate and ruined cities are now fortified and inhabited'"* (Ezekiel 36:8,30,35);

"'Behold, the days are coming,' declares the LORD, 'when **the ploughman shall overtake the reaper** [7] *and* **the treader of grapes him who sows the seed; the mountains shall drip sweet wine, and all the hills shall flow with it.** *I will restore the fortunes of my people Israel, and they shall rebuild the ruined cities and inhabit them; they shall plant* **vineyards** *and drink their* **wine,** *and they shall make* **gardens** *and eat their* **fruit**'" (Amos 9:13,14).

❖ Settled Regime

One consequence of such fruitfulness will be that there will be abundant food. Famine will become a thing of the past. Whereas now there is no-one with real influence to care for the most deprived in society, in the coming age there will be a king who cares about them and who will ensure their interests are protected and their needs met. King David anticipated what his successor would achieve – someone who would be greater than Solomon his son – when he said this:

---

[7] *This means that the harvest will be so abundant that the ploughman will be waiting to get into the field to prepare for the next crop, but will be delayed by the harvesting which is still going on.*

*"May he **defend the cause of the poor of the people, give deliverance to the children of the needy, and crush the oppressor!** ... **For he delivers the needy when he calls, the poor and him who has no helper. He has pity on the weak and the needy, and saves the lives of the needy***. From oppression and violence he redeems their life, and precious is their blood in his sight" (Psalm 72:4,12-14).*

Another consequence of a king who cares about people will be that they will be able to live securely and happily. They will not be displaced by warring factions, herded into refugee camps, or terrorised by a militia. Instead people will be able to live at peace and enjoy the fruits of their labour.

*"They shall build houses and inhabit them; they shall plant vineyards and eat their fruit. They shall not build and another inhabit; they shall not plant and another eat; for **like the days of a tree shall the days of my people be, and my chosen shall long enjoy the work of their hands**. They shall not labour in vain or bear children for calamity, for they shall be the offspring of the blessed of the LORD, and their descendants with them. Before they call I will answer; while they are yet speaking I will hear. **The wolf and the lamb shall graze together; the lion shall eat straw like the ox, and dust shall be the serpent's food.**[8] 'They shall not hurt or destroy in all my holy mountain', says the LORD" (Isaiah 65:21-25);*

*"They shall sit **every man under his vine and under his fig tree**, and no one shall make them afraid, for the mouth of the LORD of hosts has spoken" (Micah 4:4);*

*"In that day, declares the LORD of hosts, every one of you will invite his neighbour to come **under his vine and under his fig tree**" (Zechariah 3:10).*

Sitting under a vine or a fig tree might not be our immediate idea of a quiet and relaxing evening, but when those words were first spoken or written they would have conveyed exactly that idea: of a people living together in peace

---

[8] *Again there are links with the Garden of Eden, both with regard to the animals living together peacefully and the descendants of the serpent suffering the punishment God had meted out.*

and plenty. For it was often the case that in time of war these commodities were the first to go, so they became proverbial to describe a long and happy period of continuous prosperity.[9]

❖ Jerusalem Restored

Isaiah tells us more than we might at first realise, for his reference to *"all my holy mountain"* (65:25) means only one place – Jerusalem. This city, built on a mountainous site is the centrepiece of God's purpose; it is the place that God chose out of all available places in the land of Israel as the site of His temple and the centre of divine government. It was there that kings once reigned for God. It is to this place that God's appointed king – the Lord Jesus Christ – will return to rule. Jerusalem is destined to be the centre of world government: the capital city of the Kingdom of God when it is restored in the earth.

The previous verses to that passage from Isaiah chapter 65 start with these words:

> *"For behold, I create new heavens and a new earth, and the former things shall not be remembered or come into mind. But be glad and rejoice forever in that which I create; for* **behold, I create Jerusalem to be a joy, and her people to be a gladness. I will rejoice in Jerusalem and be glad in my people;** *no more shall be heard in it the sound of weeping and the cry of distress. No more shall there be in it an infant who lives but a few days, or an old man who does not fill out his days ..." (65:17-20).*

It is just one of very many passages that describe the glorious future of Jerusalem when her fortunes are restored and her present problems cease. Here are just a few of those word-pictures:

> *"Great is the* LORD *and greatly to be praised* **in the city of our God! His holy mountain, beautiful in elevation, is the joy of all the earth, Mount Zion,**[10] *in the far north,* **the city of the great King"** *(Psalm 48:1);*

<hr>

[9] *See Jeremiah 5:17; Hosea 2:12; Joel 1:7,12 and Habakkuk 3:17.*

[10] *Mount Zion is another of the names for Jerusalem. It is one of the mountains upon which the city is built. (See Isaiah 24:23, in the list of passages on the next page, where Jerusalem and Mount Zion are clearly different names for the same place.)*

"Why do you look with hatred, O many-peaked mountain, at **the mount that God desired for his abode, yes, where the LORD will dwell forever?"** *(Psalm 68:16);*

"On the **holy mount** *stands the city he founded; the LORD loves* **the gates of Zion** *more than all the dwelling places of Jacob. Glorious things of you are spoken, O* **city of God"** *(Psalm 87:1-3);*

"The LORD has chosen Zion; *he has desired it for* **his dwelling place***: 'This is my resting place forever;* **here I will dwell***, for I have desired it. I will abundantly bless her provisions; I will satisfy her poor with bread'"* *(Psalm 132:13-15);*

"Then the moon will be confounded and the sun ashamed, for **the LORD of hosts reigns on Mount Zion and in Jerusalem,** *and his glory will be before his elders"* *(Isaiah 24:23);*

"Behold Zion, the city of our appointed feasts! Your eyes will see Jerusalem, an untroubled habitation, an immovable tent, whose stakes will never be plucked up, nor will any of its cords be broken. But **there the LORD in majesty** *will be for us a place of broad rivers and streams, where no galley with oars can go, nor majestic ship can pass. For the LORD is our judge; the LORD is our lawgiver; the LORD is our king; he will save us"* *(33:20-22);*

"Awake, awake, put on your strength, O Zion; put on your beautiful garments, O **Jerusalem, the holy city***; for there shall no more come into you the uncircumcised and the unclean ... Break forth together into singing, you waste places of Jerusalem, for the LORD has comforted his people;* **he has redeemed Jerusalem"** *(52:1,9);*

"For Zion's sake I will not keep silent, and for Jerusalem's sake I will not be quiet, until **her righteousness** *goes forth as brightness, and* **her salvation** *as a burning torch ... You shall be* **a crown of beauty in the hand of the LORD***, and* **a royal diadem in the hand of your God** *... On your walls, O Jerusalem, I have set*

watchmen; all the day and all the night they shall never be silent. You who put the LORD *in remembrance, take no rest, and give him no rest until he establishes Jerusalem and makes it a praise in the earth"* (62:1,3,6-7).

❖ The Kingdom of God Restored

A glance at those passages will explain why the immediate followers of the Lord Jesus expected him to establish God's kingdom on earth there and then. So many Old Testament passages speak of Jerusalem's glorious future, when a king reigns on David's throne in the city he established as Israel's capital. When Jesus appeared, and was declared to be the long-awaited Messiah, it seemed obvious to many that the time had now come when God would fulfil His ancient promises.

↘ The **prophets of God** foretold the restoration of the kingdom. They said things like: *"And you, O tower of the flock, hill of the daughter of Zion, to you shall it come, the former dominion shall come, kingship for the daughter of Jerusalem"* (Micah 4:8); [11]

↘ **Jesus** endorsed that when – quoting Psalm 48 – he said: *"I say to you, Do not take an oath at all, either by heaven, for it is the throne of God, or by the earth, for it is his footstool, or by Jerusalem, for it is the city of the great King"* (Matthew 5:34,35);

↘ The **crowds** lining the streets, as Jesus entered on an ass, certainly hoped this was the time, for they cried: *"Blessed is the coming kingdom of our father David! Hosanna in the highest!"* (Mark 11:10) and *"Blessed is the King who comes in the name of the Lord! Peace in heaven and glory in the highest!"* (Luke 19:38);

↘ The **disciples** who had been close to Jesus for over three years expected the restoration to take place soon. Just before Jesus ascended to heaven they asked him: *"Lord, will you at this time restore the kingdom to Israel?"* (Acts 1:6);

---

[11] *When Micah made this prediction the kingdom of Israel was still in existence, for he prophesied at the time of some of its later kings. He predicted the fall of that kingdom (3:12), the return of the scattered people (4:6-7), and the re-establishment of the kingdom in Jerusalem (4:1-5,8).*

↘ **Jesus** did not rebuke them for their misunderstanding but merely replied that their timing was adrift: he said to them, *"It is not for you to know times or seasons that the Father has fixed by his own authority" (Acts 1:7);*

↘ The **apostles**, who were sent to preach the gospel, taught that the time would come when the kingdom would be restored: *"Repent therefore, and turn again, that your sins may be blotted out, that times of refreshing may come from the presence of the Lord, and that he may send the Christ appointed for you, Jesus, whom heaven must receive until the time for restoring all the things about which God spoke by the mouth of his holy prophets long ago" (Acts 3:19-21);*

↘ The **apostle Paul** writing to the Romans explained, in chapters 9-11, that God's purpose was far from finished with the Jewish people and that, when the time was right, *"all Israel will be saved, as it is written, 'The Deliverer will come from Zion, he will banish ungodliness from Jacob'; 'and this will be my covenant with them when I take away their sins.' As regards the gospel, they are enemies of God for your sake. But as regards election, they are beloved for the sake of their forefathers" (Romans 11:26-28).*

❖ The Kingdom of God on Earth

Adam lost control and was banished from Paradise and it was many generations later that God offered mankind another chance to exercise dominion and rule on His behalf. That offer was made to the descendants of Abraham, Isaac and Jacob – to the nation of Israel that God redeemed out of slavery in Egypt. It may come as something of a surprise, if this is a new idea to you, but the Bible teaches that God's Kingdom once existed on earth.

To form a kingdom you need people, land, laws and a king. It was when the law of God was being spelled out to the new nation of Israel, in anticipation of their entering the promised land, that God declared them to be a very special people – a kingdom of priests:

> *"Now therefore, if you will indeed obey my voice and keep my covenant, you shall be my treasured possession among all peoples, for all the earth is mine; and you shall be to me a **kingdom of priests and a holy***

nation" (Exodus 19:5,6).

God was their king at the time and He remained in sole control for many years. At first there was Moses and then Joshua to lead the nation; afterwards there were occasional saviours, called judges. It was not until the days when Samuel was in charge that the people demanded a king, like the other nations around them, whereupon God said they were in fact rejecting His absolute rulership:

*"The LORD said to Samuel, 'Obey the voice of the people in all that they say to you, for they have not rejected you, **but they have rejected me from being king over them'"** (1 Samuel 8:7).*

Even so, God instructed Samuel to appoint someone as king and that began a period of monarchy in Israel which lasted altogether about 450 years, though not without its problems. The first king, Saul, led the nation in a way that created unrest and internal difficulty and allowed enemies to take effective control of many parts of the land. His successor was King David; he turned things around and established a nation that was pleasing to God in most respects. He ruled as God's king, understanding that he must himself live subject to God's laws and encouraging the nation in the worship of God and in faithfulness. He was very much a religious leader, but his political accomplishments were also considerable. David conquered the Philistines and subdued them, and then enlarged Israel's territory to establish secure borders. He created a stable economy and put good administrative systems in place.

David ruled over God's kingdom, not his own, and he knew that. The law that he tried to keep was God's law, and he was as obedient to it as were his subjects. It specifically required him to do certain things and forbade other things; see, for example, Deuteronomy chapter 17, verses 14-20. If he, and his successors, remained faithful and obedient they could continue as kings. If they abandoned God's law their throne would be forfeit. Those were the terms on which God permitted kings to reign over His Kingdom as His representatives on earth.

❖ Covenant Conditions

When God made a covenant with David, swearing to him that he and his successors would continue to occupy the throne, the conditions were that they should continue to be faithful to God and to obey God's law. They did not have the right to continue indefinitely regardless of their behaviour. It was as if a landlord had given the right of occupation subject to certain conditions which, if breached, meant that the tenancy would come to an end.

This was the basis upon which Israel occupied the land,[12] and it was the same for the kings, as David understood perfectly. He knew that his throne was really God's throne; for when it was time to appoint his successor, it was God's appointment not his and God chose one of his youngest sons, Solomon. This is how that appointment is recorded:

> "*Of all my sons (for the* LORD *has given me many sons)* **he has chosen Solomon my son to sit on the throne of the kingdom of the** LORD **over Israel**. *He said to me, 'It is Solomon your son who shall build my house and my courts, for* **I have chosen him** *to be my son, and I will be his father. I will establish his kingdom forever* **if he continues strong in keeping my commandments and my rules**, *as he is today.' Now therefore in the sight of all Israel, the assembly of the* LORD, *and in the hearing of our God, observe and seek out all the commandments of the* LORD *your God, that you may possess this good land and leave it for an inheritance to your children after you forever. And you, Solomon my son, know the God of your father and serve him with a whole heart and with a willing mind, for the* LORD *searches all hearts and understands every plan and thought.* **If you seek him, he will be found by you, but if you forsake him, he will cast you off forever**" *(1 Chronicles 28:5-9).*

It was *"the throne of the kingdom of the* LORD *over Israel"* that Solomon and all his successors occupied and, in case we missed that detail first time around, it is repeated for emphasis a few verses later:

> "*Then Solomon sat on* **the throne of the** LORD **as king** *in place of David his father. And he prospered, and all Israel obeyed him*" *(29:23).*

---

[12] *See Leviticus chapter 26 and Deuteronomy chapter 28, where the terms of their occupation of the land are given in detail.*

The king's primary responsibility was to keep the faith; he must be faithful himself and lead the people in the ways of righteousness. King David was an outstanding example of what God demanded. They might have been astute politicians, excellent administrators, clever and gifted individuals; but the assessment of individual kings follows the same pattern throughout the historical record. They either did right in the sight of God, by keeping His commandments, or they did not. That was the crucial thing, and mostly they did not. When King Solomon died, he was succeeded by a foolish son, Rehoboam, who mishandled matters and ignored wise counsel, which resulted in a divided kingdom.

The larger kingdom of Israel in the north of the land had a succession of very wicked kings and eventually the kingdom was overthrown, the last king was killed and the people deported to Assyria. That was the end of that kingdom for ever. The smaller kingdom of Judah, with a king reigning in Jerusalem, fared somewhat better as there were several faithful kings who followed David's example. But there were more bad kings than good ones and eventually God's covenant conditions caught up with them.

The nineteenth and last king was a man named Zedekiah, who reigned in challenging times. He was encouraged to be faithful and God provided him with spiritual help and guidance from one of His great prophets – Jeremiah. But Zedekiah took little notice of what God instructed him to do. In far-away Babylon, another prophet declared God's final judgement upon the king who had breached the covenant conditions whereby he and his descendants occupied the throne:

> *"And you, O profane wicked one, prince of Israel, whose day has come, the time of your final punishment, thus says the Lord God: Remove the turban and take off the crown. Things shall not remain as they are. Exalt that which is low, and bring low that which is exalted. A ruin, ruin, ruin I will make it. This also shall not be, **until he comes, the one to whom judgement belongs, and I will give it to him"** (Ezekiel 21:25-27).*

❖ God's Anointed Successor

It was the end of the kingdom of God that had existed on earth ever since God rescued Israel out of Egypt. He had ruled over them as king, first directly and then indirectly. There would be no more kings *"until he comes"*. One day God would anoint a successor to sit on King David's throne in Jerusalem and he would rule for God over the restored Kingdom of God on earth. He would be the Messiah, the anointed one – which is what the Greek word *"Christ"* actually means. So it was that when God's Son was to be born to Mary these ancient promises were referred to as things that were on the verge of fulfilment.

Long ago the prophet Isaiah had foretold the virgin birth and the role of the Son who would be born:

"Behold, the virgin shall conceive and bear a son, and shall call his name Immanuel" (Isaiah 7:14, referred to in Matthew 1:23);

*"For to us a child is born, to us a son is given; and the government shall be upon his shoulder, and his name shall be called Wonderful Counsellor, Mighty God, Everlasting Father, Prince of Peace. Of the increase of his government and of peace there will be no end, **on the throne of David and over his kingdom, to establish it and to uphold it with justice and with righteousness from this time forth and for evermore.** The zeal of the LORD of hosts will do this" (Isaiah 9:6,7).*

It was the angel Gabriel who told Mary that her Son would be the one to fulfil all these promises. He told her:

*"'Do not be afraid, Mary, for you have found favour with God. And behold, you will conceive in your womb and bear a son, and you shall call his name Jesus. He will be great and will be called the Son of the Most High. And **the Lord God will give to him the throne of his father David, and he will reign over the house of Jacob forever, and of his kingdom there will be no end.**' And Mary said to the angel, 'How will this be, since I am a virgin?' And the angel answered her, 'The Holy Spirit will come upon you, and the power of the Most High will overshadow you; therefore the child to be born will be called holy – the Son of God'" (Luke 1:30-35).*

❖ Prince of Peace

The coming king will rule for God in Jerusalem, as did David's other successors, and will far exceed them in what he is able to accomplish. King Jesus is to rule the world from Jerusalem. What was once the capital city of a tiny little country is to become the capital city of the world, as the prophets of God foretold long ago:

> *"The word that Isaiah the son of Amoz saw concerning* **Judah and Jerusalem**. *It shall come to pass in the latter days that the mountain of the house of the LORD shall be established as the highest of the mountains, and shall be lifted up above the hills; and all the nations shall flow to it, and many peoples shall come, and say: 'Come, let us go up to the mountain of the LORD, to the house of the God of Jacob, that he may teach us his ways and that we may walk in his paths.'* **For out of Zion shall go the law, and the word of the LORD from Jerusalem. He shall judge between the nations, and shall decide disputes for many peoples; and they shall beat their swords into plowshares, and their spears into pruning hooks; nation shall not lift up sword against nation, neither shall they learn war anymore"** *(Isaiah 2:1-4);*

> *"***The LORD will be king over all the earth***. On that day the LORD will be one and his name one. The whole land shall be turned into a plain from Geba to Rimmon south of Jerusalem. But Jerusalem shall remain aloft on its site from the Gate of Benjamin to the place of the former gate, to the Corner Gate, and from the Tower of Hananel to the king's winepresses. And it shall be inhabited, for there shall never again be a decree of utter destruction.* **Jerusalem shall dwell in security"** *(Zechariah 14:9-11);*

> *"In his days may the righteous flourish, and peace abound, till the moon be no more!* **May he have dominion from sea to sea, and from the River to the ends of the earth!** *May desert tribes bow down before him and his enemies lick the dust! May the kings of Tarshish and of the coastlands render him tribute; may the kings of Sheba and Seba bring gifts!* **May all kings fall down before him, all nations serve him!"** *(Psalm 72:7-11);*

> *"Then I saw heaven opened, and behold, a white horse! The one sitting on it is called Faithful and True, and* **in righteousness he judges and makes war** ... *He is*

clothed in a robe dipped in blood, and the name by which he is called is **The Word of God**. *And the armies of heaven, arrayed in fine linen, white and pure, were following him on white horses. From his mouth comes a sharp sword with which to strike down the nations, and* **he will rule them with a rod of iron**. *He will tread the winepress of the fury of the wrath of God the Almighty. On his robe and on his thigh he has a name written,* **King of kings and Lord of lords**" *(Revelation 19:11-16)*.

This will be the world government of God. It will be exercised in righteousness, not to the glory of man, nor to the furtherance of his greatness and magnificence. A king will reign in righteousness and the world will be greatly blessed as a result. For one thousand years the reign of the Lord Jesus will continue until the mortal population of the world has had every opportunity to see the blessings that come from following God's law.

"Then I saw thrones, and seated on them were those to whom the authority to judge was committed. Also I saw the souls of those who had been beheaded for the testimony of Jesus and for the word of God, and who had not worshipped the beast or its image and had not received its mark on their foreheads or their hands. **They came to life and reigned with Christ for a thousand years**. *The rest of the dead did not come to life until the thousand years were ended" (Revelation 20:4,5)*.[13]

This thousand year reign of the Lord Jesus is known as the Millennium and it will be the best thousand years in the world's history to date. Those who are privileged to experience that time will have the opportunity to see the coming Prince of Peace take control of the world, gradually subdue its warring tendencies and establish true peace. Over time the nations of the world will learn peace and will come to understand the principles of true worship and the true joy of living. And the Jewish nation will have an important part to play in that Kingdom, for God's purpose with

---

[13] *As far as we can tell this reference is to a literal period of 1000 years and it is sometimes linked to the period of 6000 years of Bible history, making this the final period which aligns with the seventh day of creation in which God rested from all His work.*

them is not yet complete, as the apostle Paul goes on to explain in his Letter to the Romans.

Things to Read

📖 Psalm 72 was written by King David just before he died and it looked forward to a king who would one day sit on his throne in Jerusalem. David was succeeded by king Solomon, but this Psalm is about the time when king Jesus will reign from Jerusalem.

📖 Isaiah chapter 35 describes the time when the people of God will be gathered together to Jerusalem. It speaks of "everlasting joy", which is a good two-word description of what God's coming kingdom will be like for those who are privileged to experience it.

Questions to Think About

20.1 When Jesus was about to ascend to heaven from the Mount of Olives, near Jerusalem, his disciples asked him something. They were then told two important things, one by Jesus and one by an angel. What were they told and why were all those things important? (Acts 1:1-11; Zechariah 14:1-4)

20.2 The prophets tell us a great deal about the coming king and His kingdom. Read Micah chapter 4 and then list the things the prophet Micah says about the future of Jerusalem and the Kingdom of God when it is established again on earth.

"The LORD will be king over all the earth. On that day the LORD will be one and his name one" (Zechariah 14:9).

21
What about the Jews?

The nation of Israel was rescued from Egypt and declared by God to be *"a kingdom of priests and a holy nation"*. These were the people who first occupied Jerusalem as *"the place"* where God has said He would dwell in the midst of His people.[1]

✓ It was their king who *"sat on the throne of the LORD"*, reigning over the Kingdom of God on earth;

✓ It was to them the prophets of God came and declared the unfolding purpose of God;

✓ It was to this nation that God sent His Son, the Lord Jesus Christ.

By their unbelief and their rejection of Jesus, has the Jewish nation thrown it all away for ever? Or is there some future role it must fulfil in God's coming kingdom? What has this nation to teach us today?

❖ "Kinsmen according to the flesh"

When Paul contemplated the gracious climax of God's purpose with His creation, in that lovely passage that ends Romans chapter 8, his very next thought was about the Jewish people: his own nation. This is what he said:

"I am speaking the truth in Christ – I am not lying; my conscience bears me witness in the Holy Spirit – that I have great sorrow and unceasing anguish in my heart. For I could wish that I myself were accursed and cut off from Christ for the sake of my brothers, my kinsmen according to the flesh. **They are Israelites, and to them belong the adoption, the glory, the covenants, the giving of the law, the worship, and the promis-**

---

[1] *To follow the idea of a chosen "place", where God would dwell in the midst of His people, see Deuteronomy 12:5,14,18, 21 and 26 and any cross-references you might have.*

*es. **To them belong the patriarchs, and from their race, according to the flesh, is the Christ who is God over all, blessed forever.** Amen" (Romans 9:1-5).*[2]

The apostle then spends two chapters of the letter explaining what went wrong with the nation, so that we can avoid making the same mistakes. He explains how it will all work out for the best in the long term, when God restores the nation to His favour. To get maximum benefit from his argument we need to develop another technique which will help us in understanding the Bible for ourselves, that of summarising an argument into a few key points. Try reading the three chapters in question (Romans 9 to 11), note down what you see as the main points and then compare your list with this one:

Romans	Key Point
9:1-5	I have great sorrow for Israel because they have had so many advantages and opportunities and are missing out on so much now.
9:6-18	God's promises have not failed: only those who believed the promises of God can really be counted as His children. God has always worked through those He chooses – it's His choice.
9:19-29	God is sovereign in all these matters – like a potter who shapes the clay.
9:30-33	Gentiles have learned how to become righteous by faith (by what they believe), but the Jews are still trying to work out their own salvation: by trying to be obedient to the Law of Moses.
10:1-13	I really want the Jews to be saved but they have to accept the Lord Jesus Christ as the one who can give them righteousness – he is Lord of both Jew and Gentile and we must all believe in him and confess that he is Lord if we are to be saved.

2 *This is better rendered "to them belong the patriarchs, and of their race, according to the flesh, is the Christ. God who is over all be blessed for ever. Amen" (RSV). As we have seen before, that is a translation which is consistent with Bible teaching elsewhere.*

Romans	Key Point
10:14-21	That is why the gospel is preached; but it has long been predicted that not everyone will accept the message. Sadly, many Jews have become both disobedient and obstinate.
11:1-5	Does that mean that God has finished with the Jewish people? Far from it! God has always worked through a remnant – a small number of people who have remained faithful: that has happened throughout the ages.
11:6-10	In all that time the Jewish people have been unwilling to accept Jesus as Lord: they have been like blind people.
11:11-24	They have stumbled but have not fallen beyond recovery. Their loss has been gain for the Gentiles, who now have what Israel once had. But Israel will return to favour with God. That will also be the time of the resurrection of the dead; it will be as if the original branches are grafted back onto the stock of the tree.
11:25-36	When that happens *"All Israel will be saved"* – the nation of Israel, the people racially descended from Abraham, will at last be saved, and all this will give glory to God.

❖ The Hope of Israel

One key feature of Paul's inspired explanation is that the Gentiles have become heirs of the promises of God, which were first entrusted to Israel, by accepting and believing those very same promises. God has not started a new and different way of establishing a right relationship with Him. It is the way which was outlined in the

Old Testament, but it is the way of faith, not of works. In other words, try as we might, we can never be good enough to merit what God offers by way of salvation from sin and a place in His kingdom. We can only obtain that by God's grace and favour – as a *gift,* not as a right. This is a point that Paul makes many times in his various letters, including in Romans, as we have seen.

If we want to obtain God's favour, we have to become Jews inwardly, a point that Paul made early in the letter:

> *"No one is a Jew who is merely one outwardly, nor is circumcision outward and physical.* **But a Jew is one inwardly,** *and circumcision is a matter of the heart, by the Spirit, not by the letter. His praise is not from man but from God" (Romans 2:28,29).*

We become members of the family of God by embracing the promises first made by God to the Jewish people and thus becoming relatives of Abraham, by faith. Again that is something that Paul established as his argument was developing:

> *"He received the sign of circumcision as a seal of the righteousness that he had by faith while he was still uncircumcised.* **The purpose was to make him the father of all who believe without being circumcised,** *so that righteousness would be counted to them as well,* **and to make him the father of the circumcised who are not merely circumcised but who also walk in the footsteps of the faith that our father Abraham had before he was circumcised.** *For the promise to Abraham and his offspring that he would be heir of the world did not come through the law but through the righteousness of faith" (4:11-13).*

This is why the Bible insists that the one hope it contains is a Jewish hope through and through. The Lord Jesus once said, to a Samaritan woman:

> *"You worship what you do not know; we worship what we know, for* **salvation is from the Jews**" *(John 4:22).*

And his apostles were equally insistent that if you want to be part of God's purpose you must find and keep the *"hope of Israel".* This is the one and only hope of salvation that there is. The apostle Paul was persecuted by Jews who opposed what he was teaching and preaching. But he had no hesitation in saying that the faith he preached was, in fact, the hope of Israel; if only they would accept it themselves! He explained this at one of his trials: [3]

> "Because the Jews objected, I was compelled to appeal to Caesar – though I had no charge to bring against my nation. For this reason, therefore, I have asked to see you and speak with you, since it is because of **the hope of Israel** that I am wearing this chain" (Acts 28:19,20).

Earlier he had spelled it out even more clearly:

> "I stand here testifying both to small and great, **saying nothing but what the prophets and Moses said would come to pass**: that the Christ must suffer and that, by being the first to rise from the dead, **he would proclaim light both to our people and to the Gentiles**" (26:22,23).

There was salvation available to both Jews and Gentiles on the same basis – by faith in the promises of God and through baptism into the saving name of Jesus Christ.

❖ Jewish Hope

This hope is *"of the Jews"* or *"of Israel"* for several reasons:

1 The promises about a Saviour who would redeem mankind were made by God to Jews and were first believed by them – that is Paul's observation in Romans 9:4, when he says *"to them belong ... the promises"*.

2 The Saviour was to be a Jew, born of the tribe of Judah, in a Jewish town, to a Jewish girl, to occupy a throne in Jerusalem the capital of the nation of Israel.[4]

3 Salvation will only come to the world when the king comes to Zion (another name for Jerusalem), and at that time both Jew and Gentile will be saved.

Paul refers to these Old Testament predictions about Jesus coming to Jerusalem as Saviour of the world:

---

3 *"There is one body and one Spirit – just as you were called to the one hope that belongs to your call – one Lord, one faith, one baptism" (Ephesians 4:4,5).*

4 *See Genesis 49:10 (Jesus was to be born of the tribe of Judah); Micah 5:2 (in Bethlehem); Isaiah 7:14 (to a virgin daughter of Israel); Isaiah 9:7 (to rule on David's throne in Jerusalem).*

"In this way all Israel will be saved, as it is written, 'The Deliverer will come from Zion, he will banish ungodliness from Jacob'; 'and this will be my covenant with them when I take away their sins.'" As regards the gospel, they are enemies of God for your sake. But as regards election, they are beloved for the sake of their forefathers. For the gifts and the calling of God are irrevocable" (Romans 11:26-29).

Here the inspired apostle combines at least two Old Testament passages – Isaiah 59:20,21 and 27:9. In their original settings within the prophecy of Isaiah they are about a redeemer who would come to rescue mankind, at a time when there was nobody else who could help. He armed himself with righteousness and thus brought salvation, and he will come again to Jerusalem to destroy all opposition and save those who *"turn from transgression"* (Isaiah 59:20). The coming deliverer – the Lord Jesus Christ – will then make a new covenant or agreement with the nation of Israel: the guilt of the nation will then be atoned for, and their sin will be removed (Isaiah 27:9).

There are many such prophecies in the Old Testament Scriptures[5] about the coming of a king who will redeem and rescue God's people and make *"Jerusalem to be a joy in the earth, and her people to be a gladness"* (Isaiah 65:18). We looked at some of them in the last chapter about the place of Jerusalem in the coming Kingdom of God. But we did not then explore the role of the Jewish people when the one comes who long ago was declared to be the *"King of the Jews"*. Paul insists, in chapters 9-11 of Romans, that the Jews will have an important part to play, when *"all Israel will be saved"* (11:26).

❖ Hope for the World

There are very many passages in the Old Testament that predict the coming of a Saviour to rescue Israel and the world out of all trouble and distress. They promise that the work of Jesus will be in that order: he will come to rescue Israel out of trouble and that will result in a change in the fortunes of all nations.

Immediately prior to his ascension to heaven, Jesus was

---

[5] *For example: Leviticus 26:44,45; Jeremiah 3:14-`18; Ezekiel 37:21-23; Joel 2:32 and 3:16.*

walking with his disciples on the Mount of Olives outside Jerusalem, when they asked him about that time and whether it was near. If they had thought about it they would have known that at that very same location, just a few weeks before, Jesus had told them what would first happen to the Jewish nation and to the whole world.

Then they had asked him about the timing of his coming and of the end of the age and Jesus replied by giving them a list of things that would come to pass before his return from heaven. You can read the words of Jesus in three of the gospel accounts,[6] and you might like to compile a complete list of everything that Jesus predicted. Among the things that Jesus said would happen before his coming are the following:

✓ *The rise of false Christianity and false Christs;*

✓ *The persecution of true Christians;*

✓ *Wars and rumours of wars;*

✓ *Earthquakes, famines and diseases;*

✓ *Jerusalem surrounded by armies;*

✓ *The Jewish nation separated from Jerusalem;*

✓ *Jerusalem under foreign control, until the Jews return;*

✓ *Tribulation and distress amongst the nations.*

The Lord Jesus Christ is the greatest of all prophets and his prediction has come remarkably true over nearly 2000 years since he spoke those words. We have had occasion several times already to note how the original Christian message has been distorted and falsified. Over the years, there have been many individuals, and even Church organisations, who have claimed to be Christ, or Christ's representatives on earth. Yet the sad fact is that the churches which make these claims have often been at the forefront of the persecution of those who challenged their wrong teaching.

Whilst all that was happening, and sometimes because of it, the world has also been at war and often still is. The present conflict against terrorism in its many forms seems set to continue for many years to come and has been

---

[6] *This prophecy given by Jesus is sometimes known at the Mount Olivet prophecy and is recorded in Matthew 24; Mark 13 and Luke chapter 21.*

instrumental in increasing the level of distress and anxiety in the world. Now everybody is at risk and nobody is safe. Whilst there have been such fears before about things getting out of control, the risks are now such that people really do believe there is no way out for mankind, and that an accident or a deliberate act could wreak huge damage to the environment, even perhaps destroying life on earth.

Climate change has resulted in similar concerns and there seems to be no obvious answer. Mankind as a whole shows no willingness to curb its materialistic pursuits, regardless of the consequences for future generations. Climate change has already produced an increase in freak weather conditions – including floods, earthquakes and tornadoes – and the sea level is now rising steadily, as the ice caps begin to melt. It's no wonder that people are distressed about the present state of things and are anxious about the future.

Of course, things have been bad at many periods of human history and people have often been distressed: that's the nature of human government and human misrule. Many times in the past people have thought that the end of everything must be near and that things couldn't get any worse; but they have. This time things are different, and the Jews play an important part in indicating that the coming of Jesus is near, at long last.

❖ Jewish Witness

From the time God called the Jews to be His people, it was intended that they would be the means by which His gracious offer of salvation would be conveyed to all nations. That was made clear to Abraham at the outset when he was told that *"in you all the families of the earth shall be blessed"* (Genesis 12:3). It became increasingly clear, as time passed, that individuals from other nations could share in Israel's blessings.

➤ There was such a provision made when the Passover meal was being shared in Egypt and a mixed multitude of people left Egypt with Israel (Exodus 12:38,48,49);

➤ When they entered the Promised Land, there were opportunities for people like Rahab and Ruth to be accepted as members of the nation of Israel (Joshua 6:25; The Book of Ruth);

ᵜ When Solomon dedicated the temple at Jerusalem he expressly included a prayer about foreigners who would come to worship the God of Israel, and there were at least two prominent Gentiles[7] during his lifetime who became worshippers of the one true God (1 Kings 8:41-43);

ᵜ The prophets spoke repeatedly about the admission of the Gentiles into the congregation of Israel,[8] explaining that Messiah would enlarge the purpose of God in just that way: *"It is too light a thing that you should be my servant to raise up the tribes of Jacob and to bring back the preserved of Israel;* **I will make you as a light for the nations, that my salvation may reach to the end of the earth"** *(Isaiah 49:6).*[9]

By the time of Paul's Letter to the Romans – written both to Jewish and Gentile believers – it was an established fact in the Christian community that there was no difference between them in the sight of God.[10] There was just one way of salvation for everyone, regardless of birth, race and gender, and Jews were as much in need of it as everyone else. If they wanted salvation they had to be reborn, by baptism into Christ, and many Jewish believers accepted that opportunity.[11]

The gospel was preached by Jews to Jews in the first place, but as they gradually became unwilling to accept the message of the apostles, the focus of attention switched to the Gentiles. Sadly, many Jews are depicted in the New Testament as opponents of the gospel. Thus the Book of Acts ends with the apostle Paul rebuking the Jews at Rome for their unbelief and declaring that henceforth the gospel would be taken to the Gentiles:

---

[7] *They were Hiram, the King of Tyre and the Queen of Sheba.*

[8] *Paul cites some of those prophecies in Romans 10:19-21,which also explain that whilst the Gentiles would believe, the Jews would not at first accept what God was doing through His Son, the Lord Jesus Christ.*

[9] *The apostle Paul also quotes this Scripture to show that he was continuing the Lord's work in taking the gospel to the Gentiles (Acts 13:47).*

[10] *Paul makes this very clear in Galatians 3:26-29 and also explains his own task to preach the gospel to Gentiles in Romans 15:14-22, which is why he wanted to come to Rome.*

[11] *See Acts 2:41 and 4:4, where we read about the baptism of 5000 Jewish believers.*

> *"For this people's heart has grown dull, and with their ears they can barely hear, and their eyes they have closed; lest they should see with their eyes and hear with their ears and understand with their heart and turn, and I would heal them.'* **Therefore let it be known to you that this salvation of God has been sent to the Gentiles; they will listen.** *He lived there two whole years at his own expense, and welcomed all who came to him,* **proclaiming the kingdom of God and teaching about the Lord Jesus Christ** *with all boldness and without hindrance" (Acts 28:27-31).*

❖ Reluctant Witnesses

So it came about that the Jews, who should have been God's willing witnesses to teach the nations all about God and His gracious purpose, actually became resistant to the gospel. But that did not mean that God's purpose with His people was finished. It meant that they became witnesses of His purpose in a rather different way. They became witnesses to the severity of God, showing all nations that God's Word is not to be lightly set aside, and that He is in control of everything that happens in the world.

Long ago in Israel's history their leader Moses spelled out the options for the Jewish people. You can read the full text in Deuteronomy chapter 28 or in Leviticus chapter 26. It amounted to this – If they obeyed God and remained faithful the nation would be hugely blessed by God in every respect; but if they disobeyed they would suffer greatly at the hands of other nations. That suffering would include their conquest by another nation, their dispersion to all nations, and their continued persecution wherever they were scattered. Look at an extract from these long prophecies:

> *"The LORD will scatter you among all peoples, from one end of the earth to the other, and there you shall serve other gods of wood and stone, which neither you nor your fathers have known. And among these nations you shall find no respite, and there shall be no resting place for the sole of your foot, but the LORD will give you there a trembling heart and failing eyes and a languishing soul. Your life shall hang in doubt before you. Night and day you shall be in dread and have no assurance of your life. In the morning you shall say, 'If only it were evening!'*

and at evening you shall say, 'If only it were morning!'
because of the dread that your heart shall feel, and the
sights that your eyes shall see" (Deuteronomy 28:64-67).

This is not the place to undertake a review of Jewish history through the ages, fascinating though that is. It should be sufficient for our purposes to say that some 40 years after Jesus had been executed in Jerusalem the city was besieged and taken by the Romans, following a Jewish revolt, and the survivors were either butchered or deported. It is said that the slave markets were glutted with Jewish slaves and the end result was the dispersion of Jews all over the world. The Romans banned the Jews from Jerusalem, renamed the city, even had a plough dragged over it to declare ceremonially that it would never be rebuilt.

Over the centuries a host of other people occupied Jerusalem including Romans, Persians, Byzantines, Arabs, Egyptians, Turks, Crusaders, Muslims and the British, who conquered Jerusalem from the Ottoman Turks in 1917. Meanwhile the Jews – who were often denied the opportunity to own land in or around Jerusalem, and who were sometimes banned from even living there – suffered greatly in the lands where they had been dispersed. Often they were forced to flee from country to country in search of a safe haven; often they had to move on again as fresh persecutions broke out. There are stories of harsh treatment meted out to Jews in many countries – pogroms in Russia, burnings in Britain, the annihilation of six million Jews in Nazi Germany.

In all those events the Jews were witnesses to God's Word. He had said this would happen if they were unfaithful and disobedient and it happened exactly as predicted. It was always open to the Jews to throw themselves upon the mercy of God and to accept the Lord Jesus Christ. Their own Scriptures kept open the promise that if they inclined their hearts to God and sought His salvation, He would heed

and act to save them.[12] But there has been no such national inclination and most of the Jewish people today are persuaded, as were their ancestors, that the claims made by Jesus of Nazareth are false. Indeed many of them no longer believe that God exists!

❖ Return to the Land

Despite the continued unbelief of the Jews, and the centuries of their dispersion, the prophets of God also made it clear that there would come a time when God would act to bring this time of Jewish trouble to an end. There would come a time when – to use Paul's figure in Romans 11:12-24 – God would graft back into the ancient stock those olive branches that had been cut off for so many generations. The natural olive (the Jews) and the wild olive (the Gentiles) would then grow together and be fruitful for God, when He had mercy on the natural descendants of Abraham, Isaac and Jacob:

> *"Just as you were at one time disobedient to God but now have received mercy because of their disobedience, so **they too have now been disobedient in order that by the mercy shown to you they also may now receive mercy**. For God has consigned all to disobedience, that he may have mercy on all. Oh, the depth of the riches and wisdom and knowledge of God! How unsearchable are his judgments and how inscrutable his ways!" (Romans 11:30-33).*

This outworking of God's mercy has been apparent during the second half of the 20th century and into this one, for the Jewish people are now back in the land that God once promised to their forefathers. Having been a nation in exile for more than 1800 years, they have retained their national identity in a quite remarkable way and towards the end of the 19th century began a process of national recovery and resettlement which is unique among nations. Many ancient people like the Babylonians, the Phoenicians, the Philistines, even the Romans, have ceased to be nationally identifiable. Over time they have intermingled with their neighbours until their original characteristics have

---

[12] *See Leviticus 26:40-45; Deuteronomy 4:29-31; 30:1-20; 1 Kings 8:47-50; 2 Chronicles 6:37-39; Psalm 91:15; Isaiah 55:6,7; Hosea 5:15 - 6:1-3; Amos 5:4-6 and Zephaniah 2:1-3.*

been lost. But the Jewish people remain as distinctive and recognisable as ever they were.

The prophets had foretold all this as well, including their return to the land and their continuing unbelief. Even the brutal acts now undertaken by the Israelis and their willingness sometimes to act against their military opponents have been foretold. In all this the Jews continue to be God's witnesses to the nations that His purpose is on track and that all these happenings are the final events due to take place before the return to earth of the Lord Jesus Christ. Here are some prophecies about the regathering of the Jews and their return in unbelief: [13]

*"Return, **O faithless children**, declares the LORD; for I am your master; I will take you, one from a city and two from a family, and I will bring you to Zion. And I will give you shepherds after my own heart, **who will feed you with knowledge and understanding** ... At that time Jerusalem shall be called the throne of the LORD, and all nations shall gather to it, to the presence of the LORD in Jerusalem, and they shall no more stubbornly follow their own evil heart" (Jeremiah 3:14-17);*

*"Behold, **I will bring them** from the north country and gather them from the farthest parts of the earth, among them the blind and the lame, the pregnant woman and she who is in labour, together; a great company, they shall return here. With weeping they shall come, and with pleas for mercy **I will lead them back**, I will make them walk by brooks of water, in a straight path in which they shall not stumble, for I am a father to Israel, and Ephraim is my firstborn. Hear the word of the LORD, O nations, and declare it in the coastlands far away; say, '**He who scattered Israel will gather him, and will keep him as a shepherd keeps his flock**'" (31:8-10);*

*"Behold, **I will gather them from all the countries to***

---

[13] *Here are some more references you might care to look up, also about the regathering of the Jews to their ancient land (Isaiah 54:7; Ezekiel 20:34,41; 36:24; 37:21; Micah 2:12; Zephaniah 3:19 and Zechariah 8:4).*

*which I drove them in my anger and my wrath and in great indignation. **I will bring them back to this place,** and I will make them dwell in safety" (32:37);*

*"'Thus says the Lord GOD: I will gather you from the peoples and assemble you out of the countries where you have been scattered, and I will give you the land of Israel.' **And when they come there, they will remove from it all its detestable things and all its abominations. And I will give them one heart, and a new spirit I will put within them.**[14] I will remove the heart of stone from their flesh and give them a heart of flesh, that they may walk in my statutes and keep my rules and obey them. And they shall be my people, and I will be their God. But as for those whose heart goes after their detestable things and their abominations, I will bring their deeds upon their own heads, declares the Lord GOD" (Ezekiel 11:17-21).*

The return of the Jews to the land once occupied by their forefathers and their re-establishment as a nation among nations is a modern miracle, no less. It is part of God's witness to this generation that He is still ruling in the kingdom of men and that His purpose is working out exactly as predicted. The time is coming when Israel will accept the Lord Jesus Christ as their long-awaited Messiah and Saviour.

❖ National Resurrection

The prophet Ezekiel tells us a lot about the events that lead up to the return of Jesus and the start of the new age, when the Kingdom of God is re-established on earth. One of his visions captures the coming transformation in a very graphic way. He saw a valley which was full of very dry bones and was told to prophesy over those bones, which he duly did, as he spoke the Word of God. He told the dead bones what God was about to do – that they were going to re-assemble and become bodies once again – and as he prophesied it happened.

Bone came to bone and sinews and flesh covered them

---

[14] *Reference to a new heart and a new spirit is God's promise of a new relationship, or a new covenant to be established with the nation. This is what Paul referred to in Romans 11:26,27.*

until the valley was full of lifeless corpses. Next he was told to summon the four winds that they might breathe life into the corpses:

> *"So I prophesied as he commanded me, and the breath came into them, and they lived and stood on their feet, an exceedingly great army. Then he said to me, 'Son of man, **these bones are the whole house of Israel**. Behold, they say, Our bones are dried up, and our hope is lost; we are clean cut off. Therefore prophesy, and say to them, Thus says the Lord GOD: Behold, I will open your graves and raise you from your graves, O my people. And I will bring you into the land of Israel. And **you shall know that I am the Lord, when I open your graves, and raise you from your graves, O my people.** And I will put my Spirit within you, and you shall live, and I will place you in your own land. Then you shall know that I am the Lord; I have spoken, and I will do it, declares the Lord'"* (Ezekiel 37:10-14).

This divine prediction comes with its own explanation. Ezekiel was prophesying about the nation of Israel which, in his lifetime, had seemed to be on the point of national extinction. He spoke these words just after Nebuchadnezzar, the king of Babylon, had sent his troops into Jerusalem to kill the inhabitants and pillage the city. Some of their actions are described in Jeremiah 7:30–8:3 where Jeremiah tells of the way the tombs were rifled and the dead bodies left out in the open, drying in the sun.

We have already seen that Ezekiel prophesied that, at this time, the kingdom of Israel would be overturned and would be no more until the Messiah came.[15] In the chapter we are currently looking at, the prophet now tells us of the way the nation of Israel would be reborn prior to the coming of their king.

In the middle of the 20th century, the Jews faced extinction once again, at the time of the Holocaust. But at that point of national extremity – a circumstance more extreme than anything faced by any other nation – God rescued them and brought them back to the land. There had been earlier indications that individual nations would view sympathetically the re-establishment of a Jewish state in their original homeland. The events of the Second World War

---

[15] *Ezekiel 21:26-27*

touched the hearts and consciences of many nations. In 1947, just two years after that war ended, a majority of the League of Nations voted to support the rebirth of Israel as a nation, since when millions of Jews have returned to establish modern Israel.

❖ Act of God

Ezekiel predicted that this would not be a gesture of goodwill on the part of mankind – a sort of reparation for all the injustice the Jews had suffered in many places. It would instead be an act of God, something that had been predicted. God brought the Jews back to the land and He reestablished them there, using human political systems and national decisions as part of His purpose, as He has always done. But notice the two stages of Ezekiel's prophetic vision:

1   The Jews were to return as a body of people: they would be a national entity, recognizable among the nations of the world.

2   Later they would be energized by the Spirit of God. As God said: *"I will put my Spirit within you, and you shall live"* (37:14).

That means that the time is coming when Israel will come to a proper relationship with God. They will learn to live by faith and will then accept the Lord Jesus Christ as their Saviour and King. When that happens we will be on the brink of the Kingdom of God being established. Remember what the apostle Paul said:

> **"Now if their trespass means riches for the world, and if their failure means riches for the Gentiles, how much more will their full inclusion mean!** *Now I am speaking to you Gentiles. Inasmuch then as I am an apostle to the Gentiles, I magnify my ministry in order somehow to make my fellow Jews jealous, and thus save some of them.* **For if their rejection means the reconciliation of the world, what will their acceptance mean but life from the dead?"** *(Romans 11:12-15).*

These are such exciting matters that we need to make a slight diversion from Romans to consider just how all this is going to work out, so that *"all Israel will be saved"*.

Things to Read

📖 Read Ezekiel chapter 37 which contains a very graphic picture of the restoration of the Jews at a time when their hope seemed lost. Notice what the prophet said about their coming king.

📖 Jeremiah chapter 30 contains another colourful description of God regathering the Jews, as though He were a shepherd collecting His sheep. Notice what it says about Israel becoming the people of God once again.

📖 If you haven't already read one of the three accounts of the so-called "Olivet Prophecy," in which Jesus predicted the signs that would lead up to his coming and the end of the age, try reading Luke chapter 21.

Questions to Think About

21.1 Read Romans chapter 10 and then answer the following questions:

   a What was it that Israel failed to do? (v 1-3)

   b What was the Law of Moses unable to give them? (v 5-8)

   c What does everyone, whether Jew or Gentile, need to do in order to be right with God? (v 9-13)

   d How do we get to have faith in God? (v 14-17)

   e Did the prophets predict that the Jews would not believe in Jesus, but that the Gentiles would? (v 16-21)

21.2 In Romans 11:1-6 Paul explains that God often works through a *"remnant"* – a small number of people who believe, while the majority does not. Can you think of any other occasions when there were only a few who believed whilst the rest did not? What does it tell you about believers today? (Genesis 6; Numbers 14; Joshua 2)

22
How will it all End?

The apostle had written a lot about the purpose of God before mentioning the part the Jews still have to play. But when he asked the question: *"Has God rejected his people?"* his answer was emphatic and detailed:

> *"**By no means!** For I myself am an Israelite, a descendant of Abraham, a member of the tribe of Benjamin. **God has not rejected his people whom he foreknew"** (Romans 11:1,2).*

Paul then explained that their rejection was only temporary and that God still has the gracious intention of restoring the Jews to a special place in His affections. They have a key part to play in the events of the last days.

❖ Last Days

We have not yet encountered the phrase *"the last days"* in our look at Bible teaching, perhaps because it is not a phrase Paul uses in Romans, although he does mention it elsewhere. Writing to Timothy the apostle says this about the period in question:

> *"Understand this, that **in the last days** there will come times of difficulty. For people will be lovers of self, lovers of money, proud, arrogant, abusive, disobedient to their parents, ungrateful, unholy, heartless, unappeasable, slanderous, without self-control, brutal, not loving good, treacherous, reckless, swollen with conceit, lovers of pleasure rather than lovers of God, having the appearance of godliness, but denying its power. Avoid such people" (2 Timothy 3:1-5).*

He was writing about a world that is astray from God because of the various things he lists, beginning with the crucial one that *"people will be **lovers of self** ... rather than lovers of God"*. There are many warnings in Scripture about the dangers of the world and its deceptive ways, and it is clearly prophesied that things will get steadily worse before God intervenes to establish His kingdom on earth.

We have already seen how the Lord himself listed the events that were due to take place over the generations after the Jews had been displaced from Jerusalem, and how he said that they would return at a time of unparalleled concern for the world.[1] To predict the return of the Jews after more than 1800 years was itself marvellous; to know that the world would be in turmoil at the time of their return was also remarkable. Only God, who knows the future, could possibly have given the Lord Jesus such prophetic insight and he readily acknowledged that to be the case.[2]

He also said that his coming would be at a time of widespread immorality and increasing violence, for he likened those days to the times of both Noah and Lot:

> *"Just as it was in the days of Noah, so will it be in the days of the Son of Man. They were eating and drinking and marrying and being given in marriage, until the day when Noah entered the ark, and the flood came and destroyed them all. Likewise, just as it was in the days of Lot – they were eating and drinking, buying and selling, planting and building, but on the day when Lot went out from Sodom, fire and sulphur rained from heaven and destroyed them all – so will it be on the day when the Son of Man is revealed. On that day, let the one who is on the housetop, with his goods in the house, not come down to take them away, and likewise let the one who is in the field not turn back. Remember Lot's wife" (Luke 17:26-32).*

Jesus was not saying that there is anything wrong with eating, drinking, getting married, or with the other things he mentions, but that many people who live in the *"days of the Son of Man"* will be doing nothing else. For, in the days of Noah and Lot, the people who lived alongside them did nothing else: they had no sense of impending destruction. Death overtook them whilst they were busy with the concerns and enjoyments of everyday life. Jesus said that it will be like that again when he comes as king.

---

[1] *Chapter 21 page 317.*

[2] *Jesus was always quick to attribute his remarkable abilities to his Father, as gifts he had received (see John 14:10).*

❖ The End

The end of everything will herald a new beginning for those who are aware of God's purpose and have prepared their lives accordingly. The coming kingdom will bring to an end human government and will replace it with divine rulership all over the earth. Over time all opposition will be subdued and the influence of the new rulership – that of the Lord Jesus Christ and his immortal saints – will gradually extend.

About 600 years before Jesus was born there was a mighty monarch who ruled the then dominant kingdom of Babylon – ancient Iraq. He ruled the inhabited or civilized world but one night he had a troubling dream. When it was recalled and interpreted by the prophet Daniel, it turned out to forecast part of human history – the part that world empires would play. Nebuchadnezzar, the king of Babylon, saw in his dream a huge multi-metalled statue with a head of gold, a breast and arms of silver, a bronze belly and thighs and legs of iron. The feet were the really curious part – they were an unstable mixture of clay and iron, materials that do not stick together. So the whole thing was standing on a very shaky base and suddenly something happened which brought it all crashing down.

A stone was dislodged from a mountain without any human intervention and it fell upon the feet of the great statue and felled it. The result was that the whole thing was broken to pieces, like chaff on a threshing floor, and the wind blew all the bits of the statue away, leaving just the stone which grew and grew until it was the size of a mountain that filled the whole earth. In this one vision the future of world rulership was foretold for, as you would now expect having seen other Bible prophecies, we are not left to guess what it meant. Daniel gave the king a detailed explanation, both of what he had seen and what it meant:

> "This was the dream. Now we will tell the king its interpretation. You, O king, the king of kings, to whom the God of heaven has given the kingdom, the power, and the might, and the glory, and into whose hand he has given, wherever they dwell, the children of man, the beasts of the field, and the birds of the heavens, making you rule over them all – you are the head of gold. Another kingdom inferior to you shall arise after you, and yet a third kingdom of bronze, which shall rule over all the

earth. And there shall be a fourth kingdom, strong as iron, because iron breaks to pieces and shatters all things. And like iron that crushes, it shall break and crush all these. And as you saw the feet and toes, partly of potter's clay and partly of iron, it shall be a divided kingdom, but some of the firmness of iron shall be in it, just as you saw iron mixed with the soft clay. And as the toes of the feet were partly iron and partly clay, so the kingdom shall be partly strong and partly brittle. As you saw the iron mixed with soft clay, so they will mix with one another in marriage, but they will not hold together, just as iron does not mix with clay. **And in the days of those kings the God of heaven will set up a kingdom that shall never be destroyed**, *nor shall the kingdom be left to another people. It shall break in pieces all these kingdoms and bring them to an end, and it shall stand forever, just as you saw that a stone was cut from a mountain by no human hand, and that it broke in pieces the iron, the bronze, the clay, the silver, and the gold. A great God has made known to the king what shall be after this. The dream is certain, and its interpretation sure"* (Daniel 2:36-45).

❖ World History

The first thing to note is that the Kingdom of God, which replaces the four world empires that precede it, is as much a world power as they were: it replaces them and takes control of the world. But it does so gradually: the stone first breaks in pieces those kingdoms, removes all traces of their influence and existence, and then grows to fill the earth.

We are in a privileged position to be able to look back over history and see the way in which all this came about exactly as predicted. There were only four empires that ruled with absolute power in the world and which held control over the land and people of Israel. Three of them are clearly identified within the book of Daniel, and the fourth is indicated though not precisely identified.[3] This is how history worked out:

---

[3] *Nebuchadnezzar's dream was followed by a series of other visions. In one, the next two world empires are seen in conflict and are identified as Medo-Persia and Greece (Daniel 8:20-21) and in a very detailed forecast of future events the fourth empire (Rome) is indicated by the expression "the ships of Kittim" (11:30).*

Head
Gold
BABYLON

Chest & Arms
Silver
MEDO-PERSIA

Middle & Thighs
Bronze
GREECE

Legs
Iron
ROME

Feet
Part Iron part Clay
DIVIDED KINGDOM

Stone
GOD'S COMING KINGDOM

Babylon	606-539 BC	*Daniel 2:48*
Medo-Persia	539-334 BC	*Daniel 8:20*
Greece	334-67 BC	*Daniel 8:21*
Rome	BC 67-1453 AD	*Daniel 11:30*

After Babylon came three other empires, each power in turn having control of the nation of Israel, until the Romans conquered Jerusalem in A.D. 70 and dispersed the Jews into other countries. The Roman empire continued, later becoming two parts – East and West – until A.D. 1453. By that time[4] there were many other powerful nations and no one empire held control of the world, as Rome and its predecessors had once done. Daniel predicted that a mix of nations, some strong and some weak, would succeed those four great empires and a very unstable mix it has proved to be. For things have happened exactly as he foretold.

Many attempts have been made over the years to forge alliances, make treaties, have special agreements, create a League of Nations, a United Nations, a Commonwealth, the European Union, a bloc of nations. All sorts of arrangements have been tried and all have failed to achieve the desired outcome. National sovereignty and the rights and interests of particular nations are always the dominant feature, so the world very seldom unites with one common goal. Trade agreements, quotas, international accords and treaties all fail sooner or later, unless nations are absolutely agreed that something is wholly in their common interest.

❖ Jews in Jerusalem

The world is now exactly in the state that Daniel foretold would occur before the coming of the stone power – the one that would break all existing world powers and would gradually take control. Our world is very unstable and many people are anxious for the future. Right at the centre of three continents – Europe, Asia and Africa – the Jewish nation exists again, just as Jesus predicted would occur. Jerusalem was occupied by other powers for nearly 2000 years but in 1948 the nation of Israel was re-established and in 1967 the Jewish people conquered east Jerusalem and thus took major control of their capital city once again. Jesus made this detailed predication about Jerusalem and the world at that time:

---

[4] *The Western Roman Empire had, in fact, fallen in A.D. 476 when Rome was conquered by the Vandals, after which the Eastern part continued, with its capital at Constantinople.*

"They (the Jewish people) will fall by the edge of the sword and be led captive among all nations, and Jerusalem will be trampled underfoot by the Gentiles, **until the times of the Gentiles are fulfilled.** *And there will be signs in sun and moon and stars, and on the earth distress of nations in perplexity because of the roaring of the sea and the waves, people fainting with fear and with foreboding of what is coming on the world. For the powers of the heavens will be shaken.* **And then they will see the Son of Man coming in a cloud with power and great glory.** *Now when these things begin to take place, straighten up and raise your heads, because your redemption is drawing near"* (Luke 21:24-28).

Jesus said that when *"the times of the Gentiles"* were fulfilled, the city would no longer be trampled underfoot.[5] The Jews are God's witnesses of His unfolding purpose and their return to the land and the city signals that the end of everything is now very near. There is a power coming which will destroy all human governments and replace them with divine control – this is what the Kingdom of God is all about. And the Jewish nation is destined to play a vital part in the events of the Last Days.

Many times the Old Testament prophets described the events that would bring their Messiah to Jerusalem and always their vision was that he would come to rescue the nation from dire calamity and near destruction. They predicted that Israel's return to the land would be at a time of difficulty and distress – Ezekiel said this:

"As a shepherd seeks out his flock when he is among his sheep that have been scattered, so will I seek out my sheep, and I will rescue them from all places where they have been scattered **on a day of clouds and thick darkness.** *And I will bring them out from the peoples and gather them from the countries, and will bring them into their own land"* (Ezekiel 34:12,13).

Back in the land they were destined to be surrounded by enemies, including some who would be plotting their annihilation:

---

5 *Note how similar this expression is to that used by the apostle Paul in Romans 11:25-26, when he explained about the time when "the fullness of the Gentiles has come in".*

"Thus says the LORD God: **Because the enemy said of you, 'Aha!' and, 'The ancient heights have become our possession,'** *therefore prophesy, and say, Thus says the LORD God: Precisely because they made you desolate and crushed you from all sides, so that you became the possession of the rest of the nations, and you became the talk and evil gossip of the people, therefore, O mountains of Israel, hear the word of the LORD God ... Therefore thus says the LORD God: I swear that* **the nations that are all around you shall themselves suffer reproach"** *(36:3-7);*

"For behold, days are coming, declares the LORD, when I will restore the fortunes of my people, Israel and Judah, says the LORD, and I will bring them back to the land that I gave to their fathers, and they shall take possession of it ... **Alas! That day is so great there is none like it; it is a time of distress for Jacob; yet he shall be saved out of it.** *And it shall come to pass in that day, declares the LORD of hosts, that I will break his yoke from off your neck, and I will burst your bonds, and foreigners shall no more make a servant of him. But they shall serve the LORD their God and David their king, whom I will raise up for them"* *(Jeremiah 30:3-9).*

❖ Jerusalem under Siege

There are detailed prophecies which describe the build-up to the arrival of Israel's Messiah. One common feature is that many nations are aligned against the Jews and are intent upon their overthrow. This would have seemed unimaginable only a few years ago. Now there is a political precedent for a confederacy of nations invading the sovereign territory of another nation to bring "peace and stability"; to remove terrorism; to disarm a nation which is thought to hold weapons of mass destruction; or to replace an undesirable regime. Invasions of Afghanistan, the Balkans, Iraq and suchlike have made it more likely that international action as described by the prophets could occur soon.

Israel's political and military decisions, often made regardless of international political opinion, may well provoke international military action. And strong-minded nations around, aggravated by Israeli attitudes and actions, will take action, as they have done before,[6] if they see a suitable opportunity and reckon they can succeed.

The prophecies that tell of these terrible events, and of an eventual happy outcome, are not given so that we can work out just how and when all this will occur. If we knew this, we might relax and put off any decision about following Jesus until nearer the time – that's human nature! You should read the prophecies in Ezekiel chapters 38 and 39; Joel chapter 3 and Zechariah chapters 12-14 and note the common themes:

✿ Nations confederate against the nation of Israel;

✿ Military action being launched;

✿ Israel in grave distress and the nation at the point of extinction;

✿ The Lord Jesus Christ coming to rescue them;

✿ Their acceptance of him as their Messiah and king.

The prophet Zechariah is quite specific about the outcome, for he says this about the time when the nation of Israel at last encounters its redeemer:

> *"On that day I will seek to destroy all the nations that come against Jerusalem. And I will pour out on the house of David and the inhabitants of Jerusalem a spirit of grace and pleas for mercy, so that, **when they look on me, on him whom they have pierced, they shall mourn for him, as one mourns for an only child, and weep bitterly over him, as one weeps over a firstborn**" (Zechariah 12:9,10).*

Israel will at last recognise Jesus as their king – the one who was pierced when he was nailed to the cross – and they will then be in a position to make a new agreement with God, by faith in Jesus Christ. The prophet indicates that there will be baptisms again in Jerusalem, as at the time of the apostles, whereupon the nation will come once

---

[6] *There have been wars between Israel and her Arab neighbours in 1948, 1967 and 1973 and the Palestinian "intifada" or uprising which began in 1987. The hatred that exists between Israel and her Arab neighbours goes right back to Bible times and is there described as a "perpetual enmity" (Ezekiel 35:5).*

more into covenant relationship with God.[7] For this is what Zechariah says:

> *"On that day* **there shall be a fountain opened for the house of David and the inhabitants of Jerusalem, to cleanse them from sin and uncleanness**. *And on that day, declares the* LORD *of hosts, I will cut off the names of the idols from the land, so that they shall be remembered no more. And also I will remove from the land the prophets and the spirit of uncleanness"* (Zechariah 13:1,2).

The prophet also identifies the place to which Jesus will come to rule as king:

> *"Behold, a day is coming for the* LORD, *when the spoil taken from you will be divided in your midst. For I will gather all the nations against Jerusalem to battle, and the city shall be taken and the houses plundered and the women raped. Half of the city shall go out into exile, but the rest of the people shall not be cut off from the city. Then the* LORD *will go out and fight against those nations as when he fights on a day of battle.* **On that day his feet shall stand on the Mount of Olives** *that lies before Jerusalem on the east ...* **And the** LORD **will be king over all the earth.** *On that day the* LORD *will be one and his name one"* (Zechariah 14:1-9).

❖ When will it Happen?

It was outside Jerusalem – the city from which the coming king is going to reign – that the apostles asked Jesus whether he was going to restore the kingdom to Israel there and then. Jesus told them something important about the timing of all this:

> **"It is not for you to know times or seasons that the Father has fixed by his own authority.** *But you will receive power when the Holy Spirit has come upon you, and you will be my witnesses in Jerusalem and in all Judea and Samaria, and to the end of the earth"* (Acts 1:7,8).

---

[7] *This is what the apostle Paul also said would happen: "In the very place where it was said to them, 'You are not my people,' there they will be called 'sons of the living God' " (Romans 9:26).*

They were right as far as their expectations were concerned, but they were not to know the timing and neither are we to know. Instead, we are to keep spiritually awake and alert to watch what is happening in the world. And we should continue to talk to people about what all this means, and what God is still offering them. It is a matter of being prepared and keeping active, because we do not know precisely when Jesus will come. When he was living on earth, not even Jesus knew when he was to return as king. This is what Jesus said:

> *"**Concerning that day or that hour, no one knows, not even the angels in heaven, nor the Son, but only the Father. Be on guard, keep awake. For you do not know when the time will come.** It is like a man going on a journey, when he leaves home and puts his servants in charge, each with his work, and commands the doorkeeper to stay awake. Therefore **stay awake** – for **you do not know when the master of the house will come,** in the evening, or at midnight, or when the cock crows, or in the morning – lest he come suddenly and find you asleep. And what I say to you I say to all: **Stay awake**" (Mark 13:32-37).*

Even when Jesus gave a detailed exposition of things that were to come to pass, and described the confrontation between the combined forces of the earth and the powers of heaven – the battle of Armageddon – he gave this important aside:

> *"I saw, coming out of the mouth of the dragon and out of the mouth of the beast and out of the mouth of the false prophet, three unclean spirits like frogs. For they are demonic spirits, performing signs, who go abroad to the kings of the whole world, to assemble them for battle on the great day of God the Almighty. (**'Behold, I am coming like a thief! Blessed is the one who stays awake, keeping his garments on, that he may not go about naked and be seen exposed!'**) And they assembled them at the place that in Hebrew is called Armageddon. The seventh angel poured out his bowl into the air, and a loud voice came out of the temple, from the throne, saying, 'It is done!'" (Revelation 16:13-17).*

❖ Being Prepared

Imagine what it would be like if we had become so fascinated by world events and so determined to work out when Jesus will come that we were unprepared for that coming! Nobody knows when their life will end – it's one of the challenges of life to try to do everything that we know we should do while there is still time. The New Testament has a lot to say about the Kingdom of God but its main emphasis is on the qualities needed if we are to become citizens of the Kingdom.[8] Jesus taught that we should:

↘ *Be born again, of water and the Spirit (John 3:5);*

↘ *Become like little children if we want to enter the Kingdom of God (Matthew 18:3; Luke 18:17);*

↘ *Grow up to be fruitful and productive to the glory of God (Matthew 13:23);*

↘ *Make the kingdom our absolute priority in life (Matthew 6:33; 13:44);*

↘ *Pray for its coming (Matthew 6:9,10);*

↘ *Be spiritually prepared for the coming of the bridegroom, and keep awake! (Matthew 25:1-13);*

↘ *Realise that however hard we try, entry into the kingdom will still be God's gracious gift to us (Matthew 25:34).*[9]

If we want a new life in God's kingdom we have to start living differently now; it's no good waiting until the coming of Jesus in the hope that it will all come right when he returns – it won't. Life in the Kingdom of God is going to be so different to our present experience that any hardship or difficulty we face now will prove to be completely worthwhile. Paul was having a tough life himself, though you wouldn't know that from Romans; but he reckoned it all worthwhile when weighed in the balances alongside what is

---

[8] *The apostle Paul makes a similar comment later in Romans when he says that: "The kingdom of God is not a matter of eating and drinking but of righteousness and peace and joy in the Holy Spirit" (14:17). Notice that he is saying there's more to life than "eating and drinking", which many forgot in the days of Noah and Lot!*

[9] *It has been one of Paul's key themes that we cannot be justified by works but by faith (by the things that we believe).*

to be the final outcome.[10] This is the same for all of us –
the joys of the kingdom will far outweigh any hardships we
may suffer now as disciples of the Lord.

❖ International Opposition

When God's chosen king reigns on earth he will transform
the world and make it a fit place in which to live. So you
would expect everybody to welcome the coming of Jesus
with open arms. But they won't and we have to be prepared
for that too. The Scriptures tell us that the nations of the
world will challenge his right to rule and will oppose his
authority. The Psalmist foresaw this when he penned these
words:

> *"Why do the nations rage and the peoples plot in vain?*
> *The kings of the earth set themselves, and the rulers*
> *take counsel together, against the LORD and against his*
> *anointed, saying, 'Let us burst their bonds apart and*
> *cast away their cords from us.' He who sits in the heav-*
> *ens laughs; the LORD holds them in derision. Then he will*
> *speak to them in his wrath, and terrify them in his fury,*
> *saying, 'As for me, I have set my King on Zion, my*
> *holy hill.' I will tell of the decree: The LORD said to me,*
> *'You are my Son; today I have begotten you. Ask of*
> *me, and I will make the nations your heritage, and*
> *the ends of the earth your possession'" (Psalm 2:1-8).*

Can you imagine it? At last a king comes, a ruler for
whom many people have been longing, one who will bring
peace, righteousness, justice, security, abundant fruitfulness, excellent healthcare for all, prolonged life, restored
moral values, united worship of the one true God, and true
happiness for all mankind.[11] Yet the ruling powers resent
his arrival and challenge his authority! Put like that, it does
seem a likely, if sad, outcome. For most people take a self-
centred view about life and what matters to many is the
loss of position, status or personal influence. Such people
will oppose Christ when he comes to reign on earth, which
is why Daniel's explanation of the dream indicated that the
stone power will achieve its objective in two stages:

---

[10] *See 2 Corinthians 4:16-18 and Romans 11:33-36.*
[11] *We looked at life in God's Kingdom in Chapter 20.*

1 It will destroy all existing kingdoms and powers and remove all traces of their existence and influence (Daniel 2:44; Revelation 11:15-18);

2 The stone will grow into a mountain to fill the earth – the king will increase his authority and control step-by-step, to result in a thousand-year rule over all the earth (Daniel 2:35; Revelation 20:1-6).[12]

❖ Jesus in Jerusalem

All sorts of changes are due to take place in Jerusalem when Jesus returns and they are described in some detail in various prophecies. The city is to be the centre of world government from whence the law of God will be issued, and the rulers of the earth will come there, sooner or later, to acknowledge the new ruler of the world. The prophets say this about Jerusalem:

> "For behold, darkness shall cover the earth, and thick darkness the peoples; but the LORD will arise upon you, and his glory will be seen upon you. And **nations shall come to your light, and kings to the brightness of your rising** ...Your gates shall be open continually; day and night they shall not be shut, that **people may bring to you the wealth of the nations, with their kings led in procession.** For the nation and kingdom that will not serve you shall perish; those nations shall be utterly laid waste" (Isaiah 60:2-3,11-12);

> "At that time Jerusalem shall be called the throne of the LORD, and **all nations shall gather to it, to the presence of the LORD in Jerusalem**, and they shall no more stubbornly follow their own evil heart. In those days the house of Judah shall join the house of Israel, and together they shall come from the land of the north to the land that I gave your fathers for a heritage" (Jeremiah 3:17,18).

---

[12] *This one thousand year period is called "The Millennium", though that actual word does not appear in the Scriptures.*

It is clear that the Jewish people will have a special function in this new age of the world. They are destined to fulfil their original calling and become God's ambassadors to the nations:

> *"Thus says the LORD of hosts: Peoples shall yet come, even the inhabitants of many cities. The inhabitants of one city shall go to another, saying, 'Let us go at once to entreat the favour of the LORD and to seek the LORD of hosts; I myself am going.' Many peoples and strong nations shall come to seek the LORD of hosts in Jerusalem and to entreat the favour of the LORD. Thus says the LORD of hosts:* **In those days ten men from the nations of every tongue shall take hold of the robe of a Jew, saying, 'Let us go with you, for we have heard that God is with you'** *" (Zechariah 8:20-23).*

❖ Centre of True Worship

It is clear from these prophecies that people from many nations will want to come to Jerusalem because it will be the centre of divine worship in the age to come. Nowadays there are many different gods being worshipped and many different ways of worshipping them. But when King Jesus reigns there will be only one way of worshipping God acceptably. We looked earlier at Zechariah's prophecy about the king coming to Jerusalem to rule over all the earth and the very same chapter continues like this:

> **"Then everyone who survives of all the nations that have come against Jerusalem shall go up year after year to worship the King, the LORD of hosts, and to keep the Feast of Booths.** *And if any of the families of the earth do not go up to Jerusalem to worship the King, the LORD of hosts, there will be no rain on them. And if the family of Egypt does not go up and present themselves, then on them there shall be no rain; there shall be the plague with which the LORD afflicts the nations that do not go up to keep the Feast of Booths"* (Zechariah 14:16-18).

Here is another indication that the king's influence will gradually increase and that there will be some on-going resistance for a time. But it is also clear that Jerusalem is to be a place of public religious worship, a place where feasts are to be kept to the LORD as they were many generations ago. Other prophets tell of the erection of a magnificent temple and the reintroduction of sacrifices.[13]

These changes will serve the purpose of helping the mortal inhabitants of the kingdom learn about sin and its awful consequences, and to help them look back in time and understand more about the great redeeming sacrifice accomplished by the Lord Jesus Christ. His sacrifice for sins was *"once for all"* (Hebrews 7:27; 9:26; 10:10) and will never be repeated.

But when the 1000 year reign of Christ has come it will be much harder for the inhabitants of the earth to remember how brutal and cruel things used to be, and what Jesus suffered in order to overcome sin. So their appreciation of what Jesus did will lapse as life becomes so pleasant and people and animals live in such harmony and at peace. An occasional visit to the Jerusalem temple as a learning experience will sharpen their appreciation and cause them to rejoice at the great salvation of God. And the Jews will be the priests at that venue, thus to fulfil their age-old destiny. They will be God's *"treasured possession among all peoples ... and you shall be to me **a kingdom of priests and a holy nation"*** (Exodus 19:5,6).

❖ Mortal and Immortal

Those who have been already to the Judgement Seat of Christ, at the start of the Millennium – the 1000 year reign of the King – and who have been made immortal will have the responsibility of teaching and guiding the mortal population. They will become rulers and advisers and the indications are that they will have particular powers and insights that will make that role very effective indeed.

> *"For **a people shall dwell in Zion, in Jerusalem;** you shall weep no more. He will surely be gracious to you at the sound of your cry. **As soon as he hears it, he answers you.** And though the Lord give you the bread of adversity and the water of affliction, yet **your Teacher will not hide himself anymore, but your eyes shall see your Teacher. And your ears shall hear a word behind you, saying, 'This is the way, walk in it,'***

---

[13] *It may seem strange to think of animal sacrifices being reinstituted as a teaching aid, but the prophecies are quite clear about this. See, for example, Ezekiel 43:18-27; Isaiah 60:6-7 or Hosea 3:4-5.*

when you turn to the right or when you turn to the left. Then you will defile your carved idols overlaid with silver and your gold-plated metal images. You will scatter them as unclean things. You will say to them, "Be gone!" (Isaiah 30:19-22).[14]

In this way the mortal nations of the kingdom age will learn righteousness and will come to understand more and more about the ways of God. Laws against immorality and wrongdoing will be enforced and people will have no alternative but to live in an obedient and law-abiding way, to the advantage of all. But what chance will there be for these mortals to become immortal themselves? We are told, in graphic picture language, that sin will be restrained for the duration of the Millennium but that, at the end of that period, the restraint will be removed. The detail comes in the last book of the Bible, the Revelation of Jesus Christ:

*"Then I saw an angel coming down from heaven, holding in his hand the key to the bottomless pit and a great chain. And he seized the dragon, that ancient serpent, who is the devil and Satan, and bound him for a thousand years, and threw him into the pit, and shut it and sealed it over him, so that he might not deceive the nations any longer, **until the thousand years were ended. After that he must be released for a little while**" (Revelation 20:1-3).*

We have not yet considered Bible teaching about the Devil and Satan, because Paul has made no mention of the subject whatsoever in his Letter to the Romans. But in this passage the forces which deceive mankind are said to be restrained for 1000 years, after which they are released once more. The result of ungodliness being allowed to express itself once more will be that a division will occur between those who want to rebel against God and those who want to have eternal life under the rulership of Christ. Here's the picture language of Revelation again:

"And when the thousand years are ended, Satan will be

---

[14] *The translators of this Version of the Bible have understood the prophet to be speaking about the coming again of Jesus (the Teacher). Other versions omit the capital letter, showing that those translators understood that it will be the work of immortal saints in different localities to act as teachers to a particular community.*

*released from his prison and will come out to deceive the nations that are at the four corners of the earth, Gog and Magog, to gather them for battle; their number is like the sand of the sea. **And they marched up over the broad plain of the earth and surrounded the camp of the saints and the beloved city, but fire came down from heaven and consumed them, and the devil who had deceived them was thrown into the lake of fire and sulphur where the beast and the false prophet were, and they will be tormented day and night for ever and ever**. Then I saw a great white throne and him who was seated on it. From his presence earth and sky fled away, and no place was found for them. And I saw the dead, great and small, standing before the throne, and books were opened. Then another book was opened, which is the book of life. And the dead were judged by what was written in the books, according to what they had done" (20:7-12).*

❖ Second Resurrection

At the end of the Millennium there is therefore to be another resurrection – this time of those who have died during the thousand years; and another judgement of those still living and those who died during the Millennium who have now been raised. This will give a final opportunity for the mortal population to become immortal. Those who oppose the rulership of Christ will have shown that they prefer something else; those who have come to appreciate the gracious gift of God will now receive the privilege of living forever in a right relationship to God.

This is what Scripture says about that time – the beginning of that age of eternity when the immortal inhabitants of planet earth live in perfect harmony because of the work of God in Christ:

*"**Then comes the end, when he** (the Lord Jesus Christ) **delivers the kingdom to God the Father** after destroying every rule and every authority and power. For he must reign until he has put all his enemies under his feet. The last enemy to be destroyed is death. For 'God has put all things in subjection under his feet.' But when it says, 'all things are put in subjection,' it is plain that he is excepted who put all things in subjection under him. When all things are subjected to him, then the Son*

*himself will also be subjected to him who put all things in subjection under him, that **God may be all in all**" (1 Corinthians 15:24-28).*

Quite what it means that God will *"be all in all"* remains to be seen. One version, which amplifies each verse to offer a range of possible meanings, says:

*"When everything is subjected to him, then the Son himself will also subject himself to [the Father] who put all things under Him, so that God may be all in all [**be everything to everyone, supreme, the indwelling and controlling factor of life**]."* [15]

God means to fill the earth with His glory, and that means filling it with men and women who share His image, reflect His character, and think and behave in a truly godly way. When everything has been made subject to God's supreme will, His will and purpose will be the indwelling and controlling factor of life. God will then be *"all in all"*. As God was manifested, or made known, in the way that Jesus lived on earth, so He will be manifested in all those men and women who live in the new-made world.[16]

At last the end of mortal existence will have come. It will be the time when the earth is restored to perfection and all who live on it will be made immortal. All creation will then resound in praise to Almighty God. He has created all things for His glory and at last mankind will reflect the divine image. The time will have come which the apostle Paul described in these words:

"The creation waits with eager longing for the revealing of the sons of God. For the creation was subjected to futility, not willingly, but because of him who subjected it, in hope that the creation itself will be set free from its bondage to decay and obtain the freedom of the glory of the children of God" (Romans 8:19-21).

---

15 *The Amplified Bible.*
16 *See 1 Timothy 3:16 and 1 John 1:1-2. When Jesus lived on earth, God was manifest, or displayed, to mankind through His Son.*

Things to Read

📖 Zechariah chapters 12 to 14 give a dramatic portrayal of the events of the last days, including the repentance of Israel and the invasion of Jerusalem. The prophecy is not in chronological order, so you cannot work out the precise sequence of events, but all the elements are there which will feature prominently in the final countdown to the coming of Christ.

📖 Revelation chapter 20 gives a different sort of picture of these events, using Scriptural symbols to show, for example, how all forms of sin will be restrained when the kingdom is established.

Questions to Think About

22.1 Joel chapter 3 describes the judgement of nations by a coming king. Read it and then answer the following questions:

  a Where is this judgement due to take place?

  b Why is God angry with the nations?

  c What is due to happen to the children of Israel (the Jews)?

  d Where is the Judge said to be residing?

  e What is the predicted future for Jerusalem?

22.2 Isaiah chapter 65 verses 17 to 25 describes the coming kingdom as *"a new heavens and earth"*, or a new society which will be established. What especial blessings and benefits does the prophet foresee? Would you like to be part of this?

"'As for me, I have set my King on Zion, my holy hill.' I will tell of the decree: The Lord said to me, 'You are my Son; today I have begotten you'" (Psalm 2:6,7)

23

The Punishment of the Wicked

We have spent most of our time so far looking at what happens to those who are found faithful and are blessed with the gift of immortality. We have seen the sort of life they are to enjoy in the new world when they *"obtain the freedom of the glory of the children of God"* (Romans 8:21). In the last chapter, which was concerned with the end of this world, we saw that the last enemy to be destroyed is death, after which the Lord Jesus Christ will hand over control of the kingdom directly to his Father. Then God will become *"all in all"*. But what happens to those who are rejected?

❖ Accepted or Rejected?

In fact we have already glimpsed a few things about those who are found unworthy of life in the age to come. First, we discovered that some people will not be raised from the dead, but will remain dead forever, unconscious and oblivious. There will be no life after death for them: they will simply perish.[1] Others will be raised from the dead and be summoned to judgement together with those who are still living when the Judge returns. What will happen to those who are then rejected by Christ is described as follows:

> *"Because of your hard and impenitent heart* **you are storing up wrath for yourself on the day of wrath when God's righteous judgement will be revealed.** *He will render to each one according to his works ...* **for those who are self-seeking and do not obey the truth, but obey unrighteousness, there will be wrath and fury. There will be tribulation and distress for every human being who does evil"** *(Romans 2:5-9);*

---

[1] *Chapter 17, pages 254-256.*

*"Many of those who sleep in the dust of the earth shall awake, **some to everlasting life, and some to shame and everlasting contempt**" (Daniel 12:2);*

*"He will say, 'I tell you, I do not know where you come from. **Depart from me, all you workers of evil!**' In that place there will be **weeping and gnashing of teeth**, when you see Abraham and Isaac and Jacob and all the prophets in the kingdom of God but **you yourselves cast out**" (Luke 13:27,28);*

*"... when the Lord Jesus is revealed from heaven with his mighty angels in flaming fire, **inflicting vengeance on those who do not know God and on those who do not obey the gospel of our Lord Jesus. They will suffer the punishment of eternal destruction, away from the presence of the Lord and from the glory of his might**, when he comes on that day to be glorified in his saints, and to be marvelled at among all who have believed" (2 Thessalonians 1:7-10).*

These passages warn about the awful things that will happen to someone who is rejected at the judgement seat. They will experience the wrath of God's righteous judgement (Romans 2:8,9) and His everlasting contempt (Daniel 12:2), by being cast out of the presence of the king (Luke 13:28) to *"suffer the punishment of eternal destruction, away from·the presence of the Lord and from the glory of his might" (2 Thessalonians 1:9)*. But does that cover the entire picture, or are there other aspects to think about?

❖ What about Heaven and Hell?

You might have been expecting to discover that those rejected would suffer eternal torment in hell, in the company of the devil and his angels. When the Greek idea about an immortal soul was wrongly grafted on to true Christian teaching, it brought with it some complications. If everyone lives forever, because all souls are immortal, then those who die have to go somewhere immediately to continue their existence in a state of bliss and something has to happen to those who are unworthy of life with God. These wrong ideas led to the development of further wrong teaching – about both heaven and hell – which only goes to show that if you get one wrong idea it usually leads to even more error and confusion.

The obvious place for immortal souls to go, according to this scheme of things, was heaven, so that they could live in the presence of God, the Lord Jesus and the angels. Then there had to be a place of everlasting punishment – everlasting because souls were said to be immortal. What a muddle all this created; and there was more to come. If very good-living people died and went to heaven they were thought to be available as intermediaries who could plead with God on behalf of the living, so the idea of saints who would mediate came about. People began to adore and pray to Mary and other holy men and women, believing that such prayers were especially beneficial for certain things. St Christopher was thought of as the patron saint of travellers; St Peter was said to be the gatekeeper of heaven, and so on.

❖ Somewhere In-between?

Some people were unhappy about the thought of the rejected suffering endless torment in hell with no prospect of a second chance. What about those who had never even heard about the Bible, or the Lord Jesus Christ? Were they destined to suffer for evermore, despite that being no fault of their own? Was there no prospect of repentance for tormented sinners? How could all this be reconciled with the idea of a merciful and forgiving God who wanted to save everyone? So a whole system emerged to try and meet those problems – all of them man-made! People began to teach that there was a state of Limbo, or that Purgatory existed – ideas which are completely without any Bible basis whatsoever.

Heaven exists, of course, for it is God's dwelling place and now the Lord Jesus has ascended to live there with his Father and with the angels. They comprise the family of God who now share endless life and who dwell in a situation which is entirely free from sin. But heaven is God's realm, not man's, and the great news is that when the kingdom comes, and the rule of God has been established on earth to such an extent that sin has been destroyed, then the inhabitants of heaven will come to dwell with men.

It is God's purpose to bring together his family in heaven and believers on earth, which is why the Bible ends with a picture of the New Jerusalem coming down from heaven to earth.[2] But what about hell; how does that fit into the scheme of things?

❖ The Bible "Hell"

Just as the wrong idea about the human condition has made hell necessary as a place of punishment, the right idea about what happens to us after death makes the hell of popular belief quite unnecessary. Because there is no conscious existence after death until the resurrection, there is no need of a place of torture and everlasting punishment. Death could be considered punishment enough. The return to the grave of those who are raised to judgement to see the king in all his glory and glimpse something of his kingdom, and then are rejected and expelled, would appear to be sufficient punishment. So what does the Bible mean when it talks about hell?

The version we have been using in this study – the English Standard Version – does not mention *"hell"* at all in the Old Testament and only infrequently in the New, and that is the case with many of the more recent translations. Instead they substitute the original words – either in Hebrew or Greek – and do not translate them at all. In the Old Testament the Hebrew word is *"Sheol"* and in the New Testament it is the Greek word *"Hades"*, although there is another word as well, as we shall see.

This brings us another stage forward in learning how to read and understand the Bible, namely having to think about the meaning of particular words which can be translated in quite different ways in different Bible versions. In this case the translators have done the work for us by identifying the original words; sometimes we have to find that out for ourselves. Here we need help from the margin of the Bible (which can sometimes include helpful notes), a concordance which identifies original words[3] or even a Bible dictionary. By far the best way to work out what the word

---

[2] *See Revelation 21:1-5; 2 Peter 3:13; Ephesians 1:10 and Matthew 6:10. This is also why the "Kingdom of God" is sometimes called the "Kingdom of heaven" – because the rulership of God which now exists in heaven will then be extended to include earth as well. But you can see from Matthew 19:23-24 that they are interchangeable terms.*

[3] *These concordances are known as Exhaustive Concordances and there are two main ones, compiled by Robert Young and James Strong respectively. You might be able to consult one locally, but fortunately you are not likely to need one too often.*

in question means, once you have identified it, is to look at the passages where it occurs and just work out the meaning for yourself. That way you are letting Scripture interpret Scripture.

❖ Old Testament – "Sheol"

Let's try that with the Old Testament word *"Sheol"* by looking at some passages:

> *"The LORD kills and brings to life; he brings down to Sheol and raises up"* (1 Samuel 2:6);

> *"I call upon the LORD, who is worthy to be praised, and I am saved from my enemies. For* ***the waves of death encompassed me, the torrents of destruction assailed me; the cords of Sheol entangled me; the snares of death confronted me.*** *In my distress I called upon the LORD; to my God I called. From his temple he heard my voice, and my cry came to his ears"* (2 Samuel 22:4-7);

> *"The LORD has made himself known; he has executed judgement; the wicked are snared in the work of their own hands.* ***The wicked shall return to Sheol, all the nations that forget God"*** *(Psalm 9:16,17);*

> *"Therefore my heart is glad, and my whole being rejoices; my flesh also dwells secure.* ***For you will not abandon my soul to Sheol, or let your holy one see corruption.*** *You make known to me the path of life; in your presence there is fullness of joy; at your right hand are pleasures for evermore"* (Psalm 16:9-11);

> ***"The snares of death encompassed me; the pangs of Sheol laid hold on me;*** *I suffered distress and anguish. Then I called on the name of the LORD: 'O LORD, I pray, deliver my soul!'"* (Psalm 116:3,4);

> *"Her house is the way to* ***Sheol***, *going down to* ***the chambers of death*** *... he does not know that* ***the dead are there***, *that her guests are* ***in the depths of Sheol"*** *(Proverbs 7:27;9:18);*

> *"Moreover, wine is a traitor, an arrogant man who is never at rest.* ***His greed is as wide as Sheol; like***

352

death he has never enough. He gathers for himself all nations and collects as his own all peoples" (Habakkuk 2:5).

It doesn't take a lot of effort to work out what *"Sheol"* is by looking at these passages (and the other 58 where the word occurs). It is clearly the Hebrew word for **the grave** – the place where the dead are laid to rest. Good and bad people alike are destined to go there, the difference being that God will leave some there for ever – he will *"bring them down"* or *"abandon"* them there. The *"chambers of death"* are destined to be their homes for ever. But the righteous have a different and much better outlook. They will not be abandoned in Sheol, nor will they see corruption, but God will raise them up.

❖ New Testament – "Hades"

There is a real bonus awaiting us here, for one of the Old Testament passages we have already looked at also occurs in the Greek New Testament. The apostle Peter referred to it when he was teaching in Jerusalem and explained what had happened to Jesus when he died, was buried, and three days later rose again. This is what he said:

*"This Jesus, delivered up according to the definite plan and foreknowledge of God, you crucified and killed by the hands of lawless men. **God raised him up, loosing the pangs of death**, because it was not possible for him to be held by it. For David says concerning him, 'I saw the Lord always before me, for he is at my right hand that I may not be shaken; therefore my heart was glad, and my tongue rejoiced; my flesh also will dwell in hope. **For you will not abandon my soul to Hades, or let your Holy One see corruption.** You have made known to me the paths of life; you will make me full of gladness with your presence.' Brothers, I may say to you with confidence about the patriarch David that he both died and was buried, and his tomb is with us to this day. Being therefore a prophet, and knowing that God had sworn with an oath to him that he would set one of his descendants on his throne, he foresaw and spoke about the resurrection of the Christ, that **he was not abandoned to Hades, nor did his flesh see corruption. This Jesus God raised up,** and of that we all are witnesses" (Acts 2:23-32).*

As you can see, *"Hades"* bears exactly the same meaning in Greek as does the Hebrew word *"Sheol"* in the Old Testament. If you want to look  at some more occasions where the word *"Hades"* occurs (however it might be translated in the Bible you are using), try 1 Corinthians 15:55 and Revelation 20:13. [4]

❖ Picture Language

Mention of Revelation chapter 20 introduces another feature of Bible language which is a very helpful one for our development as Bible readers. The last book of the Bible portrays future events in vivid picture language. Nations are depicted as beasts; famine is portrayed as a horseman bringing destruction, and suchlike.

The Bible uses such pictures whenever it wants to convey something important in a way which will stick in the mind. But we cannot take those pictures literally: otherwise we will be expecting the Lord Jesus Christ to come to earth riding on a white horse with a sword protruding from his mouth and an iron rod in his hand (Revelation 19:11-15). Each part of the picture symbolises something that Jesus will do when he returns. He will come swiftly (the horse) to rule righteously (the white horse) and with great power he will crush all opposition (the sword and the rod).

Now consider what we are told about hell (the original word being "Hades"):

> *"The sea gave up the dead who were in it, Death and Hades gave up the dead who were in them, and they were judged, each one of them, according to what they had done. Then Death and Hades were thrown into the lake of fire. This is the second death, the lake of fire"* (20:13,14).

This is right at the end of the Millennium, just before God takes control of everything, and it is describing – in picture language – how death and the grave are to be destroyed forever. The lake of fire is pictured as the place of

---

[4] *Here the word "Hades" is translated "death" in the ESV; "grave" in the KJV.*

their destruction and we can identify with the idea, even though it requires us to picture "Death" and "Hades" as if they were people or things. It's a figure of speech called *personification* and this is a good example of how that is applied in practice. That picture language fits in perfectly with another quite different word used in the New Testament, which is also translated as "hell" and sometimes as "hell fire".

❖ New Testament – "Gehenna"

This Greek word is *"gehenna"* and the curious thing is that Gehenna was a place near Jerusalem which was used as a rubbish tip. In particular it was the place where the bodies of executed criminals were thrown prior to being burned, for there was always a fire burning at this tip to dispose of the rubbish.[5] Using that word was therefore a perfect way of warning people that they could come to a very sad end if they didn't come to their senses. Perhaps mothers would say that to naughty children – that they would end up "in Gehenna" if they carried on being naughty!

There are just twelve times when this word is used, seven of them by Matthew who was writing especially for Jews. It is the reference to fire which has led people to conclude that this is a place of eternal torment, but once you understand the background to the word, and appreciate that this is picture language, it all makes perfect sense and fits in precisely with what we have learned about death elsewhere in Scripture. Here are a few of the occasions when *"gehenna"* is the underlying word:[6]

> *"If your right eye causes you to sin, tear it out and throw it away. For it is better that you lose one of your members than **that your whole body be thrown into hell**" (Matthew 5:29);*

> *"Do not fear those who kill the body but cannot kill the soul. Rather fear him who can **destroy both soul and body in hell**" (Matthew 10:28);*

---

[5] *"Gehenna" comes from the Hebrew word "Ge-Hinnom" which means "the Valley of Hinnom". This was a valley just outside Jerusalem which was once used for idol worship, was cleansed in the days of King Josiah (2 Kings 23:10), and later became a rubbish tip for the city.*

[6] *All 12 occurrences are in Matthew 5:22,29,30; 10:28; 18:9; 23:15,33; Mark 9:43,45,47; Luke 12:5; James 3:6.*

*"If your hand causes you to sin, cut it off. It is better for you to enter life crippled than with two hands to go to **hell, to the unquenchable fire"** (Mark 9:43).*

The meaning is quite clear: don't behave in such a way that you will be totally destroyed and disgraced – like a common criminal. And the idea of fire is picked up to describe utter destruction in other passages too, like Revelation 20:13,14 and the "lake of fire". Again it has its basis in these ancient rubbish tips and is a very colourful and graphic image. Thus Paul talks about the coming of the Lord Jesus:

*"... with his mighty angels **in flaming fire**, inflicting vengeance on those who do not know God and on those who do not obey the gospel of our Lord Jesus. **They will suffer the punishment of eternal destruction, away from the presence of the Lord and from the glory of his might"** (2 Thessalonians 1:7,8).*

And the Lord himself talked about the wicked being destroyed in the fire, just as weeds are burned by a farmer:

*"**Just as the weeds are gathered and burned with fire**, so will it be at the close of the age. The Son of Man will send his angels, and they will gather out of his kingdom all causes of sin and all law-breakers, **and throw them into the fiery furnace**. In that place there will be weeping and gnashing of teeth"* (Matthew 13:40-42).

Jesus was using parable language and his meaning is plain once that is understood: he was describing utter destruction, as in the picture of the Lake of Fire.

❖ Parables

Jesus often taught in parables because this way of teaching immediately separated those who just wanted to hear stories from those who were prepared to take some trouble to work out what he was saying. Finding out what is true, especially now that there are so many wrong ideas about, takes time and effort; but, as we know, nothing worthwhile is ever achieved without some effort.

Jesus revealed things in his teaching which had not been understood before, for the purpose of God had advanced in an important way when the Son of God was born. Now there was an opportunity for everyone – Jew and Gentile alike – to find the way that leads to eternal life:

"He told them another parable. 'The kingdom of heaven is like leaven that a woman took and hid in three measures of flour, till it was all leavened.' **All these things Jesus said to the crowds in parables; indeed, he said nothing to them without a parable.** *This was to fulfil what was spoken by the prophet:* **'I will open my mouth in parables; I will utter what has been hidden since the foundation of the world'"** *(Matthew 13:33-35 quoting Psalm 78:2); [7]*

"Ask, and it will be given to you; seek, and you will find; knock, and it will be opened to you. *For everyone who asks receives, and the one who seeks finds, and to the one who knocks it will be opened"* (Matthew 7:7,8).

It follows that when Jesus speaks in parables we need to be able to differentiate between the picture and the meaning. In the above parable, the Kingdom of God is compared to leaven because that has such a powerful influence when mixed with flour. The kingdom of God is neither leaven nor flour, but it can be likened to those things in that limited effect.

❖ Lazarus and the Beggar

There is one parable that Jesus taught which requires a little more detailed consideration, for this has been a cause of confusion to people who insist on understanding it literally and not as Jesus intended. As we have been looking at figurative – or picture – language, reading this parable gives us an opportunity to note the difference between a parable and straight teaching. This parable is not meant to be taken literally. It is a carefully constructed picture with a very pointed meaning.

"There was a rich man who was clothed in purple and fine linen and who feasted sumptuously every day. And at his gate was laid a poor man named Lazarus, covered with sores, who desired to be fed with what fell from the rich man's table. Moreover, even the dogs came and

---

[7] *"Give ear, O my people, to my teaching; incline your ears to the words of my mouth! I will open my mouth in a parable; I will utter dark sayings from of old" (Psalm 78:1,2), again the emphasis being upon listening and thinking about what is said.*

licked his sores. The poor man died and was carried by the angels to Abraham's side. The rich man also died and was buried, and in Hades, being in torment, he lifted up his eyes and saw Abraham far off and Lazarus at his side. And he called out, 'Father Abraham, have mercy on me, and send Lazarus to dip the end of his finger in water and cool my tongue, for I am in anguish in this flame.' But Abraham said, 'Child, remember that you in your lifetime received your good things, and Lazarus in like manner bad things; but now he is comforted here, and you are in anguish. And besides all this, between us and you a great chasm has been fixed, in order that those who would pass from here to you may not be able, and none may cross from there to us.' And he said, 'Then I beg you, father, to send him to my father's house – for I have five brothers – so that he may warn them, lest they also come into this place of torment.' But Abraham said, 'They have Moses and the Prophets; let them hear them.' And he said, 'No, father Abraham, but if someone goes to them from the dead, they will repent.' He said to him, 'If they do not hear Moses and the Prophets, neither will they be convinced if someone should rise from the dead' " (Luke 16:19-31).

Certain elements in that picture are straightforward. A rich man and a poor man had lived in very different circumstances and when they died they were pictured as receiving very different rewards. One was pictured in bliss, the other in torment. Lazarus could see the rich man in torment and wanted to help him, and the righteous and the wicked could converse. All were in a conscious state after death.

❖ Why Picture Language?

We have already concluded, by looking at Scripture as a whole, that:

1   The dead are unconscious;

2   Abraham is specially mentioned as one who has not yet been rewarded, because he *"was gathered to his people"* (Hebrews 11:8-16; Genesis 25:8);

3   Their hope is resurrection from the dead – which is mentioned in the parable;

4 *"Hades"* is just the Greek word for the grave: it is not a
place of torment. In any case, those who believe in a
place of tormént would not expect any contact between
heaven and hell. That would make for considerable difficulties and much on-going sorrow for inhabitants of
heaven, if those they had loved were separated from
them, yet were visible.

So, why did Jesus use this particular picture language
to make his point? He was gently, but very effectively, pok-
ing fun at the rather silly views that some Jews had developed. We know from Jewish history that some Jews
believed in a sort of waiting area where the just and unjust
were left, pending the judgement and the resurrection.
There the just would "enjoy the prospect of the good things
they see, and rejoice in the expectation of those new enjoyments ... while they wait for that rest and eternal new life
in heaven which is to succeed this region". [8]

The place of waiting was called by those Jews *"The
Bosom of Abraham"*. Meanwhile the unjust would be
dragged to the neighbourhood of hell itself where they were
to be "struck with a fearful expectation of a future judgement" and when they looked across to 'Abraham's Bosom',
even hereby are they punished: for a chaos deep and large
is fixed between them: insomuch that a just man that hath
compassion upon them cannot be admitted".

With that information we can now see why Jesus told
this story and what his point really was. Those Jews who
believed that they were going to a waiting area after death,
where they would be tormented by the sight of what they
should have believed, but where it was now too late for
them to do anything about it, should take every opportunity to draw the right conclusions about what they had seen
and heard from Jesus. After death it would be too late. If
someone was raised from the dead and came back to life
again, they should take especial note of what that meant. It
would be a remarkable way for God to demonstrate that the
raised person was on His side.

And notice one other thing. This is the only time in all of
the parables that Jesus taught when one of the characters
is named. The beggar is named "Lazarus" and, on the eve of

---

8 *A full account of these Jewish views is given in the writings of the Jewish
historian Josephus, in his "Discourse to the Greeks concerning Hades". The
quotations that follow are from that document.*

his last visit to Jerusalem, who should the Lord Jesus raise from the dead but his friend Lazarus! You can read all about that in John chapter 11, and the reaction of the Jewish leaders in John 12:10,11. Far from believing what Jesus taught, they decided the best course of action would be to kill Lazarus as well, so they were certainly taking no notice of what Jesus taught or did.

❖ Destruction in Death

Unless we take notice of the warnings given to us by Jesus and the apostles, we will be denied everything that God wants to share with us. As the apostle Paul said earlier in Romans:

> *"The wages of sin is death; but the free gift of God is eternal life in Christ Jesus our Lord" (6:23).*

We have worked out that death really does mean death: that it is a punishment from God which will have abiding consequences. Unless we do something about it we will cease to exist for ever:

> *"For he sees that even the wise die; the fool and the stupid alike must perish and leave their wealth to others. Their graves are their homes forever, their dwelling places to all generations, though they called lands by their own names. **Man in his pomp will not remain; he is like the beasts that perish**" (Psalm 49:10-12);*

> *"For when he dies he will carry nothing away; his glory will not go down after him. For though, while he lives, he counts himself blessed, – and though you get praise when you do well for yourself – his soul will go to the generation of his fathers, who will never again see light. **Man in his pomp yet without understanding is like the beasts that perish**" (49:17-20).*

Note the difference between those two extracts. A person may be held in honour in this life, but that counts for nothing after death if there was no *understanding* of the purpose of God. Without that understanding there is little to distinguish a man from an animal. But the knowledge of God's purpose which is then acted upon makes all the difference. This gives us a real hope of resurrection from the dead when we can be given everlasting life and a place in God's kingdom, when it is established on earth.

Things to Read

📖 Ecclesiastes chapter 12 concludes the book written by King Solomon about the meaning of life. In this chapter he gives an illuminating portrait of old age and eventual death. Notice how he describes death, as a return to dust, and what he says about judgement to come.

📖 2 Thessalonians chapter 1 tells how the coming again of Jesus will separate the world into those who long for him to come and save them and those who are destroyed by him. Notice that their destruction is said to be everlasting.

Questions to Think About

23.1 Where did all these good men expect to go at death? (In each case the Hebrew word is "sheol", although it is translated differently in different Bible versions.)

a   Jacob (Genesis 37:35)

b   Job (Job 14:13; 17:13-16; 19:25-27)

c   King Hezekiah (Isaiah 38:10-18)

23.2 What does the Lord's Prayer (Matthew 6:5-13) teach us about our prospects of going to heaven at death? What are we really praying for when we pray for God's kingdom to come?

"Our Father in heaven, hallowed be your name. Your kingdom come, your will be done, on earth as it is in heaven. Give us this day our daily bread, and forgive us our debts, as we also have forgiven our debtors. And lead us not into temptation, but deliver us from evil" (Matthew 6:9-13)

24

What about the Devil and Satan?

The last two chapters have looked at Bible teaching about the end of this world. We have considered what the coming of God's kingdom will be like, both for those who are ready and who have prepared for it, and for those who do not believe the promises of God and who do not think that anything will happen, one way or the other.

This was a view being held in New Testament times as well, as the apostle Peter points out, when he taught about the worldwide flood that occurred in Noah's time. He says that people didn't believe Noah's warnings. They argued that such a disaster had never overtaken the world before, and in a similar way people were now arguing that the return of Jesus Christ would never happen either.

❖ Flood Disaster

In fact the apostle Peter teaches quite a lot about the Flood in his two letters.[1] He understood that it happened for a very good reason. God brought the flood as a punishment for sin. A commonly held view is that sin is something that is provoked inside us by the action of the Devil or Satan. Yet the Book of Genesis says nothing about that. If you read the account of the flood, in Genesis chapters 6-9, you will notice that there is no mention of the Devil or Satan anywhere. Instead, this is why destruction came:

> *"The LORD saw that the wickedness of man was great in the earth, and that every intention of the thoughts of his heart was only evil continually.* And the LORD was sorry that he had made man on the earth, and it grieved him to his heart. So the LORD said, 'I will blot out man whom I have created from the face of the land, man and animals and creeping things and birds of the heavens, for I am sorry that I have made them' ... Now the earth was corrupt in God's sight, and **the earth**

---

[1] *See 1 Peter 3:20-21; 2 Peter 2:5 and 3:1-14.*

was filled with violence. And God saw the earth, and behold, it was corrupt, for all flesh had corrupted their way on the earth. And God said to Noah, 'I have determined to make an end of all flesh, for the earth is filled with violence through them. Behold, I will destroy them with the earth'" (Genesis 6:5-13).

There is a mention of the *"sons of God"* inter-marrying with the *"daughters of men"* (in Genesis 6:1-2) which some people have said refers to fallen angels, and out of that mistake they have spun a web of confusion. But we are now well-enough equipped to sort that out if we give it a moment's thought:

➤ **Angels dwell in the presence of God**, being His messengers, and as only holy and righteous beings can survive in that situation it is impossible for angels to sin;[2]

➤ **Angels do not marry** (Matthew 22:30), which is a verse you will come across as you work through the Bible Reading Planner suggested earlier;[3]

➤ **The passage in question does not say that angels married the "daughters of men", but that the "sons of God" did.** As Genesis has been tracking two family trees in chapters 1 to 5 – the one a faithful group of believers and the other an unfaithful group, who were rebelling against the purpose of God – it is clear that Genesis 6:1-2 is telling us that those two sets of people intermarried.

Originally there had been two groups of people:

   a. mighty men and women of God, and

   b. violent and evil men and women.

When inter-marriage took place a blend of both characteristics came about and, sadly, the offspring were:

   c. mighty men who were both violent and evil.[4]

---

[2] *Remember that the reason why we cannot see God and still live is that we are sinful and His glorious presence would consume us (Exodus 33:20; 1 Timothy 6:16; Hebrews 12:29).*

[3] *Chapter 3, pages 34,35.*

[4] *Genesis 6:4.*

❖ Man's Wickedness

God destroyed the entire civilization of Noah's day because of the way that mankind had corrupted everything; they were violent, godless, heedless and thus worthless. Paul made the same observation in Romans about the way that the 1ˢᵗ century world was deliberately ignorant about God's existence and purpose and preferred impurity to holiness (Romans 1:18-32). And if you have worked through Peter's comments about the flood, in his two letters, you will have noted the same diagnosis.[5]

Paul has had a lot to say in Romans about the problem of sin and the great work God and the Lord Jesus Christ have accomplished in making a solution possible so that we, who struggle with sin, can become right with God. But have you noticed what Paul has said about the Devil and Satan? Absolutely nothing! There is no mention of the Devil at all in Romans, even though it contains the most detailed consideration of what God has done and is doing to save men and women from destruction. And there is only one passing reference to Satan in the entire letter when Paul says:

> *"For your obedience is known to all, so that I rejoice over you, but I want you to be wise as to what is good and innocent as to what is evil. **The God of peace will soon crush Satan under your feet**. The grace of our Lord Jesus Christ be with you" (Romans 16:19-20).*

This is a reference back to the first promise God ever made about the destruction of the serpent in Eden – that Eve's offspring would crush the serpent, but be bruised in the process.[6] So why does Paul make no mention of the Devil and all its supposed influence, if it is really important? It would seem that Paul understood the real problem and saw no need to refer to the Devil; that term was superfluous so far as Paul was concerned. In other letters Paul did use Devil language but not in Romans. Instead he wanted his readers to concentrate on the real problem with which we have to grapple – that of our *sinful nature* and its

---

[5] ***"They deliberately overlook this fact**, that the heavens existed long ago, and the earth was formed out of water and through water by the word of God, and that by means of these the world that then existed was deluged with water and perished" (2 Peter 3:5,6).*

[6] *Genesis 3:15 which we looked at in Chapter 12.*

powerful personal effects.

Paul's approach to all this is exactly the same as that of other inspired writers and teachers. Here's a selection of New Testament Scriptures:

*(Jesus) said, "**What comes out of a person is what defiles him. For from within, out of the heart of man, come evil thoughts, sexual immorality, theft, murder, adultery, coveting, wickedness, deceit, sensuality, envy, slander, pride, foolishness. All these evil things come from within, and they defile a person**" (Mark 7:20-23);*

*"**Sin came into the world through one man**, and death through sin, and so death spread to all men **because all sinned**" (Romans 5:12);*

*"**Sin**, seizing an opportunity through the commandment, **deceived me and through it killed me**" (7:11);*

*"I know that **nothing good dwells in me, that is, in my flesh**. For I have the desire to do what is right, but not the ability to carry it out. For I do not do the good I want, but the evil I do not want is what I keep on doing. Now if I do what I do not want, it is no longer I who do it, but **sin that dwells within me**. So I find it to be a law that when I want to do right, **evil lies close at hand**" (7:18-21);*

*"Now **the works of the flesh** are evident: sexual immorality, impurity, sensuality, idolatry, sorcery, enmity, strife, jealousy, fits of anger, rivalries, dissensions, divisions, envy, drunkenness, orgies, and things like these. I warn you, as I warned you before, that those who do such things will not inherit the kingdom of God" (Galatians 5:19-21);*

*"You have heard about him and were taught in him, as the truth is in Jesus, to **put off your old self, which belongs to your former manner of life and is corrupt through deceitful desires**, and to be renewed in the spirit of your minds" (Ephesians 4:21-23);*

"Let no one say when he is tempted, 'I am being tempted by God,' for God cannot be tempted with evil, and he

365

*himself tempts no one. But **each person is tempted when he is lured and enticed by his own desire. Then desire when it has conceived gives birth to sin, and sin when it is fully grown brings forth death**. Do not be deceived, my beloved brothers"* (James 1:13-16);

*"What causes quarrels and what causes fights among you? Is it not this, that **your passions are at war within you**?"* (James 4:1).

❖ Old Testament Confirmation

So far we have looked only at what the New Testament says about our nature, but you could easily build up a similar dossier from the Old, an exercise you might like to try. Here are some passages to start you off and if you look for cross-references in the margin of your Bible, if you have that sort of Bible, you will quickly build up an impressive list:[7]

*"Solomon did **what was evil in the sight of the LORD** and did not wholly follow the Lord, as David his father had done"* (1 Kings 11:6);

*"**There is a way that seems right to a man**, but its end is the way to death"* (Proverbs 16:25);

*"Behold, **I was brought forth in iniquity, and in sin did my mother conceive me**"* (Psalm 51:5, spoken by King David);

*"**The heart is deceitful above all things, and desperately sick**; who can understand it?"* (Jeremiah 17:9);

*"I know, O LORD, that **the way of man is not in himself**, that it is not in man who walks to direct his steps"* (Jeremiah 10:25).

This is intriguing. In all the Old Testament, which comprises two-thirds of the Bible, there is no mention of the Devil at all – not once! *Satan* gets a mention or two; *Lucifer* is referred to once in some versions of the Bible (though not in the ESV); but *"the Devil"* is completely absent. Such lan-

---

[7] *If not, here are two more references to look up (Psalm 58:3 and Ecclesiastes 9:3).*

guage appears only in the New Testament and is not that frequent there either; as we have seen, it never occurs in the whole of Romans. Instead, time and again, the Bible attributes the problem facing mankind to mankind itself. We are our own worst enemies! Our nature – human nature – is the root problem and it is that which needs to be changed, as we have already seen many times, and as Paul has argued throughout the Letter to the Romans.

❖ Old Testament Investigation

We need to do a little bit of personal research if we are to find out more about the Devil and Satan. We have already discovered that immortal souls and continual torment in a fiery hell are myths, not truths. They are human ideas and the same is true about the Devil as the supposed supernatural mastermind of evil. No such being exists. Think about this in relation to a few examples, including some Bible passages that people say teach the existence of a supernatural Devil.

❖ *Eden*

Who was to blame for what happened in Eden? Was it the fault of the Devil or Satan? Of course not! We know from what Paul said in Romans that Adam was to blame,[8] and the serpent was also responsible for its part in the proceedings because punishment was meted out to it.

If the serpent had been just a stooge, or if some external power was manipulating it to make it lure Eve and then Adam to eat the forbidden fruit, it would have been most unfair of God to have held the serpent responsible. But it most certainly was held responsible for its own actions and the New Testament both acknowledges the serpent's role and warns us against being deceived in the same way.[9]

❖ *Job's "Satan"*

The earliest occurrence of the term *"Satan"* in Scripture comes in the poetic Book of Job, the events of which probably occurred during the time the chapters of Genesis were

---

[8] *"Sin came into the world through one man, and death through sin" (Romans 5:12); and the serpent (a) was said to be crafty (Genesis 3:1) and (b) was cursed by God for its misdeeds (3:14,15). We may have never encountered an animal that could speak and think, but there is another Scriptural example – Balaam's ass (Numbers 22:28-30; 2 Peter 2:16).*

being written, though Job does not feature directly in its recorded histories. The Hebrew word *"Satan"* – which means 'adversary' or 'opponent' – occurs 14 times in the first two chapters of the Book of Job but nowhere else in the book. Indeed there are only four other occurrences of the word in the English Standard Version of the Bible, though the Hebrew word *"Satan"* occurs in another 9 places where it is translated *"adversary", "opponent"* or *"accuser".*

The opening chapters of the Book of Job set the scene for the trying times which will befall Job as he is tested to see:

1 whether or not he is good just because he is materially blessed by God, and

2 how he would react if those things were taken away.

This is the charge someone made when the *"sons of God"* met together to worship and God agrees that Job will be tested to discover the quality of his obedience and faithfulness.[10] Thus it is that God allows various calamities to befall Job and what follows is about the reaction of Job, his three friends who offer their analysis and a young man who offers a different and more helpful point of view. Finally God appears to challenge Job and then rewards him for his response to everything that he had endured.

Who could have been acting as the adversary to challenge Job's integrity? Who suggested to God that Job was only worshipping Him for what he could get out of it (see Job 1:6-2:10)? There are different views about who made those allegations and we can get some help from seeing who other adversaries (or "Satans") are elsewhere in Scripture:[11]

---

[9] *"I am afraid that as the serpent deceived Eve by his cunning, your thoughts will be led astray from a sincere and pure devotion to Christ" (2 Corinthians 11:3).*

[10] *There is no way that God could have entered into discussion with an evil being, for God is "of purer eyes than to see evil and cannot look at wrong" (Habakkuk 1:13).*

[11] *In all the references that follow the same Hebrew word "Satan" is used to describe quite different opponents. This shows that the word itself does not describe a supernatural devil. It merely describes someone in opposition to God or to someone who worships Him.*

Reference	Adversary
Numbers 22:22,32	When Balaam was prevented from going to prophesy against Israel it was *an angel* who opposed him
1 Samuel 29:4	When David joined the Philistine army to fight against his own people, the Philistines feared that *he could become their adversary* whilst the battle is taking place
2 Samuel 19:22	David himself calls *some of his relatives* his adversaries or *'Satans'*
1 Kings 11:14,23,25	God raises up several *political adversaries* against King Solomon to try to reform his conduct
1 Chronicles 21:1; 2 Samuel 24:1	*God Himself is described as an adversary* acting against King David
Zechariah 3:1,2; Jude 9 [12]	*The enemies of Israel*, who tried to stop the walls of Jerusalem being built, are described as *'Satans'* and the apostle Jude calls these opponents *'the devil'*

Now we can see how wide-open the options are! In this dramatic opening to the Book of Job the adversary – the *"Satan"* – could have been an angel acting out a part, a fellow-worshipper who was envious of prosperous Job, or an enemy who wanted to see Job suffer loss and who prayed to God for that to happen. Once the challenge had been made, God responded by allowing a chain of events to occur which brought Job to his knees and showed the true quality of Job's obedience.

---

[12] *Jude says that the opponents of Israel were challenged by the archangel Gabriel (as described in Zechariah 3:1-2, where he is called the LORD), and were told to leave the people (whom he called "the body of Moses") alone, in case God rebuked them. Jude's point is that not even the angel would rebuke them – he regarded that as God's prerogative.*

So the eventual outcome was good for Job as well as for us, for we learn a lot from the book about the ways of God. Through it all Job never once thought there was a supernatural being who was bringing calamity upon him: he knew all the time that what was happening was directly under the control of God, and the book says many times that this was the case.[13] There was no Satan in control, only God! That was what Job believed at the outset and that was what the writer of the book said had happened at the end:

*"Then his wife said to him, 'Do you still hold fast your integrity? Curse God and die.' But (Job) said to her, 'You speak as one of the foolish women would speak. **Shall we receive good from God, and shall we not receive evil**?' In all this Job did not sin with his lips" (Job 2:9,10);*

*"Then came to him all his brothers and sisters and all who had known him before, and ate bread with him in his house. And they showed him sympathy and comforted him **for all the evil that the LORD had brought upon him**. And each of them gave him a piece of money and a ring of gold" (42:11).*

When the challenge was over and Job was greatly rewarded for his steadfastness, despite the loss of everything, there is no further mention of the adversary. Job prays for his three unhelpful friends, however, and the narrator tells us that Job lived happily afterwards. The Satan has served his function at the start of the drama and nobody is bothered about the adversary's reaction to the fact that Job was hugely blessed in the end.

❖ Other Old Testament "Satan" passages

There are two other passages which are sometimes thought to teach that a supernatural monster of evil exists and they will form a helpful test to see how your Bible reading skill has developed. Have a look at them and then see whether your analysis matches that given below. They are Isaiah 14:3-23 and Ezekiel 28:11-18.

---

[13] *In addition to 2:10 and 42:11, see 6:4; 9:17,22; 13:20-22; 19:21; 22:3,4 and 27:2,3.*

❖ *Isaiah 14:3-23*

The key to understanding the first passage is Isaiah 14:4, in which the object of this song is stated. It is a taunt against *the King of Babylon*, the ruler of a powerful nation that was to become a major threat to the tiny kingdom of Judah, and which would eventually take the entire nation captive. The prophecy declares that however great and mighty the king thinks himself to be, and however he might attempt to consort with his gods, he is a mortal man and will end up dead!

There are two especially interesting points in this poem. The first is that picture language is used throughout. The whole earth, including the trees, is pictured as singing happily about Babylon's fall (14:7-8); those who are already dead are pictured as waking up to welcome the King of Babylon into their habitation (14:9-11); and the king is depicted as trying to place his throne in the heavens, as though he were lord of the universe! (14:12-14). The second thing to note is that the prophet uses the very language of Babylon as part of the satire:

> *"How you are fallen from heaven, O Day Star, son of Dawn! ... 'I will ascend to heaven; above the stars of God I will set my throne on high; I will sit on the mount of assembly in the far reaches of the north; I will ascend above the heights of the clouds; I will make myself like the Most High'"(14:13,14).*

This is the very terminology Babylonians used when they were imagining their gods in heavenly places – much as the Greeks would later come to believe that their gods lived on Mount Olympus.

❖ *Ezekiel 28:11-18*

The Ezekiel passage has a similar key to its meaning, this time Ezekiel 28:12, where we are told that it is a taunt against the *King of Tyre*. It forms part of a section of the prophecy which is describing what will happen in the future to several Middle Eastern nations[14] – Ammon, Moab, Seir, Edom, the Philistines and then Tyre (chapters 26-28). Tyre was an important trading nation at this time (about

---

14 *Ammon (25:1-7); Moab and Seir (25:8-11); Edom (25:12-14); Philistines (25:15-17).*

600 B.C.) and about 400 years earlier King Hiram of Tyre had formed an alliance with King Solomon to help him build God's temple at Jerusalem.[15]

This was more than just a trading arrangement for it seems that Hiram became a worshipper of the one true God. That meant that the entire nation could have allied itself with Israel and with the God of Israel. But they did not and Ezekiel now spells out the consequences for them. Once their king was in fellowship with God, associated with the work of the priests who ministered at the temple in Jerusalem,[16] but they abandoned all that might have been and went their own disastrous way!

❖ New Testament Investigation

There is no reference to the Devil in the Old Testament and only very few mentions of "Satan". But when describing different adversaries or opponents, the New Testament writers use both terms.[17] What had happened in the years[18] between both Testaments to bring a new vocabulary[19] into existence? The answer is quite straightforward, once you do a little digging around in ancient history.

After years of national independence, the nation of Israel became a subject people and the result was that they were brought into close contact with the religions of the Babylonians, Persians, Grecians and Romans – their various overlords. Those nations worshipped many gods and, in particular, they believed in rival gods of good and evil. Over time those beliefs influenced both the language of the Jews and the word pictures they came to use.

Here's an example to make the position a little clearer. On one occasion the religious enemies of Jesus accused

---

[15] *For the alliance in question see 1 Kings chapter 5.*

[16] *There are references to Eden, the garden of God, the cherubim that were in the temple, the stones of fire being the altar where sacrifices were offered and the holy mountain: all these are allusions to the blessings that Israel enjoyed as the people of God and to Jerusalem's special position in God's purpose.*

[17] *"Devil" occurs just 35 times in the New Testament and "Satan" 37 times. It is still infrequent.*

[18] *There is a 400 year gap between the end of Malachi and the start of the New Testament, during which there was no revelation from God.*

[19] *A close parallel is what happened during the 20th century and onwards with the arrival of radio and television. That introduced a new vocabulary including words like receivers, transistors, aerials and suchlike.*

him of using trickery when performing his miracles, but notice how they made that accusation:

> "When the Pharisees heard it, they said, **'It is only by Beelzebul, the prince of demons, that this man casts out demons.'** Knowing their thoughts, he said to them, 'Every kingdom divided against itself is laid waste, and no city or house divided against itself will stand. And if Satan casts out Satan, he is divided against himself. How then will his kingdom stand? And if I cast out demons by Beelzebul, by whom do your sons cast them out? Therefore they will be your judges. But if it is by the Spirit of God that I cast out demons, then the kingdom of God has come upon you. Or how can someone enter a strong man's house and plunder his goods, unless he first binds the strong man? Then indeed he may plunder his house'" (Matthew 12:24-29).

The accusation was made by Pharisees, who were a very strict religious group in Israel and who believed very firmly in the unity of God, and it is clear that they did not believe in "Beelzebul" as a god who had any power. They were just using this language to colour their accusation against Jesus, for Beelzebul (or Beelzebub) was the name of a disgraced god in Old Testament times – something that another nation had wrongly worshipped.[20]

Notice that Jesus uses the same language back to them, but this time he uses the term "Satan." He paints the picture[21] of Satan having a kingdom at his command and of demonic forces that fight with him. If that is the case, Jesus says, then the whole thing is absurd – evil is fighting against evil and the kingdom of evil must be about to collapse! He immediately changes the figure to that of a strong man under attack in his own home. To Jesus the term "Satan" was clearly just colourful picture language to describe the forces of evil that oppose the purpose of God.

---

[20] *See 2 Kings 1:2. The different spellings – Beelzebul and Beelzebub – occur in different versions of the Bible. The ESV uses only the first of those spellings.*

[21] *That this is indeed picture language is confirmed by Mark 3:23. Writing about this very same incident Mark says: "He called them to him and said to them **in parables**, 'How can Satan cast out Satan?'"*

❖ Picture Language

We have come across this sort of thing before when considering "Hell" and "Hell-fire". Then we found two helpful keys to unlock the puzzle.[22] We looked at the underlying Hebrew and Greek words and we noticed the use of picture language to make things more vivid and thus more important to the reader or hearer. Both those keys will help us again. Jesus had just been baptized and was about to start his public ministry when he was tempted to use his newly-acquired powers to serve himself in some way, quite understandable temptations in the circumstances. God put him to the test in private, for the record says that he was driven by the Spirit into the wilderness and was tempted in three ways:

1   He fasted for nearly six weeks and in extreme hunger he was tempted to make stones into bread.

2   He was tempted to throw himself down from the pinnacle of the temple in Jerusalem and let God's angels catch him by way of an open display of his status in God's purpose.

3   He was tempted to take the kingdoms of the world by force and establish a kingdom there and then.

Jesus resisted each temptation firmly and was then given angelic support and refreshment. If you read the gospel accounts of these temptations – in Matthew 4:1-11; Mark 1:12-13 and Luke 4:1-13 – you will see what vivid language is used. The writers describe the conflict between the Lord Jesus and the Devil or Satan and paint a graphic word picture of the contest.

A moment's thought will show it to be something that was taking place in the Lord's mind, for he could not be in the wilderness and at Jerusalem at the same time, nor is there a mountain from which *"all the kingdoms of the world and their glory" (Matthew 4:8)* can be seen instantaneously. In the mind's eye all those things are possible, but not in actuality. Nor can we imagine God subjecting His Son to the wiles of a supernatural Devil, nor Jesus agreeing to converse with a supernatural being who was God's enemy. It is important to note that the very first use of the word

---

[22] *Chapter 23, pages 351-356.*

'Devil' in the New Testament occurs in Matthew chapter 4, and concerns these temptations experienced by Jesus. The life of the Lord Jesus Christ was a battle between his inherited nature, which prompted him to do wrong, and what God wanted him to do. In this struggle against sin, which Jesus resisted right up to the point when he laid down his life (see Hebrews 12:3,4), we are to see how important it is for each of us to resist the natural human desires we have to please ourselves, rather than God.

Once we grasp the main idea that the terms *"Devil"* and *"Satan"* are ways of picturing all the forces that are in opposition to God, everything begins to make sense.

➘ *There is only One God, who is in control of everything, and He allows no power to oppose Him;*

➘ *Picture language is used to portray sin as an enemy of God so that we can see the battle that must be fought against sin in the clearest possible terms;*[23]

➘ *In the end all forms of evil, and its terrible consequences for mankind, will be destroyed and goodness will reign supreme; this too is pictured for us when all forms of evil are destroyed in the "lake of fire" (Revelation 20:1-10).*

Here are some examples of the use of this terminology in the New Testament:

Ref	Adversary
Matthew 16:23	"(Jesus) turned and said to **Peter**, 'Get behind me, Satan! You are a hindrance to me. For you are not setting your mind on the things of God, but on the things of man.'"
Luke 22:3	"Then Satan entered into **Judas called Iscariot**, who was of the number of the twelve."

[23] *A good example of this is in Revelation Chapter 12 where the enemies of God are pictured as being thrown down from their exalted positions of political power and influence and God's chosen ruler is pictured as being exalted. This is sometimes said to be the Devil being thrown out of heaven by the angels of God, but it is a prophecy of "things that must soon take place" (Revelation 1:1), not of things that happened long before.*

Ref	Adversary
John 6:70,71	Jesus answered them, "Did I not choose you, the Twelve? And yet **one of you is a devil**."
Acts 5:3,4	Peter said, "**Ananias**, why has Satan filled your heart to lie to the Holy Spirit and to keep back for yourself part of the proceeds of the land? ... Why is it that you have contrived this deed in your heart?
Acts 13:6,10	"When they had gone through the whole island as far as Paphos, they came upon a certain magician, a Jewish false prophet named **Bar-Jesus** ... and (Paul) said, 'You son of the devil, you enemy of all righteousness, full of all deceit and villainy, will you not stop making crooked the straight paths of the Lord?'"
2 Cor 11:14	"And no wonder, for even Satan disguises himself as an angel of light".[24]
2 Cor 12:7	"So to keep me from being too elated by the surpassing greatness of the revelations, a thorn was given me in the flesh, a messenger of Satan to harass me, to keep me from being too elated."[25]
Eph 6:11	"Put on the whole armour of God, that you may be able to stand against the schemes of the devil."
Rev 2:13	"I know where you dwell, where Satan's throne is.[26] Yet you hold fast my name, and you did not deny my faith even in the days of Antipas my faithful witness, who was killed among you, where Satan dwells."

[24] *This means that sometimes the opponents of God make out that they are the most righteous and upright of people.*

[25] *Paul had a disability of some sort and came to realise that it was God-given, to remind him not to trust in the flesh or in his native ability; it made him even more dependent upon God.*

[26] *This is part of a letter sent to the believers at Pergamum, in Asia Minor, and they were living in a city which was the centre of Emperor worship. The Roman Empire is seen as an opponent to Christianity in 1 Peter 5:8, where the specific reference may be to the Emperor Nero who had just begun to persecute Christians.*

❖ Original Language

The second Bible tool we used earlier was to see if the word *"Devil"* or *"Satan"* had a meaning in the original languages. We have already discovered that "Satan" is a Hebrew word which just means *"adversary"* or *"opponent"* and that it has been carried over into the Greek New Testament without being translated. "Devil" however is a translation of the Greek word *"diabolos"*. It means *"slanderer"* or *"false accuser"* and there are a few occasions where the word is translated just like that.[27] Thus the definition of the word is completely consistent with the way we have seen it being used already.

There is another way of getting a Bible definition of the word and that is by comparing one passage of Scripture with another. If one passage uses "Devil" or "Satan" terminology and the other does not, we can easily see what those terms mean when the idea is expressed in non-picture language. To an extent we have seen that already in Romans, where Paul spells out the problem of sin that we have to overcome with God's help without using the words "Satan" or "Devil" at all. And earlier in this chapter we noted that the real problem to confront us is variously described as *"wickedness"*, *"sin"*, *"evil"*, *"iniquity"*, *"transgression"*, *"disobedience"* and suchlike.

All these attitudes and inclinations find a natural home in human nature. We are inclined towards them and have been ever since Adam chose to disobey God and thought that this was the easiest way through life. As we learned in Romans: *"sin came into the world through one man, and death through sin, and so death spread to all men because all sinned" (5:12)*. Now notice how the writer to the Hebrews says the same thing:

> *"Since therefore the children share in flesh and blood, he (Jesus) himself likewise partook of the same things, **that through death he might destroy the one who has the power of death, that is, the devil**" (2:14).*

Because the devil is described as that which *"has the power of death"*, we can see straight away that the devil is another way of describing sin. This is where you can try applying a bit of simple logic to the question we are considering. The

---

[27] *See 1 Timothy 3:11; 2 Timothy 3:3 and Titus 2:3.*

writer says here that the devil "has the power of death". Now ask yourself this simple question: "Who or what is responsible for death?" Remember that we have already found the answer to that, in Romans 5:12:

> *"Therefore, just as sin came into the world through one man, and **death through sin, and so death spread to all men because all sinned**".*

We sin, therefore we die; so **SIN** is responsible for **DEATH**. If you want to check the comparison further then look up James 1:15 and Hebrews 9:26. The death of Jesus was a key part of God's saving plan to rescue mankind from sin and death. If there had been a supernatural being somewhere, who was plotting to upset God's purpose, the death of Jesus could not possibly have destroyed that being. But in dying Jesus dealt sin a death blow!

❖ What about Demons?

That leaves one remaining topic related to the Devil and Satan. If these terms are just a pictorial way of describing sin in its various forms, how do demons fit in as a part of that picture language?

We have already seen that demons are part of the picture language used both by Jesus and his religious opponents. The time when they accused him of acting by the power of Beelzebub was an occasion when:

> *"A demon-oppressed man who was blind and mute was brought to (Jesus), and he healed him, so that the man spoke and saw. And all the people were amazed, and said, 'Can this be the Son of David?' But when the Pharisees heard it, they said, 'It is only by Beelzebul, the prince of demons, that this man casts out demons'"* (Matthew 12:22-24).

Let's analyse this passage together. Notice that:

✓ *There was no obvious cause for the man's illness. When Jesus healed people who were obviously sick – people who were lame, had leprosy, suffered from a fever, or even those who were dead – we do not read of demons. But where it was not obvious what was wrong with a person who, for example, could not speak, it had become customary to use the language of demon possession.*

378

✓ *The record says that Jesus "healed" the man; not that he exorcised the demons! Sometimes when people have mental problems – such as those suffered by the madman Legion – healing the mental sickness is described as casting out the demons, as it graphically describes how Jesus could get rid of a disturbed mental state. Thus Legion was later to be found "clothed and in his right mind" (Luke 8:35).*

✓ *Just as the Pharisees did not believe in Beelzebub (the false god of Ekron) neither did they believe in a "prince of demons"; it was just a figure of speech. For the Old Testament used demon language to describe idol worship, and both Testaments insist that idols are no-gods – they do not exist.*

Here are some Old Testament references to demons and you will see how the same terminology has carried over into the New Testament as a figure of speech, not because people believed in demon possession as such:

*"So they shall no more sacrifice their sacrifices to **goat demons**, after whom they whore. This shall be a statute forever for them throughout their generations" (Leviticus 17:7);*

*"**They sacrificed to demons that were no gods, to gods they had never known**, to new gods that had come recently, whom your fathers had never dreaded" (Deuteronomy 32:17);*

*"They sacrificed their sons and their daughters to **the demons**" (Psalm 106:37).*

The very same language is used by the apostle Paul, writing to believers in Corinth, about idolatry which was widespread in that city. So it is clear that whilst people talked about demons, many Jews and the followers of Jesus recognised that there are no such things in fact.

*"What do I imply then? **That food offered to idols is anything, or that an idol is anything? No, I imply that what pagans sacrifice they offer to demons and not to God.** I do not want you to be participants with demons" (1 Corinthians 10:19,20).*

❖ Picture Power

One word of caution is needed. The Bible uses picture language for a particular purpose – to make things more graphic and dramatic than they would otherwise appear. So, for example, when Cain killed Abel he was immediately challenged by God in this way: *"What have you done? The voice of* **your brother's blood is crying to me from the ground.** *And now you are cursed from the ground, which has* **opened its mouth to receive your brother's blood** *from your hand" (Genesis 4:10,11).*

Biblical use of picture language to describe sin in its various forms has a similar purpose, to make us realise that sin is a powerful force that we need to really fight against, with God's help. If it was merely referred to as an influence which needed our attention, we would not understand what a struggle it is going to be to overcome everything. The apostle Paul does not use Devil or Satan picture language in Romans, but he most certainly deploys other colourful figures. For example, when he pictures himself in a life and death struggle against his natural inclinations:

> *"I see in my members another law* **waging war** *against the law of my mind and* **making me captive** *to the law of sin that dwells in my members. Wretched man that I am! Who will* **deliver me** *from this body of death?" (Romans 7:23,24).*

There is a battle to be fought and won. The Lord Jesus Christ was engaged in such warfare and was marvellously triumphant over the combined forces of evil. Meanwhile we have to fight the fight of faith. This is how Paul expressed the challenge, vividly and pictorially, in another of his letters:

> *"Finally, be strong in the Lord and in the strength of his might. Put on the whole armour of God, that you may be able to stand against the schemes of the devil. For we do not wrestle against flesh and blood, but against the rulers, against the authorities, against the cosmic powers over this present darkness, against the spiritual forces of evil in the heavenly places. Therefore take up the whole armour of God, that you may be able to withstand in the evil day, and having done all, to stand firm" (Ephesians 6:10-13).*

Things to Read

Jesus was wonderfully able to resist temptation and it is said of him that "he did no sin". Read the account of his temptations in the wilderness in Matthew chapter 4, when he conquered all the thoughts that occurred to him, whereby he could have used the power of God to rule the world, there and then.

Read Mark chapter 7 about the confrontation between the Lord Jesus and his adversaries. in which he explained to them that the real problem we have to tackle is inside us. Note that later in the chapter two healings are described where the language used in the first (which happened in Gentile territory) is about unclean spirits and demons, and in the second is much more matter-of-fact.

Questions to Think About

24.1 There is a great deal of emphatic repetition in Hebrews 2 verse 14 about the nature of Jesus and the consequences of his death for us. What do you understand by the statement that when he died he destroyed the "one who has the power of death"? (Hebrews 9:26; James 1:15; Romans 6:23; 8:3)

24.2 Compare the terms used in these passages of Scripture and say whether or not you think they are both talking about the same thing. If so, what conclusions do you draw about the Bible's use of picture language?

a Acts 5:3,4

b Ephesians 2:2,3

c 2 Timothy 2:26 and James 1:14

d Ephesians 6:11 and 4:22

e 2 Corinthians 4:4 and 2 Timothy 4:10

25
How should we Worship God?

The apostle Paul had been systematically explaining the gospel of salvation when he suddenly paused in wonderment, as though overtaken by the magnificence of God's grace and mercy towards fallen humanity. He had glimpsed the end of God's purpose, the salvation of all those who respond to God's invitation and choose to be saved, when he concluded that:

> "God has consigned all to disobedience, that he may have mercy on all. Oh, the depth of the riches and wisdom and knowledge of God! How unsearchable are his judgements and how inscrutable his ways! 'For who has known the mind of the Lord, or who has been his counsellor?' 'Or who has given a gift to him that he might be repaid?' For from him and through him and to him are all things. To him be glory for ever. Amen" (Romans 11:32-36).

For Paul this was an expression of worship and praise to Almighty God. It was his way of saying how much he appreciated what God had done and was doing – and his words seem quite spontaneous. When we stop to consider what God is offering us by way of salvation, we too might be overtaken with feelings of appreciation and deep gratitude. But, in Old Testament times, whilst God was pleased when His people praised Him spontaneously from receptive hearts and minds, He did not leave worship of Him to such individual gestures from His people. God knew the minds and hearts of His people – as He knows us today. He knows that without some structure and discipline in our worship and praise of Him, our feelings are more likely to turn towards pleasing ourselves than towards pleasing Him – as they did in Israel in past times.

❖ Spiritual Worship

In the final part of his Letter to the Romans, the apostle Paul turns his attention towards the way we should worship God and starts where he had left off at the end of Romans chapter 8. Chapters 9-11 were a digression by the apostle about God's longstanding purpose with the Jewish people. For you could read on from Romans 8:39 to 12:1 without noticing any break in the apostle's thought. Like this:

> *"I am sure that neither death nor life, nor angels nor rulers, nor things present nor things to come, nor powers, nor height nor depth, nor anything else in all creation, will be able to separate us from the love of God in Christ Jesus our Lord ... I appeal to you therefore, brothers, by the mercies of God, to present your bodies as a living sacrifice, holy and acceptable to God, which is your spiritual worship" (Romans 8:38,39; 12:1).*

Because of all that God has done and is doing for them, baptized believers should want to live for Him and surrender their lives in His service. It should be our aim to live a holy life, which is what God will find acceptable, and that will constitute *"spiritual worship"*. Sometimes, when there is doubt about how best to translate the original language in which a Scripture was first given the translator may offer an alternative rendering. This is one such case, where the ESV also suggests *"which is your rational service"*. [1]

We are certainly expected to make a heartfelt response to all that God has done for us; anything less would be ungrateful. It is also perfectly reasonable for God to expect us to want to live in a way that pleases Him if we really want to become members of His family and spend eternity with Him and with other members of His family, including the Lord Jesus Christ. So how do we do it? The apostle now explains that we have to get our minds right with God. In Romans chapter 8, Paul talked about the need to develop *"the mind of the Spirit" (8:5,6)*; now he explains a little more

---

[1] *Here the Amplified Bible has both possible renderings and it suggests: "I appeal to you therefore, brethren, and beg of you in view of [all] the mercies of God, to make a decisive dedication of your bodies [presenting all your members and faculties] as a living sacrifice, holy (devoted, consecrated) and well pleasing to God, which is your reasonable (rational, intelligent) service and spiritual worship."*

what that involves:

> *"Do not be conformed to this world, but* **be transformed by the renewal of your mind,** *that by testing you may discern what is the will of God, what is good and acceptable and perfect" (Romans 12:2).*

❖ Spiritual Transformation

The two things have to go together. If we want transformed bodies – made like that of the Lord Jesus, being free from sin and death – then our minds must be transformed, and that process starts now! By understanding the Bible and by making it our lifelong guide and companion, we can change the way we think. It shows us how to have a relationship with God and Jesus and teaches us how to learn to live with them and relate to them in prayer.

Once that relationship is established we will begin to alter the way we behave. We will come to learn what pleases God, as we have been doing in this book, and then we will begin to want to do it. This change will not come overnight: it takes time to cultivate – to develop a new attitude and a different set of desires from those with which we were born. Changing the way we think and feel is something we should be doing together with other believers. Paul says that together believers form the body of Christ:

> **"We, though many, are one body in Christ, and individually members one of another"** *(Romans 12:5).*

We have taken it for granted so far in our studies that there was a Christian congregation in Rome to which Paul was writing. His letter was addressed to *"all those in Rome who are loved by God and called to be saints" (1:7).* The word *"saint"* in Scripture means people who are "set apart" from the world and worldly ideas. They have chosen to serve God, and have made an agreement with Him through their involvement in the work of Christ. In Rome they were the people who believed what Paul believed and taught: it was their understanding and acceptance of the gospel that justified them in God's sight and made them sharers of the one true faith.

It is the same today. Only those who believe the gospel as Paul taught it are members of the true church. As we have seen, there are many people who believe and teach wrong things about God's purpose;[2] they are not members of the true church, for their teachings are man-made and not God-given. It is vitally important to transform the mind by believing the truth as God has revealed it. Human reasoning is useless for that purpose. What matters first is to *understand* and then to *do* the will of God.

❖ Christian Congregations

The writer of this book is a Christadelphian. He belongs to a group of people who have from earliest times sought to rediscover exactly what the Bible teaches. This community was established in the 19th century and its founder members all sought to practise what we have been learning to do – to read the Bible for themselves and then do what God requires of them. There are now Christadelphian[3] congregations[4] in most parts of the world and we can put you in touch with your nearest group if you write to the address given at the back of this book. Sometimes, of course, you may be the first believer in your locality, in which case we can help and support your spiritual development while you are teaching others in the locality. For this is what the apostle now says to the Roman believers that they should do. They should work together to build one another up.

Notice that Paul doesn't write to the *clergy* at the Church of Rome, as though they were the only ones who would understand what he was saying. He wrote to *"all those … who are loved by God" (1:7)*. The early Christians did not have professional teachers or priests. All the believers worked together and contributed to the spiritual development of their congregation as they were able. For God

---

[2] *Some of the wrong teachings we have considered were about the immortality of the soul; heaven-going at death; hell as a place of torment; the existence and power of a supernatural Devil or Satan; the existence of demons; the denial of the Unity of God; confusion about the nature and work of the Lord Jesus and the Holy Spirit – the power of God; and not believing that baptism by immersion is essential for salvation. In all these things Christendom in general is astray from the Bible.*

[3] *The word Christadelphian means 'Brothers in Christ' – a phrase we meet in Colossians 1:2.*

[4] *To remain Bible-based and to distinguish themselves from Christian churches that have strayed far away from true Bible teaching, Christadelphians call their congregations "ecclesias", this being the Greek word for "congregations". They believe that people are the really important thing, not the "church" building itself.*

had called them all to be holy; as the apostle Peter expresses it:

> *"You are a chosen race, a royal priesthood, a holy
> nation, a people for his own possession, that you may
> proclaim the excellencies of him who called you out of
> darkness into his marvellous light. Once you were not a
> people, but now you are God's people; once you had not
> received mercy, but now you have received mercy" (1
> Peter 2:9,10).*

All members of the congregation were to be holy and
were to work together to worship God. So Paul tells the
Romans that they should see what they can contribute:

> ***"Having gifts that differ according to the grace
> given to us, let us use them***: *if prophecy, in proportion
> to our faith; if service, in our serving; the one who teach-
> es, in his teaching; the one who exhorts, in his exhorta-
> tion; the one who contributes, in generosity; the one who
> leads, with zeal; the one who does acts of mercy, with
> cheerfulness" (Romans 12:6-8).*

Everybody has something to give, says the apostle, and
that is as true now as it was when he first wrote those
words. When we are able to understand the Bible we can
do a great deal to help others who also are learning, and
this is a wonderful way of growing together and developing
spiritually as we prepare for the coming of the Lord Jesus
Christ.

❖ Congregational Worship

Paul does not spend time in this letter explaining how worship should be arranged, but he does this in other letters.
For example, in his letters to the believers at Corinth he
deals with problems they were having in their communal
worship. It is something to watch out for as you are reading
the Bible, to see how congregations (or "ecclesias") were
organised in the First Century and to note that there are a
lot of differences from the organisational structure that
exists in some churches today.

The early church had overseers, elders and deacons, but
those terms described a simple arrangement in which some
members of the congregation were appointed to look after
arrangements, to care for the sick and needy and to make
sure that matters were organised properly. The entire con-

gregation had similar responsibilities, for all the members were to love and care for one another. The notion of paid clergy with different layers of responsibility and importance is not a New Testament idea at all.[5] It is another of those things that got incorporated from the way other non-Christian religions had organised their affairs, and it can have more to do with business planning and career development than with the House of God. The Lord Jesus was very strongly opposed to such matters, as he once demonstrated in spectacular fashion when he overturned the tables of the moneychangers in the temple at Jerusalem (Matthew 21:12,13).

We have a priest in heaven – the Lord Jesus Christ, who sits at the right hand of the Father and who is our go-between. We have no need of earthly priests. For if they were to be appointed they would distance the believer from his or her direct contact with God through Christ. The writer to the Hebrews, who wrote to people who were used to such an arrangement, explained carefully why priests are no longer appropriate. The Lord Jesus Christ, he explains, is now the only priest we need.

In First Century times there were people who had Holy Spirit gifts and they were able to speak as prophets, including in foreign languages, or interpreting such languages. Those gifts have now passed, having served their purpose, but even in those times it was possible for a congregation to become disorganised or over-excited, so Paul wrote about such matters at length to the Corinthians.[6] We should not seek to be over-emotional or to get over-excited in our worship, but should use the time to sing hymns, to read from God's Word, to pray together and to listen to an exposition of God's Word. There is so much to learn and so much encouragement that we can give one another that we will greatly benefit from such times and are encouraged to meet together regularly. This is what the writer to the

---

[5] *To read about church organisation you might want to look at 1 Timothy 3:1-13; 5:17-19 and Titus 1:5-9. Christadelphians have no paid ministers or missionaries: all the work is done voluntarily and the congregations are self-financing. Sometimes there are funds to help new meetings get established and to deal with welfare needs. Members contribute towards these various funds if they are able to, but non-members are never asked to contribute any money.*

[6] *Paul's advice about how the First Century believers were to exercise their Holy Spirit gifts is in 1 Corinthians chapters 12-14.*

UNDERSTAND THE BIBLE FOR YOURSELF

Hebrews said:

> *"Since we have a great priest over the house of God, let us draw near with a true heart in full assurance of faith, with our hearts sprinkled clean from an evil conscience and our bodies washed with pure water. Let us hold fast the confession of our hope without wavering, for he who promised is faithful. And let us consider how to stir up one another to love and good works, not neglecting to meet together, as is the habit of some, but encouraging one another, and all the more as you see the Day drawing near" (Hebrews 10:21-25).*

❖ Preachers and Teachers

There is one Scriptural requirement, not observed nowadays in many churches, concerning those who are to teach and preach in a congregation when there are both men and women present. Because of what happened in Eden, the apostle Paul explains that it is men who are now charged with the responsibility of public teaching from God's Word.[7]

> *"Let a woman learn quietly with all submissiveness. I do not permit a woman to teach or to exercise authority over a man; rather, she is to remain quiet. For Adam was formed first, then Eve; and Adam was not deceived, but the woman was deceived and became a transgressor" (1 Timothy 2:11-14).*

This does not preclude women teaching children, or from speaking when there are only other women present, but it shows that the legacy of Eden is far-reaching and will not be wholly resolved until the Lord Jesus comes again. Nor does it limit the role that women can play in the Christian community; it merely defines that role as excluding public speaking in mixed assemblies. In the last chapter of Romans Paul sends personal greetings to those members of the congregation he already knew and nine out of the twenty six persons greeted by name are women. We know that from their names. Four of the nine are described as prominent in the work of the congregation at Rome. For example, it is said of Priscilla (or Prisca) that she is Paul's *"fellow-worker"* and of Phoebe that they were to give her whatever help she needed *"for she has been a patron of*

---

[7] *See also 1 Corinthians 14:34,35.*

388

many and of myself as well" (16:2). So there is evidently plenty for everyone to do in the Lord's service, whether we are men or women.

When baptized believers meet together to worship week-by-week, they are to remember the Lord Jesus Christ. So the exposition of God's Word should always be helpful in that respect and should direct the minds of those present towards some aspect of Christian discipleship. Early believers broke with the Jewish practice of meeting on a Saturday – Sabbath keeping by the Jews began at sunset on Friday and ended at sunset on Saturday. Jesus rose on the first day of the week and, to celebrate that great victory over sin and death, Sunday morning marked the start of the day when believers met together to remember Jesus.[8]

❖ The Breaking of Bread

Jesus commanded that baptized believers should remember the death and resurrection of their Lord by sharing together some bread and wine, just as he and his disciples did at the Last Supper. This act is described in the New Testament as the Breaking of Bread, or sometimes as an act of communion (the word simply means fellowship or sharing together); and the bread and wine are symbols of the body and blood of the Lord. They are not his actual body and blood – that is another of those pagan ideas that some people have wrongly taught and believed. And this act is to be done, as a matter of commandment, by all the believers, not by a select few, and both bread and wine should be shared. Scripture is quite clear about that:

> *"The cup of blessing that we bless, is it not a participation in the blood of Christ? The bread that we break, is it not a participation in the body of Christ? Because there is one bread, **we who are many are one body, for we all partake of the one bread**" (1 Corinthians 10:16,17);*

> *"For I received from the Lord what I also delivered to you, that the Lord Jesus on the night when he was betrayed took bread, and when he had given thanks, he*

---

[8] *See John 20:1; Acts 20:7 and 1 Corinthians 16:2. As Paul explains in Colossians 2:16, any day will do in which to remember Jesus and in some parts of the world work-practices make it easier for believers to meet on a Friday or a Saturday.*

broke it, and said, 'This is my body which is for you. **Do this in remembrance of me.***' In the same way also he took the cup, after supper, saying, 'This cup is the new covenant in my blood.* **Do this, as often as you drink it, in remembrance of me.***' For as often as you* **eat this bread and drink the cup, you proclaim the Lord's death until he comes.** *Whoever, therefore, eats the bread or drinks the cup of the Lord in an unworthy manner will be guilty of profaning the body and blood of the Lord.* **Let a person examine himself, then, and so eat of the bread and drink of the cup"** *(11:23-28).*

Ideally, of course, it is an act of remembrance to be undertaken with fellow baptized believers. Where there are unbaptized people present they would not share the bread and wine, for it is the closest expression there is that the partaker is in covenant relationship with God and that, week-by-week, that covenant is renewed in this way. It is a sharing together of the love of God and of the Lord Jesus Christ.

❖ "Love one another"

When Jesus instituted this meal in remembrance of himself, he shared it with his disciples. He began by telling them how important it was that they should love one another and he washed their feet to show that he was among them as somebody who had come to serve. Paul, who has just written to the Romans about the "one body" of Christian believers, now stresses the importance of living the new life that began at baptism. In chapter 7 he spoke of it in terms of a fierce struggle to overcome; in chapter 8 of the development of a spiritual mind, so that our thinking is right. Now he turns his attention to what our conduct should be towards one another, believers and unbelievers alike:

"Let love be genuine. Abhor what is evil; hold fast to what is good. Love one another with brotherly affection. Outdo one another in showing honour. Do not be slothful in zeal, be fervent in spirit, serve the Lord. Rejoice in

hope, be patient in tribulation, be constant in prayer. Contribute to the needs of the saints and seek to show hospitality. Bless those who persecute you; bless and do not curse them. Rejoice with those who rejoice, weep with those who weep. Live in harmony with one another" (Romans 12:9-16).

Believers should live together as befits members of the family of God: that's why Paul writes about *"brotherly affection"*. It is a great thing that Jesus is happy to call all new members of God's family his brothers and sisters.[9] We should be careful for the material and spiritual needs of all our fellow believers, and should live in a way which supports and builds up one another. If we have more than we personally need, we should contribute to the needs of others. For this reason it is usual to have a collection at those meetings when believers are together remembering Jesus, but not at public meetings when the gospel is being preached. For whilst Jesus said that *"It is more blessed to give than to receive"* (Acts 20:35), he also said *"You received without paying; give without pay"* (Matthew 10:8).

❖ Christian Behaviour

The way we behave – with believers and unbelievers alike – is a very important expression of the change that has taken, or is taking, place inside us. For the things we say and do are outside indicators of our inner state of mind. We have to try to live a transformed life, as though we had stopped living for ourselves and are now living entirely for others as servants of the Lord Jesus Christ. That is what Paul means by living sacrificially – putting the needs and feelings of others before our own.

There are two reasons for this. The first is that we are commanded to do this as followers of the Lord Jesus Christ, because that is how he lived. In a masterful understatement, Paul says this:

*"We who are strong have an obligation to bear with the failings of the weak, and not to please ourselves. Let each of us please his neighbour for his good, to build him up. **For Christ did not please himself"*** (Rom 15:1-3).

---

[9] *"He is not ashamed to call them brothers"* (Hebrews 2:11) and that is why Christadelphians are so called, for the name comes from Greek words which mean "brothers in Christ".

Jesus set the standard and we have to do the best we can to follow his example. We will not achieve the same level of obedience, of course, for the Lord was perfect in everything he did. He never once sinned. But we have to try hard to follow his lead. Just what that means in practice is explained here (in Romans chapters 12-15), and by the Lord Jesus himself in the long talk he gave to his disciples, recorded in Matthew chapters 5-7, sometimes called the Sermon on the Mount. Paul's encouragement to the believers at Rome is closely modelled on what Jesus taught. For example, he says that we should not retaliate when people do unfair or unreasonable things to us, but should suffer wrong for Christ's sake:

"Repay no one evil for evil, but give thought to do what is honourable in the sight of all. If possible, so far as it depends on you, live peaceably with all. Beloved, never avenge yourselves, but leave it to the wrath of God, for it is written, 'Vengeance is mine, I will repay, says the Lord.' To the contrary, 'if your enemy is hungry, feed him; if he is thirsty, give him something to drink; for by so doing you will heap burning coals on his head.' Do not be overcome by evil, but overcome evil with good" (Romans 12:17-21).

In these verses Paul gives us the second reason why we should try to live just as Jesus did. We need to live in a way that encourages other people to want to know about Jesus, so that they too can believe the gospel and be saved. The greatest good we can do to anyone is to share with them the faith that saves from eternal death. This is why Paul wrote the Letter to the Romans, so that they too would know what he believed and benefit from that knowledge. His gift to us, centuries later, is priceless; for without this knowledge we could not obtain eternal life. Now it becomes our responsibility to share that faith with others – and how we live is a vital part of that sharing.

❖ In Relationships

The apostle Peter wrote about partners in a marriage where only one of them was a believer and this is what he advised:

"Likewise, wives, be subject to your own husbands, so that even if some do not obey the word, they may be won

without a word by the conduct of their wives – when they see your respectful and pure conduct. Do not let your adorning be external – the braiding of hair, the wearing of gold, or the putting on of clothing – but let your adorning be the hidden person of the heart with the imperishable beauty of a gentle and quiet spirit, which in God's sight is very precious" (1 Peter 3:1-4).

Again it was a question of the outward behaviour of the believer being such that it would influence for good those with whom the believer lived, whether husband, wife or children. Quite what that involves today depends greatly upon individual circumstances. Perhaps only one brother or sister in a house is able to read easily. In such a case he or she can help the others to learn to read the Bible and can give helpful advice from it. In other cases husband and wife might have different opinions. Perhaps one is strongly opposed to religion, or wants to do things which are not in accord with the teachings of Jesus. There might be some hard choices then that have to be made. But in the first place at least the believer must seek to live in accordance with the life of Christ – to be honourable in behaviour, to live at peace, to be respectful and pure in conduct, and to cultivate a gentle and quiet spirit.

We will look at what the Bible says about marriage later. For the moment it is important to note that both the apostles Peter and Paul say that we should respect and work for a demanding employer with just the same attitude of mind as if we were in a difficult marriage. For the working relationship is another opportunity to demonstrate to others that we have changed our thinking and our behaviour. It gives us the discipline that we sometimes need to make sure that we are putting into practice Christian values and attitudes. So if people are unfair to us, we will not be unfair back, but will return their unkindness with kindness. And if things are hard, it is an opportunity for us to remember just how hard things were for the Lord Jesus.

❖ New Life in Christ

None of this is easy of course and you may be wondering how you could possibly keep it up, even if you started living in this way. It seems an impossible standard to achieve. It is exactly for this reason that the apostle structured his letter in the way he has done. Think how you would have responded if in the opening chapter of this book you had been challenged to live like this – to be nice to people who are nasty; to love those who hate you; to pray for those who treat you badly. You would probably not even have finished that first chapter!

But all through the opening part of the letter Paul was busy telling us about the purpose of God – what God has done to make salvation possible, how much we need it, and how it will all come together when the Lord Jesus returns from heaven to establish God's kingdom on earth. We have seen that God is at work in the world and that He wants us to be part of His great purpose. In the middle of his explanation the apostle said that we can join that purpose by believing and being baptized into the saving name of Jesus. Then he started to explain what that means inside our minds as we begin to change the way we think and become focused on spiritual things.

It is only now, towards the end of the letter, that he spells out what this will be like as we start to live differently – as our new life in Christ is shown to other people. He started this section by reminding us that the driving force of that transformation is the mind; that it needs to be transformed every day as we understand more fully what God's will involves. We need to keep in constant touch with God through Christ. These are the things which will enable us to start to live like this – like Jesus – and these are the ways in which that new life can be sustained. Here they are again:

> *"Be transformed by the renewal of your mind, that by testing you may discern what is the will of God, what is good and acceptable and perfect" (Romans 12:2);*

> *"Do not be slothful in zeal, be fervent in spirit, serve the Lord. Rejoice in hope, be patient in tribulation, be constant in prayer" (12:11,12).*

❖ Renewing the Mind

The Bible is going to be our guidebook and companion along life's journey and it will help to mould and shape our thinking and our feelings. It does not merely change our mind about things – as this book might have changed your mind about the things you believe as you have been reading. The Bible *renews* our mind. The more we read it, the more we understand about God and His purpose and the more we shall want to be part of that purpose, whatever the personal cost. It is a life-giving Word from God which is quite unlike any other book you might read. Because the Bible comprises a large and complicated collection of books, it takes time fully to understand it, and there are endless avenues to explore. It is meant to be a life-long study for the man and woman of God.

But it is a two-way process when we start to learn about God and want to get to know Him more and more. This is why Paul says we should be persistent in prayer. He means that we should keep praying. Prayer is our opportunity to talk to God and to tell Him how we are feeling about things. We can thank Him for all He is doing in our lives; ask Him for help and guidance and praise Him. When we become baptized believers we can pray for forgiveness to a Father who is always ready to help and to forgive when we fail. For it is not only in the act of baptism that our sins are forgiven. When, after baptism, we fail to achieve the sort of behaviour at which we are aiming, as we all do, then God is ready to forgive us through our Lord Jesus Christ and to help us to keep going forward in our next attempt:

> *"My little children, I am writing these things to you so that you may not sin. But if anyone does sin, we have an advocate with the Father, Jesus Christ the righteous. He is the propitiation for our sins, and not for ours only but also for the sins of the whole world. And by this we know that we have come to know him, if we keep his commandments" (1 John 2:1-3).*

There are commandments to be kept as part of our new life in Christ and we will gradually become more obedient and more faithful if we are striving to live as followers of Jesus. Over time we will see a change taking place and, at the coming of Christ, it will be completed by the transformation of our bodies.

❖ Transfiguration

There was an event in the life of Jesus when he had climbed a mountain with three of his disciples and there he was transfigured before them. The gospel accounts say that he was completely transformed: *"he was transfigured before them, and his face shone like the sun, and his clothes became white as light" (Matthew 17:2).* For the disciples and for the Lord it was a glimpse of what things will be like in God's kingdom, when all our present problems will be completely removed and we will begin life at a higher level in every respect.

When Paul asks us to be *"transformed by the renewal of your mind" (Romans 12:2)*, the word *"transformed"* is the same Greek word as that translated *"transfigured"* in Matthew's account of the transfiguration of Jesus. Just as Jesus was transformed, so we are to be changed inwardly so that, in due course and in the mercy of God, we too can be changed outwardly to be just like Jesus. When we resolve to follow Christ we are beginning to live a completely new life: we have started a life that will never end if we remain faithful and become obedient children in God's heavenly family.

Things to Read

📖 Read Ephesians chapter 5 to see the practical way the apostle Paul addresses the changes that have to take place in our lives.

📖 Galatians chapters 5 and 6 show us how our lives should change inwardly and outwardly. It is a regular feature of the apostle Paul's letters that he deals first with what we should believe and then with the change of behaviour that must follow.

Questions to Think About

25.1 What is the driving force of the new life in Christ and how will we be able to keep up a good standard of behaviour as we try to follow the example set by Jesus? (John 13:34; Romans 12:10; Ephesians 5:2; Colossians 3:14; 1 Thessalonians 4:9)

25.2 How should we pray to God? What will make our prayers effective in His sight? (Luke 18:1; Matthew 6:6-7; 7:7; 26:41; Ephesians 6:18; Philippians 4:6)

26

The Believer and the State

Paul has written about the personal challenges that face the believer and has told us that we must live the life of Christ – the new life. Now he directs our attention to our relationship with the present order of things in the world and, in chapter 13 of Romans, lays down some important guidelines for believers in all ages.

Rome was the capital city of the empire that then ruled the world and the Christian community at Rome, the "ecclesia" there, was right at the centre of things. The brethren and sisters would have seen the emperor from time to time and might even have known members of the Roman Senate. It is even possible that some of the believers may have worked for the state. Erastus was the city treasurer, for example (Romans 16:23), and Paul included him in the greetings that he sent.

❖ God Rules!

Paul told believers they must live transformed lives and not be *"conformed to this world"* (12:2), but what did he mean by that? Should they take part in government or legal matters, or should they separate themselves from such things now that they were God's people and looked for His kingdom to come? Should the followers of Jesus protest against the established order if they found its rule contrary to the principles of the gospel? If so how should they do this? How would this fit in with their understanding that God is in charge of everything and that He will change things for good when the time is right for Him to do that? These are the very questions that Paul now writes about. For, at the start of chapter 13, this is what he says:

> *"Let every person be subject to the governing authorities.* ***For there is no authority except from God, and those that exist have been instituted by God.*** *Therefore whoever resists the authorities resists what*

*God has appointed, and those who resist will incur judge-
ment. For rulers are not a terror to good conduct, but to
bad. Would you have no fear of the one who is in authority? Then do what is good, and you will receive his
approval, for he is God's servant for your good. But if you
do wrong, be afraid, for he does not bear the sword in
vain. For he is the servant of God, an avenger who carries
out God's wrath on the wrongdoer" (Romans 13:1-4).*

Long before Paul wrote that, under the direction of God's
Holy Spirit, the same lesson had been learned by a young
Jewish exile in Babylon. The prophet Daniel was given an
insight into future world history by the God who was
directing operations, and this is the profound truth that
Daniel learned:

*"Blessed be the name of God for ever and ever, to whom
belong wisdom and might. He changes times and seasons;* **he removes kings and sets up kings;** *he gives
wisdom to the wise and knowledge to those who have
understanding" (Daniel 2:21);*

And later:

**"The Most High rules the kingdom of men and gives
it to whom he will and sets over it the lowliest of
men"** *(4:17).*

We saw this principle to be especially true of God's kingdom, when it existed on earth – God then appointed His
kings and made them administrators of His law, giving
them the remit to rule over His people in His land. Now we
are being told that, in a somewhat different way, God over-
sees the rulership of the world and establishes powers and
authorities which are in accordance with His purpose.
Quite how that works we shall never know, though there is
a hint given, later in Daniel's prophecy, that God's angels
are at work behind the scenes to make sure that everything
works out as God requires it.[1]

So the powers that now exist – for good or ill so far as we
are concerned – are in place because that is God's will, and
they are playing a part in His purpose, as everything moves
towards the end of human rule and the beginning of the
worldwide rulership of the Lord Jesus Christ. This does not

---

[1] *See Daniel 10:12-20 where we are told about angels making preparations
for the transfer of world power from the Persian to the Greek Empire.*

mean that God is responsible for the errors or the atrocities that are sometimes committed by human rulers, for Daniel said that sometimes *"the lowliest of men"* are either appointed to rule, or seize power. Yet, in some way or other, God overrules and directs the entire process.[2]

❖ Discovering God's Will

Imagine what it would be like to oversee the government of the world and put in place its rulers - and only those who would achieve what you wanted to happen. Humanly speaking, such world government is an impossible task, as many who have attempted it have found out, to their cost. Even the very best of men would not know how to rule if given the authority to do so.

A believer in the gospel would also fail at this, for we do not know the mind of God in these matters. there are secret things which are hidden from us (Deuteronomy 29:29), and just how God rules in the kingdoms of men is one of them. Notice that Paul says two things that come together to solve our difficulty:

1 That we must *"discern what is the will of God, what is good and acceptable and perfect"* (Romans 12:2).

2 Given that it would be impossible for us to know how God wants the politics of the world to be arranged at any particular time, Paul tells us to be subject to the powers that God puts into place.

He goes on to say that we should pay any taxes that are levied upon us, and that our conduct should always be good and submissive. We are not here to change governments, but to await the coming government of God.[3] We should to use the opportunity we now have to change our own behaviour and help others to come to an understanding of what is about to happen on earth.

Here is a really sobering thought. In the first century, believers were being persecuted for their faith. The Roman emperor Nero wanted someone to blame for the great fire that had destroyed much of Rome which, incidentally, gave him great opportunities to redesign the city and extend his

---

[2] *If you want to follow this up, look at John 19:11; Acts 17:26; 2 Peter 2:10,11 and Jude v8.*

[3] *This is an Old Testament truth too – Proverbs 24:21.*

palace. He decided to blame the Christians and some awful things were done to early believers. Yet, writing to Jewish believers, including those in Rome, the apostle Peter said this:

> **"Be subject for the Lord's sake to every human institution, whether it be to the emperor as supreme, or to governors as sent by him to punish those who do evil and to praise those who do good.** For this is the will of God, that by doing good you should put to silence the ignorance of foolish people. Live as people who are free, not using your freedom as a cover-up for evil, but living as servants of God. Honour everyone. Love the brotherhood. Fear God. **Honour the emperor"** (1 Peter 2:13-17).

There was no question of resistance or of political protest in the apostle's mind. Whatever was happening was in accordance with God's will and would eventually work out for the best, so the followers of Jesus must obey his teaching and accept his example.[4] For when Jesus was reviled, he did not retaliate, but put himself completely in God's hands; he was always submissive and obedient. The apostles say that that is how we should be too.

❖ Citizenship

The reasoning behind the commands we are being given is twofold:

1 We do not know what God's will is in any given situation, so we are best advised to take no part whatsoever in political activity of any sort.

> Instead we should be bystanders and should concentrate on using the opportunities we have to develop our characters and to preach the gospel, being grateful for the things that come our way, under God's good hand. Indeed, we are commanded to pray for the authorities and to be thankful:
>
> > *"First of all, then, I urge that supplications, prayers, intercessions, and thanksgivings be made for all people, for kings and all who are in high positions, that we may lead a peaceful and quiet life, godly and dig-*

---

[4] *We are reminded many times of the Lord's teaching and example: see Matthew 22:21; 1 Timothy 6:13; 1 Peter 2:23.*

nified in every way. This is good, and it is pleasing in the sight of God our Saviour, who desires all people to be saved and to come to the knowledge of the truth" (1 Timothy 2:1-4).

2 Once we are baptized we accept Jesus as king and pledge to be citizens of his kingdom, waiting for the time when he will return to rule as "King of kings and Lord of lords".

This is a very important change and one that brings with it all sorts of other considerations. All who are baptized, and who become the servants of Christ, are under his command from then on.[5] In truth, they are citizens of his heavenly kingdom and are subject to his command. They can never exchange his lordship for the rulership of man, not can they give allegiance to anyone else instead.

This is how the apostle Paul expresses the position of all who have become followers of the Lord Jesus Christ:

> *"**Our citizenship is in heaven**, and from it we await a Saviour, the Lord Jesus Christ, who will transform our lowly body to be like his glorious body, by the power that enables him even to subject all things to himself" (Philippians 3:20,21).*

> *"You are no longer strangers and aliens, but **you are fellow citizens with the saints and members of the household of God**" (Ephesians 2:19).*

Although we live in a world which is alien to God and which is opposed to His will and purpose, and which will resist the coming of the Lord when he returns from heaven, we have to be excellent citizens under this jurisdiction. Our position is just like that of an ambassador from another country who represents his ruler and his government. The way ambassadors conduct and behave themselves is an important way of conveying the values and standards of the country they represent. We are God's ambassadors. For once we are bap-

---

[5] *This was what we looked at when considering Romans chapter 6 (see Chapter 14).*

tized into Christ we become His representatives on earth, showing, by the way we live, the values and standards of God's kingdom, So, Paul said:

"If anyone is in Christ, he is a new creation. The old has passed away; behold, the new has come. All this is from God, who through Christ reconciled us to himself and gave us the ministry of reconciliation ... Therefore, we are ambassadors for Christ, God making his appeal through us. We implore you on behalf of Christ, be reconciled to God" (2 Corinthians 5:17-20).

❖ What all this Means

Scripture does not suggest that baptized believers should formally change their nationality, for there are no passports or identity documents issued for the Kingdom of God. We remain as we are, with our various national identities and responsibilities, and should be very thankful for the facilities and provisions of the state in which we live. As good citizens we are to do everything that is required of us, provided that it is in harmony with the law of God, which is more important than the mere commandments of men. Here are two examples from Bible times when there was a clash between what God commanded and what the law of the land said.

❖ **Daniel** once held an important position in the Persian Empire and was influential in helping one of the Persian kings to fulfil God's will by sending the Jewish exiles back to their land. Other courtiers resented his influence and plotted to overthrow him, but he was such a good-living man they knew the only way they could trap him would be to get the king to pass a law that was contrary to Daniel's beliefs. So they flattered the king and got a law passed that banned prayer to anyone other than the king himself, for a specified period of time. It was a direct challenge to Daniel's worship of God, so he had to disregard it whatever the consequences were. The result was that he was thrown into a den of hungry lions, but God delivered him because he had been faithful and obedient.

❖ Years later, the Jerusalem authorities tried to stop people believing in Jesus so they forbade the apostles

Peter and John to preach or teach about him. This is what happened, for the law was expressly contrary to the commandment that Jesus had given – that the apostles were to preach the gospel in Jerusalem:

"Peter and John answered them, 'Whether it is right in the sight of God to listen to you rather than to God, you must judge, for we cannot but speak of what we have seen and heard.' And when they had further threatened them, they let them go, finding no way to punish them, because of the people, for all were praising God for what had happened" (Acts 4:19-21).

It follows that it may be all right for us to work for the government, or in the public services, as did Erastus the city treasurer and the prophet Daniel, but only in a capacity where we will not come into conflict with the law of Christ. No disciple of Jesus should be in a position where he or she could take absolute orders, which have to be obeyed regardless of conscience or other considerations. For example, service in the armed forces, or associated services,[6] would be quite inappropriate, partly because it may involve swearing an oath of allegiance to the monarch or the government, and partly because such a role requires total obedience to military commands.

As the law of Christ has to come first and demands our absolute obedience, it is equally inappropriate to become involved in work which is on the fringe of military life, where believers could be drafted in to work in conjunction with armed forces, or who would work in support of them. Thus police work is to be avoided. There are other jobs such as being a prison warder or a security guard where violent conduct may be a necessary part of the jobs; indeed such people carry weapons to protect themselves and enforce their authority. These jobs should be avoided also.

Some soldiers once came to John the Baptist and asked him about their employment, as they were thinking about becoming his followers. It would have been very difficult for him to say "Stop working in that capacity"; that would have been seen as traitorous and he would probably have been

---

[6] *Those services would include anything that is in support of military or political objectives, such as providing armaments, building or designing military vehicles or planes, producing parts which will go into such vehicles, working in army camps or with military personnel. All those are things to be avoided by the follower of the Lord Jesus.*

imprisoned much earlier than actually happened. So he
gave them this advice instead:

> *"Soldiers also asked him, 'And we, what shall we do?'*
> *And he said to them, 'Do not extort money from any-*
> *one by threats or by false accusation, and be con-*
> *tent with your wages'" (Luke 3:14).*[7]

He gave them the moral teaching of the gospel that was
applicable to their situation so that, as they thought about
the implications of it in their lives, they would know what
to do. They would soon see that their occupation was
incompatible with gospel teaching and, if committed to it,
would seek other work.

❖ Conscience First

We are to live as model citizens in a world order which is
passing away, whilst we wait for a new world order and our
coming king. If we do wrong under this human administration we will be punished for it here and now. For the insti-
tutions of human government, which often give us safety
and stability and which look after many of our needs, also
act as a restraint upon our wildest and silliest actions. The
law of the land helps all of us to behave in a way which is
helpful to others: for our safety and well-being as well as
for that of everybody else. Imagine what it would be like if
there were no laws regulating which side of the road vehicles were to drive on; or if there was no law to stop people
killing or seriously hurting one another. We are all grateful
for that protection. But notice what else Paul says:

> *"Rulers are not a terror to good conduct, but to bad ... For*
> *he is the servant of God, an avenger who carries out*
> *God's wrath on the wrongdoer. Therefore one must be*
> *in subjection, not only to avoid God's wrath but also*
> *for the sake of conscience. For the same reason you*
> *also pay taxes, for the authorities are ministers of God,*
> *attending to this very thing. Pay to all what is owed to*
> *them: taxes to whom taxes are owed, revenue to whom*
> *revenue is owed, respect to whom respect is owed, hon-*
> *our to whom honour is owed" (Romans 13:3-7).*

---

[7] *The King James Version renders the verses: "Do violence to no man, nei-*
ther accuse any falsely; and be content with your wages". That would mean
that soldiers would have to find another occupation straight away!

We have to live in a way which is right with our conscience. So, for example, it would be wrong for a believer to fight in a war, or to support a war by some form of active involvement. We have to be "conscientious objectors" to such activity because it is contrary to the law of Christ.[8] Remember that we do not know what God's will is in any given situation – who God might want to win a battle and who not – and none of us would want to be found fighting against the will of God. There have been dreadfully confusing times in the past when people professing to be Christians have fought against one another, each group praying to God for deliverance and asking for His help. That wrong thinking has done much to discredit Christianity and has resulted in people losing their faith and confidence in the gospel. But it is not the gospel that is then at fault; the people to blame are those who act in a way which makes the gospel of salvation seem contradictory.

Paul says that we should obey human law and be good citizens, as we are able, but on matters of Christian conscience we are to obey God rather than man. As we cannot imagine Jesus putting on the armour of a Roman soldier and going about killing people, neither should we. The time might come when we are asked to join the forces of righteousness and fight with the Lord Jesus and God's holy angels. If that were ever to happen it would be the will of God that we should do so, and it would be against our conscience *not* to take part. But for the moment it is clear that we are the soldiers of Christ fighting a spiritual battle against the forces of darkness and ignorance, and that is the only battle in which we should be engaged.[9]

❖ **Politics and the Courts of Law**

Everything that applies to involvement in armed warfare, directly or indirectly, applies also to any active involvement in politics. We belong to another leader and are looking to

---

[8] *Our conscience has to be instructed by the Word of God, otherwise we might all take different views about things. For example, in Matthew 5:43-46 Jesus commands his followers to love their enemies, not to hate them, and (in 5:39) not to resist evil, but to accept it for the time being, in the knowledge that he will right all wrongs in due course.*

[9] *Paul uses this language in Ephesians chapter 6, where he looks at all the equipment of a Roman soldier and likens it to the things that we should do fighting for Christ, as we battle against sin in all its forms.*

him to rule on earth and resolve all the present problems there are here. Therefore we should not put our allegiance in earthly rulers, nor should we vote for them or support their political organisations. That would be a denial of what we believe for we do not belong to this order of things, but to a heavenly kingdom.

We must obey man-made laws when they are not in opposition to God's law, but we should neither try to change those laws nor seek to enforce them to our advantage. Courts of law are not places where believers should be found, either practising in the legal profession or seeking to get the law enforced to their advantage. Some believers find this hard to accept but the Bible is quite clear about it. It is better to suffer wrong than to go to a court of law to get things decided by a human administration. The apostle Paul said:

> *"When one of you has a grievance against another, does he dare go to law before the unrighteous instead of the saints? Or do you not know that the saints will judge the world? And if the world is to be judged by you, are you incompetent to try trivial cases? ... Can it be that there is no one among you wise enough to settle a dispute between the brothers, but brother goes to law against brother, and that before unbelievers? To have lawsuits at all with one another is already a defeat for you. Why not rather suffer wrong? Why not rather be defrauded? But you yourselves wrong and defraud – even your own brothers" (1 Corinthians 6:1-8).*

If we do find this principle hard to accept, and want to justify ourselves if wronged, we should look to the example of Christ. The apostle Peter wrote these words of the Lord to help us in such situations:

> *"Christ also suffered for you, leaving you an example so that you might follow in his steps ... when he suffered, he did not threaten, but continued entrusting himself to him (God) who judges justly" (1 Peter 2: 21-23).*

The law courts of this world are not places to frequent because they administer human law and it is not always in harmony with God's law. This is a very important distinction to understand. What man decides as acceptable for society and appropriate in terms of personal behaviour may or may not be acceptable in the sight of God. At all times, we should remember God's code of conduct and must try to live according to that. If there are problems and disputes between believers they should be resolved between believers within the ecclesia, drawing upon the wisdom and experience of other members if necessary. The believer has a much higher standard by which to live, for he or she will ultimately be judged by the Lord Jesus Christ.

❖ The Law of Love

It is this standard that the apostle Paul now refers to in his letter:

> *"Owe no one anything, except to love each other, for the one who loves another has fulfilled the law. The commandments, 'You shall not commit adultery, You shall not murder, You shall not steal, You shall not covet,' and any other commandment, are summed up in this word: 'You shall love your neighbour as yourself.'* **Love does no wrong to a neighbour; therefore love is the fulfilling of the law**" *(Romans 13:8-10).*

If we live according to the guiding principle that we should love one another we will not go wrong, says the apostle. For he explains that it is the guiding principle in everything that God has done and that love was the driving force in everything that Jesus said and did. The Lord made it clear that love is not an optional extra – something we could do if we feel like it. It is a matter of command. Once, having washed his disciples' feet as an act of humble service, Jesus said:

> *"A new commandment I give to you, that you love one another: just as I have loved you, you also are to love one another.* **By this all people will know that you are my disciples, if you have love for one another**" *(John 13:34,35).*[10]

This is a very far-reaching law indeed but it can be summarized quite easily. We should always do to others as we would want them to do to us, and we should always try to act in a way that we think Jesus would have acted. Paul gives some specific illustrations in those few verses of things we should not want to do. He mentions adultery, murder, stealing and wanting other people's things, as

---

[10] *This commandment was repeated in John 15:12 and 17.*

matters that would be against the law of love, and elsewhere he talks about other things too.

❖ Separation

Just after the passage where Paul said we are to be God's ambassadors on earth, he goes on to say:

> *"Do not be unequally yoked with unbelievers. For what partnership has righteousness with lawlessness? Or what fellowship has light with darkness? What accord has Christ with Belial? Or what portion does a believer share with an unbeliever? What agreement has the temple of God with idols? For we are the temple of the living God"* (2 Corinthians 6:14-16).

Believers should marry believers, says the apostle, and should avoid any situation where they are affected by the unlawful and ungodly behaviour of others.[11] This means that, in trying to live a Christ-like life, we should spend our time with other believers and make them our companions. When we are with other people we should be very careful to live according to the law of Christ – the law of love – so that our way of life will itself witness to the things we now believe and do.

We live in the world, but the world is a very dangerous place for believers. It is organised according to human ideas and is inhabited by people who have very different values, and it has always been like that. Before his death Jesus prayed to his Father for his followers in these words:

> *"I am praying for them. **I am not praying for the world but for those whom you have given me**, for they are yours ... I have given them your word, and the world has hated them because **they are not of the world, just as I am not of the world. I do not ask that you take them out of the world,** but that you keep them from the evil one. **They are not of the world, just as I am not of the world"** (John 17:9-16).

The challenge of Christian discipleship is to live in the

---

[11] *Whilst marriage is an obvious example of two people joining together in a lifelong relationship – being "yoked together" – it is also important that believers don't get entangled in things like business partnerships, which can lead them into difficulties because their unbelieving associates have a very different standard of behaviour.*

world as though we were just visitors here; biding our time until our future permanent home arrives. That is how the faithful managed in ancient times, some of them preferring to be tent dwellers rather than living in a house, so that they would never forget they were just *"strangers and pilgrims"*. They lived in the world but they didn't belong to the world and that is how we must try to live as well. Then, when the Lord Jesus Christ returns, we shall be ready to leave everything we know now and go with him, wherever he leads. This is precisely the point that Paul now makes in his letter:

> *"Love does no wrong to a neighbour; therefore love is the fulfilling of the law. Besides this you know the time, that the hour has come for you to wake from sleep.* **For salvation is nearer to us now than when we first believed**. *The night is far gone; the day is at hand.* **So then let us cast off the works of darkness and put on the armour of light**. *Let us walk properly as in the daytime, not in orgies and drunkenness, not in sexual immorality and sensuality, not in quarrelling and jealousy. But put on the Lord Jesus Christ, and make no provision for the flesh, to gratify its desires" (Romans 13:10-14).*

The coming of Jesus is nearer than we might imagine. We tend to think that things will go on for ever, as they are now, but the purpose of God is drawing towards its intended end. God rules in the kingdoms of men. He has put in place people who will work things out as He requires and as His will directs and He is now engaged in the final act of His divine drama. Many of us now living should see the coming of the Lord Jesus, or so it would seem. But even if we die first, our next conscious moment will be resurrection from the dead at the appearance of the Lord. No wonder Paul could say: *"Salvation is nearer to us now than when we first believed"*, for he was that much older and that much nearer his own death. And so are we – all of us! Time marches on and the more time we spend thinking about things the less time there is left in which to do the right things.

❖ A Change of Clothes

When Paul warns about the nearness of the coming of the Lord Jesus he uses military language to remind us that we are engaged in the Lord's battles, not those of men. The armour we are to wear is *"the armour of light"* and we are fighting against the forces of darkness and ignorance. That is a big challenge that affects our daily behaviour in all sorts of ways – big things as well as little. That is why he goes on to list some of the daily dangers that could lead us astray – *"orgies and drunkenness"*, *"sexual immorality and sensuality"*, and *"quarrelling and jealousy"*.

The believer has to live a holy life, one free from immorality and sexual licence, a life where we remain in control of our feelings. Our fleshly feelings will not change overnight: the flesh still has desires and an appetite which it would like us to satisfy.[12] The challenge for the believer is to put those feelings to death – to *"make no provision for the flesh, to gratify its desires"*. We do this, says the apostle, by putting on the Lord Jesus Christ.

This picture is one the apostle has used before. Writing to the believers at Philippi, in Asia Minor, Paul said:

> *"**Put to death** therefore what is earthly in you: sexual immorality, impurity, passion, evil desire, and covetousness, which is idolatry. On account of these the wrath of God is coming. In these you too once walked, when you were living in them. But now you must **put them all away**: anger, wrath, malice, slander, and obscene talk from your mouth. Do not lie to one another, seeing that you have put off the old self with its practices and have **put on the new self**, which is being renewed in knowledge after the image of its creator ... **Put on then**, as God's chosen ones, holy and beloved, compassion, kindness, humility, meekness, and patience, bearing with one another and, if one has a complaint against another, forgiving each other; as the Lord has forgiven you, so you also must forgive. And above all these **put on love**, which binds everything together in perfect harmony"* (Colossians 3:5-14).

When we are baptized into Christ we declare publicly that we want to change our way of life and start to live like Jesus. Day by day the baptized believer has to put into practice the life of Christ – by putting away the things that belonged to the old life and putting on the things that

---

[12] *In fact those feelings inside us, that prompt us to do wrong, will be with us all through our lives as the flesh never changes. But we will gradually become less inclined to want to follow those promptings as we want more and more to do the will of God and live so as to please Him.*

belong to the new self, the new life. From our baptism we have to try to live as did Jesus in holiness and purity. That will affect, says Paul:

➥ our sexual appetites – *"Put to death therefore what is earthly in you: sexual immorality, impurity, passion";*

➥ our wants and desires for things, including those things that others have but we do not – *"evil desire, and covetousness, which is idolatry";*

➥ our feelings – *"anger, wrath, malice";*

➥ the things we say – *"slander, and obscene talk from your mouth";*

➥ our truthfulness – *"Do not lie to one another".*

❖ **New Life in Christ**

Paul tells us that we should replace the feelings with which we were born – our natural affections and desires – with a new set of values and desires – those that belong to the life in Christ. Looking at one example should make things clear.

Sexual immorality is forbidden, but sex is not: it is recognised as a God-given gift. It is possible that the apostle Paul did not marry, but he recognised that others were made differently and that they would need a companion. God had provided one for Adam, and men and women were meant for each other, but sex is only to take place within marriage.

If you want to look up some of the Scriptures that talk about this, here are some helpful references: *Genesis 2:23-24; Proverbs 18:22; Malachi 2:14-16; Matthew 19:3-9; Mark 10:6-12; Romans 7:2; 1 Corinthians 6:16,17; 7:2-4,10,11; 11:8-9; Ephesians 5:28-31; 1 Timothy 5:14; 1 Peter 3:1-7.*

There are some churches that forbid marriage. That is quite wrong, for Paul declares marriage to be something *"that God created to be received with thanksgiving by those who believe and know the truth" (1 Timothy 4:3).* It is something to be held in honour (Hebrews 13:4), and both husband and wife are commanded to live within that relationship, each in a way that respects and honours the other. For the relationships and friendships we have form a vital part of living a new life, and it is about our relationship with others that the apostle now writes as he brings his

Letter to the Romans towards its conclusion.

Things to Read

📖 Psalm 110 gives us a picture of the Lord Jesus Christ who has ascended to heaven where he sits in glory at his Father's right hand. Notice what it says about those who are the people of this coming king.

📖 Philippians chapter 4 tells us how to focus our minds upon those things that are lovely and fulfilling and shows us the way we should live joyfully and contentedly.

Questions to Think About

26.1 We are to live apart from the world and its values and interests. What does that mean in terms of our employment, and active participation in things like politics and the legal system? (Ephesians 4:17; 5:7-11; Romans 12:2; 2 Corinthians 6:14-18)

26.2 If marriage is a God-given relationship, how should a man and woman live together in a way which is pleasing to God and in harmony with the law of Christ? (Ephesians 5:21-33; Colossians 3:18-19; 1 Peter 3:7; 1 Corinthians 7:12-15,39)

"A new commandment I give to you, that you love one another: just as I have loved you, you also are to love one another. By this all people will know that you are my disciples, if you have love for one another" (John 13:34,35).

27
Living together as Believers

The apostle John was given several visions of the events that were to happen before the return of the Lord Jesus Christ to earth, to set up God's kingdom. They are described in "The Revelation of Jesus Christ", the last book of the New Testament. In one of them he saw a huge crowd of people who were following Christ in the coming age. When he enquired who they were, he was told:

> "These are the ones coming out of the great tribulation. They have washed their robes and made them white in the blood of the Lamb. Therefore they are before the throne of God, and serve him day and night in his temple; and he who sits on the throne will shelter them with his presence. They shall hunger no more, neither thirst anymore; the sun shall not strike them, nor any scorching heat. For the Lamb in the midst of the throne will be their shepherd, and he will guide them to springs of living water, and God will wipe away every tear from their eyes" (Revelation 7:14-17).

They were the redeemed of God, the very people that we should want to be part of – if we want to share in the joys of the coming age. They were a huge multitude and, the record says, they had come:

> "**From every nation, from all tribes and peoples and languages,** standing before the throne and before the Lamb, clothed in white robes, with palm branches in their hands, and crying out with a loud voice, 'Salvation belongs to our God who sits on the throne, and to the Lamb!'" (7:9,10).

❖ Jew and Gentile

There was once a time when God showed Himself to be especially close to the Jewish nation. He dwelt in the very middle of their encampment and later His presence made their capital city a very special place. That arrangement was intended to bring other nations also into a relationship with God and now the gospel has been made freely available to all nations so that, Jew and non-Jew alike, we can share in God's gracious plan of salvation.

It does not matter now, so far as our salvation is concerned, where we originate[1] although, as we have seen,[2] the nation of Israel will still have a special role to fulfil when the Kingdom of God is established on earth. But all those who are to be saved out of that nation will have to accept Jesus just like anyone else – by belief and baptism into his saving name. It was like that in Jerusalem in the first century and it will be like that again when Jesus returns. There is no other way of obtaining eternal life.

Paul brings his Letter to the Romans to a close with many personal greetings to people he already knew or knew about.[3] But first he refers again to his special role as the apostle to the Gentiles and shows how the original scope of God's purpose has now been enlarged:

> *"For I tell you that Christ became a servant to the **circumcised** to show God's truthfulness, in order to confirm the promises given to the patriarchs, and in order that the **Gentiles** might glorify God for his mercy. As it is written, 'Therefore I will praise you among the **Gentiles**, and sing to your name.' And again it is said, 'Rejoice, O **Gentiles**, with his people.' And again, 'Praise the Lord, all you **Gentiles**, and let all the peoples extol him.' And again Isaiah says, 'The root of Jesse will come, even he who arises to rule the **Gentiles**; in him will the **Gentiles** hope'" (Romans 15:8-12).*

It is an interesting exercise to track down the Scriptures[4] the apostle cites and to note that God's inten-

---

[1] *"There is neither Jew nor Greek, there is neither slave nor free, there is neither male nor female, for you are all one in Christ Jesus" (Galatians 3:28).*

[2] *Chapter 21*

[3] *Those greetings take up the sixteenth chapter of Romans which we will not examine in this study of Romans.*

[4] *You can do this by using the cross-references in your Bible, if you have any. They should lead you to 2 Samuel 22:50; Psalm 18:49; Deuteronomy 32:43; Psalm 117:1; Isaiah 11:10 and 42:3. Just glancing at that spread of references gives an idea of how widely the truth was announced in advance that God would save both Jew and Gentile from sin and death.*

tion of redeeming a multitude *"from every nation, from all tribes and peoples and languages"* is a long-standing promise. It had been announced from the time of Moses, some 1400 years before the birth of Jesus, and it was the birth and work of Jesus that made it possible. The saddest thing was that many Jews resented the inclusion of Gentiles into a relationship that they had come to think of as theirs alone – a special status and position in the purpose of God. They wanted to keep their God to themselves!

❖ Living Together

Paul was writing to a mixed congregation of believers who worshipped in Rome, both Jews and Gentiles. He has been careful in the letter to address both and to be sensitive about their particular concerns. Early on,[5] he defined a Jew as someone who was inwardly circumcised – who had resolved to cut off "the flesh" from their lives, not just a small part of the flesh from their bodies. Thus he encourages all his readers to think of themselves as Jews, and to share the *"hope of Israel"* as their own hope.

In his final words of encouragement in this letter, Paul writes about the importance of living together in harmony and at peace, so that we can help and encourage one another. He reminds his readers that nobody should exist by himself or live for himself. We should all see ourselves as part of the community or family of God.

It is worth noting how the apostle approaches this subject, for it will help us when we have specific problems to think through. First, he outlines the key principle that should govern all our behaviour – love for one another (Romans 13:8-10). Then he reminds us that everything we do now will be subject to scrutiny at the coming of Christ, so that we should be careful how we apply the principle of loving one another in practice in our lives:

"The night is far gone; the day is at hand. So then let us cast off the works of darkness and put on the armour of light" (13:12).

And now he returns to that idea when he says:

"For we will all stand before the judgement seat of God;

---

[5] *See Romans 2:28,29 and Acts 28:20, where he declared "the hope of Israel" to be his hope, even though he was an apostle to the Gentiles.*

415

for it is written, 'As I live, says the Lord, every knee shall bow to me, and every tongue shall confess to God.' So then each of us will give an account of himself to God"14:10-12).

It is not that we should live in fear of the judgement seat of Christ; but the apostle does not want us to forget that there is a day of reckoning coming when all wrongs will be put right – a day of final accounting for the way we have lived our lives. In between those two references to the coming of the Lord Jesus, the apostle does two things.

1 He uses some specific examples to explain how we should live in a way that is right with God: we will look at those shortly.

2 He reminds us about the way that Jesus lived and the example he has set for all of us. His point is that if we want to live like him in the age to come we have to live like the Lord Jesus now.

❖ Specific Examples

This will be the last opportunity, as we work through Romans, for you to try out your skills as a Bible student. But by now you will have learned to understand the Bible for yourself, so this should be easy. Read through Romans chapters 14 and 15 again, this time looking for the particular illustrations Paul uses to explain what living-by-love means in practice. Then ask yourself these questions:

◥ Why does Paul refer to things eaten, or not eaten, and to the observance of certain special days?

◥ What is his advice about how the believer should respond to such concerns which are genuinely held by other believers?

◥ What reasons does he give for the advice he offers?

◥ What does this course of conduct mean for the way we should behave towards other people?

The clue to answering these questions is to remember that Jews and Gentiles were living together side-by-side in Rome. All Jews had been brought up to observe strict dietary laws, sometimes to fast, and occasionally to keep special feast days, like the Feast of Passover or Tabernacles. In time, believing Jews came to realise that

416

this observance was now unnecessary. But it took a while for the change of practice to work through, and God allowed for that. So it was that Paul went to Jerusalem for the Feast of Pentecost (see Acts 20:16) and made offerings in the temple, just before he was arrested by the Roman authorities (Acts 21:17-26).

Paul's advice to the Gentile believers in Rome was that they should be tolerant and sympathetic towards their Jewish brethren, and vice versa. He stressed that what really mattered was that they should live together in peace. They should not pass judgement on one another, nor despise one another – because of what they ate or did not eat; and they should not do anything that would be a hindrance or an obstacle to their fellow believers. There were things the Gentiles might eat – including meat that had been routinely offered to idols – which could cause the Jews deep offence. Paul said that both Jew and Gentile believers should be sensitive to the needs of others and should do nothing that might damage the faith of their brothers and sisters in Christ. [6]

❖ "For whom Christ Died"

The reasons given by Paul for this Christian tolerance are at the heart of what it means to be in fellowship with others who share the same faith and have also been baptized into Christ. They give us a glimpse into the way of thinking about those with whom he was in fellowship. Here are some extracts:

*"For **none of us lives to himself, and none of us dies to himself**. If we live, we live to the Lord, and if we die, we die to the Lord. So then, whether we live or whether we die, **we are the Lord's**" (Romans 14:7,8);*

*"If your brother is grieved by what you eat, you are no longer walking in love. By what you eat, **do not destroy the one for whom Christ died**. So do not let what you regard as good be spoken of as evil" (14:15,16);*

*"We who are strong have an obligation to bear with the failings of the weak, and not to please ourselves. **Let***

---

6 *It seems to have been New Testament practice to call fellow-believers "brother" and "sister" and that is the practice of Christadelphians to this day (see Matthew 12:50; 1 Corinthians 7:15 and James 2:15).*

each of us please his neighbour for his good, to build him up. For Christ did not please himself, but as it is written, 'The reproaches of those who reproached you fell on me'" (15:1-3);

"Therefore welcome one another as Christ has welcomed you, for the glory of God" (15:7).

Paul here reminds his brothers and sisters what the Lord Jesus Christ has done for them and what that should mean to them. It should stimulate all believers to try to follow his wonderful example and to live selflessly and sacrificially. We must try to care as much about others as we do about ourselves: to put them and their needs first. Notice that all believers should try to be like this – whether they are Jew or Gentile, bond or free, male or female. All believers have a duty of care and love towards their fellow believers. It would not be right for one believer, or a small group, to insist on their own way when, in fact, they held a minority point of view.

This is where careful Bible reading helps, for the language used by the apostle is very telling. He says that believers should be most tolerant towards those who could lose their faith if something is done that deeply offends them. For example, if Jews who believed they must still keep the feasts were despised by their Gentile brethren for so doing, that could force them back to Judaism, and they would lose their new-found faith. Paul does not say that the moment anybody says they are unhappy about a course of action the brother or sister involved should stop. As ever, with so much that happens in life, it all depends. These are the critical words Paul uses:

*"As for the one who is weak in faith, welcome him, but not to quarrel over opinions ... It is before his own master that he **stands or falls** ... Therefore let us not pass judgement on one another any longer, but rather decide never to put a **stumbling block or hindrance** in the way of a brother ... For if your brother is grieved by what you eat, you are no longer walking in love. By what you eat, **do not destroy** the one for whom Christ died ... So then let us pursue what makes for peace and for mutual upbuilding. Do not, for the sake of food, **destroy** the work of God. Everything is indeed clean, but it is wrong for anyone to make another **stumble** by what he eats. It is*

*good not to eat meat or drink wine or do anything that causes your brother to **stumble*** *(14:1,4,15,19-20).*

❖ Christian Fellowship

We should behave towards others as we would want them to behave towards us. Being in fellowship with other believers means that we would want to do nothing that could cause them such offence that they would stumble, fall and lose their faith. Paul was quite clear that there were no real reasons why people should not eat certain foods; but for the sake of nurturing and developing the faith of others he was willing to abstain. It is that spirit of mutual tolerance and sympathetic understanding towards each other that should typify the fellowship that exists between brothers and sisters in Christ. This was how Paul summed up his desire for all believers, of whatever race or background:

*"May the God of endurance and encouragement grant you to **live in such harmony with one another, in accord with Christ Jesus, that together you may with one voice glorify the God and Father of our Lord Jesus Christ**" (15:5,6).*

This is a prayer for the unity and harmony of all *true* believers. Paul is not praying that *all* people everywhere who claim to be Christians should live together in harmony or that they should be in fellowship with one another. This would be quite contradictory to what we have already discovered – that saving faith is the vital and only way into God's favour.

There have been attempts made to bring churches together on the basis that doctrinal differences are unimportant and that what matters is that everyone is worshipping the same God and Lord Jesus Christ. But, as we have seen, that is not the case. It really *does* matter what you believe and the differences are very substantial. Some people understand that God is a trinity and not a unity, and many other beliefs that people hold are man-made and are not in harmony with what God has revealed in His Word.

Notice that Paul's prayer is that all believers should live *"in accord with Christ Jesus"*, which means believing what he believed and obeying his commandments, not the commandments and teachings of men. It follows from this that Christadelphians take no part in inter-church discussions,

419

believing instead that what you believe and how you then act are vitally important if we are to be found acceptable to God at the coming of the Lord Jesus Christ.

Believers should be courteous and considerate towards members of other churches and faiths, but they should take every opportunity to explain to them what constitutes saving faith. There is a responsibility on all who follow Jesus to try to assist others who have not yet come to understand the gospel of salvation, so that at the coming of Jesus there will be many others who join with them in welcoming him. This is the only proper way of enlarging the fellowship of true believers. But until that proves possible, a new believer could be the only person in a locality who holds the faith and will have to keep the faith alone. But he or she will soon become aware of the fellowship of many other believers elsewhere in the world.

❖ Single or Married?

It makes a difference, of course, whether a new believer is single or married when he or she learns to understand the Bible and decides to act on what is true. If married, there will be an immediate challenge to live in such a way that the other partner recognises the difference and is encouraged to learn more himself or herself. The apostle Peter was thinking about a believing wife married to an unbelieving husband when he gave advice in 1 Peter 3:1-7, but it is equally important advice for a believing husband. In some societies not all members of the family may be able to read and there is then a real opportunity, and responsibility, to teach other family members by reading the Bible together and talking about it. And if there are children, there is nothing better to share with your children than the knowledge of saving truth that leads to eternal life.

The Bible has clear teaching about the state of marriage, which is a God-given arrangement, as is clear from the early chapters of Genesis when, in Eden, God said:

> *"Therefore a man shall leave his father and his mother and hold fast to his wife, and they shall become one flesh" (Genesis 2:24).*

This is a New Testament truth as well, for the verse is cited in the gospels, where it is endorsed by the Lord himself, and in the letters of the apostle.[7] Marriage is an arrangement recognised both by God and by human society. Nowadays society has become very tolerant about less formal arrangements, by recognising "common-law marriage"; [8] partnerships; same-sex relationships and even certain civil ceremonies to "marry" homosexuals and lesbians.[9]

This is another of those cases where human law is out of line with that which is acceptable to God. Marriage between one man and one woman is the only acceptable arrangement, so far as God is concerned. Ideally marriage should be between believers and it should be for life. Jesus explained that divorce was an arrangement that was introduced because some couples could not live according to the ideal but marriage should be for life, except in very exceptional circumstances.

> "Because of your hardness of heart Moses allowed you to divorce your wives, but from the beginning it was not so. And I say to you: whoever divorces his wife, except for sexual immorality, and marries another, commits adultery. The disciples said to him, 'If such is the case of a man with his wife, it is better not to marry.' But he said to them, 'Not everyone can receive this saying, but only those to whom it is given'" (Matthew 19:8-11).

Jesus was saying that not everyone needs to marry, but some people do need to. He was also recognising that not everyone who marries will be able to stay married: some will need to separate. But the Lord also commanded that once a married relationship has ended the separated couple should stay single.

❖ Coping with Difficulties

The Bible sets a high standard of behaviour and encourages us to aim high. But it also recognises that even the best people sometimes fail and need help to recover. If we

---

[7] *See Matthew 19:5; Mark 10:7; 1 Corinthians 6:16 and Ephesians 5:31.*

[8] *"Common-law" marriage is a term that describes the arrangement where two people just live together and have never been married; the state however can recognise their relationship and give some protection to it in common law, even though there is no marriage contract as such.*

[9] *God declared from early times that sex between members of the same sex, whether man or woman, was an abomination in His sight and His standards never change. See Leviticus 18:22; 20:13; Romans 1:26,27; 1 Corinthians 6:9,10; 1 Timothy 1:9,10.*

take marriage as an example, the ideal which was stated right at the outset was one man for one woman. But people like Abraham and King David had several wives – and all the problems that went along with that situation. In those cases, and many others, God worked through the situation with the people concerned. Even when David lusted after another married woman and conspired to have her husband killed so that he could take her, when he was completely repentant, God forgave him and restored them both to favour.

We may have similar difficulties to cope with, either in our own relationships, with things that have happened in the past, or with other people that we know, including with fellow believers. In the next chapter we will look at how to cope with some of those problems if something has to be done about them before baptism. But Paul, in Romans, as in many of his letters, has been encouraging believers to be tolerant, understanding, sympathetic and loving in the way they deal with such difficulties between themselves. We are all in need of God's forgiveness and His mercy, for none of us can live a good enough life to deserve eternal life; it is God's gift to us.

The way we respond to the problems of others is an indication of our appreciation of what God and Jesus have done for us. We must try to live together as members of God's family in a way which encourages and upbuilds one another but, at the same time, we all need to uphold the standards of behaviour and conduct that befit those who are baptized believers and members of the family of God.

This is not always an easy balance to strike, as Paul indicates in these last chapters of Romans. On the one hand he urges the followers of Christ to be sympathetic, loving and caring. On the other hand they are to be discriminating and careful to uphold the standards of behaviour and belief which are right in the sight of God. We can see that process of trying to balance things up if we gather some verses together from the last four chapters:

Show Love to all	Uphold Proper Standards
	"Be transformed by the renewal of your mind, that by testing you may discern what is the will of God, what is good and acceptable and perfect" (12:2)
"Let love be genuine ..." (12:9)	"... Abhor what is evil; hold fast to what is good" (12:9)
"Love one another with brotherly affection. Outdo one another in showing honour" (12:10)	
"Live in harmony with one another. Do not be haughty, but associate with the lowly. Never be conceited" (12:16)	
	"If possible, so far as it depends on you, live peaceably with all" (12:18)
	"Do not be overcome by evil, but overcome evil with good" (12:21)
"You shall love your neighbour as yourself." Love does no wrong to a neighbour; therefore love is the fulfilling of the law" (13:9,10)	
	"Let us walk properly as in the daytime, not in orgies and drunkenness, not in sexual immorality and sensuality, not in quarrelling and jealousy" (13:13)
"As for the one who is weak in faith, welcome him, but not to quarrel over opinions" (14:1)	
"Why do you pass judgement on your brother? Or you, why do you despise your brother? For we will all stand before the judgement seat of God" (14:10)	
"So then let us pursue what makes for peace and for mutual upbuilding" (14:19)	

Show Love to all	Uphold Proper Standards
	"The faith that you have, keep between yourself and God. Blessed is the one who has no reason to pass judgmeent on himself for what he approves" (14:22)
"We who are strong have an obligation to bear with the failings of the weak, and not to please ourselves. Let each of us please his neighbour for his good, to build him up" (15:1,2)	
"May the God of endurance and encouragement grant you to live in such harmony with one another, in accord with Christ Jesus, that together you may with one voice glorify the God and Father of our Lord Jesus Christ" (15:5,6)	
	"I myself am satisfied about you, my brothers, that you yourselves are full of goodness, filled with all knowledge and able to instruct one another. But on some points I have written to you very boldly by way of reminder" (15:14,15)
	"I appeal to you, brothers, to watch out for those who cause divisions and create obstacles contrary to the doctrine that you have been taught; avoid them. For such persons do not serve our Lord Christ, but their own appetites, and by smooth talk and flattery they deceive the hearts of the naive. For your obedience is known to all, so that I rejoice over you, but I want you to be wise as to what is good and innocent as to what is evil" (16:17-19)

❖ Finding the Balance

Sometimes in these matters it seems difficult to keep the right balance. We know that we must love each other and forgive each other, as God has forgiven us. Yet we may see things in the lives of other Christians that we know are wrong. What should we do? As ever, it is to the example of the Lord Jesus Christ that we should turn. He was *"full of grace and truth*". He didn't sometimes show grace[10] and at other times practise truth: he demonstrated both all the time. What the Lord wanted for everyone was that they would be in the Kingdom of God – but he knew this could only happen by acceptance of the true gospel and a new life of discipleship. So it should be in our lives. It may be that we decide that we ;annot meet with other Christians because they do not believe the true gospel or they practise things which are wrong in God's sight. But this does not mean that we do not love them or do not want them to be in God's kingdom and all our words and actions should show both 'grace and truth' towards them.

Paul acknowledges that it is not always easy to balance the two sides of the issue in this way. Notice that in the closing words of this letter (16:17-19) he is still adamant that *"the doctrine that you have been taught"* is absolutely vital to salvation and must be carefully protected and preserved. This is why he has written the letter – to set out his understanding of what constitutes saving faith. Now he says that efforts will be made by others to change those teachings and to substitute human thinking; such a process is inevitable, but it will be "evil" and not good.

Centuries on from the time when the apostle Paul wrote those words we are in a position to see just what has happened to the doctrine that he taught. It has been changed in very many important respects. Things have been added to it which are man-made ideas and many important things have been taken away. People who now call themselves "Christian" often believe things that would not be recognised as Christian teaching by the apostles. And people who still believe what is taught in the Bible and nothing else are often treated as though they were not followers of the Lord Jesus Christ. That's how the apostle was treated by many of his contemporaries, including his fellow countrymen, many of whom regarded him as a traitor and a blasphemer. But he preached God's true gospel of salvation, and has passed that saving truth on to us through this letter.

We are now faced with the challenge that confronted the first readers of the letter. Do Paul's views match those we once had, or now have? Would we be happy to meet him and to discuss our beliefs with this great man of God, con-

---

[10] *"Grace" means undeserved favour from God.*

fident that we believe the same things that he believed, share the same hope, and serve the same Lord? Make no mistake about it, the gospel that Paul preached is the one true gospel – there is no other. This is how he concludes the letter we have been using as the basis of our own exploration:

> *"Now to him who is able to strengthen you according to my gospel and the preaching of Jesus Christ, **according to the revelation of the mystery that was kept secret for long ages but has now been disclosed and through the prophetic writings has been made known to all nations, according to the command of the eternal God, to bring about the obedience of faith** – to the only wise God be glory for evermore through Jesus Christ! Amen"* (16:25-27).

Things to Read

Now that our study of Romans is finished take the opportunity to read the whole letter again. If you haven't read it through at one sitting before, you will now have the opportunity to follow the apostle's argument as he develops it. Now we have looked at it in some detail you should have a very good understanding of what the gospel really is.

Questions to Think About

27.1 Paul was on his way to Jerusalem when he met with the elders of the Ephesian ecclesia at a place called Miletus. What were the important things that he told them (in Acts 20:17-35) at what he thought would be his last meeting with them, and what do we learn about our own situation in the 21st century?

27.2 Now that we have finished working through Romans, what do we need to do to continue our understanding of the will of God? (Colossians 3:16; 1 Peter 2:2; 1 Timothy 4:15; Romans 12:1-2)

28
What should I do now?

We have come to the end of the Letter to the Romans but not, of course, to the end of learning to understand the Bible for ourselves. Using the tools you now have at your disposal, there are another 65 books to explore, and as you continue to read and understand things more fully your appreciation of what God has revealed for our learning will grow and grow. It's one of the wonderful things about God's Word that it never becomes dull or repetitive; there are new things to learn and re-learn all the time.

❖ Bible Reading

Daily Bible reading is a structured way to absorb Bible teaching. Some people prefer to read a book at a time, considering that approach to give them better continuity and letting them follow through the inspired writer's argument. Another way is to read systematically by taking readings every day from different parts of the Bible – starting with the beginning and middle of the Old Testament and the start of the New. That allows for another of Scripture's wonders to work; for one part of Scripture often throws light on another part. We have seen in Romans that the apostle often referred to what had been written earlier, for example about Abraham, and then interpreted that statement or promise in the light of the work of the Lord Jesus Christ. Scripture does that sort of thing all the time.

Appended to this chapter, is a table of daily Bible readings which Christadelphians have been using for nearly 150 years. Using it every day you will read the Old Testament once and the New Testament twice each year. You may find it helpful; if you do and would like a copy in a separate format just write to the address on page 451, and a free copy will be sent.

❖ Belief and Baptism

If you have been satisfied with the explanations offered in this book and have been persuaded that baptism is an important next step for you, we now need to consider some of the practicalities of that.

Baptism into Christ is a straightforward matter and is nothing to be worried about; but because it begins the new life of a believer it is important that it is done properly. That means being sure that your faith is soundly based and that you understand true Bible teaching. Remember that Jesus commanded his disciples to go and teach the gospel in all nations, adding *"Whoever believes and is baptized will be saved" (Mark 16:16).*

To make sure that your belief is such that your baptism would be right with God you first need to check through the things you now believe and see if they are in line with what the Bible teaches. The next chapter summarises Bible teaching, highlighting the things that you would be expected to know about. It also mentions some of the things that have been wrongly introduced into the gospel message by others: things you should now recognise as *not* part of the original gospel. Work through those and you will have a good idea whether or not your beliefs are the same as those held by Christadelphians.

You may well have some problem areas: things you would like to discuss in detail with others. It often takes time to adjust to different ideas, especially if you have believed things for a long time, perhaps since childhood. If that is the case there are different options available.

❖ Attending a Christadelphian Meeting

You may live near to a group of believers, in which case you would be best advised to make contact and go to meet them. You will be sure of a warm welcome and nobody will put you under any pressure. In our meetings we aim to present the gospel as it is taught in the Bible. Procedures vary a little from place to place, as there are Christadelphian meetings all over the world, but the general pattern is that one meeting is held for baptized believers, usually called the "Breaking of Bread", during which bread and wine is shared in remembrance of the Lord Jesus Christ and in accordance with his commandments. Only baptized believers who are Christadelphians are able to take the bread and wine, but you would be very welcome to attend the service even so. Often there is a separate Bible talk at which the gospel is preached and that is for everyone to attend. No collection will be taken at that meeting.

Just making contact will start you on your way and if

you go with a list of questions and queries you are likely to get some helpful answers. Christadelphians love talking about the Scriptures, as it is the thing that sustains and encourages them in their faith. They read the Bible all the time. Sometimes there are Seminars or Bible Classes being held and these could also be of real help, especially if you still want things sorted out or need to know more about the background and general teaching of the Bible. But nobody is expected to know everything about the Bible when they first ask to be baptized. You are not going to be asked to list the kings of Israel or to give the names of the twelve disciples of Jesus! The aim is to help you be sure that you believe what the Bible teaches.

❖ Correspondence or the Internet

If you are not living near any other Christadelphians at present, somebody will talk to you before your baptism. But first you might want to have some of your queries sorted out and any doubts dispelled. You might even prefer to contact us in writing first, even if you live near to a meeting. That's no problem: we are keen to help in any way possible.

The address at the back of this book will put you in touch with someone who will help.

↘ If you want, you can work through a correspondence course, with a personal tutor to guide you; you can ask for free literature on a specific topic or topics; or just list your questions, ask for someone to answer them, and we will do our best. We have a monthly Bible magazine called *"Glad Tidings"* which might help and there are other books you might want to read, including one which looks at Bible teaching book-by-book. These can give you a solid grounding in parts of the Bible we haven't examined at all.

↘ If you have children that you would like to be taught about the Bible, we can arrange for them to have Sunday School lessons.

↘ If you have access to the Internet, there is a wealth of Bible resource at your fingertips there, which can assist with any queries, including an on-line correspondence course you might want to work through. Start at the website which is mentioned on page 454 and follow the various links until you find what you need.

429

❖ Lifestyle Issues

It may be that your concerns are not about Bible teaching as such. Perhaps you have read this book and found yourself agreeing with everything. It may even be that these are things you had already come to believe from your own reading. That has happened quite often in the past. But you may be concerned that your present lifestyle is not in harmony with Bible teaching, and perhaps you feel that little can be done about it. Yet most things can be changed for the better, given goodwill on all sides and the Lord's help. Remember what we learned from Romans about the help that God gives to those who seek Him:

> "We know that for those who love God all things work together for good, for those who are called according to his purpose" (Romans 8:28).

It is certain that some changes will have to be made in your life if you are engaged in practices which are wrong according to the commandments of Christ. Perhaps you will have to change your companions or change your habits. That might be hard at first, but as your beliefs and desires change, so will your interests and feelings towards things and people. The apostle Paul once wrote to believers in a city which had a worldwide reputation for loose living and immoral behaviour. He warned them that such conduct would lead to destruction, not to salvation, and then he added a comment which showed how powerfully the gospel had changed the lives of the believers in Corinth:

> "Do you not know that the unrighteous will not inherit the kingdom of God? Do not be deceived: neither the sexually immoral, nor idolaters, nor adulterers, nor men who practise homosexuality, nor thieves, nor the greedy, nor drunkards, nor revilers, nor swindlers will inherit the kingdom of God. **And such were some of you. But you were washed, you were sanctified, you were justified in the name of the Lord Jesus Christ and by the Spirit of our God**" (1 Corinthians 6:9-11).

That's the remarkable difference the gospel can make in a person's life. But the change has to start before baptism. There can be no question of our carrying on with such practices and then expecting God to go on forgiving us for wrong behaviour. Paul was very clear about that in

430

Romans:

> *"What shall we say then? Are we to continue in sin that grace may abound? By no means!* **How can we who died to sin still live in it? Do you not know that all of us who have been baptized into Christ Jesus were baptized into his death?"** *(Romans 6:1-3).*

Baptism is a death to sin, but we must first be willing to die to self – to put to death those things that are wrong in God's sight. You may not feel able to do that straight away, in which case you need to think about what we have been learning together and make it a matter of earnest prayer. Perhaps you will need some help or advice about certain aspects, in which case that is something to be thinking about at this stage. Remember that what God offers is eternal life, the forgiveness of sins, a real and living hope, fellowship with Him through the Lord Jesus Christ and fullness of being. These are things that should not be set aside lightly even though it may be difficult at first to change your present lifestyle and develop another.

This is the reason why baptism is often coupled in Scripture with another word – *"Repent!"* It means that we have to turn around and go a different way.[1] Renouncing the past, we have to resolve with God's help to leave it behind and strike out in a new and better direction. One New Testament writer was about to list a host of people in ancient times who made huge personal sacrifices for the sake of what they believed, but before doing so he offered these words of encouragement:

> *"You have need of endurance, so that when you have done the will of God you may receive what is promised. ... But we are not of those who shrink back and are destroyed, but of those who have faith and preserve their souls" (Hebrews 10:36-39).*

Nothing worthwhile was ever accomplished without effort. There have often been difficult times in the past when people wanted to follow Jesus. The apostle Paul knew all about that. He would eventually get to Rome, but not in the way he had hoped when he wrote the letter.[2] He arrived as a prisoner, because of his Jewish enemies who were

---

[1] *Repentance is taught in such Scriptures as Matthew 4:17; Acts 2:38; 3:19 and 2 Peter 3:9.*

plotting to kill him. He was in the city for two years, always under guard, before being released, then later imprisoned once more, and then executed. He thus became one of many faithful people who have died for their faith. They died full of faith that this life is nothing by comparison with the life that is to come in God's Kingdom, when Jesus returns to the earth.

❖ **Relationships**

There might, of course, be some complications in your life that need attention. It is almost the normal custom in some countries for people to live together although they are not married and there could well be children in the family and other dependants. What should be done then?

Marriage is a state that God has instituted and it comes about when two people make promises to one another about their life-long relationship as man and wife. Nowadays those promises should be registered officially with the state, so the marriage is properly recognised in the sight of all. The best course of action is for a person who is not legally married to discuss the matter with their partner, explain that their views have changed, and arrange to be married before being baptized. This may not be possible, perhaps because the other partner does not want to get married, or because of other complications. Then the situation will need to be talked through or corresponded about, to decide the best course of action and the one that best meets the commandments of Christ.

Being a follower of the Lord Jesus does not mean abandoning all previous responsibilities and just walking away from them. Those who follow the law of love will be more caring and considerate than ever. A solution will need to be found which meets the needs of all concerned and which upholds the requirements of a holy life in the sight of God.

❖ **What Then?**

Once preliminary issues like these have been sorted out, and that could take a little while in certain cases, the next step is to talk through with someone what you have come to understand and believe. This stage of the process is a safeguard for you, for baptism is the greatest decision you will ever make and it is important that you have really

---

2 See Romans 15:22-29 and Acts chapters 27 and 28.

thought it through beforehand. Remember that Jesus commanded the sequence of events in the words: *"Whoever (1) believes and (2) is baptized will be saved"*.

Straightforward questions will be asked to guide you through a confession of faith, and any necessary help and further instruction can be given at that time. For example, you might be asked this sort of thing about Jesus:

✓ What does it mean that Jesus is the Son of God?

✓ How was he born?

✓ When did he come into existence?

✓ What do we know about Mary, the mother of Jesus?

✓ Was Jesus tempted in just the same way that we are?

This would not be an examination, but a friendly chat to guide you through your understanding and to make sure that you are happy about what you now believe. The summary of beliefs in the next chapter will act as a reminder of the various things we have thought about as this book has progressed. You could work through those topics and check on how satisfied you are yourself about your own views. You could also explore any of those areas further if you feel the need to do so, using the Scripture references by each point.

Bear in mind that you will not stop learning when you are baptized. If you continue reading the Bible and thinking about its teaching your knowledge will steadily increase and lots of things that may seem a bit disjointed at present will slot into place. Baptism is the beginning of your journey not the end of the road!

❖ Baptism

Once you have given a good confession of your faith and have sorted out any concerns you might have about lifestyle issues, baptism itself will be straightforward. Baptism is a burial in water and is best done as a public act, though that is not always possible or advisable. If there is a Christadelphian meeting room nearby it may have a facility for baptisms and a simple service would be held in the company of other people who share your faith. People being baptized usually bring other members of their family along to witness the event. It's an excellent way of introducing them to the meeting and they too will be warmly welcomed.

In the absence of a local meeting, suitable arrangements will be made for a baptism. Sometimes a river, the sea, public baths, or a bath in a hotel room or a private house, might be used. Where the act takes place is not important; the act itself is what matters. Sitting or standing in the water you will be asked:

"Do you believe the things concerning the Kingdom of God and the name of Jesus Christ?"

When you answer *"I do"*, the baptizing brother will say something like:

"Then, upon your confession of faith, I baptize you in the name of the Lord Jesus Christ for the remission of your sins".

Having said that, he will gently lower and immerse you for a moment, and bring you safely up again. That's baptism! It's that straightforward to obey the commandment to *"Repent and be baptized" (Acts 2:38)*. And what a difference it then makes in life, as we saw in detail when we were studying Romans.[3]

❖ What Happens Then?

As a baptized believer you will become a member of the family of God and a Christadelphian as well. That means if there are Christadelphians in your locality you would meet with them week-by-week to remember the work of Jesus and to share bread and wine in remembrance of all he has done. You would also join with them in the various other activities in which the meeting is engaged, including sharing the gospel with others and studying the Bible together.

The ecclesia exists to help believers prepare for the coming of the Lord, whatever that might require, and to worship God. All believers are part of a holy congregation which seeks to worship God in an acceptable way. There is no paid ministry but all members share the various duties. Brothers (the male members) will help with Bible readings, other brothers will pray and another will give a few words of explanation and encouragement from God's Word. Everything is very Bible-based and concentrates on developing the understanding of the congregation and of giving God thanks and praise.[4]

---

[3] *See Chapters 14 and 15.*

You may not be near any other believers, at least not until you have had opportunity to share your faith and to encourage others to learn to understand the Bible for themselves. But you will still be part of a worldwide congregation or brotherhood. When people are visiting your locality they will come and meet you, and you can then break bread together. Otherwise you will need to break bread just by yourself, week by week, for it is a commandment of Jesus that we should remember him in this way. We will give some guidance about the best way of doing that and arrangements can be put in place which will provide a regular supply of material to help you with that remembrance.

❖ Preparing for the Kingdom

We are now nearing the end of human government and the beginning of God's coming kingdom when all faithful, baptized believers can expect to be together with the Lord, working with him in the development of the world and enjoying the gift of eternal life. That will be a wonderful time, full of fellowship and with everything directed towards the praise and worship of Almighty God.

The apostle Paul looked forward to that time when everything would at last be made right and good. He had a sense of urgency which drove him on, for he lived a life which was beset with many dangers. He could have died at any time, so it is no wonder that he said this with such force:

> *"Besides this you know the time, that **the hour has come for you to wake from sleep**. For salvation is nearer to us now than when we first believed. The night is far gone; the day is at hand. So then let us cast off the works of darkness and put on the armour of light. Let us walk properly as in the daytime, not in orgies and drunkenness, not in sexual immorality and sensuality, not in quarrelling and jealousy. But **put on the Lord Jesus Christ, and make no provision for the flesh, to gratify its desires**" (Romans 13:11-14).*

There is nothing more urgent in life.

---

[4] *Don't worry that you might be expected to do any of these things. None of them are compulsory and the people who do read, pray or speak do so only if and when they feel ready to do any of those things.*

435

Bible Reading Tables

JANUARY

Day			
1	Gen. 1, 2	Psa. 1, 2	Matt. 1, 2
2	... 3, 4	... 3, 5	... 3, 4
3	... 5, 6	... 6, 8	... 5
4	... 7, 8	... 9, 10	... 6
5	... 9, 10	...11, 13	... 7
6	...11, 12	!4, 16	... 8
7	...13, 14	... 17	... 9
8	...15, 16	... 18	... 10
9	...17, 18	...19, 21	... 11
10	... 19	... 22	... 12
11	...20, 21	...23, 25	... 13
12	...22, 23	...26, 28	... 14
13	... 24	...29, 30	... 15
14	...25, 26	... 31	... 16
15	... 27	... 32	... 17
16	...28, 29	... 33	... 18
17	... 30	... 34	... 19
18	... 31	... 35	... 20
19	...32, 33	... 36	... 21
20	...34, 35	... 37	... 22
21	... 36	... 38	... 23
22	... 37	...39, 40	... 24
23	... 38	...41, 43	... 25
24	...39, 40	... 44	... 26
25	... 41	... 45	... 27
26	...42, 43	...46, 48	... 28
27	...44, 45	... 49	Rom. 1, 2
28	...46, 47	... 50	... 3, 4
29	...48, 50	...51, 52	... 5, 6
30	Exod. 1, 2	...53, 55	... 7, 8
31	... 3, 4	...56, 57	... 9

FEBRUARY

Day			
1	Exod. 5, 6	Psa.58,59	Rom. 10, 11
2	... 7, 8	...60, 61	... 12
3	... 9	...62, 63	... 13, 14
4	... 10	...64, 65	... 15, 16
5	...11, 12	...66, 67	Mark 1
6	...13, 14	... 68	... 2
7	... 15	... 69	... 3
8	... 16	...70, 71	... 4
9	...17, 18	... 72	... 5
10	...19, 20	... 73	... 6
11	... 21	... 74	... 7
12	... 22	...75, 76	... 8
13	... 23	... 77	... 9
14	...24, 25	... 78	... 10
15	... 26	...79, 80	... 11
16	... 27	...81, 82	... 12
17	... 28	...83, 84	... 13
18	... 29	...85, 86	... 14
19	... 30	...87, 88	... 15, 16
20	...31, 32	... 89	I Cor. 1, 2
21	...33, 34	...90, 91	... 3
22	... 35	...92, 93	... 4, 5
23	... 36	...94, 95	... 6
24	... 37	...96, 99	... 7
25	... 38	100, 101	... 8, 9
26	...39, 40	... 102	... 10
27	Lev. 1, 2	... 103	... 11
28	... 3, 4	... 104	... 12, 13

MARCH

Day			
1	Lev. 5, 6	Psa. 105	I Cor. 14
2	... 7	... 106	... 15
3	... 8	... 107	... 16
4	... 9,10	108, 109	2 Cor. 1, 2
5	... 11	110, 112	... 3, 4
6	...12, 13	113, 114	... 5, 6, 7
7	... 14	115, 116	... 8, 9
8	... 15	117, 118	... 10, 11
9	... 16	119,v.40	... 12, 13
10	...17, 18	v. 41-80	Luke
11	... 19	v.81-128	...
12	... 20	v.129-176	...
13	... 21	120, 124	...
14	... 22	125, 127	...
15	... 23	128, 130	...
16	... 24	131, 134	...
17	... 25	135, 136	...
18	... 26	137, 139	...
19	... 27	140, 142	10
20	Num.	... 143, 144	11
21	... 2	145, 147	...
22	... 3	148, 150	13, 1
23	... 4	Prov. 1	15
24	... 5	... 2	1
25	... 6	... 3	1
26	... 7	... 4	1
27	... 8, 9	... 5	1
28	... 10	... 6	2
29	... 11	... 7	2
30	...12, 13	... 8, 9	2
31	... 14	... 10	2

JULY

Day			
1	I Sam. 13	Isa. 56,57	Rev. 21,22
2	... 14	... 58	Matt. 1, 2
3	... 15	... 59	... 3, 4
4	... 16	... 60	... 5
5	... 17	... 61	... 6
6	... 18	... 62	... 7
7	... 19	... 63	... 8
8	... 20	... 64	... 9
9	...21, 22	... 65	... 10
10	... 23	... 66	... 11
11	... 24	Jer. 1	... 12
12	... 25	... 2	... 13
13	...26, 27	... 3	... 14
14	... 28	... 4	... 15
15	...29, 30	... 5	... 16
16	... 31	... 6	... 17
17	2 Sam. 1	... 7	... 18
18	... 2	... 8	... 19
19	... 3	... 9	... 20
20	... 4, 5	... 10	... 21
21	... 6	... 11	... 22
22	... 7	... 12	... 23
23	... 8, 9	... 13	... 24
24	... 10	... 14	... 25
25	... 11	... 15	... 26
26	... 12	... 16	... 27
27	... 13	... 17	... 28
28	... 14	... 18	Rom. 1, 2
29	... 15	... 19	... 3, 4
30	... 16	... 20	... 5, 6
31	... 17	... 21	... 7, 8

AUGUST

Day			
1	2 Sam. 18	Jer. 22	Rom. 9
2	... 19	... 23	... 10, 11
3	...20, 21	... 24	... 12
4	... 22	... 25	... 13, 14
5	... 23	... 26	... 15, 16
6	... 24	... 27	Mark 1
7	I Kings 1	... 28	... 2
8	... 2	... 29	... 3
9	... 3	... 30	... 4
10	... 4, 5	... 31	... 5
11	... 6	... 32	... 6
12	... 7	... 33	... 7
13	... 8	... 34	... 8
14	... 9	... 35	... 9
15	... 10	... 36	... 10
16	... 11	... 37	... 11
17	... 12	... 38	... 12
18	... 13	... 39	... 13
19	... 14	... 40	... 14
20	... 15	... 41	... 15
21	... 16	... 42	... 16
22	... 17	... 43	I Cor. 1, 2
23	... 18	... 44	... 3
24	... 19	...45, 46	... 4, 5
25	... 20	... 47	... 6
26	... 21	... 48	... 7
27	... 22	... 49	... 8, 9
28	2 Kings 1,2	... 50	... 10
29	... 3	... 51	... 11
30	... 4	... 52	... 12, 13
31	... 5	Lam. 1	... 14

SEPTEMBER

Day			
1	2 Kings 6	Lam. 2	I Cor.
2	... 7	... 3	...
3	... 8	... 4	2 Cor. 1,
4	... 9	... 5	...
5	... 10	Ezek. 1	... 3,
6	...11, 12	... 2	... 5,
7	... 13	... 3	... 8,
8	... 14	... 4	... 10,
9	... 15	... 5	Luke 12,
10	... 16	... 6	...
11	... 17	... 7	...
12	... 18	... 8	...
13	... 19	... 9	...
14	... 20	... 10	...
15	... 21	... 11	...
16	...22, 23	... 12	...
17	...24, 25	... 13	...
18	I Chron.1	... 14	...
19	... 2	... 15	...
20	... 3	... 16	...
21	... 4	... 17	13,
22	... 5	... 18	...
23	... 6	... 19	...
24	... 7	... 20	...
25	... 8	... 21	...
26	... 9	... 22	...
27	... 10	... 23	...
28	... 11	... 24	...
29	... 12	... 25	...
30	...13, 14	... 26	...

Read the Old Testament once and the New Testament twice each year

Read God's Word every day and grow

APRIL

Day			
1	Num. 15	Prov. 11	Luke 24
2	... 16	... 12	Gal. 1, 2
3	...17,18	... 13	... 3, 4
4	... 19	... 14	... 5, 6
5	...20,21	... 15	Eph. 1, 2
6	...22,23	... 16	... 3, 4
7	...24,25	... 17	... 5, 6
8	... 26	... 18	Phil. 1, 2
9	... 27	... 19	... 3, 4
10	... 28	... 20	John 1
11	...29,30	... 21	... 2, 3
12	... 31	... 22	... 4
13	... 32	... 23	... 5
14	... 33	... 24	... 6
15	... 34	... 25	... 7
16	... 35	... 26	... 8
17	... 36	... 27	... 9, 10
18	Deut. 1	... 28	... 11
19	... 2	... 29	... 12
20	... 3	... 30	... 13, 14
21	... 4	... 31	... 15, 16
22	... 5	Eccl. 1	... 17, 18
23	... 6, 7	... 2	... 19
24	... 8, 9	... 3	... 20, 21
25	...10,11	... 4	Acts 1
26	... 12	... 5	... 2
27	...13,14	... 6	... 3, 4
28	... 15	... 7	... 5, 6
29	... 16	... 8	... 7
30	... 17	... 9	... 8

MAY

Day			
1	Deut. 18	Eccl. 10	Acts 9
2	... 19	... 11	... 10
3	... 20	... 12	... 11, 12
4	... 21	Song 1	... 13
5	... 22	... 2	... 14, 15
6	... 23	... 3	... 16, 17
7	... 24	... 4	... 18, 19
8	... 25	... 5	... 20
9	... 26	... 6	... 21, 22
10	... 27	... 7	... 23, 24
11	... 28	... 8	... 25, 26
12	... 29	Isaiah 1	... 27
13	... 30	... 2	... 28
14	... 31	... 3, 4	Col. 1
15	... 32	... 5	... 2
16	...33,34	... 6	... 3, 4
17	Joshua 1	... 7	1 Thes. 1, 2
18	... 2	... 8	... 3, 4
19	... 3, 4	... 9	... 5
20	... 5, 6	... 10	2 Thes. 1, 2
21	... 7	... 11	... 3
22	... 8	... 12	1 Tim. 1,2,3
23	... 9	... 13	... 4, 5
24	... 10	... 14	... 6
25	... 11	... 15	2 Tim. 1
26	... 12	... 16	... 2
27	... 13	...17,18	... 3, 4
28	... 14	... 19	Titus 1, 2
29	... 15	...20,21	Philemon
30	... 16	... 22	Heb. 1, 2
31	... 17	... 23	... 3, 4, 5

JUNE

Day			
1	Joshua 18	Isaiah 24	Heb. 6, 7
2	... 19	... 25	... 8, 9
3	...20,21	...26,27	... 10
4	... 22	... 28	... 11
5	...23,24	... 29	... 12
6	Judges 1	... 30	... 13
7	... 2, 3	... 31	James 1
8	... 4, 5	... 32	... 2
9	... 6	... 33	... 3, 4
10	... 7, 8	... 34	... 5
11	... 9	... 35	1 Peter 1
12	...10,11	... 36	... 2
13	...12,13	... 37	... 3, 4, 5
14	...14,15	... 38	2 Pet. 1, 2
15	... 16	... 39	... 3
16	...17,18	... 40	1 John 1, 2
17	... 19	... 41	... 3, 4
18	... 20	... 42	... 5
19	... 21	... 43	2 & 3 John
20	Ruth 1, 2	... 44	Jude
21	... 3, 4	... 45	Rev. 1, 2
22	1 Sam. 1	...46,47	... 3, 4
23	... 2	... 48	... 5, 6
24	... 3	... 49	... 7, 8, 9
25	... 4	... 50	... 10, 11
26	... 5, 6	... 51	... 12, 13
27	... 7, 8	... 52	... 14
28	... 9	... 53	... 15, 16
29	... 10	... 54	... 17, 18
30	...11,12	... 55	... 19, 20

OCTOBER

Day			
1	1 Chron.15	Ezek. 27	Luke 24
2	... 16	... 28	Gal. 1, 2
3	... 17	... 29	... 3, 4
4	...18,19	... 30	... 5, 6
5	...20,21	... 31	Eph. 1, 2
6	... 22	... 32	... 3, 4
7	... 23	... 33	... 5, 6
8	...24,25	... 34	Phil. 1, 2
9	... 26	... 35	... 3, 4
10	... 27	... 36	John 1
11	... 28	... 37	... 2, 3
12	2 Chron.1,2	... 38	... 4
13	... 3, 4	... 39	... 5
14	... 5, 6	... 40	... 6
15	... 7	... 41	... 7
16	... 8	... 42	... 8
17	... 9	... 43	... 9, 10
18	...10,11	... 44	... 11
19	...12,13	... 45	... 12
20	...14,15	... 46	... 13, 14
21	...16,17	... 47	... 15, 16
22	...18,19	... 48	... 17, 18
23	... 20	Daniel 1	... 19
24	...21,22	... 2	... 20, 21
25	... 23	... 3	Acts 1
26	... 24	... 4	... 2
27	... 25	... 5	... 3, 4
28	...26,27	... 6	... 5, 6
29	... 28	... 7	... 7
30	... 29	... 8	... 8
31		... 9	... 9

NOVEMBER

Day			
1	2 Chron.30	Dan. 10	Acts 10
2	... 31	... 11	... 11, 12
3	... 32	... 12	... 13
4	... 33	Hosea 1	... 14, 15
5	... 34	... 2	... 16, 17
6	... 35	... 3	... 18, 19
7	... 36	... 4	... 20
8	Ezra 1, 2	... 5	... 21, 22
9	... 3, 4	... 6	... 23, 24
10	... 5, 6	... 7	... 25, 26
11	... 7	... 8	... 27
12	... 8	... 9	... 28
13	... 9	... 10	Colos. 1
14	... 10	... 11	... 2
15	Neh. 1, 2	... 12	... 3, 4
16	... 3	... 13	1 Thes. 1, 2
17	... 4	... 14	... 3, 4
18	... 5, 6	Joel 1	... 5
19	... 7	... 2	2 Thes. 1, 2
20	... 8	... 3	... 3
21	... 9	Amos. 1	1 Tim. 1,2,3
22	... 10	... 2	... 4, 5
23	... 11	... 3	... 6
24	... 12	... 4	2 Tim. 1
25	... 13	... 5	... 2
26	Esther 1	... 6	... 3, 4
27	... 2	... 7	Titus 1, 2, 3
28	... 3, 4	... 8	Philemon
29	... 5, 6	... 9	Heb. 1, 2
30	... 7, 8	Obadiah	... 3, 4, 5

DECEMBER

Day			
1	Esth. 9,10	Jonah 1	Heb. 6, 7
2	Job 1, 2	... 2, 3	... 8, 9
3	... 3, 4	... 4	... 10
4	... 5	Micah 1	... 11
5	... 6, 7	... 2	... 12
6	... 8	... 3, 4	... 13
7	... 9	... 5	James 1
8	... 10	... 6	... 2
9	... 11	... 7	... 3, 4
10	... 12	Nahum 1,2	... 5
11	... 13	... 3	1 Peter 1
12	... 14	Hab. 1	... 2
13	... 15	... 2	... 3, 4, 5
14	...16,17	... 3	2 Pet. 1, 2
15	...18,19	Zeph. 1	... 3
16	... 20	... 2	1 John 1, 2
17	... 21	... 3	... 3, 4
18	... 22	Hag. 1, 2	... 5
19	...23,24	Zech. 1	2 & 3 John
20	...25,26	... 2, 3	Jude
21	...27,28	... 4, 5	Rev. 1, 2
22	...29,30	... 6, 7	... 3, 4
23	...31,32	... 8	... 5, 6
24	... 33	... 9	... 7, 8, 9
25	... 34	... 10	... 10, 11
26	...35,36	... 11	... 12, 13
27	... 37	... 12	... 14
28	... 38	...13,14	... 15, 16
29	... 39	Malachi 1	... 17, 18
30	... 40	... 2	... 19, 20
31	...41,42	... 3, 4	... 21, 22

By courtesy of 'The Christadelphian'

29
The Gospel Truth

This final chapter offers an overview of the gospel. Right at the start we took an overall look at the Letter to the Romans and summarised its teaching. To do that we read through the letter before listing its key ideas, after which we examined it in greater detail. We could do that because it is a detailed and carefully constructed explanation of the gospel which the apostle Paul believed and taught.

As we worked through that explanation we have diverted, here and there, to see what other parts of the Bible have said about particular subjects and topics. We should now be in a position to summarise our findings and, in so doing, should get a detailed picture of what the Bible teaches on all the important matters that have to do with our salvation and the unfolding purpose of God.

Here is that summary, topic by topic. Should you want to do some further research into particular items, Scriptural references are also included that will help you explore things in more detail.

"I am not ashamed of the gospel, for it is the power of God for salvation to everyone who believes, to the Jew first and also to the Greek"
(Romans 1:16)

❖ The Bible

The Bible is the basis of all our knowledge about God and His gracious purpose. It consists of the Old Testament (containing the writings of Moses and the prophets), and the New Testament (containing the gospels and the epistles, or letters). This book, or library of books, was given by inspiration of God. God's power operated in such a way that what the different writers recorded is wholly inspired and without error. The only errors that might now exist in the Bible are those that have resulted from the process of copying or translation out of the original languages.

The Bible can give us all the understanding we need about God and His purpose to save us from sin and death. It is the foundation of our faith and it is vitally important that we read it regularly and in that way inform and transform our minds, so that we know what is pleasing to God.

Scriptures: 2 Timothy 3:16; 1 Corinthians 14:37; Nehemiah 9:30; John 10:35

❖ God

There is only one true God who has revealed Himself to mankind in different ways. In past ages He communicated through angels, by visiting people like Abraham, Isaac, Jacob and Moses. When the time was right, God sent His Son, the Lord Jesus Christ, so that we could see, by the way that Jesus lived and from the things he said and did, just what God wants us to become, and what He wants us to understand about His purpose and His character.

God is supreme and unequalled. He has always existed and always will, for He is eternal. He dwells in unapproachable light yet He is everywhere present by His Spirit, or power.

By that Spirit God created heaven and earth and everything that is in them. It was the Spirit of God that operated through the patriarchs, prophets and apostles to reveal the Bible to mankind. Because it was a revelation intended to lead men and women to holiness, that divine power is called God's Holy Spirit. The power was occasionally given to people to show that they were working on God's behalf: it was a way of confirming their authority as the servants of God. But when the Bible had been fully revealed those Holy Spirit gifts were withdrawn. They do not exist today as they once did.

Isaiah 40:13-25; 43:10-12; 44:6-8; 45:5; 46:9,10; Job 38,39 and 40; Deuteronomy 6:4; Mark 12:29-32; 1 Corinthians 8:4-6; Ephesians 4:6; 1 Timothy 2:5; Nehemiah 9:6; Job 26:13; Psalm 124:8; 146:6; 148:5; Isaiah 40:26,27; Jeremiah 10:12,13; 27:5; 32:17-19; 51:15; Acts 14:15; 17:24 1 Chronicles 29:11-14; Psalm 62:11; 145:3; Isaiah 26:4; 40:26; Job 9:4; 36:5; Psalm

92:5; 104:24; 147:4-5; Isaiah 28:29; Romans 16:27; 1 Timothy 1:17; 2 Chronicles 16:9; Job 28:24; 34:21; Psalm 33:13,14; 44:21; 94:9; 139:7-12; Proverbs 15:3; Jeremiah 23:24; 32:19; Amos 9:2,3; Acts 17:27,28; Psalm 123:1; 1 Kings 8:30,39,43,49; Matthew 6:9; 1 Timothy 6:15,16; 1:17; Hebrews 2:1-4; 1 Corinthians 12:1-11; 13:8-13

❖ Jesus

God is the Father of the Lord Jesus Christ. Jesus is the Son of God who was begotten of Mary by God's Holy Spirit power, without the involvement of man. He is God's only begotten Son and was able to do and say so many powerful things because God anointed him with the Holy Spirit without measure when he was baptized. Although God had known from the beginning that He would need to save mankind by sending His Son, Jesus only came into existence when he was born of his mother Mary.

Matthew 1:23; 1 Timothy 3:16; Acts 2:22-24,36; Matthew 1:18-25; Luke 1:26-35; Galatians 4:4; Isaiah 7:14; Matthew 3:16,17; Isaiah 11:2; 42:1; 61:1; John 3:34; 7:16; 8:26-29; 14:10-24.

God needed to intervene by sending His Son because of the desperate state of the human race. This condition had come about because of the events that occurred in Eden and the choices that were there made by Adam, who chose to please himself rather than God. In so doing he brought sin and death into the world and destroyed his fellowship with God. Jesus came to restore man's relationship with God and was wholly successful in that mission. Because of his faith and his obedience to his Father's will, Jesus was raised from the dead and exalted to glory.

1 Corinthians 15:21,22; Romans 5:12-19; Genesis 3:19; 2 Corinthians 5:19-21

❖ Mankind

The first man was Adam, whom God created from the dust of the ground and made a living being. God placed him under a law – whereby the fruit of one tree in the garden was forbidden both to Adam and Eve. If they wanted to stay in that garden and stay alive they had to be obedient. If they ate of the forbidden fruit they would die.

440

Genesis 2:7; 18:27; Job 4:19; 33:6; 1 Corinthians 15:46-49; Genesis 2:17

Adam broke God's law, and was judged unworthy of immortality. He was sentenced to return to the ground from which he had been taken and that sentence became part of his everyday experience, and the experience of all his descendants. Two problems resulted. Firstly, we are all born mortal and are therefore destined to die. We do not have an immortal soul and when we die we are unconscious and our bodies corrupt. The only hope of life is resurrection from the dead at the second coming of Jesus. Those who are not resurrected will remain dead forever.

Secondly, all men and women are now inclined, like Adam, to disobey God. By nature we now prefer to serve self rather than God. The source of all temptation is inside us, but outside influences may also tempt us to disobey God. There is no supernatural devil or Satan who does the tempting; those Bible terms are picture language for sin in its various forms.

Genesis 3:15-19,22,23; 2 Corinthians 1:9; Romans 7:24; 2 Corinthians 5:2-4; Romans 7:19-23; Galatians 5:16,17; Romans 6:12; 7:21; John 3:6; Romans 5:12; 1 Corinthians 15:2; Psalm 51:5; Job 14:4; Isaiah 45:5-7; Jeremiah 17:9; Mark 7:21-23; James 1:13-16

❖ God's Plan of Salvation

In His kindness, God had a plan of restoration by which He was able to rescue the human race from destruction and eventually fill the earth with people who are both sinless and immortal. Because He is holy and righteous in everything He does, and cannot be otherwise, God has made this possible in a way which upholds His righteousness and justice. In no way has God changed His attitude towards sin; rather, in all that was done God showed how terrible sin is and how determined and how right He is to destroy it absolutely.

Revelation 21:4; John 3:16; 2 Timothy 1:10; 1 John 2:25; 2 Timothy 1:1; Titus 1:2; Romans 3:26; John 1:29

❖ His Promises

This plan of salvation was the subject of great promises made at first to people like Adam and Eve, Abraham, and

441

David, which were afterwards given in even greater detail through the prophets. Those promises are a vital part of the gospel of salvation and have not been overtaken by later developments, nor have they yet been fulfilled altogether.

Genesis 3:15; 22:18; Psalm 89:34-37; 33:5; Hosea 13:14; Isaiah 25:7-9; 51:1-8; Jeremiah 23:5

❖ Centred in Jesus

These great promises point forward to the Lord Jesus Christ. It was necessary that he should be born in the line of Abraham and David, and that he should share the very same human nature with which we are all born. That was what happened when he was born of Mary by the power or Spirit of God. During his lifetime Jesus was tempted in the same way that we are tempted, but he remained sinless and lived a life of perfect obedience to his Father. The climax of his life of obedience was that he died on the cross. This destroyed the power of sin and made available a way of escape from sin and death, both for him and for all who would choose to believe and follow him. Because of his perfect obedience God raised Jesus from the dead and exalted him to sit in glory at His right hand in heaven. That is where he is now.

1 Corinthians 15:45; Hebrews 2:14-16; Romans 1:3; Hebrews 5:8,9;1:9; Romans 5:19-21; Galatians 4:4,5; Romans 8:3,4; Hebrews 2:14,15; 9:26; Galatians 1:4; Hebrews 7:27; 5:3-7; 2:17; Romans 6:10; 6:9; Acts 13:34-37; Revelation 1:18; John 5:21,22,26,27; 14:3; Revelation 2:7; 3:21; Matthew 25:21; Hebrews 5:9; Mark 16:16; Acts 13:38,39; Romans 3:22; Psalm 2:6-9; Daniel 7:13,14; Revelation 11:15; Jeremiah 23:5; Zechariah 14:9; Ephesians 1:9,10

❖ His Birth and Rebirth

It was to fulfil God's great plan of salvation that Jesus was miraculously begotten of a human mother. The sinless Jesus carried the burden of our sins to the cross to make it possible for our sins to be forgiven. Then, because he had been perfectly obedient in all things, the righteousness of God required that he be raised from the dead. Jesus did not die instead of us (as a substitute); he died on our behalf (as our representative) so that we, through his death, might have our sins forgiven.

Matthew 1:18-25; Luke 1:26-35; Galatians 4:4; Isaiah 7:14; Romans 1:3,4; 8:3; 2 Corinthians 5:21; Hebrews 2:14-17; 4:15; 1 Peter 2:21-25

❖ His Life on Earth

Jesus was begotten of God and showed us, in his life and by everything that he did, just what God is like. It was as if God was speaking to us through His Son, who gave the fullest ever disclosure of what godliness is like in day-to-day terms. Father and Son worked together to accomplish God's great plan of salvation and Jesus willingly obeyed his Father's commandments. During his life on earth, he was a mortal man who shared all the problems of our humanity, including death itself. He chose to lay down his life as a matter of obedience and was not compelled to do so. It follows that any suggestion that Jesus had existed beforehand in heaven, or that he was part of a three-in-one godhead, is unscriptural and does a great disservice to the Lord Jesus Christ.

Matthew 1:23; 1 Timothy 3:16; Hebrews 2:14; Galatians 4:4; Hebrews 2:17; John 10:17,18; 17:3

❖ His Teaching

The message that Jesus delivered from God called men and women to repentance. That means turning away from sin and turning towards God by abandoning every evil work and seeking to transform our thinking and the direction of our lives towards God, so as to be in harmony with His revealed will. Jesus first made that appeal to his own nation, the Jewish people, explaining in the process his part in God's purpose, as God's Son. He showed that i.e was the long-awaited Messiah who could deliver them from sin and death. He said that he had come to fulfil all that was written in the law and in the prophets.

Mark 1:15; Matthew 4:17; 5:20-48; John 10:36; 9:35; 11:27; 19:21; 1:49; Matthew 27:11-42; John 10:24,25; Matthew 19:28; 21:42,43; 23:38,39; 25:14-46; Luke 4:43; 13:27-30; 19:11-27; 22:28-30; Matthew 5:17; Luke 24:44

❖ His Death

For delivering this message, Jesus was put to death by the Jews and Romans. Nothing had gone wrong with God's purpose; for God had intended that in this way He would demonstrate His love for mankind and show the awfulness of sin. By his death on the cross, Jesus showed how right God has always been to condemn sin; demonstrated what sin is really like; and revealed how great God's love is in rescuing us from ourselves, and our own choices. That sacrificial death thus declared the righteousness of God, and made it possible for God to forgive repentant sinners. It showed God to be both righteous and forgiving. All believers who become related to God by baptism, through this crucified but risen representative of Adam's disobedient race, can be forgiven. The Scriptures use several different words to refer to God's gracious work through His Son, including "reconciliation", "redemption" and "atonement".

Luke 19:47; 20:1-16; John 11:45-53; Acts 10:38, 39; 13:26-29; 4:27,28; Romans 8:3; Hebrews 10:10; Acts 13:38; 1 John 1:7; John 14:6; Acts 4:12; 1 Peter 3:18; 2:24; Hebrews 9:14; 7:27; 9:26-28; Galatians 1:4; Romans 3:25; 15:8; Galatians 3:21,22; 2:21; 4:4,5; Hebrews 9:15; Luke 22:20; 24:26,46,47; Matthew 26:28

❖ His Resurrection

On the third day after his crucifixion God raised Jesus from the dead, and exalted him to the heavens to be a priestly mediator between God and man. He is there now, at God's right hand, working to gather together from all nations a people who can be saved from sin and death by believing and obeying the saving truth that God has revealed.

1 Corinthians 15:4; Acts 10:40; 13:30-37; 2:24-27

❖ His Priesthood

Jesus is the only priest who is acceptable to God. There is no need for human priests; for the Lord Jesus is the God-given mediator and intercessor between God and man. He lives in heaven to make intercession for those who have accepted the gospel and who become his brothers and sisters. If they confess and forsake their sins, those sins can be forgiven.

Luke 24:51; Ephesians 1:20; Acts 5:31; 1 Timothy 2:25; Hebrews 8:1; Acts 15:14; 13:39; Hebrews 4:14,15; John 17:9; Hebrews 10:26; 1 John 2:1; Proverbs 28:13

❖ His Apostles

Jesus sent forth apostles to proclaim salvation through him, as the only name under heaven whereby men must be saved. That salvation was available for both Jew and Gentile, but it is necessary for all who want that salvation to approach God in the one way that has been provided.

Acts 1:8; Matthew 28:19,20; Luke 24:46-48; Acts 26:16-18; 4:12.

❖ The Only Way of Salvation

The only way to obtain salvation from sin and death is to believe the gospel as it was preached by the Lord and his apostles, and to take on the saving name of the Lord Jesus Christ. This is done by baptism, which is an act of burial or immersion in water, and that must follow a satisfactory confession of faith. Baptism which takes a different form, or one that occurs before a person has a saving faith, is unacceptable to God.

Baptism begins a new life in Christ, one which requires patient observance of all that he commanded, none being recognised as his friends except those who do what he has commanded.

Acts 13:48; 16:31; Mark 16:16; Acts 2:38,41; 10:47; 8:12; Galatians 3:27-29; Romans 6:3-5; 2:7; Matthew 28:20; John 15:14.

The gospel of salvation consists of *"the things concerning the kingdom of God and the name of Jesus Christ"*.

❖ The *"name of Jesus Christ"* expresses those things about the nature and work of the Lord Jesus which have been outlined above.

❖ The *"kingdom of God"* consists of that truth which is revealed in the writings of the prophets and by the Lord Jesus and the apostles, as outlined below.

Acts 8:12; 19:8,10,20; 28:30,31

❖ The Kingdom of God

God will set up a kingdom on earth, which will overthrow all others, and change them into *"the kingdom of our Lord and his Christ"*.

Daniel 2:44; 7:13,14; Revelation 11:15; Isaiah 32:1,17; 2:2-4; 11:9,10

For this purpose God will send Jesus Christ to the earth. He will come visibly, personally and powerfully.

Acts 1:11; 3:20,21; Psalm 102:16,21; 2 Timothy 4:1; Acts 1:9,11; Daniel 7:13

The kingdom which he will establish will be the kingdom of Israel restored, in the territory it formerly occupied, namely the land that was gifted by covenant for an everlasting possession to Abraham and his seed. Abraham's seed is the Lord Jesus Christ.

Micah 4:6-8; Amos 9:11,15; Ezekiel 37:21,22; Jeremiah 23:3-8; Genesis 13:14-17; Hebrews 11:8,9; Galatians 3:16; Leviticus 26:42; Micah 7:20

This restoration of the kingdom to Israel will involve the ingathering of God's chosen but scattered nation, the Jews. It was predicted by the prophets that after years of dispersion they would be reinstated in the land of their fathers, which would be reclaimed from *"the desolation of many generations"*. Long ago the Bible predicted that Jerusalem would be occupied once again by Jews. This was to happen prior to it becoming *"the throne of the Lord"* and the capital city of the whole earth.

Isaiah 11:12; Jeremiah 31:10; Zechariah 8:7,8; Ezekiel 36:34,36; Isaiah 51:3; 60:15; 62:4; Jeremiah 3:17; Micah 4:7, 8; Joel 3:17; Isaiah 24:23

The governing body of the kingdom of God which is to be established will be the brothers and sisters of Christ – those people from all generations who have believed the promises of God and have been obedient to His commands. They will be made immortal rulers in that age and, with Christ at their head, will comprise the collective "seed of Abraham", in whom all nations will be blessed,

Daniel 12:2; Luke 13:28; Revelation 11:18; 1 Thessalonians 4:15-17; John 5:28, 29; 6:39, 40; Luke 14:14; Matthew 25:34,46.

❖ **Resurrection and Judgement**

At the appearing of Christ, prior to the establishment of the kingdom, those who know the revealed will of God, and have been called upon to submit to it, will be summoned before his judgement-seat. This will necessitate those from times past being raised from the dead. They will be raised mortal. It will be a time of reckoning for both faithful and unfaithful alike.

2 Corinthians 5:10; 2 Timothy 4:1; Romans 2:5,6,16; 14:10-12; 1 Corinthians 4:5; Revelation 11:18

As a result of that judgement, the faithful will be given the gift of immortality and will be exalted to reign with the Lord Jesus Christ as joint heirs of the kingdom. The unfaithful will be consigned to shame and *"the second death"*. Their punishment will be that they are excluded from the presence of the Lòrd and the glories of his reign.

The Bible does not teach that people will be endlessly punished in hell or with hell fire. Such terminology is picture language for the total destruction of those who are rejected by God as unworthy of the life to come.

Matthew 7:21; 8:12; 25:31-46; Daniel 12:2; Galatians 1:8; 5:21; 2 Thessalonians 1:8-10; Hebrews 10:26-29; 2 Peter 2:12; Revelation 21:8; Malachi 4:1; Psalm 37:29-38; Proverbs 10:25-30; 1 Corinthians 15:51-55; 2 Corinthians 5:1-4; James 1:12; Romans 2:7; John 10:28; Matthew 5:5; Psalm 37:9,22,29; Revelation 5:9; Daniel 7:27; 1 Thessalonians 2:12; 2 Peter 1:11; Revelation 3:21; 2 Timothy 2:12; Revelation 5:10; Psalm 49:7-9; Luke 22:29, 30

❖ **The Millennium**

The Kingdom of God, thus constituted, will continue a thousand years, during which sin and death will continue among the earth's subject inhabitants, though in a much milder degree than now. It will be the mission of the kingdom to show the mortal inhabitants of that age how best to live in a way that pleases God and makes their own lives happy and contented.

Revelation 20:4-9; 11:15; Isaiah 65:20; Ezekiel 37:22,25; 1 Corinthians 15:24-28.

A law will be established, to which all nations will become subject, for their *"instruction in righteousness"*. This will result in the abolition of war to the ends of the earth; and the *"filling of the earth with the knowledge of the glory of the LORD, as the waters cover the sea"*.

Micah 4:2; Isaiah 11:1-5; 2:3,4; Habakkuk 2:14

The work of the kingdom will be to subdue all God's enemies and finally death itself, by opening up the way of life to the nations. Men and women will have the opportunity to live in this kingdom during the thousand years.

1 Corinthians 15:25,26; Revelation 21:4; 20:12-15; Isaiah 25:6-8

At the close of the thousand years, there will be a general resurrection and judgement, resulting in the final extinction of the wicked, and the immortalisation of all those who have lived during the thousand years who are now considered worthy of eternal life.

Revelation 20:11-15; 1 Corinthians 15:24

The government will then be delivered up by Jesus to the Father, who will manifest Himself as the *"all-in-all"*. Sin and death will have been taken out of the way, and the human race will be completely restored to a fit state for fellowship with Almighty God.

1 Corinthians 15:28

❖ Life in Christ

All who believe these things and who are baptized as Jesus commanded must live in obedience to the Lord's commandments. This will require them to have the right attitude towards God and the Lord Jesus Christ by putting their requirements first, and by loving them more than anyone or anything else. We should always seek to care for and respect our fellow believers, putting their interests in front of our own, and loving other men and women as ourselves.

❖ We should love God first and foremost, putting Him before all else. We should pray to Him frequently and worship Him regularly.

   Matthew 22:37; Luke 18:1; Matthew 6:7; Ephesians 5:20

❖ We should always highly regard the Lord Jesus Christ and honour him in all things. He is our role-model in life. In everything we should seek to be Christ-minded and to live as he lived – selflessly and in the best interests of others.

1 Peter 2:21; Luke 14:26; Colossians 3:16; Ephesians 3:17

❖ We are to love even our enemies and not to be aggressive or vengeful, not exercising legal rights or going to law but seeking agreement and reconciliation at all times, seeking to overcome evil with good. It should always be our aim to do to others as we would have them do to us.

Matthew 5:25,39-44; 7:12; Romans 12:17-21; 1 Corinthians 6:7; Hebrews 12:14

❖ We should choose employment which is in harmony with the things we believe, not taking an oath of allegiance to any other king or ruler except the Lord Jesus Christ and showing a conscientious objection to those things which are contrary to our beliefs. That means that we should not work in the armed forces or in the police.

❖ We should not vote to elect political parties, because our allegiance is to Jesus Christ alone, and we await his government, when he rules as king in Jerusalem.

John 18:36; Philippians 3:20-21; 2 Timothy 2:4; Hebrews 11:13-16; 13:14; 1 Peter 2:9,11-14

❖ In employment we should be diligent, honest and conscientious employees, not complaining or causing trouble but working for our employer as unto the Lord.

Matthew 7:1; Ephesians 6:5-8; Colossians 3:23; James 5:9

❖ Our personal relationships should always be appropriate to our calling as a follower of Jesus. We should choose friends carefully. Sexual relations are only permissible within marriage and believers should marry believers. Marriage is for life and divorce is to be avoided. In all our relationships we should be gentle, meek, kind-hearted, compassionate, merciful and forgiving. Our behaviour should always be courteous and caring. We should always be ready to talk about the things we believe.

2 Timothy 2:24; Titus 2:2; Ephesians 4:32; Colossians 3:12; Matthew 18:35

❖ Our words should always be appropriate and seemly. We should never use the name of God or the Lord Jesus in vain. We should not be angry or engage in speaking evil about others but we should be sincere, truthful and honest at all times.

Ephesians 4:25,31; Titus 2:2; Philippians 4:5; 1 Peter 1:13-16; 2:1; 5:8; Colossians 3:8; 4:6

❖ Our behaviour should always be above reproof, for we are to be an example to others, showing by the way we live that we serve the Lord Jesus and do not live to please ourselves. We should therefore have nothing to do with adultery, fornication, rude jesting, foolish talking or immoral behaviour of any sort, but should seek things that are pure and wholesome at all times.

Philippians 2:15; 4:8; Ephesians 5:3,4; Romans 12:2; Titus 2:12

❖ We are to do good to all as we have opportunity, the greatest good being to share our knowledge of the gospel with others.

Matthew 5:16; Philippians 2:4,16; Galatians 6:2,10; Matthew 6:1-4; Romans 12:13; Hebrews 13:16

❖ We are to obey rulers, pay taxes and in every respect be model citizens as we wait for the coming of the Lord Jesus from heaven, to reign from Jerusalem. Nothing that we do should dishonour God's name or bring his Word into disrepute.

Titus 3:1; 1 Peter 2:13; 1 Timothy 5:14; 1 Corinthians 3:17; 10:31

❖ Whilst we await the Lord's coming we should be diligent about his business, watchful for his appearance and careful in all things to give God the glory due to His holy name.

1 Corinthians 16:13; Philippians 4:4; 1 Thessalonians 5:6-10; Titus 2:14; 1 Corinthians 15:58; Galatians 6:9

30
Answers to some Questions

There may be lots of questions that have occurred to you whilst you have been working your way through this book and we would like to help you further your Bible studies if we can.

You can write to us at –

Christadelphian Bible Mission,
404 Shaftmoor Lane,
Birmingham, B28 8SZ
UK

You might want a personal tutor who will help you through some of the things you are unsure about or would like to discuss.

❖ You might want further literature to clear up some areas of confusion or to deal with topics that have not been covered here. If so, write and say what particular topics you have in mind.

❖ If you have access to the Internet you can also get further help by logging on to our web-site or looking at any of the linked sites. Log on at *www.thisisyourbible.com.*

❖ You might want to talk to someone about baptism or find out where your nearest Christadelphians are located. Write to us at the above address or e-mail us at *requests@cbm.org.uk* and we will be in touch.

If you have had difficulty with any of the questions at the end of the chapters, you can both ask for a tutor and then send in your answers, together with any questions you have, or you can get help from the answers included in this chapter. But do try and answer things first, otherwise you don't get the full benefit of thinking things through for yourself. Remember that the aim of this book is to help you understand the Bible for yourself by providing you with the skills you need for understanding the whole of God's Word.

Answers to Questions at the End of each Chapter

The numbering system for these answers is as follows. The first number in each case is the number of the chapter and the second number is the number of the question. Look up each question and then read the answer.

1.1 The gospel was first preached in the Old Testament, so people who say it is only New Testament teaching that matters are likely to believe only part of the gospel. To understand the full teaching from God we need to look at all the Bible: it is all God's inspired Word. A part of what God has revealed is not enough (see Acts 20:27).

1.2 This very important teaching is that Jesus was Son of God on two counts. First, the Lord Jesus was born a Jew, descended from King David. At his baptism God declared him to be His Son (see Matthew 3:17), for he had no human father. God was His Father. Second, when God raised Jesus from the dead, he again declared him to be His Son (Romans 1:4). So Jesus was born "of the flesh" and "of the spirit". There is more about this in Chapter 7.

1.3 Paul says that the gospel is powerful to save all those men and women who believe it. As the Letter to the Romans proceeds, he shows that the gospel can change our lives and give us real hope, both now and in the age to come.

2.1 Paul firmly believed the Old Testament and constantly taught from it (as the supplied references in the Book of Acts show). For example, when some of the Jews in Rome were reluctant to accept his interpretation of the Scriptures, that Jesus was their Messiah, he said to them that even in their unbelief they were fulfilling what the prophet Isaiah had foretold about them (Acts 28:25-28).

2.2 Jesus demonstrates quite superbly that he believed the Scriptures to have been given by God. He refers to the Book of Leviticus (in Mark 1:44) and tells a healed leper to go and offer those things that Moses commanded, and to the Book of Exodus and the giving of the law (in Matthew 15:4 and Mark 7:10): he clearly believes that the law given to Moses was from God. Some people say there are two accounts of creation (in Genesis chapters 1 and 2), but Jesus accepts that there is just one account, more detail about what happened being given in chapter 2. Jesus quotes from both chapters of Genesis (in Matthew 19:3-9) and thus shows clearly that the creation of Adam and Eve and the law of marriage were divine arrangements. In Luke 20:37, Jesus not only accepts the appearance of the angel in the bush as a true happening, but he accepts that the words then spoken, as recorded by Moses, are so accurately recorded that he bases his entire argument on the precise words spoken.

2.3 Jesus promised his disciples that he would give them the help of the Holy Spirit – God's supernatural power – to make sure that the gospel accounts would be absolutely accurate (John 14:26). When writing letters of instruction and encouragement, the apostles knew they were writing with God-given authority and their writings were inspired (1 Thessalonians 2:13 and 1 Corinthians 14:37). The apostle Peter even refers to the writings of the apostle Paul in such a way that it is clear that he regarded them as "Scripture", for he says of some people that: *"there are some things in them that are hard to understand, which the ignorant and unstable twist to their own destruction, as they do the other Scriptures"* (2 Peter 3:15-16).

3.1 The command to the kings of Israel shows that they were to be as much subject to God's law as were their subjects. They were not above the law, as some people now reckon themselves to be. Copying it out (as Deuteronomy 17:18-20 required) would impress God's law on the king's mind and that is what regular Bible reading should also do for us. When the family were meeting together they were to make the Word of God their daily delight (Deuteronomy 6:6-12); it was to be more than something they remembered, they were to enjoy thinking about God's revealed purpose. That's how the Word of God should be to us as well; something we come to love and enjoy as we learn more and more about God's character and His gracious ways.

3.2 Jesus might have been educated in a synagogue school where he would have learned to read, and the Scriptures would have been the reading book that was used there. He evidently knew a lot about Bible teaching and made excellent progress (Luke 2:51-52). Aged twelve he was found in the Temple at Jerusalem talking to the religious teachers and they were amazed at his understanding (Luke 2:47). Tempted to do what was wrong he rebutted those temptations by referring to what the Scriptures said (Luke 4:2-12), showing that they had a really practical application in his life. When he attended the synagogue in Nazareth he did what he usually did – he read from the Scriptures, and went on to explain their meaning in a very dramatic way (Luke 4:16-21). So, if it took Jesus time to become acquainted with the Old Testament, we need to give ourselves some learning time too. God has designed His Word in such a way that we can only take it into our lives bit by bit. There is no such thing as an overnight believer.

4.1 The Flood did not come immediately to destroy mankind; God gave the people who lived then a lot of warning, but they chose not to believe that anything would happen. Peter says they were *"wilfully ignorant"* (2 Peter 3:5) and he warns that the same thing will happen again before God destroys the world order that now exists. We need to be aware of what is happening in the world and be ready for God's rescue plan. Noah and his family made proper provision for what was coming and they were saved (Hebrews 11:6-7) and God wants to save all those people who listen to His Word and act on it (2 Peter 3:9). But most people will carry on regardless, without a thought about God, until it is too late (Matthew 24:34-42). We need to taken action now, while there is still time.

4.2 There are many warnings in Scripture that the things God revealed would be corrupted and distorted by men and women. 1 Timothy 4:1-5 gives some examples, and some of those things are now practised in some churches. The Bible says that is a warning sign that the true faith has being corrupted. Paul then catalogues a lot of things that now describe our society and says that these are dangerous times in which to live (2 Timothy 3:1-7). The root problem is that people love themselves more than they love God (3:2-4) and we must be careful not to be led astray by our own feelings and desires. We need to find out what God wants us to do and then make that our first choice.

5.1 The hope of faithful men and women in all ages was that after their death they would be raised from the grave at the time of resurrection. King David recognised that this was his only hope: that he would awake from the sleep of death (Psalm 17:15) to be made immortal like God. Being a prophet, he predicted that the Lord Jesus Christ would be raised from death to sit at God's right hand (Psalm 16:8-11, as interpreted by Acts 2:25-32). Other Psalmists shared the same hope, of being rescued from the grave (49:15) and of being raised from the dead (71:20).

5.2 A careful comparison between Psalm 49 verses 12 and 20 shows that the key difference between mankind and the animal kingdom is that we can understand the purpose of God, and animals cannot. So they die and cease to exist, and so will all those who do not understand and believe God's purpose. After listing several of God's people who have gone before us, in Hebrews chapter 11, the writer says this: They all died not having received what was promised to them, for they are waiting to be made perfect, together with all God's people, at the resurrection of the dead (Hebrews 11:13,39-40). The key to their future hope is that all those listed had faith, or belief, in what God had promised, and they acted accordingly.

5.3 In the Bible the word *"soul"* has quite a wide range of meaning. As we saw in the chapter, in Genesis 2:7 it means "creature" or "person" and that meaning holds good for all the passages listed. For example, Noah and 7 other people were saved in the ark (1 Peter 3:20). Thus it should not come as a surprise that souls (or people) can both sin (Leviticus 4:2) and die (Joshua 10:28).

6.1 In Psalm 90 we learn that God has always existed (verse 2). In the beginning He was already there (Genesis 1:1); and He always will be. Moses says that God is *"from everlasting to everlasting"*. It follows that God is not limited by time (verse 4), whereas we are; we only have a short time to live (verses 3,5,10). God is holy and if His righteous anger is directed at us, we have no chance of surviving it (verses 7-11). But God is merciful and loving and will save us from sin, if we turn to Him (verses 14-17).

6.2 It is a key teaching of the Bible that God is one. It follows from this (a) that we should love Him with our whole being, for no one or nothing else so deserves our love (Deuteronomy 6:4,5) and, (b) that there is no-one or nothing that could ever exist to rival God (Isaiah 45:5,6). This passage is especially interesting in that it was written about a Persian king who would be appointed by God to fulfil His will (45:1) and the Persians believed in a god of good and a separate god of evil. God's prophet explained that the God of the Bible admits no such rivalry; there never was and there never will be any other supernatural power to rival Almighty God. He has total control of the forces of good and evil (45:7). It really matters that we understand this about God, for our eternal life depends upon it (John 17:3). So, if we want one word to sum up the nature of God as described in these three passages it would have to be that God is a "Unity". He is complete, unique and supreme.

7.1 The Bible insists (see, for example, Hebrews 2:14) that Jesus was tempted in just the same way that we are tempted. That means that he was tempted from inside – by his natural thoughts and feelings – as well as from outside, by the things he saw and by what he heard and experienced. We are tempted when thoughts naturally occur to us, then we are drawn away by those feelings (James 1:13-16). Temptations are not sins: we only sin when we give in to those feelings. Jesus never did. But all the feelings we get, he would have got too. If he had yielded to those things which come naturally from the heart of man (Jeremiah 17:9), it would have resulted in all sorts of wrong actions and characteristics – those described in Mark 7:18-23 and Galatians 5:19-21. The marvellous thing is that Jesus never once gave way to those inner feelings or to any suggestions made to him. He was tempted like us, but he never once sinned! (Hebrews 4:15).

7.2 Because he was so faithful and obedient, God his Father raised Jesus from the dead and exalted him to glory and honour (Acts 2:32-36). He gave him the power of the Holy Spirit with no limitations whatsoever (Matthew 28:18) and set him in glory at His own right hand in heaven, where he is now. It was not that Jesus had been there before coming down to earth. Jesus was exalted to glory because he had been obedient (Philippians 2:9-

11). It is now appropriate for us to highly honour the exalted Lord Jesus Christ, to the glory of God his Father, for even the angels in heaven reckon him worthy of honour, glory and blessing (Revelation 5:11,12). When Jesus returns to earth he will be acclaimed by those believers who greet him as their Lord (2 Thessalonians 1:10).

8.1 When Jesus said that he and his Father were one (John 10:30) he clearly did not mean that they were one and the same person, for the preceding verse says *"My Father, who has given them to me, is greater than all" (10:29).* The whole passage is one in which Jesus explains to his accusers that he is God's Son (see 10:17-18,25-39). His key point is that the works he was doing were works that God had empowered him to do: he was not working alone. In fact they were working together; that was his real point when he said that he and his Father were one. They had one purpose, one mind and one aim. In his prayer for disciples in all ages, Jesus prays that we might have the same attitude of mind and heart; that, like him, we too might want to serve the Father and love Him with all our hearts. He wants us to be one with the Father: *"I do not ask for these only, but also for those who will believe in me through their word, that they may all be one, just as you, Father, are in me, and I in you, that they also may be in us" (John 17:20,21).* This is the unity of purpose and intent that we must all strive to achieve, with God's help.

8.2 The very first thing we read about God is that He created the heavens and the earth by uttering words of command (Genesis 1:1-3; Psalm 33:6-9). Those words made things happen and as they were spoken they revealed something about the power and purpose of the speaker. For step-by-step God created an ordered and designed Universe, a fit dwelling place for mankind. It was all part of His plan and the result of His wisdom. King Solomon tells us this when he urges us to follow in Wisdom's way (Proverbs 8:1-32), reminding us that God had wisdom from the very beginning and by that wisdom He created the world. Solomon pictures Wisdom as though it were a woman sitting alongside God: that is quite a typical way in which the Bible depicts things, making them easier to remember in the process. So the apostle John is telling his readers that God had a plan and purpose from the beginning (he calls it God's "Word") and, in course of time, that purpose took shape in the form of His only begotten Son (John 1:14,18), when Jesus was born. Because Jesus had to inherit characteristics from his mother Mary as well as from his Father, he could not have existed before he was born. If he had lived in heaven before his birth on earth, Mary would have contributed nothing to his personality and character. But, in fact, Jesus had to be the *"seed of the woman"* (Genesis 3:15; Galatians 4:4) as well as the only begotten Son of God.

9.1 It is one of the wonderful things about the Lord Jesus Christ that he willingly and voluntarily laid down his life for us. There was nothing automatic about the process, as there would have been if he had lived in heaven before and had conceived the plan to come to earth. Can you imagine what failure would have meant in that case? It would have been unthinkable! But Jesus said that he was a volunteer and that God had given him the option whether to die or not (John 10:17-18), though his natural inclination was not to die. Like us, he had inbuilt instincts of self-preservation, but he set them aside, hard though it was for him to do that (Luke 22:42). Now if Jesus was willing to do all that for us, we should highly honour and love him for his kindness and love (John 5:23) and we should try to follow his example. We too should want to do the will of God (Romans 12:1-2) and will be keen to work out exactly what God's will is for us. That means we will be keen readers of the Bible, for that is where we find out God's will and purpose.

9.2 Paul sums up his feelings for Jesus in a wonderful verse in which he says that he realises Jesus died for him. He died for everyone else as well, of course, but Paul sees the sacrifice of Jesus as a very personal thing. He reasons (in Galatians 2:20) that as Jesus died for him, he too will die to self and live for Christ. That meant for Paul that every day he would try to love God and his neighbour, making those twin aims the law of his life and in that way he would seek to let the life of Jesus continue in him.

10.1 When asked if only few would be saved, Jesus replied: "Do your best to go in through the narrow door; because many people will surely try to go in but will not be able." He added that, whatever works people claimed to have done in his name, the key thing was whether or not they knew him. That explanation was made clearer in Matthew's account where Jesus explained there are two ways we can choose, and only the narrow way leads to life. He added: *"and there are few people who find it" (Matthew 7:14).* The key thing is that there is only one way that leads to life and we have to seek it out if we want to find the things that are true. Eternal life is not something we can earn; it is a gift from God. It is impossible for any of us to gain access into God's kingdom through our own efforts. Only He can give us that gift of life for evermore.

10.2 Cornelius is described as *"a religious man; he and his whole family worshipped God. He also did much to help the Jewish poor people and was constantly praying to God" (Acts 10:2).* If good living was enough for God, Cornelius might have been good enough, but he knew that more was required. Instructed by an angel, he sent to ask the apostle Peter to come to Caesarea, where he lived. Peter came, after receiving instructions from God, and preached the gospel to him and his household (Acts 10:34-43). This was a huge turning point for the early believers as a Gentile had not been received as a member up to now. So God gave the Holy Spirit to this household just as He had to the apostles, and that convinced the apostle Peter that Cornelius was accepted by God. Then he *"ordered them to be baptized in the name of Jesus Christ"* *(10:48).* There is no other way into God's family except to believe and be baptized.

11.1 God chose Israel as His special nation because of the promises he made to Abraham about his descendants, who were to be as numerous as the sand on the sea shore (Genesis 13:14-17; Deuteronomy 9:5). They were to possess the land that God showed Abraham (12:7) and through them all nations would be blessed (12:1-3), for into that nation Jesus would be born. The promises about the coming blessing are only partially fulfilled, so Israel still has a part to play in God's purpose, as Paul explains in Romans chapter 11 (see Chapter 21).

11.2 The special descendant promised both to Abraham and David will:

a   Give Abraham as many faithful descendants as there are stars in the sky or grains of sand along the seashore;

b   Conquer all their enemies;

c   Let people from all nations share in the blessing promised to Abraham (the forgiveness of sins: Acts 3:26);

d   Occupy David's throne in Jerusalem;

e   Establish an everlasting kingdom;

f   Build God a temple;

g   Ensure that David's dynasty will last for ever. Jesus brings real hope of eternal life in the future (see 2 Samuel 7:19).

12.1 Adam was the man who brought sin and death into the world through his disobedience and it had control over mankind for a long time; but Jesus was the man who made amends for Adam's mistakes and made a way of escape possible. He was everything that Adam was not – obedient, righteous and faithful. He can set us free from the bondage of sin and death and that really matters if we want to live forever.

12.2 To match Adam's situation, Jesus had to be a man like us and Scripture insists that he was made like us and was tempted like us (Hebrews 2:14; 4:15). If Jesus had not inherited those tendencies from Mary, she would have contributed nothing to his character or personality. Jesus had to be the *"offspring of the woman"* (Genesis 3:15) and be *"born of woman"* (Galatians 4:4), because that is what Scripture said must happen. He was to be a willing and obedient sacrifice, because he had chosen to do God's will – not like the animals sacrificed under the Law, who had no choice. And because Jesus knows how we feel, he is able to act as a priest (Hebrews 5:1,2) who can understand our circumstances. The marvellous thing about this is that Jesus was faithful and obedient to his Father in all things. Therefore he was able to undo all the mischief that Adam's disobedience brought into existence.

13.1 Becoming like Jesus is something we have to start doing now, beginning with the way we think, which is why it is so important to understand the Bible for yourself. The more we understand about the way Jesus thought about things, the better able we shall be to change our way of thinking (which is what Paul says in Philippians 2:1-5). He was humble and faithful to God, and so should we be. But we are not like that naturally. So we have to put to death our natural feelings and desires and replace them with better and more satisfying feelings and desires. That's what Paul explains in Colossians 3:1-6: that we try to live life at a higher level, as Jesus did. It all starts when we are touched by the great love that God and Jesus have for us and want to do those things that we are commanded to do to show our love for them (John 15:12-15). Baptism into Christ is the first of those commands.

13.2 We will never be completely like Jesus until our present human nature has been changed to be like his. For some of us this change will not take place until we die and are raised from the dead. Those of us who are still alive at the return to earth of Jesus will be "changed" after we have been accepted by him. The end of that process of change will be that our bodies will be transformed to be like that of the risen Jesus – forever free from sin and death (1 Corinthians 15:51-58).

14.1 In 1 Peter 3:18-22 the apostle Peter draws a parallel between baptism and the flood at the time of Noah. Then the whole earth was destroyed, except for those in the ark (as described in Genesis 6-8). First, he says that Jesus died for us to bring us to God and that he rose again by the power of God (His Holy Spirit power). That was the power by which Jesus had preached the gospel during his lifetime, as he often declared (e.g. John 3:34; 6:63), preaching to people who were in the prison house of sin and death. Sadly, says Peter, the same Spirit was operative in the days of Noah, when there were people imprisoned by darkness and ignorance. Noah was preaching the gospel of salvation in his days and God had provided a way of escape from destruction (just as Jesus would later provide one from sin and death). But only 8 people, out of an entire civilisation, wanted to know about God's escape plan. All the others perished. Now it's the same with baptism. We can either be saved by belief and baptism, or we will be destroyed like the foolish people in Noah's day. Baptism is that important; it's a matter of life and death!

14.2 There are no examples in the Bible of infants being baptized or of anybody of any age being christened. When we read that entire households were baptized, as recorded in the Acts (e.g. Acts 18:7,8), they were first instructed about true Bible teaching. We should remember that in those days households would have included servants and perhaps slaves, so they were not just a family with children. Scripture does not tell us what age we should be to be baptized, but clearly we must be old enough to understand the gospel and to believe it. As baptism requires us to change the way we behave, we need to be old enough to know what we are doing so that our lifestyle really will change as we seek to keep the commandments of Christ.

15.1 When the apostle talks about the "flesh" in Romans chapter 8, he is referring to that way of life which is natural to the human condition. It is how we all are by birth and how we think and act naturally because of the promptings of our human nature. In that condition we are "weak" when it comes to obeying God's Law (8:3); we think the wrong things, we are hostile to God and will eventually die in our sins (8:5-8). Left in that condition we cannot please God. But life *"in the Spirit"* is quite different. When we fill our minds with the things taught by God's Spirit and become spirit-minded (8:5-7), we are in the process of developing an attitude of mind and heart that will be inclined towards God. Over time we will find ourselves wanting to please God and wanting to do what is right in His sight. That will result in our being at peace with God (8:6) and the eventual outcome will be eternal life in God's kingdom on earth.

15.2 When Jesus told Nicodemus he had to be born again (John 3:3-8) he said that rebirth had to be of water (which means baptism by immersion) and of the Spirit. That second process is the one we were just thinking about in Question 15.1. It means getting our minds right with God and seeking to live in a way which is spiritual, or Bible-based. It also means that our natures are to be transformed at the coming of Jesus, when those who please him are given the gift of eternal life and their nature is changed. When that happens they will have spiritual bodies (1 Corinthians 15:44; Philippians 3:20,21).

16.1 The word *"spirit"* can mean lots of different things. In the passages referred to it means:

- ❖ The power by which God created the world, when He spoke words of command (Genesis 1:1-3) and by which, in the process of Creation, He began to reveal what He is like;
- ❖ The attitude of mind and heart that Caleb had: he was a faithful man who was said to have another spirit, for most of his fellow Israelites had a spirit of unbelief (Numbers 14:24);

❖ The force of life that sustains us all without which, if God was to withdraw, we would all be lifeless (Job 34:14);

❖ That is the same life-force which we share with animals, who are also said to be empowered by the spirit or breath of life which is in their nostrils (Ecclesiastes 3:21; Genesis 7:15; Acts 17:25);

❖ It was the power of God that enabled God's prophets to convey the message that He gave them to proclaim (2 Samuel 23:2; 2 Peter 1:21). That power has now passed because God's revelation is complete;

❖ There was also a special gift of Holy Spirit power in the first century (Acts 2:1-4) which enabled the apostles to preach the gospel. Among the gifts given was the ability to speak in foreign languages (Acts 2:7-11).

❖ Put in just one sentence: "The Holy Spirit is the power of God by which He does everything and through which God seeks to make men and women holy, like Himself."

16.2 Holy Spirit gifts were transmitted by the laying on of hands by the apostles and in no other way. For example, when Philip the evangelist had preached in Samaria he was unable to confer those gifts himself. The apostles Peter and John had to come from Jerusalem, and it was clear that only their laying on of hands could pass the power on (see Acts 8:14-20). So, when the apostles died, the power to pass on the gift died with them. This agrees with what the early Church fathers said: that the gifts died out during the second century A.D.

17.1 John chapter 11 tells us first that when Jesus spoke about death he used the language of "sleep", for death is an unconscious state like a dreamless sleep (John 11:11-14). He also spoke of resurrection as an awakening from sleep (11:11), which was his consistent practice (Mark 5:39-42). When Jesus reached Bethany he found two grieving sisters who believed in resurrection at the last day (verses 21-24) and who believed in Jesus. He said that he was *"the resurrection and the life"* and that if a person believes in him they need not stay forever dead, but can be raised to life. Jesus then demonstrated that by raising Lazarus from the dead (11:25-44). He was raised a mortal man and would, in course of time, have died again. But, for as long as he lived, Lazarus was a testimony both to the power of Jesus to raise the dead and to our need of resurrection. It is never suggested that Lazarus was better off dead than alive! He had not gone to heaven; he was asleep in the grave and his body was undergoing the process of corruption. Resurrection was his only hope, as it is ours.

17.2 God told Adam that if he ate of the forbidden fruit he would die: *"in the day that you eat of it you shall surely die"* (Genesis *2:17).* Death was going to be a punishment, not a reward, and it would mean that Adam and Eve would return to the ground from which Adam had been taken (3:14-19). They would forfeit the prospect of living forever, because of sin. But God held out some hope for them and for us, because first He made a covering for their sin and shame, by having an animal or animals slain (Genesis 3:21). Then He made them a wonderful promise (3:16) about a special descendant who would be born – the offspring of the woman (not of the man). That descendant was to be Jesus, though he was not born to the virgin Mary for thousands of years. But his coming was already in God's mind and formed an important part of His purpose. By his perfect obedience, Jesus undid the harm that Adam had done and although he died, as a sacrifice for sin, he was raised from the dead to a new life. He is therefore the perfect solution to all the problems Adam brought (1 Corinthians 15:21-26). If we die *"in Adam"* we can be raised *"in Christ":* it's all about making sure we belong to Jesus and we do that by believing in him, being baptized and learning to live with him now.

18.1 In the seven letters that Jesus wrote to the believers in Asia he mentioned the following rewards for his faithful followers:

1 eating of the tree of life, which is in the paradise of God (Revelation 2:7) – that means having eternal life in the Kingdom of God;
2 wearing *"the crown of life"* (2:10);
3 being sustained by God's own provision (hidden manna); being found faultless (a white stone) and having a new character and personality (a new name) (2:17);
4 having authority over the nations, by helping Jesus with the work of administering God's Kingdom (2:26-28);
5 being found to be right with God and being held in God's everlasting remembrance (3:5);
6 being forever part of a body which worships and praises Almighty God and which glorifies His name (3:12);
7 being with the Lord Jesus Christ and working with him (3:21).

18.2 Jesus was specific about what had to be done by those Christian congregations if they were to inherit these things. Here's another list:

❖ They were to remain loving and to repent of any failure or shortcoming (Revelation 2:4-5);
❖ They were to be faithful, if necessary unto death (2:10);
❖ They must believe the right things and not believe wrong things (2:14-16);
❖ Their behaviour must be consistent with their beliefs (2:20-25);

❖ They must have a living faith and must remain watchful and vigilant against evil (3:1-2);

❖ They had to continue to be faithful to the end (3:11);

❖ They should be earnest and enthusiastic about their faith, always ready to welcome Jesus into every aspect of their lives and wanting, more than anything, to have fellowship with him (3:15-20).

19.1 John chapter 14 records a promise that Jesus made to his disciples shortly before his death on the cross. He was encouraging them to believe in him whatever happened, for none of them really understood that he had to die on the cross, and Jesus knew it was going to be a huge setback for them. So he told them not to be afraid, because God's house has many rooms and he was going to prepare a place for them. The Scriptures often talk about the *"House of God"*, the Temple, and it had apartments alongside it where some of the priests lived when they were serving at the temple complex (see 1 Kings 6:5-7). That was a lovely picture of people living close to God and serving Him in the process. Now, Jesus told his disciples, he was going to make such a dwelling place possible for mankind in general (not just for priests) and when the time was right he *"will come again and will take you to myself, that where I am you may be also" (John 14:3)*. So this passage does not promise that we go to heaven. It promises that when Jesus returns to earth he will make it possible for believers to dwell with God (see Revelation 21:3).

19.2 Psalm 146 explains that when we die, we are unconscious. It says of the dead: *"When his breath departs he returns to the earth; on that very day his plans perish" (verse 4)* and encourages us to worship God while we still have time. Notice that it holds out no second chance, such as limbo or purgatory might offer. There is no second chance, which is why we should use every opportunity now to learn about the things of God. But this is not a Psalm without hope for it proceeds to say that we are happy indeed if we have hope in God (verse 5). He can reverse the process of death by resurrection and He can remake the world. God will do all those things, bringing justice and righteousness in the process, and setting His king in Jerusalem (verses 7-10). That is a real hope and it is a blessing indeed.

20.1 The disciples asked Jesus if he was now about to restore God's kingdom to Israel, for they clearly understood that it was to come in due course (see, for example, Mark 11:10). Jesus had been talking to them for the past forty days about the coming Kingdom of God (Acts 1:3), so they clearly had a good understanding of what was going to happen. But they didn't know when it would happen, so they asked Jesus. He didn't say they were wrong to ask, or that they had got it all wrong. He said that it was not for them to know when the kingdom will come. God had fixed the time and they had work to do meanwhile (1:6-8). The two angels who appeared as Jesus was ascending to heaven told them that: *"This Jesus, who was taken up from you into heaven, will come in the same way as you saw him go into heaven" (1:11).* They had seen him go, so he will be visible when he returns; he had gone in bodily form (Luke 24:38-42) and he will come back in the same way: a spiritual body (1 Corinthians 15:44-45). He ascended from the Mount of Olives and he is due to return to that very place when he comes again to Jerusalem (Zechariah 14:1-4).

20.2 This is what Micah chapter 4 tells us about God's coming kingdom:

1 Jerusalem is to be physically lifted up above the surrounding hills (see also Zechariah 14:10,11);

2 People from many nations will come to Jerusalem to worship God there and to learn His ways (4:1-2);

3 God's law will be administered from Jerusalem, when it becomes the capital city of God's worldwide kingdom;

4 The result will be that peace will be established and instead of making weapons of war the nations will turn to peaceful pursuits. That will greatly benefit people who will be able to enjoy life once again;

5 God will gather His people together and Jesus will reign over them in Jerusalem (verses 6-7);

6 The Kingdom of God will be restored to Jerusalem (verse 8);

7 That will only come about after there is more suffering and sorrow in Jerusalem and for the Israeli people. Eventually, and only with God's help, they will overcome that opposition and will dedicate the things they then gain to the worship of God. Israel will then be a wholly religious nation once again.

21.1 Romans chapter 10 tells us the following:

a That Israel failed to accept the way that God now devised whereby they could become right with Him because of what Jesus had achieved. Instead they were determined to stick to the old way, given in the Law of Moses, and to prove themselves righteous by their godly conduct. The irony was that they had proved themselves the opposite by rejecting their God-given Messiah.

b The law of works could not give them righteousness, because they couldn't keep it. It was designed to show that we cannot solve our own problems, but that we need God's help. Moses explained that to them (in Leviticus 18:5, quoted in Romans 10:5), and urged them to live by faith (in Deuteronomy 30:12-13, quoted in Romans 10:6-8). Paul said that what Moses was looking forward to had arrived now that Christ had come.

c To be right with God both Jews and Gentiles now need to believe in Jesus and to confess that belief before men. There is no other way of being reckoned righteous before God.

d We can get faith in God from His Word the Bible because that tells us all we need to know; but we must understand the true message it contains and not rely on what others tell us it says (Romans 10:17).

e The Old Testament prophets did indeed predict both that the Gentiles would believe and that the Jews would not. That was exactly as it has worked out. In Romans 10:16-21, Paul quotes from Isaiah 53:1; Psalm 19:14; Deuteronomy 32:21 and Isaiah 65:1,2, to demonstrate that truth.

21.2 It is often the case that God has worked through a remnant – a small group of people who were faithful while the majority was unfaithful. There were only 8 people saved at the time of the flood, out of an entire civilization (Genesis 6; 1 Peter 3:20); only 2 of the 12 spies said that it was possible to enter the Promised Land there and then (and the people believed the other 10, which is why the entire generation of unbelievers died in the wilderness, see Numbers 14). Only Rahab and her family were saved when the walls of Jericho fell down (Joshua 2). Jesus said that only a few people will be saved when he comes, but that most will choose to go down the broad way that leads to destruction (Matthew 7:13,14).

22.1 Joel chapter 3 shows us clearly that God's purpose still has very much to do with the nation of Israel and the city Jerusalem, for the following reasons:

a The judgement of the nations who oppose the rulership of Christ is due to take place in the "valley of Jehoshaphat" (Joel 3:2,11), a place in Israel (the precise location of which is unknown but one which is associated with the victory of King Jehoshaphat over his enemies; see 2 Chronicles 20:20-25).

b God is angry with the nations because of the way they have treated Israel and the Jewish people (Joel 3:2-8), treatment which includes displacing them from their ancient land, scattering them among the nations and then dividing their land (3:2), as happened, for example, in 1947 when the nations partitioned the land of Israel between Jews and Palestinians.

c This prophecy is set at a time when the dispersion of the Jews has ended and when Jerusalem is once more in Jewish hands (3:1). Once the nations have been judged, the prophet says, God's people will once again dwell in the land and inhabit Jerusalem, for God will purify and redeem the Jewish people. He will again dwell in their midst, when Jerusalem becomes the "city of the great king" (Joel 3:20-21; Matthew 5:35).

d The Judge who is coming to rule all nations will be resident in Jerusalem (Joel 3:16-17) and that will be the centre of his administration.

e Jerusalem will become a holy place, God's "holy mountain", for a Temple will be established there and the nations of the world will come there to learn about God's Law and to worship Him (Joel 3:17-18; Zechariah 14:16-21).

22.2 The new society that Isaiah describes in 65:17-25 brings the following special blessings:

❖ We shall forget any painful and hurtful things that may have happened to us (verse 17);

❖ Joy and rejoicing will utterly replace weeping and crying (verse 19);

❖ Life will be prolonged – children will not die at birth and the mortal inhabitants of God's kingdom will live for well over 100 years (perhaps right through the Millennium) (verse 20);

❖ People will live safely and comfortably in their own houses without any fear of displacement, and those who are immortal (God's chosen) will be richly blessed, they and their families (verses 21-23);

❖ Theirs will be a very close relationship with God (verse 24);

❖ God's creatures will live in harmony, without hurt or destruction (verse 25).

23.1 *Jacob* expected to go to the grave when he died, for he said: "I will go down to Sheol to my son mourning" (Genesis 37:35);

Job was distraught that he would have to die and be laid in the grave without ever having his reputation restored, but he hoped for something afterwards: *"Oh that you would hide me in Sheol, that you would conceal me until your wrath be past, that you would appoint me a set time, and remember me!" (14:13).* If there was no resurrection after death, he was gong to be consigned to darkness, corruption, hopelessness, imprisonment and dust (17:13-16). But, in fact, Job believed in resurrection (19:25-27).

Good *King Hezekiah* expected to go to Sheol (the grave), to *"the pit of destruction"* (Isaiah 38:17), to the place where nobody can either thank or praise God (verse 18), because they are unconscious.

23.2 The Lord's Prayer teaches us clearly that heaven is God's dwelling place, where His name is held in reverence (Matthew 6:9). It contains no requests for us to go to be with God in heaven; quite the contrary. The Lord teaches us to pray for God's kingdom to come from heaven to earth (verse 10), so that His will shall be done here as now it is perfectly done in heaven (verse 10). When we are praying for the kingdom to come, we are asking God to take over the rulership of the world and to send His king (the Lord Jesus Christ) to reign from Jerusalem (Zechariah 14:9).

24.1 Hebrews 2:14 could just have said that when Jesus was born he shared our nature, but it really emphasizes that truth. It says that as we are flesh and blood, *"he himself likewise partook of the same things"*. So it really matters that Jesus was the same as us, for Scripture never wastes words. By his death, Jesus is said to have destroyed the devil, and that is defined as *"the one who has the power of death, that is, the devil"*. It is sin that has the power of death (Romans 6:23; James 1:15). One result of the death and resurrection of Jesus is that he can never again be tempted to sin (Hebrews 7:26). Because he died willingly, as sacrifice for sins (Hebrews 9:26), he condemned sin, showing it up for what it really is (Romans 8:3); he made it possible for sin to be rendered powerless.

24:2 Comparing Scripture with Scripture is an excellent way to discover when picture language is being used and when it is not. That is certainly the case with the Devil and Satan, as we have seen. Here are some more parallel passages where the picture is quickly explained:

Picture Language	Explanation
"Ananias, why has Satan filled your heart to lie to the Holy Spirit and to keep back for yourself part of the proceeds of the land?" (Acts 5:3)	"Why is it that you have contrived this deed in your heart? You have not lied to men but to God" (5:4)
"You once walked, following the course of this world, following the prince of the power of the air, the spirit that is now at work in the sons of disobedience ..." (Ephesians 2:2)	"... among whom we all once lived in the passions of our flesh, carrying out the desires of the body and the mind, and were by nature children of wrath, like the rest of mankind" (2:3)
"And they may escape from the snare of the devil, after being captured by him to do his will" (2 Timothy 2:26)	"each person is tempted when he is lured and enticed by his own desire" (James 1:14)
"Put on the whole armour of God, that you may be able to stand against the schemes of the devil" (Ephesians 6:11)	"put off your old self, which belongs to your former manner of life and is corrupt through deceitful desires" (4:22)

Picture Language	Explanation
"In their case the god of this world has blinded the minds of the unbelievers, to keep them from seeing the light of the gospel of the glory of Christ, who is the image of God" (2 Corinthians 4:4)	"Demas, in love with this present world, has deserted me and gone to Thessalonica" (2 Timothy 4:10)

Picture language is being used in these passages, as elsewhere, to make the struggle against sin seem that much more important and vital. It is going to be a real battle to overcome the natural impulses with which we are born. But we can learn to do that with God's help.

25.1 The driving force of the new life has to be love, both the love that God and the Lord Jesus Christ have for us (1 Thessalonians 4:9; Ephesians 5:2); the fact that we are commanded to love one another, just as Christ first loved us (John 13:34), and the fact that love is the thing that should bind believers together (Colossians 3:14). This is what Paul directs us to in Romans 12:10: that we should *"Love one another with brotherly affection. Outdo one another in showing honour"*. We shall only be able to keep up our new life and our good intentions if we continue to reflect on these things and remember week-by-week just what God and Jesus have done for us.

25.2 Our personal prayers to God should be the private way we have of talking to Him and giving Him praise and thanksgiving (Matthew 6:6-7). Prayers can include requests for the things we need (Matthew 7:7; Philippians 4:6), but it is well that we remember that our spiritual needs are the most important things in our lives (Matthew 26:41). Prayer should be an important and continuing part of our spiritual development (Luke 18:1) and it will help us to be alert to dangers and pitfalls that might otherwise beset us (Ephesians 6:18). But we should never forget that prayer is also for praise and thanksgiving, not just for asking for things or for help (Philippians 4:6). The Lord's Prayer that Jesus taught his disciples puts God, His kingdom, and His will, before our own needs or desires.

26.1 Believers in Christ are called to live separate and holy lives, free from the world and its allurements. Paul said that we are to be *"transformed"* not *"conformed"* (Romans 12:2) and that means that we must be careful about our companions, especially about people we might marry or go into business with (2 Corinthians 6:14-18). We should avoid anything or anyone who seems likely to get us into trouble or to lure us away from following Jesus (Ephesians 5:7-11). If people try to associate us with evil things we should have nothing to do with them, but should rebuke them, for our minds have been instructed by the law of Christ and we must obey him (Ephesians 4:17). We should not become involved in political parties and should not take anyone to court.

26.2 Marriage is a God-given relationship and we might already be married when we get to understand the Bible. If so, we should continue in that relationship and do all we can to help our partner come to an understanding that will also lead him or her to obtain eternal life (1 Corinthians 7:12-15). That might mean helping our husband or wife to read the Bible, or reading it with other family members. If not married, believers should marry unbelievers where that is possible or teach someone about the gospel before they marry (1 Corinthians 7:39). Marriage is for life. Believers who are married should have a loving and sharing relationship with their partner which is governed by love. The pattern and example is the love that Jesus showed to his followers – who are likened to a bride (Ephesians 5:21-33). Both husband and wife should care for and honour one another at all times (1 Peter 3:7).

27:1 When Paul met the elders of Ephesus at Miletus he made the following points, which are just as helpful to us today:

❖ He had lived with them in a way which gave them a good example of behaviour at all times (Acts 20:18-20,33-35);
❖ He had taken every opportunity to preach and teach them (v 19-21), urging them to repent and to believe the gospel, and he had proclaimed the Kingdom of God (verse 25);
❖ He had taught them the whole counsel of God, holding nothing back (verse 27);
❖ There would be false teachers who would lead many astray, as true Christianity was distorted and corrupted: that would do people grave harm (v 28-30); The key thing was to read and understand the Bible, because God's Word can confer an inheritance on those who believe its promises (verse 32).

27.2 If we now understand what Romans is all about we should use the same tools and study techniques to read the rest of the Bible, so that we can understand the *"whole counsel of God"* (Acts 20:27). We need continually to renew our minds (Romans 12:2) and think about those things that are lovely and wholesome (Philippians 4:8-9). Thinking about what Jesus said and did will be really helpful (Colossians 3:16) and we have also to put what we learn into practice (1 Timothy 4:15). For example, if we really do believe that baptism is essential for salvation then we should make arrangements to be interviewed for baptism and not delay. When we have been reborn in the waters of baptism, we should want to feed on the Word of God, much like an infant longs for its mother's milk (1 Peter 2:2).

Subject Index

471

**Christadelphian Bible Mission,
404 Shaftmoor Lane,
Birmingham, B28 8SZ, UK**

Website: *www.thisisyourbible.com*
e-mail: *requests@cbm.org.uk*